The Buddha's Middle Way

The Buddha's Middle Way
Experiential Judgement in His Life and Teaching

Robert M. Ellis
with a foreword by Stephen Batchelor

SHEFFIELD UK   BRISTOL CT

Published by Equinox Publishing Ltd

UK: Office 415, The Workstation, 15 Paternoster Row, Sheffield,
        South Yorkshire S1 2BX
USA: ISD, 70 Enterprise Drive, Bristol, CT 06010

www.equinoxpub.com

First published 2019

© Robert M. Ellis 2019

All rights reserved. No part of this publication may be reproduced or transmitted in any form or by any means, electronic or mechanical, including photocopying, recording or any information storage or retrieval system, without prior permission in writing from the publishers.

British Library Cataloguing-in-Publication Data

A catalogue record for this book is available from the British Library.

ISBN-13 978 1 78179 819 5 (hardback)
         978 1 78179 820 1 (paperback)
         978 1 78179 821 8 (ePDF)

Library of Congress Cataloging-in-Publication Data
Names: Ellis, Robert M., author.
Title: The Buddha's middle way : experiential judgement in his life and
   teaching / Robert M. Ellis.
Description: Bristol : Equinox Publishing Ltd., 2019. | Includes
   bibliographical references and index. | Description based on print version
   record and CIP data provided by publisher; resource not viewed.
Identifiers: LCCN 2018049701 (print) | LCCN 2019014956 (ebook) | ISBN
   9781781798218 (ePDF) | ISBN 9781781798195 (hb) | ISBN 9781781798201 (pb)
Subjects: LCSH: Eightfold Path. | Gautama Buddha.
Classification: LCC BQ4320 (ebook) | LCC BQ4320 .E45 2019 (print) | DDC
   294.3/444—dc23
LC record available at https://lccn.loc.gov/2018049701

Typeset by S.J.I. Services, New Delhi, India

If we want to head north, we can use the North Star to guide us, but it is impossible to arrive at the North Star. Our effort is only to proceed in that direction.

Thich Nhat Hanh

Acknowledgements

I'd like to thank the following individuals for helpful reading and comments on the manuscript prior to publication: Jim Champion, Barry Daniel, Susan Averbach, Viryanaya Ellis, Eric Hoogcarspel, Mark Leonard, Kamalashila Matthews, Francis Gastmans, Winton Higgins, and Stephen Batchelor. I'd also like to thank Tony Morris for his support in facilitating publication.

Robert M. Ellis

Foreword

For the past twenty years, Robert M. Ellis has been steadily developing his Middle Way Philosophy. His ideas can be found in his more popular books such as *Migglism* and *Truth on the Edge*, as well as in the recently published omnibus edition of *Middle Way Philosophy*, which runs to more than 700 pages of demanding argument and reflection. In order to translate his ideas into forms of practice that meet the challenges of living in the modern world, Ellis has also established the Middle Way Society, which offers podcasts, online discussions, retreats, and other events: http://www.middlewaysociety.org

Ellis is a rigorous thinker in his own right. While acknowledging his debt to the Buddha as the first proponent of the Middle Way, he has distanced himself from Buddhism and no longer identifies as a Buddhist. He has sought to uncover the principles of the Middle Way as they are found throughout human culture: in Christianity and Judaism, in various secular philosophies, as well as in psychology and the natural sciences. Moreover, since the Middle Way is to be practised in the context of our actual lives as ethical beings, Ellis applies its principles to our political and economic existence, our understanding of history, and our engagement with the arts.

In *The Buddha's Middle Way*, Ellis returns to Buddhist sources and presents us with a compelling account of how Buddhism as it is currently taught can serve both to obscure and to illuminate the Middle Way. In becoming a world religion based on metaphysical beliefs, Buddhism has, for Ellis, frequently lost touch with the very principle of the Middle Way that it claims to embody. Through focusing on the pragmatic and sceptical dimensions of Buddhist thought, in recovering the potency of its classical metaphors, and by highlighting how Gotama interacted with his own contemporaries, Ellis reveals how the principle of the Middle Way infuses the totality of what the Buddha taught.

To practise the Middle Way entails more than just avoiding the extremes of self-indulgence and self-mortification, as it is defined in the Buddha's First Sermon in the Deer Park at Sarnath. Avoiding such extremes provides no more than a useful example to illustrate a far broader principle. For Ellis, the Middle Way is a metaphor for an entire way of life that relinquishes all metaphysical absolutes. It is, in Ellis's words, 'a principle of judgement, focusing on how we respond to our experience rather than claims about how things finally are.' As such, the Middle Way unfolds entirely within the provisional, ambiguous world of our lives as uncertain yet ethical beings.

I hope this provocative book will encourage Buddhists to reconsider the Middle Way that lies at the core of their tradition and to appreciate how this principle links their tradition to many others, both ancient and modern, secular and religious. *The Buddha's Middle Way* will at the same time provide an excellent critical introduction to the Buddha's life and teaching for those less familiar with Buddhism. As a result of Ellis's groundbreaking work, the Middle Way may cease to be thought of as an exclusively Buddhist idea and instead may be recognised as a universal legacy of being human.

Stephen Batchelor
Aquitaine, September 2018

Contents

Acknowledgements vi
Foreword by Stephen Batchelor vii

Introduction 1

1. **The Middle Way in the Buddha's Early Life** 8
   a. The Story of Siddhartha Gautama 8
   b. The Palace 10
   c. The Four Sights and Going Forth 14
   d. The Forest: Spiritual Teachers 21
   e. The Forest: Asceticism 27
   f. Discovery of the Middle Way 31
   g. The Assaults of Mara 38
   h. Awakening: Meaning versus Belief 41

2. **The Middle Way in the Buddha's Ministry** 50
   a. The Decision to Teach 50
   b. The First Address and Four Tasks 56
   c. The Buddha's Educative Approach 63
   d. The Buddha's Discourses 72
   e. The Buddha's Politics 78
   f. The Buddha's Death 88

3. **The Buddha's Metaphors** 94
   a. Beyond Allegory 94
   b. The Middle Way as Metaphor 100
   c. Provisionality: The Raft and the Lute Strings 102
   d. Absolutisation: The Arrows 109
   e. Incrementality: The Ocean 117
   f. Agnosticism: The Elephant and the Snake 121
   g. Integration: The Wet Piece of Wood 129

4. Issues in the Buddhist Interpretation of the Middle Way — 135
    a. The Misunderstanding of Scepticism — 135
    b. The Ontological Obsession — 141
    c. The Range of Absolutes — 148
    d. The Clustering of Absolutes: 'Eternalism' and 'Nihilism' — 157
    e. Even-handedness and the Preference for Eternalism — 163

5. Interpreting the Eightfold Path — 170
    a. The Eightfold Path and Integration — 170
    b. The Middle Way in Meditation — 173
    c. The Middle Way in Ethical Practice — 180
    d. The Middle Way of Wisdom — 187

6. Interpreting Buddhist Teachings — 193
    a. Conditionality — 193
    b. The Three Marks of Conditioned Existence — 200
    c. Craving and Absolutisation — 207
    d. Karma and Rebirth — 212
    e. The Buddha's Authority and Status — 218
    f. The Meaning of 'Dharma' — 226
    g. The Community and Monastic Tradition — 229
    h. Faith and Going for Refuge — 236

7. Alternative Sources of the Middle Way — 242
    a. The Blind People and the Elephant Again — 242
    b. Pyrrhonian Scepticism — 244
    c. Christian Incarnation — 247
    d. Jungian Individuation — 251
    e. Scientific Falsificationism — 255
    f. Systems Theory and Biology — 258
    g. Embodied Meaning — 262
    h. Brain Lateralisation and Absolutisation — 265
    i. Cognitive Bias and Absolutisation — 269
    j. Ellen Langer's 'Mindfulness' — 272
    k. The Authentic Individual — 276

Conclusion — 281

Bibliography — 284

Index — 291

Introduction

The Middle Way, as far as we know, was probably first explicitly taught by the Buddha. The Buddha was a man who is said to have lived in the northeastern Indian subcontinent about 2,500 years ago. However, it's important to understand and practise the Middle Way in relation to the issues, not of his time, but of ours. The Middle Way can provide a key to living our lives more adequately in every sphere of experience.

How can we deal with stress whilst maintaining effectiveness in a demanding job? By practising the Middle Way in meditation, maintaining an interval of effective relaxation between fixed, wilful ways of operating and inadequate surrender. How do we make moral judgements in a world where old certainties have dissolved? By finding the Middle Way in which no moral principle is absolute, but all moral principles can potentially provide us with reflective tools to promote moral adequacy. How do we deal with a polarised political debate? By following a Middle Way of critical reflection, in which we expect to find some conditions addressed in all perspectives. Nevertheless, we'll recognise a need for decisive judgement to meet the present conditions as well as we can. In personal practice, in science, in ethics and politics, in work, in relationships, and in our response to environmental crises, we need the Middle Way today.

For a long time I have been writing about the Middle Way itself, but avoided writing about the Buddha. Why? Because too many people think of the former only in dependence on the latter. The Buddha did not create the Middle Way, any more than Newton created gravity. It's the Middle Way itself that needs the primary attention. This point also gets forgotten far too readily in partisan debates between scholars or schools of Buddhism. To write about the Buddha is often to subject oneself to much irrelevant partisan reaction.

However, there are also some strong positive reasons to write about the Buddha. As humans, we are storytelling creatures, and we need stories to inspire us. Not only does the Buddha provide a great archetypal story through which to start to understand the Middle Way, but many people will only have heard of the Middle Way in the first place because they have heard of the Buddha and Buddhism. Buddhism, for all the complex issues it raises as a tradition, also remains a major source of understanding of the Middle Way. It is only through Buddhism that I myself first started to understand it. People who approach the Middle Way from this direction often need clarification of the issues.

It is in this spirit that I am setting out to write about the Middle Way in relation to the Buddha. Though there are critical issues at many turns, my main goal is to provide a clear and positive account of the Middle Way *through* its exemplification in the stories about, and teachings of, the Buddha. Starting with what the Buddha did and said is one way of gaining a basic appreciation of the Middle Way. We can then move on to consider other possible directions from which we can understand it. I will be narrating the early life of the Buddha as a demonstration of the process of discovering the Middle Way, leading up to the first detailed account of its meaning in chapter 1.f.

The helpful reinterpretation of the Buddha and of Buddhism for today has taken considerable steps forward in recent years through the work of several Western and Secular Buddhist teachers and writers. These have inched their way towards a clearer and more helpful account of the Buddha's teachings free of dogmatic accretions. Foremost amongst them, Stephen Batchelor must particularly be mentioned. Batchelor's recent book *After Buddhism* offers in my view the best attempt yet to disentangle the helpful path from the traditional dogmas.

However, none of these writers seems to have yet managed to divest themself of the final encumbrance to discussion of the Buddha – that of appealing to historical authority. They want the Buddha they argue for to be the *real* Buddha, who is more authoritative because he is found in the earliest (or most canonical) texts. All such arguments are hostages to fortune, dependent on changing historical or textual claims. However well-justified these claims may seem now, they are subject to ambiguous evidence, and endless scholarly disputes over the interpretation of that evidence. Moreover, they have no relevance to the *content* of the Buddha's insights, which – if they are worth anything at all – should certainly be able to stand in their own right. So, in this book, I want to offer the book that I wish someone else had written before now: an interpretation of the Buddha's recorded teachings based only on practical criteria, rather than on disputable assumptions of how we could know about the 'real' historical Buddha.

Why am I concerned with the Middle Way primarily, rather than the Buddha's other teachings? The ones that generally receive more emphasis in Buddhist accounts are the Four Noble Truths, the Eightfold Path, the Threefold Refuge, Conditioned Arising, and so on. The argument for this emphasis will emerge more completely as the book goes on. The key point of this argument will be that *all these other teachings require the Middle Way to be interpreted helpfully*. If we begin with them and interpret the Middle Way in their terms, we may end up with dogma that is inadequate to helping humans in their changing conditions. The Middle Way, however, is a genuinely universal teaching which focuses on human judgement rather than on claims about reality. It thus provides a starting point for the helpful interpretation of every other teaching.

The Middle Way, as I shall understand it and present it here, is a metaphor for a practical method of improving our judgements at every point that conditions present to us. The way begins right now at whatever point you have reached, and stretches indefinitely into the judgements of the future. That way is the 'middle' way not because it is necessarily moderate or compromising in any conventional sense. Rather it is 'middle' because it avoids either positive or negative absolute claims. As we will see, the Buddha's life and teachings provide many inspiring demonstrations of this basic, practical, universal Middle Way. However, the Middle Way has also been presented in less helpful ways. Issues of comparison between different models of the Middle Way in Buddhism will be tackled later in the book (section 4).

Positively, then, this book aims first to offer an account of the Middle Way through the Buddha. However, there are various other things that I should point out at the outset that it is *not*, to avoid any possible misunderstanding. It is not a promotion of, nor an apology for, Buddhism. I have learnt a great deal from Buddhism, and at an earlier stage of my life was formally committed to it, but am so no longer. I am aiming to communicate some things I have learnt from the practice of Buddhism, and relate them to other sources of insight, rather than to promote the Buddhist tradition as such.

Nor, on the other hand, is this a scholarly book in the tradition of Buddhist Studies, even though it does have a serious academic case to make. As already mentioned, I am not aiming to uncover the 'true' or 'historical' Buddha by the examination of texts, nor indeed by any other method. I will refer to texts about the life and teachings of the Buddha (mainly those from the Pali Canon) so as to acknowledge sources of inspiration. *I will not be trying to prove anything through their authority, whether explicitly or implicitly.* This point needs to be stressed at the outset, because it is one that seems likely to be easily forgotten by readers who are familiar with traditional Buddhism and its scholarship as they read through this book. An appeal to authority should not be read into my arguments at any point, and it should not be assumed from the texts I select that I accord them more historical authority than others.

I will generally select what are commonly held to be earlier texts, only because they tend to offer a clearer, more consistent, and more balanced view of the Buddha, not because of their age per se. Rather than a 'proof' in the terms of the tradition or of its academic interpretation, I am seeking a *practically* helpful interpretation of what the traditions about the Buddha offer us. Cultural acceptability is thus also a factor in my selection of texts, because I want to encourage such helpful interpretations of texts that are already widely meaningful to people.

This means that, for the most part, I will be working with the translated texts available to English readers. I won't be getting too involved with questions about the origins or translations of those texts. This is not because I am unaware of the linguistic and textual questions that surround the texts (I have studied Pali at Cambridge with the great scholar, K.R. Norman). Rather it is because I consider those questions as for the most part having little practical consequence. It is only if we absolutise the authority of religious texts, assuming that they are the unquestionable source of truth, that we need to start worrying unduly about their authenticity. As I shall argue, the practically helpful message of the Middle Way itself precludes giving that kind of absolute authority to texts.

I am primarily a practical philosopher rather than a scholar. I am grateful for the past labours of scholars in translating the Buddhist scriptural texts. However, my experience of Buddhist scholarship has led me to the conclusion that its general impact is often an unnecessarily conservative one. By constantly focusing people's attention on questions of the language and historical authority of texts, it reinforces the unhelpful belief that we should give these texts pre-eminent authority as sources of belief. In my experience, scholars usually avoid exploring the *practical content* of texts critically, or even appreciating it symbolically.

I am interested in the *practical content* of the texts in the sense of what they can tell us that will help us to develop and improve our lives. Much other material regarding texts can and should be dispensed with – not before the texts have been acknowledged as sources, but long before the discussion of them starts to become an end in itself. Of course, it is always possible that we could be mistaken in our interpretation of ancient texts (as, indeed, we could with modern ones). However, a reasonable attempt to understand the range of meaning of key Pali, Sanskrit or other words is enough, before it becomes an end in itself. We should reach a point where it is acknowledged as far more important to find a *practically* helpful interpretation than one that is merely justified by 'accuracy', howsoever determined.

I am undertaking this task fresh from the completion of a similar one in relation to Christianity (*The Christian Middle Way*[1]). If you believe that the Middle Way is *essentially* Buddhist, please look at my discussion of Christianity for a disproof through counter-example. There I similarly offered an interpretation of the gospels and the Genesis Creation story that was led by the practically-helpful meaning we could get from them. I took context into account sufficiently to offer a coherent interpretation of the text, but not so as to be drawn into irrelevant scholarly or sectarian disputes. The Middle Way *can* be articulated in relation to any tradition whatsoever, whether religious, philosophical, political, or artistic, and is not the sole preserve or monopoly of any one tradition. That can be the case even though traditions engage with it to greatly varying degrees ('The Middle Way in Nazism' might be rather a limited study).

So what I am aiming to do in this book is to explore the elements of the Middle Way that I find in the traditions about the Buddha, not to adopt uncritically any Buddhist account of the Middle Way. Buddhism, like any tradition, offers elements of the Middle

---

1   Ellis (2018).

Way through which it addresses the conditions it encounters, but lapses into dogma in others. A critical process is necessary in order to distinguish these elements in any tradition. However, when considering Buddhism, a special appreciation is nevertheless necessary for just how far and how explicitly Buddhist tradition has conveyed the Middle Way.

So who is this book for? The primary people whom I expect to read it will be Buddhists. Such Buddhists will need to be open to the possibility of understanding the Buddha in ways that are *led* by the Middle Way. That means led by a case about the practical value of the teachings and the need to avoid abstract absolutes. I hope that they will then be able to adopt, or at least be influenced by, such a practical reading of the significance of the Buddha. In the process they will have a new resource to counteract both traditionalist dogma on the one hand and scholarly distraction on the other. It's quite possible to be inspired by the Buddha's Middle Way in a way that is held in common with every human being, Buddhist or not. Thus we can also understand the significance of that inspiration in a way that, via the Middle Way, is compatible with the inspiration and guidance found in other traditions of discourse.

However, this book could also be of interest to people who are not Buddhist, who have been put off by the predominance of traditional authority and dogma in Buddhism. I hope this book might help such people to isolate what is most helpful and relevant to their lives in Buddhist tradition, and more readily chart its relationship to what can be found in other traditions. Again, it should be humanity that comes first, Buddhist tradition second. Tackling things that way round may help people engage with Buddhist tradition who would not otherwise do so.

The course of this book, then, begins with the basic stories of the Buddha's life and teachings. These are selected from their original context with an eye to their practical understanding in relation to the Middle Way. Discussion of some of the Buddha's most famous analogies, and of the Eightfold Path, should then also help to offer Middle-Way-led interpretation of some other key Buddhist teachings. Unavoidably, in relation to this, I will then need to engage more fully and critically with the limitations of traditional Buddhist teaching and the ways in which it has developed that are evidently in conflict with the Middle Way. Very often this is a matter of interpretation, but nevertheless it needs to be clearly acknowledged that some very common interpretations of Buddhist teachings are incompatible with the Middle Way. These criticisms were the theme of my earlier book, *The Trouble with Buddhism*.[2] However, in this one I hope to put those criticisms much more in the wider context of a positive account of the valuable resources Buddhist teachings do offer.

The last part of the book offers parallels between the Buddha's Middle Way and a number of other possible models for the Middle Way. Some of these go back to ancient philosophy and religion, but the majority are due to more recent advances in scientific theory. Even those who started off being mainly interested in the Buddha alone, then, should finish the book with an awareness of the manifold forms that the Middle Way can take, and its variety of expressions in human experience.

---

2   Ellis (2011a).

1. The Middle Way in the Buddha's Early Life

1.a. The Story of Siddhartha Gautama

In this first section of this book I shall be concerned with the traditional story of the life of the man who became known as the 'Buddha' or Awakened One – Siddhartha Gautama – up to the point of what Buddhists refer to as his enlightenment or Awakening. My main source for this story will be the Pali Canon, with occasional reference to the later and much more elaborate account in Ashvaghosha's 'Acts of the Buddha' from the first century CE.[1] The context of this story is the northeastern part of the Indian subcontinent, approximately 2,500 years ago.

This is a *story*, albeit a symbolically important story. The story grew in the telling, but I have tried to stick to its simpler and more basic elements as found in the Pali Canon. In outline, the story is that of a prince leading an over-protected life, who became dissatisfied with that life, dropped out and sought religious truth in the forest. However, in the forest he also became dissatisfied with the answers he was given. He then only found a further way forward by navigating between the extremes represented by both the palace and the forest.

My goal here is only to explore the *significance* of that story, not to examine its historicity. To examine that significance, I will be drawing out the ways in which Siddhartha Gautama's position is very much like that of every other person. I will also be drawing analogies between that ancient situation and the modern one in which the Buddha's Middle Way needs now to be understood and applied. The things I have to say about the significance of the story would be just as valuable if the whole story turned out to be entirely a work of fiction.

The universality of this story is emphasised in the Buddhist tradition by the fact that it is considered to be merely one in a

---

1 Ashvaghosha, *Buddhacarita*. Johnston (1972).

long line of repeated stories. These stories are concerned with the development of successive Buddhas in successive past aeons. These past Buddhas are said to have the same basic story in outline, with only minor variations in details. In fact many of the details of the widely-circulated story about Siddhartha Gautama are actually only found in the Pali Canon as part of a story about an earlier Buddha, Vipassi.[2] Let's leave aside the beliefs about history and cosmology here and consider what this repetition of the story communicates to us today. It is primarily that the path of development taken by a Buddha is available to anyone at any time or place. We should thus *not* expect Siddhartha Gautama's own path to be unique, or to be bound by the specific expectations of one culture or religion.

The story is one that has been deservedly accorded special (but not unique) significance by Buddhists. That's because of what it has to tell us about the human condition and the best way of responding to that condition, even though there may also be other ways of communicating those same points. So, please don't allow cultural expectations of an irrelevant kind to interfere with your understanding of this universally-significant story.

Imagine yourself at a threshold. At the threshold you might take off your muddy boots. Along with your muddy boots, please divest yourself of any obsessions with an unattainable historical 'truth' (which will encourage you to dwell on Siddhartha as *uniquely* significant, which he isn't). Also divest yourself of dependence on the authority of the Buddhist tradition or its teachers (which will close your mind to the universality of the story – a story that is not only for Buddhists). If you shed these things at the entrance for the time being, you can always pick them up again on your way out if you like, but inside the house they will just be a nuisance. You are now entering the house of meaning, in which we are solely concerned with the practical significance of the story for our lives.

---

2 *Digha Nikaya* 14. Walshe (1995) pp. 199 ff.

1.b. The Palace

Siddhartha Gautama is said to have been a prince with a highly sheltered upbringing in a palace, in the land of the Shakyas, north of the Ganges valley. Ashvaghosha gives an elaborate account of the luxury and comfort of this upbringing. The Pali Canon, though, gives a much briefer account that is nevertheless enough to give us a strong impression of it:

> *I was delicately brought up, O monks; highly delicate, exceedingly delicate was my upbringing. At my father's house lotus ponds were made: in one of them blue lotuses bloomed, in another white lotuses, and in a third red lotuses, just for my enjoyment. I used only sandal unguent from Benares and my head dress, my jacket, my undergarment and my tunic were made of Benares Muslin. By day and night a white canopy was held over me, lest cold and heat, chaff or dew should trouble me. I had three palaces: one for the summer, one for the winter and one for the rainy season. In the palace for the rainy season, during the four months of the rains, I was waited upon by female musicians only, and I did not come down from the palace during these months. While in other people's homes servants and slaves receive a meal of broken rice together with sour gruel, in my father's house they were given choice rice and meat.*[1]

Overflowing resources are suggested by the lotus ponds and the palaces, luxury and comfort by the clothes, over-protectiveness by the canopy, isolation by the fact that he did not leave the palace during the rainy season. There is a hint of sexual indulgence in the 'female musicians', which are excessively elaborated into a whole chapter of sexual temptation in Ashvaghosha.[2] There is also generosity, or at least munificence, in the treatment of the servants by comparison with the social norm of the time.

Siddhartha Gautama is also us. If we want to appreciate the full significance of a story drawn from a context remote in time and space, we need to explore its significance in relation to our own experience at each stage. So what is our palace?

The most obvious aspect of the palace to alight on is its wealth and luxury, which has led Buddhists through the ages to identify it with self-indulgence. We could parallel that self-indulgence with that of the consumerist lifestyle of all those who are at least

---

1 *Anguttara Nikaya* 3.38. Nyanaponika and Bodhi (1999) pp. 53–4.
2 Ashvaghosha, *Buddhacarita* 4. Johnston (1972).

comfortably off, or better, in the modern world. We may not have three palaces, but we can divert ourselves by going on holiday to different locations where there are new pleasures. We may not have servants, but machines do much of the work that they would have undertaken in ancient times. We may not have three lotus ponds, but we have substantial control over our home environment, to decorate it as we wish. We can also increasingly extend this control over our actual environment into virtual environments where wish-fulfilment is practically unlimited. We may not have 'female musicians', but we have music, dating apps, sensual movies and even pornography readily available whenever we want it.

Nevertheless, it is not the physical environment of the palace itself that marks its full significance. Rather it is the cultural assumptions and habitual psychological states that accompany it. Those who are rich in a poor society will need to be highly protective of their wealth. Since their lives will differ so much from those around them, they will also develop ideological ways of defending those values. As Marx identified, the social and economic interests of those who control wealth and resources are often maintained by the control of theories that the rest of society are led to accept, through social conditioning from infancy. Inequality is maintained by the whole of society accepting that such inequality is natural and necessary.

There are two slightly varying ways that such a ruling ideology can be maintained. One way is to identify your privileged position with some universal source of absolute value – God has decreed it, it is 'natural', or it is 'inevitable'. Another is to present your position as a uniquely justified one for you and your group only. That means adopting plural values that define different positions for different groups ('it's our custom to run things like this, even if others' customs are different'). These two approaches are not always entirely distinct, because of course plural values can be claimed as part of a greater overriding final value. Either way, though, the effect of the ideology is to prevent awkward questions precipitating the possibility of change in the social order.

Siddhartha Gautama's context seems to have been one in which there were already competing values available in society. We know this simply because of the number of debates the Buddha later became engaged in with those of various other views, all recorded in the Pali Canon. Where there are differing values available, it is harder for the ruling classes to simply claim that their position is ordained, natural, and necessary. The alternative, however, is not to engage with universal questions at all, but rather to base one's values on those of a particular limited context. The more isolated and insulated that context, the easier it is to maintain those limited values as the only ones open to consideration. The isolation of Siddhartha's life in the palace represents a way of keeping one's beliefs immune from criticism.

A modern analogy to this is probably not so much one of geographical isolation as the 'echo chamber' effect in social media. This effect is created by people only seeing content on social media that has been selected for them – either targeted advertising or friends that they have selected as being like them or sharing their interests. If people don't come into contact with opposing views in a way that obliges them to engage with those views, they will come to regard their assumptions as the only possible and reasonable ones. Once again, then, the palace seems to represent key aspects of modern life: not just the consumerist comfort, but also the intellectual insulation.

As a product of those conditions, the palace also represents the belief that there is no better or more universal value to work for that goes beyond that of the specific context. The palace is thus a deeply conventional place, where the values of the royal family take total precedence. That conventionality could conceivably be very much duty-bound and ritualistic, as the British royal family is often depicted as being. However, it could also support a good deal of hedonistic self-indulgence, as it is depicted as doing in Ashvaghosha's more developed version of the Buddha's life.

The belief that there are no justifiable values higher than convention is *relativism*, which I understand as the view that no one given value is better justified than any other. One can imagine Siddhartha being urged by his parents, other relatives, or even loyal servants, to 'be a proper prince'. That would mean maintaining the values of his forefathers solely because of his position. To be a priest or a religious seeker, they would say, may be right for others, but not for you. There is no more general moral goal that should encompass all humans, they would imply, nothing higher to seek.

Once again, that relativism is a standard feature of modern life too. To defuse conflict when we do come into contact with people of different values, we fall back on it all too readily: 'That's OK for you, but not for me.' Hindus may have arranged marriages,

Muslims may eat halal meat, and the Vietnamese may eat dogs – not my custom, but each to his own. Such an attitude may often consist only of an appropriate tolerance for harmless differences, but it can also cut off further evaluation or judgement when these are needed. Relativism may be less obviously appropriate towards Nazis who massacre Jews, or towards traditional mutilators of female genitalia across many parts of northern Africa today. We cannot afford to cut off the very possibility of judgement.

So, we're now beginning to identify, not a single belief or kind of belief that the palace stands for, but rather a whole set of interdependent ones. There is self-indulgence, but that self-indulgence needs the support of insulated conventionality. That conventionality is also able to deflect any conflict with other values through relativism.

Perhaps you'll have noticed, too, that these values really have quite a close relationship with what are often regarded as their opposites. It's the fact that both these values and their opposites are isolated and not open to challenge that is the most significant thing about them. It would not be at all difficult to imagine Siddhartha being austere and duty-driven as a result of the isolation of palace life, as many palace-dwellers have in fact been. The conventionality could also just as easily be associated with absolutism as with relativism. That is, the palace-dwellers could be convinced that they had the universal truth (about God's commands, or nature, or whatever else) and that this gave them their exalted social position.

In the end, the most significant thing about the palace is its relationship with power. Those with power will maintain an ideology that helps them to maintain their social position. Power is maintained by ceasing to recognise the alternative claims of those who might challenge it. We maintain power, whether over others or over rejected parts of ourselves, by refusing to recognise alternative values that would challenge that power. The palace is in power, and it stays in power by isolating itself and maintaining the belief that it has the whole story.

1.c. The Four Sights and Going Forth

As long as we feel secure, there is little motive to change our attitudes. We tend to interpret the world in terms of the complacent world-view that maintains that security. It takes something at least uncomfortable and challenging, perhaps even traumatic, to stir that complacency and force us to re-examine our assumptions. Thus it was with Siddhartha Gautama. His life in the palace was stable and secure as long as it remained unchallenged by interfering conditions from outside. But that challenge did arise – in the form of what are known as the 'Three Considerations' or the 'Four Sights'.

The 'Three Considerations' are given in the Pali Canon as part of the story of Siddhartha himself. The 'Four Sights', on the other hand, are only found as part of the story of Vipassi, the earlier Buddha from a past aeon. The 'Three Considerations' consist only in new thoughts that come to Siddhartha, in the form of a recognition that his attitudes to ageing, sickness, and death are inadequate. There are some major conditions that his life in the palace is shutting out, and, perhaps in a rush, repressed recognitions come to him.

> *Amidst such splendour and an entirely carefree life, O monks, this thought came to me: 'An uninstructed worldling, though sure to become old himself and unable to escape ageing, feels repelled, humiliated or disgusted when seeing an old and decrepit person, being forgetful of his own situation. Now I too am sure to become old and cannot escape ageing. If, when seeing an old and decrepit person, I were to feel repelled, humiliated or disgusted, that would not be proper for one like myself.' When I reflected thus, monks, all my pride in youthfulness vanished.*[1]

Exactly the same point is then made about attitudes to sickness (removing Siddhartha's 'pride in health') and death (removing his 'pride in life'). What is particularly interesting about this version is that it focuses only on Siddhartha's recognition that his repulsion, humiliation, and disgust at age is based only on limited awareness. He has been taking youthfulness, along with health, age, and life, to be the whole story, taking his current assumption that they are permanent as absolute.

The 'Four Sights' is an alternative version of the same recognitions. It dramatises the 'Three Considerations' as actual people seen

---

1 *Anguttara Nikaya* 3.38. Nyanaponika and Bodhi (1999) p. 54.

in the world beyond the palace. It also adds a fourth person – a *shramana* or homeless religious seeker who provides a new model for alternative ways of thinking and living. This version of the story is told in the Pali Canon of the earlier Buddha Vipassi.[2] Here, the hero's encounter with age, sickness, and death are made into a new recognition when it is dramatized outwardly in this way. So he is presented as naively unacquainted with them. He makes his first excursion by chariot from a palace environment where he has been kept in total ignorance that ageing, sickness, and death occur at all.

This story is elaborated even further in Ashvaghosha. Here it becomes one in which the Gods *cause the appearance* of an old man, a sick man, and a corpse rather than Siddhartha encountering them in actuality.[3] In Ashvaghosha's version, everything is a theatrical set-up or mere appearance, created to manipulate the direction of Siddhartha's thoughts. While Siddhartha's parents try to set everything up so that he is not disturbed from his complacent security in the palace, the Gods, seeking the welfare of the world, set up their own counter-appearances to shake him out of that complacency. His parents are motivated to keep Siddhartha unperturbed because of a prophecy made at his birth. This prophecy was that he would either become a great king or, if he went forth from royal life, instead become a great enlightened figure. Their motive is obviously to make him into a great king, and thus avoid the unconventional and disruptive possibility of their son entering into a personal spiritual quest.

It is very easy to be distracted by these elaborations of the story into thinking of Siddhartha's insights here as part of an apparently predestined development for the world as a whole. But the grand theatre merely emphasises the importance of the kind of insights that Siddhartha is having. It would be easy to assume that they are important because they are the basis of unique revelatory claims in the Buddhist tradition. However, if we focus on the insights themselves they gain much more simplicity and universality. They are important *because* of that universality. If we start to think of them only in terms of the claims of one tradition, they actually start to lose that importance. They then become merely remote historical events of anthropological interest in specific cultures.

2   *Digha Nikaya* 14.2.1–15. Walshe (1995) pp. 207–10.
3   Ashvaghosha, *Buddhacarita* 3. Johnston (1972).

Buddhist tradition also tends to present Siddhartha here as recognising the truth of 'suffering' (*dukkha*) represented by impermanence (*anicca*). Old age, sickness, and death, after all, are changes that cause suffering, and our denial of them could take the form of ignoring the fact of change. If that was indeed the whole of the message, the story would still have universal significance. We have probably all experienced the intoxication by youth, health, or life that Siddhartha's 'considerations' move him beyond. A failure to recognise suffering through change, however, is only one possible form of the wider pattern of delusion that Siddhartha here moves beyond. If that were not the case, his story would not be relevant to those who have consistently faced up to old age, sickness, and death rather than tried to repress recognition of their impact on us. Siddhartha does not only recognise 'suffering' – the significance of his recognition has a wider scope than that. It is rather a recognition of the limitations of absolutisation and the need to take a critical stance beyond it, whatever assumption it is that we have absolutised. We might well think that youth, health, or life is the whole story. We might also think that our nation, or our beloved partner, or Catholic dogma, or the overthrow of capitalism, or even Buddhism is the whole story. In any of these cases we could experience a rude awakening in which the limitations of what we took to be total are suddenly revealed. It is only by interpreting Siddhartha's Three Considerations in that way that we find a symbol of universal relevance and complete flexibility.

The fourth sight also adds an element not present in the Three Considerations – an alternative. It is only by having an alternative to the limited options we were previously considering that we are able to move beyond them. If we imagine Siddhartha only recognising the limitations of his assumptions about youth, health, and life but not having any alternative view of them, the result could be merely a feeling of being trapped. To have negative feelings about the assumptions we hold, but no way out of those assumptions, could be torturous. That is exactly the state we are often trapped in when we have become dissatisfied with a view that no longer meets our needs. Our experience or imagination can then be too limited to move us beyond the mere negation of that view. Think of a religious believer whose whole life has been based on absolute beliefs but then 'loses his faith' in the sense of no longer being able to hold those beliefs. He may start to think that God is, in theory, impossible and absurd. At the same time, though, without God, he can only see a nullity – a life without the only kind of meaning he is used to being able to experience. As a result, he feels left with a choice between clinging to a belief he finds intellectually bankrupt, or abandoning it for a world of meaninglessness. What a terrible fate! But one caused only by our false restriction to two opposed options (one view and its bare negation) and a failure to even consider the possibility of third options.

The Buddha, fortunately, does have a third option between continuing life in the all-encompassing constraints of the palace-view and the potential nullity that might lie beyond the palace. That third option is revealed by the Fourth Sight:

> And as he was being driven to the pleasure-park, Prince Vipassi saw a shaven-headed man, one who had gone forth, wearing a yellow robe. And he said to the charioteer: 'What is the matter with that man? His head is not like other men's, and his clothes are not like other men's.'
>
> 'Prince, he is called one who has gone forth.' 'Why is he called one who has gone forth?'
>
> 'Prince, by one who has gone forth we mean one who truly follows Dhamma, who truly lives in serenity, does good actions, performs meritorious deeds, is harmless and truly has compassion for living beings.'[4]

It is the sheer difference of the *shramana* from what he has known before that sparks the prince's interest. He looks different, and his differing appearance also indicates a different lifestyle with different assumptions. In the context of ancient India, that difference may be much more than just a difference of chosen profession, but rather a whole difference of tradition and culture. The tradition of going forth as a homeless wanderer has often been associated with the aboriginal groups in ancient India – those who preceded the dominant invaders from whose descendants Siddhartha Gautama may well have sprung. Whatever the historical explanation for the cultural differences between Siddhartha's background and the *shramana*'s, what counts universally is the shocking size of the cultural gap. Perhaps the nearest analogy today might be the offspring of a member of the socio-economic elite 'dropping out' of Oxford or Harvard and joining a community of disreputable vagrants.

---

4   *Digha Nikaya* 14.2.14. Walshe (1995) pp. 209–10.

In addition to the cultural gap, though, there is also an idealisation of the *shramana*. Whatever this man does, he does 'truly'. He is not seen as a person going through a developmental process *aiming* to be better and more harmless, but simply as an absolute embodiment of goodness and compassion. The idealisation is not found only in the charioteer's words, but in the alacrity with which Siddhartha subsequently decides to adopt the same alternative lifestyle for himself. So, although the *shramana* offers a genuine alternative, it is an idealised alternative. As the story continues, we will see the further limitations created by this idealisation, and how Siddhartha overcomes them.

As Siddhartha adopts this alternative life by 'going forth' from the palace into the forest, he is already implicitly modelling the preliminary stages of engaging with the Middle Way. He is doing so even though the Middle Way itself is not yet explicit in his thinking. For the Middle Way begins from wherever we start, and is the most helpful path ahead of us. It may be impossible to go directly from seeing the limitations of one set of assumptions to a balanced position in which we also see the limitations of the opposite set. We have to free ourselves from the first set of absolute assumptions before we can even understand the second and opposing ones clearly enough. In order to begin to engage with the Middle Way, then, we probably need to start by 'going forth' from the initial context with its load of absolute assumptions. In the process it is difficult to avoid idealising the alternative, because all our expectations become loaded onto it.

In Ashvaghosha's elaborated version of the 'going forth', the conflict caused by absolute assumptions on both sides is emphasised by an additional moral conflict. It is made clear that by 'going forth' Siddhartha was abandoning his wife and young son as well as his parents and future royal responsibilities. Siddhartha's charioteer, Chanda, reminds him of these social responsibilities and unsuccessfully tries to dissuade him from his renunciation of worldly life.[5] This often creates a moral difficulty for modern readers who would like to wholly identify with Siddhartha as a hero, for he has broken what for many modern readers is a central moral taboo. Ancient Indians might judge the abandonment of one's family more leniently (provided they were looked after by other relatives), especially because of their tendency to idealise 'going forth' by comparison.

5   Ashvaghosha, *Buddhacarita* 6. Johnston (1972).

However, this may be little comfort to a modern reader who finds it difficult to find the universal spiritual hero they seek in such a pre-feminist figure – one who apparently does not even consult his wife to gain her support and consent before abandoning her.

But there is another way of reading the going forth that lets go of that wish to idealise Siddhartha. In such a reading, Siddhartha does not have to be perfect, and thus we do not have to rationalise away his failings. He is finding ways forward that are unavoidably messy and unsatisfactory, and that involve sacrifices of various sorts. However, in the very messiness of that process the universality of the Middle Way can be found. Siddhartha is questioning what he has considered up to that point to be absolute – the values of the palace. He has invested in those values for the whole of his life. In order to get free of the absolute power of those values he has to adopt the extreme of tearing himself away. Perhaps we can imagine other possible paths he could have taken that would have involved more compromise. Would it have been so difficult to stay in the palace for the moment whilst learning about alternatives, and even using his power in the palace to gradually change its values? But the likelihood is that Siddhartha would not have been able to do this in practice. Instead his psychological habituation to the values of the palace would continue to dominate him. It is only by getting away, and initially by trying out the extreme of opposing values, that he can cease to be sucked into the all-consuming absolute environment he is in. To get away he has to make sacrifices, even ones that affect others, and it may well prove a mistake or a later matter of regret to do this. Thus, all we can do is try to take into account the total conditions at the time we make our judgement. If we only follow a rigid rule, moral or otherwise, we may fail to address important conditions by doing so.

One universal value that the Four Sights communicates is that of provisionality. If we are provisional when we judge, we are capable of adopting a critical view of our habitual assumptions (as represented by the Three Considerations). Crucially, though, we can also recognise and consider new alternatives (as represented by the Fourth Sight).

In moving beyond an absolutising context where he would be continually forced to think in the old way, Siddhartha's 'going forth' also involves the first step of other constituent principles that I shall argue (as we go on) are aspects of the Middle Way. These include scepticism, where we recognise our fallible human state and thus question the certainties we have adopted only by ignoring that fallibility in the past. They also include integration, the actual healing of conflict by reaching out beyond entrenched positions, either in ourselves or in others. Healing of entrenched divisions is relatively easy if we already have civilised conditions of dialogue and reflection set up for us. It is very much harder when we are caught in the power of a group that exerts a huge amount of pressure on us to keep thinking in a certain absolute way in accordance with its values. The first step towards integration has to be separating ourselves from the values of that group sufficiently to allow wider awareness to emerge. At this stage, Siddhartha still has a way to go both in his scepticism and his integration, but he is beginning to implicitly recognise and apply them.

This first step is probably the hardest and most risky one in the Middle Way. It opens us to frustration, rejection, ridicule, moral ostracisation, or almost any punishment the group can throw at us. It is also the hardest step to feel confident or serene in taking, because we are still being buffeted around by absolute thinking. We may have only a weak and preliminary awareness of our wider experience.

But there are always some courageous people who are willing to take those first steps. Think of the whistleblower who uncovers corruption in a large and powerful organisation. Think of the priest who starts to examine the founding assumptions of his church at the risk of all the vested status as a believer he has built up in his whole life and career. Think of the junior officer who decides to disobey orders at the risk of execution for treason. These people are not aware that they are the heroes of stories, nor do they know that it will turn out well when they do it. Instead they take risks – they reach out and dare to think in a different way. In that way they stay in touch with the heart of moral motivation even if they disobey its letter. The 'going forth' can represent all of that if we open our minds to those meanings, rather than thinking of them only as the actions of the Buddha predestined for enlightenment. It is better to think of the 'going forth' as a mistake than it is to rationalise it with the assumption of hindsight, for its chief significance lies in a willingness to make mistakes.

1.d. The Forest: Spiritual Teachers

The 'forest' represents the uncultivated, uncivilised areas that in ancient India were obviously far more extensive than they are today. In going to dwell in the forest, then, one begins by facing up to those areas of experience that have previously been repressed by civilised conventions and assumptions. The forest is often associated with fear – of wild animals, of starvation, of disorientation. Thus it is also the best place to go in order to encounter one's fears so as to begin integrating them.[1] Those who 'go forth' into the 'homeless life', then, should create an opportunity to leave behind the normal assumptions of human society. Along with these go the safety and security of the environment society creates, even though in practice they need to stay close enough to human habitations to get food.

There are many ways today that people 'go forth' into the 'forest' to seek the same suspension of social assumptions and thus broaden their awareness beyond the limitations of their social context. There are wilderness experiences and expeditions, solitary or shared retreats, hikes and pilgrimages – whether long or short, 'religious' or 'secular'. Religious buildings such as churches, mosques, and temples often evoke the forest in their construction and use of space. They offer islands of reflection in the midst of the obsessive atmosphere of modern cities. In some ways museums, art galleries, gardens, and parks can offer the same opportunities. Even within a home, a meditation or prayer space, a study, or a bedroom can offer a space in which the press of social expectation and belief can be temporarily suspended. We can go forth on a larger or a smaller scale, perhaps initially for relaxation. But relaxation restores and re-opens the imagination and enables alternative meaning to arise, so that, in turn, alternative beliefs become possible.

Siddhartha Gautama, however, went forth into the forest in a highly committed and idealised way. Rather than going there temporarily to gain a different perspective on his normal life, he completely abandoned that earlier life:

> ...*Though my mother and father wished otherwise and wept with tearful faces, I shaved off my hair and beard, put on the yellow robe, and went forth from the home life into homelessness.*[2]

1 *Majjhima Nikaya* 4. Ñanamoli and Bodhi (1995) pp. 102 ff.
2 *Majjhima Nikaya* 26.14. Ñanamoli and Bodhi (1995) p. 256.

In the process he embraced a set of cultural conventions that were established in ancient India at the time: those of the *shramana*. The *shramana* provided the rest of society with valuable access to the otherwise repressed alternative perspective, beyond the norms, conventions, and responsibilities of the household life. Within Indian culture this totalising vision of religious life was (and remains) in tension with the Brahminical model. A brahmin is a priest providing ritual services from a point of leadership *within* society. The Brahminical model must appeal to dogmatic certainties about a natural order in which proper Hindu rituals are observed. The *shramana* is in a position, instead, to question all those certainties. In the Buddha's time, there were evidently a wide range of *shramana* schools offering very different theories about the religious life.[3] However, it is the contrast between the *shramana* and householder lifestyles itself that has created a huge dichotomy. That dichotomy occurred both in the Buddha's context, and in the model of the religious life that became established in early Buddhism.[4] By going forth into the forest, Siddhartha crosses a big divide into an alternative, and much more open, religious lifestyle.

In that open lifestyle, defined only by an individual quest, the individual *shramana* was free to meditate and reflect alone, or to join groups of other *shramana*s. However, there was an obvious attraction for a new *shramana* in seeking the relative security provided by a spiritual instructor. A teacher could help the fresh dropout to engage effectively with these new conditions. However, the context of instruction (and of solidarity with other disciples) was also likely to create the same conditions in miniature as those that had lately been abandoned in mainstream society, and that are found in all similar human circumstances: fixed leadership and social roles, assumptions and conventions shared by the group, and boundary questions about who should be accepted into it. Those who leave their original social context in such a decisive way are vulnerable to new kinds of exploitation by what we might now call a 'religious cult'. That's because they have not yet developed sufficiently rooted alternative ways of meeting their human needs for social support.

Such is the context in which we need to interpret the next stage of Siddhartha's story. Here there are successive encounters with two

---

3   Ling (1973) ch. 5.
4   Ray (1994) pp. 15 ff.

spiritual teachers called (in their Pali versions) Alara Kalama and Udaka Ramaputta. In the Pali Canon account,[5] the two encounters are told using exactly the same words, with the only difference being the 'base' declared by each teacher: 'nothingness' for Alara Kalama and 'neither perception nor non-perception' for Udaka Ramaputta. In each case, Siddhartha comes to the teacher concerned seeking instruction on how to lead 'the holy life in this Dhamma and Discipline'. He quickly learns 'to speak with knowledge and assurance' of the teachings offered by each. He then realises that the teachers have achieved more than this, having 'direct knowledge' of the 'base' that they teach. Siddhartha then also learns this 'direct knowledge' to the same level as his teachers. In each case, the teacher recognises this, and then honours Siddhartha by offering to share the leadership of his community. In each case, however, Siddhartha remains dissatisfied, and goes away seeking further wisdom.

The 'base' appealed to by each teacher needs to be understood in relation to the formula of the four 'immaterial states' or 'higher *jhanas*' (or *dhyanas*, levels of meditative absorption) found in Buddhist teaching. The four lower *jhanas* consist of levels of absorption that can be achieved with persistent meditation in good conditions. They have certain definable features (one-pointedness, initial and sustained thought, rapture, bliss, and equanimity) increasingly present. The higher *jhanas* are then presented in the early Buddhist literature as higher and more subtle attainments. They can be reached by monks who continue to apply skill and effort to meditation beyond the fourth *jhana*. These higher *jhanas* are described as 'the base consisting of boundless space', 'the base consisting of boundless consciousness', 'the base consisting of nothingness', and 'the base consisting of neither perception nor non-perception'.[6] Nevertheless, these higher *jhanas* are perceived as falling short of final Awakening. Their traditional significance in the story of Siddhartha's encounters with his teachers is to show that they guided Siddhartha to extremely subtle levels of meditative attainment, but no further than that. Traditionally, then, the explanation for Siddhartha moving on was that his teachers

---

5 *Majjhima Nikaya* 26.15–16. Ñanamoli and Bodhi (1995) pp. 257–9. Also repeated almost exactly in *Majjhima Nikaya* 36, 85, and 100.

6 *Vibhanga* 245, *Visuddhimagga* of Buddhaghosa. Ñanamoli (1991) ch. 10, pp. 320 ff.

had not gone far enough, not being able to teach him the whole path to final Awakening.

However, such accounts of the path begin with assumptions about the final achievement of Awakening and deduce understanding of the path backwards from them. These risk undermining the universality of the Middle Way. They turn it into, at best, a technical description of the achievements to be sought in the limited cultural context of Buddhist monasticism. At worst they turn it into a dogma that undermines the Middle Way itself. I would argue that a rather different, and much more universal, significance can be drawn from the episodes with Alara Kalama and Udaka Ramaputta than that Siddhartha merely surpassed them because they weren't enlightened yet. What matters in the Middle Way is not *what is achieved*, but rather *how we judge it*. The way in which judgements are made about the conclusions we can draw from meditative experience is far more significant here than what category of meditative experiences they were.

Alara Kalama and Udaka Ramaputta each had profound experiences which, one must assume, transformed their lives positively and perhaps enabled them to develop new levels of wisdom and compassion. Nevertheless, the failure of judgement in each case is that *they concluded that these experiences were the whole story*. Any experience of a finite being is bound to be limited both in terms of the information it provides, and in the extent to which it makes mental states adequate and reliable. These experiences, *however profound*, can be no exception. The Buddhist tradition tends to conclude that the instructions of these two teachers were only inadequate because they had not yet reached the true and final goal. However, a more profound and universal conclusion would be that they were inadequate only because they thought they had reached the true and final goal.

Obviously this same point must also be applied to Siddhartha himself, however beneficial, positive, and awe-inspiring his experiences. Being human and finite, whatever experiences he goes on to have must be subject to the same criteria that Siddhartha is said to have applied to Alara Kalama and Udaka Ramaputta. We must conclude that they are not perfect, absolute, or final. In doing so we will not be diminishing him or his achievements in any way, but merely recognising that they are great *human* achievements. To follow the Middle Way we need to follow Siddhartha's example rather than idealise him.

As Siddhartha leaves each teacher, he says:

> But it occurred to me: 'This Dhamma does not lead to disenchantment, to dispassion, to cessation, to peace, to direct knowledge, to enlightenment, to Nibbana, but only to reappearance in the base of nothingness [or neither-perception-nor-non-perception].' Not being satisfied with that Dhamma, I left it and went away.[7]

This raises a central conceptual question that is important in understanding the Middle Way. When we make a negative claim, there is a crucial ambiguity. That claim can be understood either as asserting a negative opposite, or as simply failing to affirm a positive. For example, 'I don't believe that dogs always eat meat' can either mean that I believe dogs don't always eat meat, or that I don't have enough information on the subject to definitely conclude that they do. In the above quotation attributed to the Buddha, his belief that the teaching (Dhamma, or Dharma) of Alara Kalama and Udaka Ramaputta does not lead to disenchantment etc. can on the one hand be interpreted as meaning that there is a Dhamma that leads to disenchantment etc., but this isn't it. On the other, it can be read as meaning that he simply can't conclude that this Dhamma does not lead to disenchantment etc., whilst remaining uncertain as to whether there is any alternative that does.

Siddhartha is *on a quest*. He has a goal in mind that is meaningful to him. However, that does not require the fulfilment of his quest to consist in the achievement of that goal as he initially conceived it. Nor does it necessarily mean that the failure to achieve enlightenment in an absolute sense would be a failure of that quest. It is in the episodes with Alara Kalama and Udaka Ramaputta that he first has to re-examine the nature of that quest. If he imagined that it would lead to the finding of a complete answer in the forest that was not available to him in the palace, he has been disappointed, not once, but twice. That does not mean that he is no further forward in his quest. Rather it means it is beginning to turn from a quest for absolute answers into a quest to overcome delusions that he can identify in experience. It seems to me here that the meaning of that

---

7 The Noble Search, *Majjhima Nikaya* 26.15–16. Ñanamoli and Bodhi (1995) pp. 258–9.

quest is already beginning to change into one defined by the Middle Way, rather than defined by the positive absolute represented by the idea of Awakening.

Siddhartha's disappointment with religious teachers is reflected in the experience of every other person who has ever idealised an authority figure and been disillusioned. Most of us, to disengage from the authority of our parents, find substitutes, but these are also then found wanting. It may be when we recognise the limitations of a school-teacher or college-lecturer whom we knew or idealised in youth. It may come in the fall from grace of a guru caught in sexual misconduct. It may come in the critical perspective offered by historical scholarship or philosophy on fundamentalist beliefs about Jesus or the Buddha, so they cease to be the absolutely flawless figures we projected.

Nevertheless, the archetype remains. We do not have to cease finding Awakening meaningful, or cease to be inspired by it or to work in the direction it represents, just because we recognise our lack of justification for beliefs about its instantiation. Idealisations fall, but they do not have to take ideals with them. In many ways, the ideals grow stronger when they cease to be projected, when we cease to assume perfection in persons or things that are imperfect. We are then better able to detect the messy and imperfect elements of them that we are more likely to find in experience.

1.e. The Forest: Asceticism

The episode of Siddhartha's sojourn with the two teachers does not yet complete the forest phase. Nor has Siddhartha yet discovered the Middle Way explicitly, even if he is moving towards it. In going beyond the absolute authority of the two teachers and developing his own authentic and autonomous response, he has progressed towards the Middle Way in one respect. However, he has yet to apply this to the judgements about his practice itself. In the episode in which he tries and abandons his ascetic practices, Siddhartha not only needs to move beyond his teachers' authority, but also to move beyond the tendency to impose the will of one voice within himself over another.

> *Just as a strong man might seize a weaker man by the head or shoulders and beat him down, constrain him, and crush him, so too, with my teeth clenched and my tongue pressed against the roof of my mouth, I beat down, constrained, and crushed mind with mind, and sweat ran from my armpits. But although tireless energy was aroused in me and unremitting mindfulness was established, my body was overwrought and uncalm because I was exhausted by the painful striving.*[1]

Asceticism typically involves an 'act of will': the attempt to force the beliefs of a 'higher' or 'true' self who is judged right, onto a lower self who is subject to rejected qualities such as greed, hatred, and ignorance. This is a process that can also be described as *repression*, and involves the maintenance of conflict within one's own psyche. Repression may be seen in terms of conscious desires versus unconscious desires. Alternatively it can be seen simply as a clash between desires that emerge more strongly at one time and those that arise more strongly at another. As the extract above makes clear, a conflict between parts of the psyche is also a bodily conflict that has the effect of inflicting undue stress on the body. If we stimulate our nervous systems to respond to a danger that is not threatening us externally but only internally, there is potentially no rest from the imaginary fight with one's own weaknesses. It is hardly surprising if we cannot keep up this fight for very long.

The standpoint for asceticism is also that of a certainty that we cannot justify: the certainty that the wilful and repressive self is the right and 'true' self. Given the variability of our experience, we

---

1   *Majjhima Nikaya* 36.20. Ñanamoli and Bodhi (1995) p. 337.

can never be sure that we will not come to regret and revise any such certainty. This unjustified certainty is often reinforced by the interdependent assumptions of a whole set of justificatory absolute beliefs. For modern ascetics, that is likely to involve beliefs about the overriding value of their work or of their duty to perform it, regardless of the cost to their minds and bodies. In the Buddha's time, it was an ideology of personal merit accrued from the practice of austerities, which would lead to a better rebirth in future. Absolutised ideas about endlessly deferred gratification tend to form the common factor in asceticism. For ascetics, pleasure in the future is always more important than pleasure now, even though the *idea* of pleasure may be just as dominant as it is for the most self-indulgent hedonist.

Siddhartha is accompanied by five companions who urge him on to ever more severe austerities. These companions represent the surrounding ascetic culture of those *shramana*s with its ideology of salvation.[2] However, the Pali Canon account focuses much more on his apparently isolated attempts to impose the will of part of himself on the other part.

The ascetic practices of Siddhartha described in the Pali Canon include 'breathingless meditation' and self-starvation, each attempted at different levels. He holds his breath again and again with dogged persistence, but he just encounters increasing levels of suffering and stress due to it, from 'a loud sound of winds coming out of my earholes' to 'violent winds carving up my belly' and 'a violent burning in my body'.[3] As for the self-starvation, after giving up the attempt at not eating at all, Siddhartha tries taking only 'very little food, a handful each time', which results in extreme emaciation that is graphically described:

> *Because of eating so little my backside became like a camel's hoof. Because of eating so little the projections on my spine stood out like corded beads. Because of eating so little my ribs jutted out as gaunt as the crazy rafters of an old roofless barn. Because of eating so little the gleam of my eyes sank far down in their sockets, looking like the gleam of water that has sunk far down in a deep well....*[4]

---

2 *Majjhima Nikaya* 36.33. Ñanamoli and Bodhi (1995) p. 340.
3 *Majjhima Nikaya* 36.21–5. Ñanamoli and Bodhi (1995) pp. 337–9.
4 *Majjhima Nikaya* 36.28. Ñanamoli and Bodhi (1995) p. 339.

The ascetic is caught in an obsessive and abstracted set of goal-driven beliefs. But each time he tries to impose his will on his body, his recalcitrantly embodied nature is reaffirmed by the resulting pain. Yet, so entrenched is the delusion of the separate, will-driven self that the ascetic will not learn from this experience, but rather assumes that he has not yet tried hard enough. There can hardly be a more vivid illustration of the delusions of the self that thinks itself independent of the body, or of the completely fruitless conflict that arises from that delusion. This kind of response involves a closed feedback loop, in which obsessive desire feeds rigid belief that then feeds obsessive desire, always based on the same assumptions. This conflict is created by the over-dominance of the linguistic and goal-driven centres of the brain's left hemisphere (see chapter 7.h), which holds the individual in an assumed frame and endlessly confirms it.

It has now become doubly clear that the 'forest' is subject to exactly the same absolutising delusions as the 'palace', because Siddhartha has brought those delusions with him. In order to get beyond the power of the assumptions of the palace, with its conventionality and hedonism, he has embraced their opposites: religious absolutism and asceticism. Neither of these has proved adequate, not because the beliefs and practices in each context don't address some conditions, but because they don't address all conditions in the way he wants them to. The palace addresses the conditions of social organisation. The cults of his spiritual teachers in the forest address the conditions of learning spiritual practices. Asceticism in the forest addresses the conditions of temporary self-control – the need to be able to suppress current desires for the moment in order to focus energy on one action at a time. However, none of these addresses all the conditions involved in the development of human beings, including their ability to avoid suffering. Human beings have a complex set of inter-related needs and goals that cannot be simply met by one formulaic prescription.

The way in which Siddhartha finds his way out of the closed ascetic loop is indicative of some of the most basic of those conditions:

> *I considered: 'I recall that when my father the Sakyan was occupied, while I was sitting in the cool shade of a rose-apple tree, quite secluded from sensual pleasures, secluded from unwholesome states, I entered upon and abided in*

the first jhana, which is accompanied by applied and sustained thought, with rapture and pleasure born of seclusion.'[5]

The experience of meditation based on mindfulness, in contrast to ascetic practices, is based not on rejection of the body, but on sympathetic awareness of it. Anyone who has ever experienced the first *jhana* (state of absorption) in meditation (which I believe I have), will be aware that its most basic condition is a full acceptance of the body as part of one's experience. Our *experience* of the body as at the basis of all meaning and thought is quite distinct from beliefs *about* the body, and its changeability as an object. Indeed, *jhana* could be defined as a temporarily integrated state of the body, in which all the energies that we experience from any part of our body become unified. The unification of energies produces the rapture mentioned in the text. Barriers and conflicts temporarily melt away, so that other recalcitrant desires not fitting the dominant desire can no longer be treated as internal enemies. In such a state of integration, it becomes grotesque to return to the kind of conflictual and self-destructive assumptions found in asceticism.

There are also other features of the rose-apple tree experience that offer a way beyond the closed loop of ascetic assumptions. The fact that it was secluded, away from all duties and distractions, makes it a potential context for wider awareness to arise apart from the assumptions of the context. Yet the episode did not occur in the forest, but back in the palace. It becomes clear that the palace is not quite so absolutely to be rejected as it was before. In some ways Siddhartha's life there at times allowed conditions to be addressed that were not addressed during his life in the forest. The rose-apple tree episode thus becomes a unifying point, beyond the assumptions associated with either the palace or the forest. There, wider experience can be gathered to meet the new conditions. This unifying point becomes the gateway to the recognition of the Middle Way.

---

5   *Majjhima Nikaya* 36.31. Ñanamoli and Bodhi (1995) p. 340.

1.f. Discovery of the Middle Way

The explicit discovery of the Middle Way may not be easily reducible to one moment of recognition. However, if there is a good candidate for such a moment in the Pali Canon, it follows immediately on Siddhartha's remembrance of the *jhana* experience under the rose-apple tree. The text then continues:

> '*Could that be the path to enlightenment?*' *Then, following on that memory, came the realisation: 'That is the path to enlightenment'.*[1]

In terms of the universal value of the story, it is this, not the enlightenment itself, that is the most crucial point. It offers a recognition about the nature of the path rather than a claim about the destination. The path is something that we all need to judge and re-judge at each instant, the destination merely an abstract idea of the purpose of treading the path. Crucially, Siddhartha recognises the path before he claims to have reached the destination. This makes it clear that the path is only dependent on the destination insofar as the destination becomes a symbol standing for the path; the destination does not tell us what direction the path is to take. The path, because of its universal nature in every individual's experience, can only ever consist in a way of judging the circumstances we find ourselves in, whatever they are. That path can be followed even if the individual concerned does not have any final beliefs about the destination. All that is needed are practical beliefs about the path itself.

From the passage above, however, it looks superficially as though the path consists only in the *jhana* experience itself. If one assumed this, it would be easy to draw the conclusion that the path consists only of ascension through *jhanas*, until one arrives at Awakening as a kind of super-*jhana*. The role of the 'higher *jhanas*' in relation to Alara Kalama and Udaka Ramaputta earlier in the story might have also encouraged this kind of interpretation. It might lead us to imagine Siddhartha roaring past his teachers (who have *only* achieved those higher *jhanas*) to win the race to the finishing post before them. But all of this would be to fix on and absolutise particular elements of the story whilst missing its more universal significance. The path is available for *everyone*, offering a way forward from wherever they are. Not everyone is in a position even to attain the lower *jhanas*, let

---

1   *Majjhima Nikaya* 36.31. Ñanamoli and Bodhi (1995) p. 340.

alone to surpass the higher ones. We must not mistake the particular details of the path of Siddhartha for the path itself that the story helps to more widely symbolise.

I have already argued that, instead, the significance of the way in which Siddhartha surpasses his two spiritual teachers lies in the way that they absolutise their achievements. They believe them to be the whole story or the totality of the path. The remembrance of the earlier experience of *jhana* under the rose-apple tree, then, is significant in another way, because it gives Siddhartha wider, more grounded awareness. That awareness enables him to stop absolutising the assumptions of asceticism. He has now recognised that awareness is what enables us to move beyond absolutisation. *Jhana* is a source of increasingly integrated awareness, but it is not a permanent state: rather it is attained in meditation and then lost as one re-engages with other activities outside meditation. *Jhana*, then, is a very useful state for Siddhartha to cultivate in order to avoid absolutisation – but it is not the only possible way of avoiding absolutisation. Nor does his attainment even of the very highest state of *jhana* guarantee that he will never absolutise again. *Jhana* is important to his individual path, and may be important in many others, but it is contingent to the whole path in general, not definitive of that path.

Siddhartha's recognition of the path here is also a recognition of the *Middle Way* because of the nature of the story that has preceded it. The path he has found does not consist in a return to the values of the palace. Nevertheless it adopts as valuable an experience he had in the context of the palace, as well as its positive valuation of pleasure. The path he has found also avoids the absolutisation of the values of the forest, both those of his spiritual teachers and those of asceticism, but nevertheless it maintains the wider value of the spiritual quest, which is the central value of the forest. The Middle Way, then, consists most basically here in the avoidance of absolutisation on either side. It seeks a path that distinguishes what is helpful in mutually opposed sets of beliefs without their wholesale acceptance.

The opposition between the palace and the forest may have symbolic resonance far beyond the Buddha's context. However, it does not offer a complete key to all the absolutising oppositions that might occur in human life, but rather *an example* of such opposition. It also helps to represent some of the structural features of absolutising opposition and how to avoid them. The example must not be mistaken for a universal statement of the Middle Way. This is clear not only from its dependence on the Buddha's specific context, but also from the issues of interpretation raised by the palace and the forest. Does the palace stand for social conventionality or for individualistic self-indulgence? These could easily be in conflict with each other in a different context, where asceticism has become a conventional duty. Does the forest stand for the absolutisation of particular religious experiences, or for the authority of religious teachers, or for asceticism? Again, these could be in conflict, for example if an authoritative religious leader was a scriptural fundamentalist who forbade giving any credence to experience. It is not always clear what the palace and the forest stand for, nor that they are really independent of each other. It would be very easy to attribute religious motives to the palace, or introduce royal sponsorship to corrupt the forest.

What is clear, however, is that, in the mind of Siddhartha at the point when he made the judgements he made, the palace and the forest represented values that were in conflict. He modelled an approach to the Middle Way that any other person might make when in a similar position of engulfment by absolute values. He first separated himself from that context to embrace the opposite, but then also remained critically aware of the limitations of that opposite, using it to work towards a more helpful and adequate third option. In becoming aware of the limitations of the opposite, a recollection of the strengths of the first set of values also proved crucial.

Such a strategy, modelled in this way, can be transferred to all sorts of apparently very different scenarios, across the whole range of human experience. Let me suggest a few examples:

- An alcoholic is struggling with addiction that assumes the absolute value of alcohol in giving meaning to his life. He goes forth to a rehabilitation centre where he 'dries out' and gains a different perspective on the motives of his addiction. The rehabilitation centre is helpful to him, but it relies on a medical model. It is only when he ceases to be dependent on that model and takes fuller responsibility for his own recovery that he begins to find longer-term ways out of alcoholism.
- A girl brought up in a conservative Muslim family runs away and throws herself into a life that enjoys everything forbidden

by her upbringing: living alone, drinking, going to night clubs, having a variety of sexual relationships, reading atheist books and so on. However, after a couple of years she burns out and starts to miss the security and discipline of her background. She then goes to a mindfulness class and starts to meditate, beginning to rediscover that sense of purpose even though her family has disowned her.

- A scientist has been researching the evidence for a certain type of theory all his life, has become well-known in that field and has made it the basis of his career and reputation. However, a younger colleague makes a breakthrough that offers a completely different type of theory. The new theory explains the same phenomena, as well as clearing up lots of puzzling discrepancies and offering a whole new line of research. Much of the older scientist's work is now looking like a waste of time. Feeling bitter, he remains attached to his old theory and tries to argue for it, but his position becomes increasingly untenable. So eventually, in a dramatic public announcement, he announces that his younger colleague is right and that he will give up the old line of research. Humiliated, he serves a subordinate role in a research programme now headed by his younger colleague. However, after a few years his continuing critical perspective on the new line of research enables him to identify some weaknesses in the new theory, so that it can be helpfully modified.

All of these disparate examples involve opposed pairs of absolute beliefs. In some cases those beliefs may completely dominate a particular social context, along with a number of other interdependent beliefs (e.g. Conservative Islam). In others they may be only one relatively isolated belief creating a blockage in a context where many other beliefs are provisional (e.g. attachment to a theory in science). The beliefs may be concerned with presumed facts, or with values, or with both. They can be scientific, ethical, or aesthetic (or more likely a combination of all of these). The groups that reinforce these absolute beliefs may be large or small, formal or informal, and their beliefs may be highly systematised or completely incoherent. The absolute beliefs may get a lot of support from obsessive desire or anxiety that may have past causes (e.g. alcoholism). Alternatively, they may be relatively abstract and contextually dependent (e.g. attachment to a theory). What allows the Middle Way approach to resolving them is the movement beyond the limitations of that pair of absolutes, not completely accepting the assumptions of either. Though it may begin as a relatively crude movement from one position towards its opposite, it grows in subtlety and becomes less dependent on one side as it proceeds.

The Middle Way, understood in this way, is a *principle of judgement*, not a metaphysical claim or a natural law of the universe. It is distinguished by the structural features of the way we judge, rather than any particular content to our judgements. It does not guarantee any particular results from judging in this way, but only allows for greater adequacy in the judgement itself. It does this by ensuring that we remove absolutisations that are likely to block that judgement and leave us in fixed patterns of response to our environment. This idea of greater adequacy of judgement by avoiding absolutisations can be justified in many other ways, as we will see particularly in section 7. I recognise that this is not the conventional Buddhist account of what the Middle Way consists in, but will leave it until section 4 to argue against the limitations of those traditional Buddhist accounts. For the moment I want to focus on only on a positive account of the Middle Way related to the Buddha.

The elements of the Middle Way are worthy of precise analysis to show more clearly how it operates, both in the Buddha's life and in universal practice. I have identified five key elements in the Middle Way which I will now list and relate to the story of the Buddha so far:

1. **Scepticism** This is the basic recognition of uncertainty (not to be misunderstood as in any respect a negative position – see chapter 4.a). It follows from our finite, embodied experience. In the Buddha's early life this scepticism is shown in the way in which he fails to accept the dogmas of either the palace or the forest, but continues to relate to them as uncertain.
2. **Provisionality** This is the capacity, not only to be critically aware of the limitations of any given belief, but to have alternatives to it available to us (which requires imagination). In the Buddha's early life this is particularly represented by the Fourth Sight that provided an alternative to the palace, and the *jhana* experience under the rose-apple tree that provided an alternative to asceticism.

3. **Agnosticism** This is the ability to suspend our beliefs in either of an opposed pair of absolutes. We don't involve ourselves in the mutual recrimination between them. We steadfastly avoid absolute beliefs that we realise will only provoke conflict either internally or externally. This quality can only start to be developed once we have got beyond an initial rejection of the first extreme. We then begin to weigh its absolutisations equally with those of the second, rather than privileging one absolutisation over the other. In the Buddha's early life, that agnosticism starts to be shown when Siddhartha moves decisively beyond asceticism without re-embracing the values of the palace.
4. **Incrementality** This is the prioritisation of judgement of qualities as a matter of degree rather than as absolutes that must be true or false. You may also have come across this in the idea of recognising shades of grey as opposed to 'black-and-white' thinking, dualism or dichotomy. Siddhartha embraces incrementality in relation to the *jhanas* when he moves on from Alara Kalama and Udaka Ramaputta. What he rejects is their absolute interpretations of their achievements. Thus by implication he sees those achievements only as points in a spectrum of meditative achievement. As he abandons asceticism he also begins to acknowledge an incremental view of pleasure. Pleasure is then no longer something to be wholly avoided, but rather seen as an experience that may create degrees of attachment.
5. **Integration** Whilst the sceptical and agnostic principles of the Middle Way emphasise avoidance of absolutes, integration is the positive counterpart of these. It consists of the process of unification of previously opposed desires, meanings, and beliefs. Integration is made possible by the avoidance of absolutes and the conflict they create. A particular judgement can become more integrated, and thus more adequate, depending on the habitual psychological states of the individual. These states in turn are influenced by the degree of integration between individuals in the social and political context. Siddhartha's experience of *jhana* provides an example of integration, and shows the centrality of integration as the psychological effect of the practice of the Middle Way. I will have much to say in section 5 about the ways that practices taught by the Buddha can aid the development of

The Middle Way in the Buddha's Early Life 37

integration. As we will see, Siddhartha's further progression after discovering the Middle Way continues to reflect a process of integration.

All five of these elements of the Middle Way will have a central place in the exposition of its meaning and practice to be found in the rest of this book. They are primarily justified, not by their explicit presence in any authoritative text, but by their practical value: one that can be applied by humans without appeal to metaphysical assumptions. But one may seek sources of inspiration for practising them, and perhaps respected sources of information to boost their credibility. One can find that inspiration or credibility in the Buddhist tradition, and the story I am telling here about their place in the life of the Buddha may help you find it. So may the things I have to say in the rest of this book about their place in the Buddha's teachings.

To return to the Pali Canon text, it is also worth noting that Siddhartha's discovery of the Middle Way is enacted immediately by an action that is of symbolic as well as practical importance:

> I considered: 'It is not easy to attain that pleasure with a body so excessively emaciated. Suppose I ate some solid food....' And I ate some solid food – some boiled rice and porridge. Now at that time five bhikkhus were waiting on me, thinking: 'If our recluse Gotama achieves some higher state, he will inform us.' But when I ate the boiled rice and porridge, the five bhikkhus were disgusted and left me, thinking: 'The recluse Gotama now lives luxuriously; he has given up his striving and reverted to luxury.'[2]

In Ashvaghosha's version, this food takes the daintier form of 'milk rice', and is offered by the daughter of a cowherd named Nandabala.[3] Whichever version one imagines, this acceptance of food is significant as marking a recognition of the needs of the body. This marks a return to the basic conditions of our experience after fruitless straining towards absolutised abstractions. If one accepts that the discovery of the Middle Way is by far the most significant event in the life of the Buddha, it seems that this event should be ritually celebrated much more than it is. Once could imagine a kind of Buddhist Eucharist in which small quantities of boiled rice and porridge are mindfully consumed, in remembrance of the Buddha's most significant and universal achievement.

---

2 *Majjhima Nikaya* 36.33. Ñanamoli and Bodhi (1995) p. 340.
3 Ashvaghosha, *Buddhacarita* 12.109. Johnston (1972). Buddhist tradition more frequently names the woman as Sujata.

1.g. The Assaults of Mara

The explicit discovery of the Middle Way, however great its importance, is of course not the end of the story. Practising the Middle Way then remains an ongoing challenge for the rest of our lives. In the traditional accounts of the life of the Buddha, the interval between the discovery of the Middle Way and the achievement of Awakening is normally depicted as a relatively brief one. During that time Siddhartha sits resolutely in meditation, determined not to shift until he has gained Awakening. However, at this point the deepest forces emerge to distract him, and it is only by remaining steadfast that he is undistracted.

Siddhartha's practice of the Middle Way is now being tested by the assaults of *Mara*. Mara is the Buddhist equivalent of Satan, who is depicted as both assaulting and tempting Siddhartha in order to prevent him gaining Awakening. The tests of Mara are symbolic of the tests that confront all of us constantly as we attempt to practice the Middle Way, whatever stage of development we may have personally reached. The accounts of these assaults in the Pali Canon are ambiguous in relation to the chronology of the Buddha's life: it is not entirely clear whether they are meant to happen before or after the Awakening. The fact that this matters little should alert us to the fact that Awakening cannot change the basic conditions of the practice of the Middle Way, which are those of human experience.

Mara first tries to undermine Siddhartha's confidence by warning him that he could die if he over-exerts himself while he is still in such an emaciated state from his earlier austerities.[1] In this he seems to represent the procrastination tendency that we can all experience, to put off real engagement with the path because the time is not yet optimal. Yet the Middle Way can be practised at any instant, starting from where you are now.

When this does not succeed, Mara assaults Siddhartha with his army, which is a representation of his fears.[2] In one version, they appropriately assault him from behind,[3] symbolising the way in which fear can unexpectedly arise from the unconscious. Ashvaghosha gives an extended account of these fearsome assaults,

---

1 *Sutta Nipata* 3.2.426–7. Sadhatissa (1985) p. 48.
2 *Sutta Nipata* 3.2.442–3. Sadhatissa (1985) p. 49.
3 *Jataka Nidana* 72. Jayawickrama (1990) p. 95.

imagined as hordes of fiends with animal faces surrounding Siddhartha as he sits beneath the *bodhi* tree.[4] These fiends shower hot coals at him, but they turn into red lotus petals.[5] Crucially, Siddhartha does not defeat these assaults by fighting back, but through his equanimity, due to which he is not afraid of them.

Finally, Mara is also depicted as tempting Siddhartha using his daughters – Tanha, Arati, and Ragha – who try to ensnare Siddhartha with lust in all sorts of different ways.[6] Siddhartha's potential sexual fantasies are given an externalised form. Of course they fail: they have 'tried to batter a mountain with the stalks of lotus flowers'.[7] Siddhartha's lack of response is presented as due to him having 'cut off craving'.[8] However, such terms do not necessarily convey the balanced (rather than repressive) nature of the equanimity that is needed to avoid such 'temptation'.

Mara represents the forces of absolutisation within us, that lead us to be overwhelmed when confronted by fear or desire. On the one hand they lead us to believe, whether implicitly or explicitly, that our projected fears (as opposed to the conditions behind them) can hurt us. On the other they make us believe that our projected objects of desire (as opposed to the conditions behind them) can be possessed. Our tendency to think of things in terms of opposed absolutes is constantly reinforced by the powerful motives of fear and desire coming from the amygdala and striatum at the back of our brains. Those motives are ones that in extreme circumstances may save us from being eaten or from starving. In more stable and civilised circumstances, though, they are much more likely to create unnecessary conflict and stress within us. When confronted, say, with the unexpected roar of a tiger or the deliberately seductive uncovering of a breast, we have basic instincts that are liable to take over. But it is the constant re-imagining of such events when they are not occurring that disrupts our ability to respond appropriately to the much more common and ambiguous events of human life: the harmlessly challenging talk of a stranger, the harmless roar of an aeroplane above, or the unprovocative eye contact a man might

---

4 Ashvaghosha, *Buddhacarita* 13.27. Johnston (1972).
5 Ashvaghosha, *Buddhacarita* 13.41.
6 *Samyutta Nikaya* 1.4.505–18. Bodhi (2000) pp. 217–20.
7 *Samyutta Nikaya* 1.4.516. Bodhi (2000) p. 220.
8 *Samyutta Nikaya* 1.4.514. Bodhi (2000) p. 219.

have with a woman in the street going about her everyday business. It is our over-reactions that threaten the equanimity that needs to be part of the practice of the Middle Way.

We thus need to interpret Mara's tests in terms of the need to avoid absolutisation in a practical and emotionally grounded way. We will then not be upset by these extreme emotional responses. In accordance with the principle of agnosticism, we cannot deal effectively with either fear or obsessive desire simply through repression. Instead we need to acknowledge it as part of our embodied situation, while we absorb it and contextualise it within a wider awareness seated in the body. Repression doesn't work, because it takes us only into a temporary state of forced self-control, where we have to continue exerting energy to keep the undesirable emotion at bay. In those circumstances it is only a matter of time before we lose the repressive energy that is required to keep Mara in check. So if he keeps working away at us and our only response is repression, he will eventually goad us into craving or hatred.

Siddhartha's achievement is not one of forced repression, but rather one of integration. The hot coals thrown by Mara's army turn into petals, because they no longer have the power to stimulate new conflict and are thus harmless to Siddhartha. As long as he keeps focusing on an integrative practice, based on his body as a unifying basis of awareness, Siddhartha is able to avoid the reactions of fear and craving. In so doing he becomes a potent symbol of the potential power of our own equanimity. It is not that he needs no effort at all, or that he can simply accept the disrupting emotions. *Suppression*, in the sense of a deliberate resolve not to respond to or act on those emotions whilst accepting their presence, is indeed needed. Nor on the other hand is it simply a matter of courage and steadfastness in the normal sense, for he is not dealing with a normal enemy. His success in integrating his disruptive emotions depends on him being able to embrace them as part of himself without accepting their separate and disruptive form. It depends on his wisdom and compassion as well as his courage.

1.h. Awakening: Meaning versus Belief

The Awakening or enlightenment of the Buddha is a highly ambiguous event, subject to a great variety of interpretations and yet seen as central to the identity of Buddhism. I want to argue that there is a simple question of priorities involved in how we choose to understand the Awakening. On the one hand, we can explain it in ways that are compatible with the Middle Way, as the most basic and universal insight to be gained from the Buddha's life and teachings. On the other, we could work on the basis of some other, more traditional, interpretation of Awakening and then apply that interpretation to the Middle Way.

For the reasons given so far and throughout this book, the first of these priorities has to be preferable, for entirely practical reasons. Awakening needs to be interpreted in terms that are compatible with the Middle Way, not only because the Middle Way is the distinctive principle of judgement offered by the Buddha, but because it *works* as the best chance for anyone, anywhere, to improve the adequacy of their responses to their experience. To interpret the Awakening in a way compatible with the Middle Way implies that Awakening cannot be understood as an absolute or discontinuous state giving access to any form of absolute truth. It implies that as we consider the Buddha's achievement, we should follow the Buddha's *method* in his encounters with Alara Kalama and Udaka Ramaputta. That method is to learn from the methods and achievements of a spiritual teacher, but not take them to necessarily have the ultimate attainment or final word.

On the other hand, you might choose to interpret Awakening in a way that puts the authority of tradition before the practical value of the Middle Way. If you do this *only* because it is traditional rather than because of any practical advantages in the views offered by tradition, then you are committing the fallacy of irrelevant appeal to tradition. A particular approach is not right because of the number or the authority of people who have taken it in the past, but because of its general adequacy for human experience. Our understanding of what is most adequate for human experience does need to take into account our degree of ignorance. However, the most effective way to take current ignorance into account is not to give absolute authority to a traditional source. That source is one that we have unavoidably chosen and interpreted for ourselves, and it may subsequently turn out to be the wrong one. Rather, an effective course is to make our judgements provisionally and incrementally as we develop greater degrees of integration.

A determination to interpret the Awakening in terms compatible with the Middle Way, however, does not mean that we cannot be deeply inspired by the story of the Buddha's Awakening. As with any story, its meaning to us extends much further than the beliefs that might be generated by it. Awakening provides a meaningful symbol of the goal at the end of the Middle Way, and the Buddha himself may also provide that symbol (see chapter 6.e). The idea that we, too, could be awakened provides a glimpse into our own potential integration. The Pali Canon accounts of the Buddha's realisations at the time of his Awakening also provide us with a provisional idea of the kinds of insight we might reach by becoming more integrated.

The recognition that we can find Awakening *meaningful* without holding *absolute beliefs* about it is central to the Middle Way. That's because the role of the body in providing us with meaning is our starting point in avoiding absolutisation. We have already noted that Siddhartha's recollection of his experience under the rose-apple tree provided him with an alternative to asceticism precisely because *jhana* is an experience that is rooted in awareness of an acceptance of the body. The body is not only essential for our lives to be sustained, but also for us to be able to relate symbols to experiences through associations. The symbols may include words as well as other sense experiences, and the associations are also synaptic links in the brain. Embodied accounts of meaning have been developed since the 1980s.[1] In these the meaning of even the most abstract language can be understood as the metaphorical development of very basic association experiences that often began in infancy. For example, the very idea of the Middle Way is a metaphorical one that is dependent on our associations between that term and our experiences of walking along a path of some kind between objects on either side (see chapter 3.b). In this way of thinking about meaning as based in our bodies (discussed further in chapters 3.a and 7.g), meanings are prior to beliefs. That's because beliefs are built up from meanings, not the other way round.

---

1 See Lakoff (1987); Johnson (2007); Lakoff and Johnson (1980); Ellis (2013b).

What does 'Awakening' or 'enlightenment' mean for us? It may be an extrapolation of our limited experiences of integration – perhaps of meditative, religious, or aesthetic experience – to their furthest possible conclusion. We think of it as being like that absorbed, clear, ecstatic experience that we had, but more so. Given that our energies are often in conflict with one another, it may also mean a glimpse of a potential greater self without that conflict that we intuit in ourselves. This could be like a flash of lightning that makes us aware of a whole landscape where we previously thought there was nothing, but only for an instant. Awakening in our experience, then, may be closely related to actual or potential integration. It may be the overcoming of conflicts within ourselves that make us more able to focus all our energies and tackle the world around us with maximal wisdom. Or our sense of Awakening may come mainly from stories like that of the Buddha: but that also is a sense of meaning based in our bodies, as we have an inspired response to the character we encounter. Given the scepticism that needs to go with that integration, we can never assume that the integration is total, whether it is our own or that of the Buddha. Nevertheless, the fact that it is accessible to our experience makes it meaningful.

If Awakening means any of these things (and perhaps many other things, too), it consists in *meaning*. That means not only that 'Awakening' is a word that we can use in communication (whatever, if anything, it communicates to others), but also one that has emotional impact on us, that moves us. That impact is independent of any beliefs we may have about it. Indeed the beliefs we attach are probably a subsequent response to relating it to a web of conceptual information. We may use it to formulate provisional, non-absolute beliefs that can be easily checked in experience, such as that 'Buddhists associate Awakening with the Buddha'. However, Buddhists and others also often use it to formulate absolute beliefs that are not entirely relatable to experience in the same way, such as that 'The Buddha gained the highest truth', or 'The Buddha saw things as they really are', or 'The Buddha stopped the rounds of rebirth'. These beliefs are not a necessary part of finding Awakening inspiring – they are an afterthought dependent on an abstract set of assumptions in which we have placed the immediate meaning of 'Awakening'. Frequently they are a way of gaining admission to a group that uses such beliefs as a shortcut to social acceptance. They have much more importance in the currency of that group than in personal experience of spiritual practice.

Absolute beliefs about Awakening are clearly incompatible with the Middle Way as Siddhartha discovered it. Siddhartha went forth from the palace precisely because of the absolutising of the assumptions in that conventional environment. He realised that this greatly constrained his ability to address the conditions around him. For the same reasons, Siddhartha rejected the absolute assumptions of spiritual teachers and of asceticism. Are we really going to work through the Buddha's early life, appreciating these points before the Awakening, and then swap them for a set of ad hoc rationalisations when we come to the Awakening? Are we really going to treat the Awakening in a completely inconsistent way from the rest of the story?

With this point in mind, let us examine the passages in the Pali Canon that describe the Buddha's experience of Awakening. Let us do so whilst considering what they might contribute to the *meaning* of Awakening for us, and perhaps also what *provisional* beliefs they might justify.

The most detailed account of the Awakening in the Pali Canon occurs in the *Mahasaccaka Sutta*.[2] This begins with the Buddha's ascension through the four lower *jhanas*, at each stage adding 'But such pleasant feeling that arose in me did not invade my mind and remain'.[3] This suggests that the increasingly refined and pleasant experiences were not absolutised, and the Buddha maintained his balanced and investigative approach to his experience. His realisations only then began when 'my concentrated mind was thus purified, bright, unblemished, rid of imperfection, malleable, wieldy, steady, and attained to imperturbability'[4]: clearly a highly integrated state.

The Buddha's realisations are then explained in terms of the 'three knowledges', each of which is allocated to one of three watches of the night. These consist of 'knowledge of the recollection of past lives', 'knowledge of the passing away and reappearance of beings', and 'knowledge of the destruction of the taints'.

---

2 *Majjhima Nikaya* 36.34-44. Ñanamoli and Bodhi (1995) pp. 340-2.
3 *Majjhima Nikaya* 36.34-7.
4 *Majjhima Nikaya* 36.38.

'Past lives' are, of course, normally interpreted cosmologically: as the Buddha's recollection of whole past biological lives in a sequence of rebirths. However, just as the Buddha's life itself does not have to be historical, in terms of its value for the development of insight, it does not matter when these past lives occurred. Nor does it matter whether they are biological rebirths or psychological experiences of cyclic processes within one life. What is important is that the Buddha learnt from his past experiences. *Jhana* can, indeed, put one in touch unexpectedly with experiences from the past, perhaps because a new access of energy surges through neglected synaptic connections. The Buddha was able to review his previous experience, and this provided him with a great resource for reflection (as a scientist might put it, a big set of data). Reflecting on that information helped him to recognise the ways in which remaining within limited spheres of assumption was restricting or damaging to him in a context of changing conditions. It also showed how he had been able to take a step forward on the path where he had avoided the absolutisation of assumptions in those past situations, and been able to integrate his response to the conditions. Reflecting on our past experience may similarly help us to understand the Middle Way.

Of course he would not only have experience of his own past life, but also of others'. It is not necessary to attribute omniscience to Siddhartha, that would enable him to know of 'the passing away and reappearance of all beings', to recognise the meaning of the second watch of the night for us. All the Buddha would need to do was to recognise the ways in which those already known to him, to a greater or lesser degree, appeared to have moved forward in the path. When they moved forward, he would see that this was because of overcoming absolutisation and addressing conditions. The Middle Way provided him with a new key to history, enabling him (and us) to get beyond a relationship to history as sets of facts to be dispassionately assembled or ideologically appropriated. Instead, he was able to see past events as a rich source of data on the kinds of states and beliefs that tend to address conditions and those that do not.[5] If we also acknowledge our degree of uncertainty about

---

5 Ellis (2013a) section 7 contains some limited attempts to interpret information about past history in this way, with examples from my own life, those of Sangharakshita and Margaret Thatcher, and the wider histories of the Ottoman Empire and Northern Ireland.

past events, we can never assemble from this the kind of certainty over a law of karma that past Buddhist tradition has pretended to. However, we can use the lives of all beings both to inform and confirm a developing understanding of the best ways in which humans can generally address conditions.

The 'taints' (*asavas*) referred to in relation to the Buddha's third 'knowledge' in the third watch of the night are craving for pleasure, craving for existence, and views.[6] These closely relate to the features of the Middle Way that have already been discussed. 'Craving' (*kamasava*) as a taint can be readily understood as the absolutisation of desire (including hatred and fear, which are inverted desire). The craving for ourselves or other people or things to 'exist' or 'not exist' (*bhavasava*) can be seen as the most basic form of absolutisation. 'Views' (*ditthasava*) can be readily interpreted as absolutised beliefs.

The very idea of 'knowledge' is one that can be formulated in a provisional or an absolute way. Is 'knowledge' a representation of how things really are (in which case it would be absolute), or is it merely a provisional representation? A provisional representation is acknowledged to be subject to limiting assumptions, models, and metaphors, developed in a particular time and place, but attempting universality as far as it can be understood. In general parlance, 'knowledge' is sometimes understood as provisional, but more often assumed to be absolute. In its most common philosophical definition, as 'justified true belief', it reinforces the common assumption that 'knowledge' is certified as true. In terms of our understanding of the Middle Way, though, it is vital to make a distinction, so that general but provisional claims do not slide into absolute ones. They have too often done so, including in Buddhist tradition. In my development of Middle Way Philosophy, I have avoided the use of the term 'knowledge' to signify provisional belief for that reason.[7] I would argue that the Buddha's insights in the Awakening are best described as justified general beliefs. Anything stronger than that starts to undermine the insights themselves.

The Buddha's crucial insight at Awakening, then, is that of conditions and the need to face up to them. This is reflected in the alternative account of the Buddha's Awakening that focuses on his

---

6   *Majjhima Nikaya* 9.70. Ñanamoli and Bodhi p. 144.
7   For more details see Ellis (2012) sections 1 and 5.

The Middle Way in the Buddha's Early Life   47

recognition of the twelve *nidana*s, or links of conditionality.[8] I will be looking in more detail at the interpretation of Buddhist teachings on conditionality in chapter 6.a. For the moment, though, it is most important to understand the relationship between the Middle Way and *addressing conditions*, without an absolute belief in conditionality as a cosmic law.

We address conditions most effectively by avoiding absolutisations, including as an important example that of self (the subject of a third canonical account of the Awakening[9]). We will *generally* produce better outcomes by addressing those conditions than we will by remaining in delusions. We create delusions by absolutising some particular limited condition and assuming it is the whole story. A *general* claim about the human situation, however, can always be interpreted provisionally. We recognise that it seems to be the case so far, but that we do not have all possible information about all human situations, so can have no certainty about it.

On the other hand, conditionality is often interpreted absolutely, creating conflict with the very conduct of the path that the doctrine is urging us towards. Absolute interpretations of conditionality tend to be deductive. They start with a general claim about the way that conditions work, accepting it on the authority of Buddhist tradition, but ignoring our role in interpreting that tradition. They then deduce other general claims about what we should believe, or how we should act, from that general claim. The belief in a law of karma that ensures people will always benefit from good deeds or suffer for bad ones is an example of such an absolute deduction from an understanding of conditionality. Rebirth, in turn, is a further deduction from karma, required to make karmic effects consistent when they have not been received within one lifetime.

Suppose you take a general claim that addressing conditions leads to better results than not addressing them. Suppose you then *deduce* from this that there is a law of karma according to which all bad actions (including mental actions) that I perform now will necessarily rebound on me negatively in the future. This is an absolute deduction that considerably oversteps the limits of justified belief for an embodied human being. We cannot have sufficient

---

8 *Samyutta Nikaya* 12.10. Bodhi (2000) pp. 537 ff.
9 *Samyutta Nikaya* 22.27. Bodhi (2000) pp. 873–4.

understanding of every case, especially those cases remote from our own context, to draw any such conclusion. More importantly, on every occasion I might try to apply such an absolute law of karma to a specific case, it will be subject to ambiguities of interpretation. Those ambiguities make it in practice useless as a guide to action. Does the law of karma imply that I should act kindly, tell the truth, not kill, or not lie? Yes, but only if I make further assumptions about the effects of these types of actions that are not evident from the law of karma alone.

However, the same general assertion about conditions can alternatively be taken as a meaningful claim that I accept for the moment, whilst being open to alternative possibilities. If I tell someone else a lie, for example, that seems *likely* to spread a misunderstanding of conditions that I actually understand myself, in the process producing conflict with the person I lied to. There may be exceptional cases in which lying actually addresses the conditions better. I will need to carefully interpret the specific conditions of the case in order to judge this. However, if I am primed to generally *expect* lying to have bad effects on a provisional basis, then this is a potentially useful application of the general recognition of conditionality.

The interpretation of Buddhist teachings on karma and rebirth, as well as conditionality, in a way compatible with the Middle Way will be discussed in more detail in section 6. However, for the moment there are two important points. First, Awakening needs to be interpreted in terms compatible with the Middle Way. Second, such an interpretation requires that conditionality and karma offer a general expectation that makes our expectations provisional rather than a cosmic law. It is one thing to always consider the possibility that our good deeds may be rewarded and our bad deeds punished. That will give us the chance to turn away from destructive actions through greater awareness. However, it is quite another to always impose that requirement in our interpretation of the evidence, which narrows our awareness. The Buddha's 'knowledge' (i.e. justified general belief) that the destruction of the taints is required to progress on the path amounts to a clear confidence in the Middle Way. However, the 'knowledge' of karma and rebirth that is often attached to it must be read as a culturally-conditioned and unnecessary deduction from conditionality interpreted in absolute terms.

As we move on past the Buddha's Awakening into the period of his ministry, one of our major concerns will be not only what the Buddha taught, but how he applied his teachings. That will also give us an indication of their active meaning for him. Is the Middle Way the evident basis of the Buddha's judgements? Or does his ministry instead give us a picture of someone inclined to control others through the use of absolute teachings as tools of power? I shall argue that a non-absolute interpretation of the Awakening is not only a practically helpful approach for us, but is much more consistent with the Buddha's subsequent actions.

2. The Middle Way in the Buddha's Ministry

2.a. The Decision to Teach

Awakening was not the end of the Buddha's problems, but only the opening to the next phase: one in which he would need to practise the Middle Way more than ever. In the Pali Canon, the Buddha is depicted as confronting the same kinds of doubts when he thinks he has made a breakthrough as the rest of us would. Should he try to work with an existing group, or follow the much harder road of starting his own? Can he really communicate the insight that he believes he has found? How much rejection can he take before doubting his own perspective? These doubts also shift the focus of the story from what so far has been a very individualised struggle to one of social relations. Even if it turned out to be true that Siddhartha had attained a state of total integration with his Awakening, this would still be out of harmony with the lack of integration of everyone else. Can he really be integrated himself in isolation from his degree of integration in his environment? That would become an ongoing issue in the history of Buddhism, and greatly contributed to the split between Theravada and Mahayana interpretations of it.

In one episode shortly following the Awakening, the Buddha is depicted as reflecting on the need for role models for his continued development:

> *While the Blessed One was alone in seclusion, a reflection arose in his mind thus: 'One dwells in suffering if one is without reverence and deference. Now what ascetic or brahmin can I honour and respect and dwell in dependence on?'*
>
> *Then it occurred to the Blessed One: 'It would be for the sake of fulfilling an unfulfilled aggregate of virtue that I would honour, respect, and dwell in dependence on another ascetic or brahmin. However, in this world...I do not see another ascetic or brahmin more perfect in virtue than myself, whom I could honour and respect and dwell in dependence on.'*[1]

---

1   *Samyutta Nikaya* 6.2.561. Bodhi (2000) p. 234.

This reflection is then repeated in relation to concentration, wisdom, liberation, and knowledge and vision of liberation in place of virtue. Here the Buddha seems to clearly acknowledge the need we have, as social beings, to be influenced by the models offered by others in order to be able to make spiritual progress. If we are to interpret it in a charitable spirit of provisionality, we should not take the Buddha's statement that he does not see another person more perfect than himself as conceit or self-inflation. Rather we should take it as an appropriately accurate summary of his experience which avoids false modesty. He does not deny the possibility of greater role models, but he doesn't see any. How, then, is he to reconcile his human need for role models with his perception of the absence of worthy role models?

This is a position that many people find themselves in today, whether or not this is due to delusion about the lack of worthier role models than themselves. If we do not perceive and acknowledge greater role models it is not possible for us to trust them. We may fail to perceive worthy role models for a variety of reasons. There may not be any within range. We may have a misplaced relativism according to which we are prevented from recognising that anyone else is worthy of moral or spiritual imitation. Or we may have reasonable doubts about the reliability of any possible role model because of their faults. The development of investigative journalism, and the easy sharing of information in modern times, means that the faults of any possible role model are likely to easily come to light. There are few gurus without a sex scandal or two in the background. So more of us are in the Buddha's position than it might at first appear.

The Buddha's answer to his own question (subsequently reinforced by the symbolic figure of Brahma Sahampati, whom we can take to be a further voice in the Buddha's own mind) is this:

> 'Let me then honour, respect, and dwell in dependence on this very Dhamma to which I have fully awakened.'[2]

However, the word *Dhamma* raises a number of problems, despite being the common currency of Buddhists to refer to the teachings of their tradition. It can mean both how things are and also the Buddhist teaching about them. Thus its use, without further

---

2 Ibid.

analysis of its meaning, can at every turn encourage Buddhists to assume an absolutisation of the Buddha's method by taking it to be a complete representation of reality (this point is discussed more fully in chapter 6.f). In this context, however, we can interpret it as meaning the Buddha's method – the Middle Way. The Buddha recognises the way in which this Middle Way stands separately and beyond himself, due to its universality. He also recognises that in the absence of human role models he needs to find his inspiration in the process of following that Middle Way itself. The Buddha does not have the final truth, or he would not still be learning and following the Middle Way. Nor, however, can he subordinate himself to someone else's authority, which would mean absolutising that authority and betraying the Middle Way. Here we have, then, a further reflection of the method that led him to move on from Alara Kalama and Udaka Ramaputta. We also have an exemplification of the Middle Way, avoiding the absolutisation either of his own beliefs or of another's authority.

This episode tracks how the Buddha developed the confidence to teach in his own right, rather than joining an established spiritual group of any kind. If the cultural changes going on in modern society are any indication, this is a balance that many people today are following him in. There is a trend towards fewer people adhering to established religions or political parties. However, there are also increasing numbers writing their own blogs and books, or creating videos on YouTube to publicise their ideas and arguments. There are, it seems, increasing numbers of leaders but fewer followers. Not all of these leaders will have balanced reasons for attempting intellectual leadership, and not all of them will be worth listening to. However, we should celebrate the fact that increasing numbers of people are acting as the Buddha did here. They are thinking autonomously and using creative self-expression as an active form of development.

However, like many others in the position of attempting creative leadership, the Buddha also encounters doubts about the difficulty of getting his message across. These doubts are redoubled by the difficulties of what he has to communicate – the Middle Way.

> *I considered: 'This Dhamma that I have attained is profound, hard to see and hard to understand, peaceful and sublime, unattainable by mere reasoning, subtle, to be experienced by the wise. But this generation delights in adhesion [or attachment], takes delight in adhesion, rejoices in adhesion. It is hard for*

> such a generation to see this truth, namely, specific conditionality, dependent origination.... If I were to teach the Dhamma, others would not understand me, and that would be wearying and troublesome for me.' ... Considering thus, my mind inclined to inaction rather than teaching the Dhamma.³

But once again, his voice of objection takes the form of Brahma Sahampati, who pleads with him to teach the Dhamma. The Buddha reconsiders.

> Surveying the world with the eye of a Buddha, I saw beings with little dust in their eyes and with much dust in their eyes, with keen faculties and with dull faculties, with good qualities and with bad qualities, easy to teach and hard to teach, and some who dwelt seeing fear and blame in the other world.⁴

This is a superb demonstration both of provisionality and of incrementality. To begin with, the Buddha has considered the matter only in terms of absolutisations. He thought of people as a single mass, entrenched in absolutisations, so that he would not be understood in trying to communicate the Middle Way. He considered only two possibilities: having a very difficult time trying to teach the unreceptive, or not teaching at all. That dualism of absolutisations is a further indication, should one be needed, that the Buddha is not all wise and does not instantaneously 'know' the correct answer in every circumstance. Rather, his distinctive contribution consists of the direction he is heading in, which is one that enables him to reconsider and correct his previous mistakes in the light of further awareness. The voice of Brahma Sahampati offers that further awareness. The Buddha's provisionality consists both in his having that voice available to him (perhaps assisted by his history of practice up to that point) and his not rejecting it. Instead he recognises its greater adequacy, due to the awareness with which he is able to weigh up the alternatives. The Buddha here explicitly admits his mistake in the light of further awareness:

> Thinking it would be troublesome, O Brahma,
> I did not speak the Dhamma subtle and sublime.⁵

This judgement is also *incremental*. Whereas initially he thought of the people he might teach as a single mass with one attribute, when thinking again he differentiates them as having differing

---

3   *Majjhima Nikaya* 26.19. Ñanamoli and Bodhi (1995) p. 260.
4   *Majjhima Nikaya* 26.20. Ñanamoli and Bodhi (1995) p. 262.
5   Ibid.

qualities along a series of spectrums: the amount of dust they have in their eyes (meaning how much conditions have subjected them to absolutising delusions), how intelligent they are, how moral they are, and how receptive they are. This incrementalisation allows him to access a compassion that he did not previously access. He is beginning to relate to his potential hearers as imagined individual people, rather than simply an abstract unreceptive mass.

The Buddha's new-found confidence and determination to communicate the Middle Way is immediately put to the test. First he reflects that his previous two teachers, Alara Kalama and Udaka Ramaputta, are now dead, and sets off to find his previous five companions in asceticism instead.[6] On the road, he encounters a *shramana* called Upaka, who seems to admire the Buddha's confident appearance and asks him about his religious allegiances. But the Buddha immediately goes into overdrive:

> '*I am the one who has transcended all, a knower of all....*
>
> *I have no teacher, and one like me*
> *Exists nowhere in all the world....*
>
> *I alone am a Fully Enlightened One....*'

The reaction this produces is richly comic. How do we respond politely to someone who is so deluded?

> *When this was said, the Ajivaka Upaka said: 'May it be so, friend.' Shaking his head, he took a bypath and departed.*[7]

One can put this episode down to the Buddha's inexperience of speaking appropriately to people. However, the way he speaks of himself here is not exceptional in the Pali Canon, and certainly not exceptional in terms of the way the Buddhist tradition speaks of him. What it communicates, once again, is the dangers of absolutising the Awakening, and it suggests that the Buddha himself might have fallen into that trap. He seems to have absolutised by interpreting what was probably a highly integrated and transformative experience in terms of an absolute revelation. Surely, if the Buddha had spoken to Upaka about his *method* instead of his supposed *status*, he would have been much more likely to be convincing?

---

6 *Majjhima Nikaya* 26.22–4. Ñanamoli and Bodhi (1995) pp. 262–3.
7 *Majjhima Nikaya* 26.25, Ñanamoli and Bodhi (1995) pp. 263–4.

He would also have been more accurate, and thus more helpful to Upaka in his own quest.

Whatever degree of integration the Buddha may have attained as an individual, it is obvious from his subsequent behaviour that it was a point on a scale. It may also have been asymmetrically available to different parts of him in different contexts. His decision to teach, and first attempts at doing so, highlight the interdependence between whatever kind or degree of integration he achieved and that of the surrounding society. He could not simply continue to enjoy solitary bliss without interacting with that society. As soon as he started to teach others, however, the wider integration both of other individuals and of society as a whole became implicitly part of his goal. Social integration thus also became a further implication of the Middle Way. Social and political conflicts have their counterparts within the individual, and individual conflicts can also get writ large as social ones. The Buddha's Middle Way became unavoidably a way of addressing a whole new and wider set of conditions.

2.b. The First Address and Four Tasks

The first recorded instance of the Buddha actually teaching is the encounter with his former five companions, at Sarnath near Benares, and his delivery of what is often known as the 'First Sermon'. This occasion sets a template for the Buddha's subsequent recorded teaching by laying down the central formulae. However, we need to bear in mind that it indicates the way in which he communicates the Middle Way to that audience at that place and time. That is not necessarily the way it needs to be communicated to people in other times and places. We see the Buddha's inexperience as a teacher, but we also see the importance of gaining people's trust and confidence, and communicating in a way they can understand. In that way it's possible to help them begin to address whatever conditions they need to address to move towards a balanced practice.

When the Buddha first arrives, the five ascetics regard him as a luxurious backslider. As he approaches, they agree amongst themselves not to 'pay homage to him or rise up for him or receive his bowl or outer robe'[1] – in other words not to give him the courtesy and respect he might have expected, but merely to offer him a seat. However, as he approached 'those bhikkhus found themselves unable to keep their pact'[2] and performed exactly the same courtesies they had agreed not to offer. We are obviously intended to credit this to the power of the Buddha's presence. Traditionally this would be attributed to the transforming effects of Awakening. However, he did not need to have achieved any discontinuous state for the effects of his practice to be highly evident from his bodily movements and demeanour even before he spoke. Others might then intuit this readily and respond to it.

Nevertheless, the ascetics address the Buddha as 'friend'. The Buddha takes exception to this, claiming that 'an Accomplished One, a Fully Enlightened One' should be addressed much more respectfully. Even taking into account the much greater formality of the Buddha's context than is normally employed in the modern West, this insistence seems to be an indication of the Buddha's inexperience as a teacher. Why should he be so concerned about how he is addressed? Does he really want to lay such emphasis on his

---

1 *Majjhima Nikaya* 26.26. Ñanamoli and Bodhi (1995) p. 264.
2 Ibid.

own status at the possible expense of helping to further his auditors' understanding of the way? There are objections from the ascetics, who don't understand why they should treat him so respectfully. He resolves this issue, eventually, only by saying, 'Bhikkhus, have you ever known me to speak like this before?'[3] This would focus their attention on their previous personal experience of him rather than on absolutisations of his status. Thus he manages to overcome the negative effects of his earlier mistakes just by developing an atmosphere of trust.

When the Buddha begins his address, however, it is noteworthy that the very first thing he talks about is the Middle Way. Indeed, he even describes the Middle Way as what he has awakened to:

> 'Bhikkhus, these two extremes should not be followed by one who has gone forth into homelessness. What two? The pursuit of sensual happiness in sensual pleasures, which is low, vulgar, the way of worldlings, ignoble, unbeneficial; and the pursuit of self-mortification, which is painful, ignoble, unbeneficial. Without veering towards either of these extremes, the Tathagata [Buddha] has awakened to the middle way, which gives rise to vision, which gives rise to knowledge, which leads to peace, to direct knowledge, to enlightenment, to Nibbana.'[4]

In teaching thus, in this situation, he begins the Buddhist tradition (which I will discuss further in section 4) of only discussing the Middle Way in terms of specific instances of absolutising extremes to be avoided. To talk in these terms, rather than the avoidance of absolutisation in general, unfortunately obscures (through selectivity) the potential conflicts between the Middle Way and the absolutisations that have developed within Buddhist tradition. In this situation, where he is explicitly addressing 'one who has gone forth into homelessness', it is surely understandable why the Buddha did this. He was addressing a group of people who had been previously obsessed with self-mortification. His first priority was to enable them to move beyond that particular absolutisation, rather than being confronted with the wider problem of absolutisation in general.

The Buddha then continues:

> 'And what, bhikkhus, is that middle way awakened to by the Tathagata, which gives rise to vision, which gives rise to knowledge, which leads to peace, to

---

3   *Majjhima Nikaya* 26.28. Ñanamoli and Bodhi (1995) p. 265.
4   *Samyutta Nikaya* 56.11.421. Bodhi (2000) p. 1844.

> *direct knowledge, to enlightenment, to Nibbana? It is this Noble Eightfold Path; that is, right view, right intention, right speech, right action, right livelihood, right effort, right mindfulness, right concentration.'[5]*

The identification of the Noble Eightfold Path with the Middle Way here often seems to have led Buddhists to assume that the latter can be understood in the terms of the former. However, the Eightfold Path is a formulation of how one might follow the Middle Way rather than a substitute for understanding the Middle Way in its own right.

The Eightfold Path provides an analysis of the kinds of integrative practices that can aid one in avoiding absolutisation. Its eight limbs can be roughly grouped into three areas of practice known as the Threefold Path: wisdom (right view and intention), ethics (right speech, action, and livelihood) and meditation (right effort, mindfulness, and concentration). Wisdom enables the avoidance of absolutisation through awareness of assumptions and their limitations: the practices of scepticism and agnosticism about both positive and negative absolutes. Ethics enables the avoidance of judgements about action that assume absolutised beliefs (and thus also tend to reinforce them). 'Meditation' (in a broad sense of the term) enables the avoidance of absolutisations through opening our minds to alternatives and thus enabling provisionality. More positively, though, all these practices are also integrative. They generally support adequate awareness of the world, individual happiness and social harmony by overcoming conflicts and projections.

The Eightfold Path is not the only possible way of formulating the path, but it is an extremely useful one, and worthy of more detailed discussion in its own right. I will be devoting the whole of section 5 to discussion of the Eightfold Path in relation to the Middle Way.

After introducing the Eightfold Path, the Buddha's First Address then moves on to expound the Four Noble Truths. Once again, the way these are introduced *after* the path encourages us to see their recognition as part of the path, and thus to interpret them in a way that is compatible with the Middle Way.

In the traditional translation used by Bhikkhu Bodhi, the Four Noble Truths are suffering, the origin of suffering, the cessation

---

5 Ibid.

of suffering, and the way leading to the cessation of suffering.⁶ However, given how unsatisfactory 'suffering' is as a translation of *'dukkha'*, I am surprised how much Buddhist translators and teachers continue to use the term. *Dukkha* is not only concerned with suffering in the normal sense, but also the ways in which our desires and expectations generally remain unfulfilled. Alternative renderings are unsatisfactoriness, frustration, or (my suggestion here) inadequacy. However, I will resist the temptation to tamper with Bodhi's translation, which nevertheless goes a long way towards revealing the breadth of what is meant:

> *'Now this, bhikkhus, is the noble truth of suffering: birth is suffering, ageing is suffering, illness is suffering, death is suffering; union with what is displeasing is suffering; separation from what is pleasing is suffering; not to get what one wants is suffering; in brief, the five aggregates subject to clinging are suffering.'*⁷

If we read this with the Middle Way in mind, then it is clear that we are being pointed towards the *general effects of absolutisation*. There is much 'suffering' in human experience that no practice can do anything to change (including ageing, illness, and death). However, there is also a good deal of inadequate judgement that makes our experience of not getting what we want worse than it might otherwise be. The Buddha uses a particular analysis of the elements that lead us to absolutise beliefs about the self (the five aggregates) to reinforce this point: we have these experiences of unsatisfactoriness, because our judgements are constantly changing and one unintegrated state undermines the ends of another. If we are to interpret this in accordance with the Middle Way, it is not a cosmic law that has been discovered. It is not even a 'truth'. However, it is a powerful statement of the need to face up to the constant disruption of conditions to our assumptions about both 'reality' and 'value'.

The second truth is the origin of suffering:

> *'It is this craving which leads to renewed existence, accompanied by delight and lust, seeking delight here and there; that is, craving for sensual pleasures, craving for existence, craving for extermination.'*⁸

6 Ibid.
7 Ibid.
8 Ibid.

Craving (*tanha*) is another term for absolutisation, but should not be identified with desire as a whole (see chapter 6.c). We have already seen the Buddha encounter desires that 'did not invade my mind and remain'. So the kinds of desires that are being pointed to are ones to which absolutisation is attached, those that are obsessive (lust) and unintegrated ('seeking delight here and there'). These unintegrated obsessions may be about sense pleasures (for example, when they are addictive). They may also be about states of existence in which we would like to be in the future (narrow ambitions). Or they may be about things we would like to destroy, whether these are in ourselves or beyond us.

Absolutisation here is a crucial concept to enable us to readily distinguish between what makes desires helpful or unhelpful. Without it, there is likely to be one of two misunderstandings. One is that Buddhism condemns all desire, making it difficult to understand how it is compatible with life and its enjoyment. The other is the attempt to distinguish between desires that are conducive to Awakening and those that are conducive only to the continuation of unhelpful cycles of obsession. Telling us that one set leads to Awakening and another not does not help us to identify which ones are helpful and which ones not so in experience – a point I will take up again in chapter 6.c. Nor is it particular kinds of desire alone that are the problem: there is a bigger context of surrounding beliefs.

We can *generally* claim that absolutising desires *tend to* lead to inadequacy or frustration, but how far and in what ways they do so in any particular case can only be judged more specifically through experience. If we *deduce* that this must occur in a particular case from an absolute law of karma, we are likely to misjudge the complexity of the conditions at work. We will also not take our own degree of ignorance of them sufficiently into account. It is likely, for example, that if I entertain possessive feelings about my partner when she is talking happily to another man, the habits of jealousy that this encourages will only serve to narrow my own awareness and make me unhappy (as well as others, if I express or act on such thoughts). But there is always uncertainty about any such effect, not only what it will consist in and when it will happen but whether it will occur at all.

The Middle Way in the Buddha's Ministry

The third noble truth is the cessation of suffering:

> *'It is the remainderless fading away and cessation of that same craving, the giving up and relinquishing of it, freedom from it, nonreliance on it.'*[9]

This cessation is commonly identified with Awakening, but the Buddha does not make that identification here. Indeed, the cessation of craving does not have to be seen absolutely at all. A particular craving ceases when we integrate it and it is no longer in conflict with its opposite, either within us or outside us. This is not a hard-edged destruction of that craving, just a drop of water entering a larger stream. 'Fading away' is thus an appropriately incremental term to use. The giving up of our obsession is not a repression, but a placing of that obsession within a larger context that frees us from the exclusivity of its claims. Cessation thus happens every time we practise the Middle Way to avoid an absolute judgement and integrate opposed beliefs.

The fourth noble truth, of the cessation of suffering, is identified with the Eightfold Path once again, bringing us full circle. This also reminds us that the way to bring about the fading away of absolutisation at each moment lies in practising the Middle Way. Too often the Four Noble Truths are presented as deductions from an initial cosmic truth, but the Buddha's First Address does not present them in that way at all. We are only introduced to the Four Noble Truths after the Middle Way, in a way that indicates their interdependence with it.

The later parts of the Buddha's First Address are very repetitive in the Pali Canon text, but they involve the Buddha's account of the impact of the Four Noble Truths on him. He says that he not only formulated them, but 'fully understood' them 'in regard to things unheard before'[10] – which suggests a flexibility and universality in his understanding that allows him to apply them to each new situation. He then connects each of the Four Noble Truths to the way in which we need to respond to it: suffering is to be *understood*, the origin of suffering is to be *abandoned*, the cessation of suffering is to be *realised*, and the path leading to the cessation of suffering is to be *developed*.[11] It is these four activities that Stephen Batchelor

---

9 Ibid.
10 *Samyutta Nikaya* 56.11.422, Bodhi (2000) pp. 1844–5.
11 Ibid.

emphasises as the basis of the insight behind the Four Noble Truths as they have been transmitted. That's why he presents them as the *Four Tasks* rather than four *truths*.[12] Whether or not you accept Batchelor's historical contention that the four tasks preceded the four truths, and were thus representative of the 'original' Buddha, his interpretation offers a far more *helpful* approach to interpreting this text.

It is his 'knowledge and vision of these Four Noble Truths as they really are', the Buddha says, that leads him now to 'claim to have awakened to the unsurpassed perfect enlightenment in this world'.[13]

There is no way of avoiding the contradictions in this last statement. The Buddha may be over-stating his own status out of inexperience, as he did with Upaka. Perhaps he adopted this approach because he thought it was necessary to convince his hearers. Perhaps the most likely explanation is just that he had inconsistent beliefs about the insights he had had. That inconsistency need not distract us too much from the insights themselves, because the Buddha does not *have* to be perfect. The Middle Way is always a messy practice pursued by fallible humans. The account of the Middle Way and its implications that the Buddha has already given before this point is already world-shaking enough for the 'Wheel of the Dhamma' to be thoroughly set in motion.

---

12 Batchelor (2015) pp. 120 ff.
13 *Samyutta Nikaya* 56.11.423, Bodhi (2000) pp. 1845–6.

2.c. The Buddha's Educative Approach

From this point, I must take leave of the sequential narrative approach I have followed so far, and be more selective in the features of the Buddha's life I comment on. According to the Pali Canon, the Buddha had a long ministry, wandering around northeastern India for about fifty years. During this time, however, it is not so much what happened to him in narrative terms as his teachings that become most significant. The bulk of this book, from sections 3 through to 6, will be concerned with the discussion of these teachings in relation to the Middle Way. In the next few chapters, however, I want to pick out a few examples (from the many possible) that reflect the way the Buddha practised the Middle Way in his conduct through his ministry. These examples will consider the way in which he taught, how he related to his disciples and to local political leaders, how he responded to conflict, and even how he approached death.

To begin with the Buddha's teaching, then, I want to bring out how the Middle Way shapes the whole way in which the Buddha tries to communicate his insights to others. If they are to follow the universal shape of the path that he followed, then his auditors must be able to identify their own palaces and forests. The teaching needs to have an entirely practical end, which is to be merely a stimulus or inspiration to the development process. If it is to do that, it must help its auditors to avoid absolutisations and move towards more integrative states that overcome conflicts. The *suttas* (*sutras* or discourses) of the Pali Canon provide example after example of the Buddha following this method. By stimulating others to follow the Middle Way, he also helped his society in general to become more integrated by addressing the psychological causes of conflict.

The entirely practical goals of the Buddha's teaching are emphasised by the comparison he makes between teaching and the treatment of a sick patient. Some patients, the Buddha says, will recover from their illness regardless of treatment, whilst others will not recover regardless of treatment: but it is those for whom treatment will make a difference, without which they won't recover, who should get priority of treatment. Similarly, in teaching we should focus attention most on those to whom it will make a difference – though that doesn't mean that others should be denied it.[1] This intensely practical focus makes clear the

---

1 *Anguttara Nikaya* 3.22. Nyanaponika and Bodhi (1999) pp. 46–7.

Buddha's determination to address the conditions, rather than to simply launch his message into the world as an end in itself. These conditions include the limited energy and attention of the teacher, who cannot help everybody, as well as the limited capacities of different auditors. The implication here, then, is also that the ethics of teaching are found in the path itself – namely, in the optimisation of judgement in the circumstances. There is no overall dogmatic principle dictating the priorities of a teacher apart from what will enable better judgement.

The language of the Buddha's teaching also set him apart from his contemporaries because it was focused on the needs of his auditors, rather than the fulfilment of dogmatic tradition. He used the vernacular of his context, which could be described as 'Magadhi', except that this tells us little, because it is just a label for the language of the area the Buddha lived in. Because of its preservation in a transmission of oral teachings that were eventually written down, this language is now known as Pali. 'Pali' is originally supposed to have meant 'a row of letters', and it is only after being written that it became the dead scriptural language that it is today. However, given the dominance of the high, priestly language of Sanskrit in all religious contexts in the Buddha's time, the Buddha's use of the language actually used every day by his hearers was significant. 'Sanskrit' means 'complete' or 'perfect', and this perfection was commonly ascribed to the language along with the power of those who used it – in contrast to the imperfection of the vernacular. Obviously, the language of everyday life would be much more directly meaningful and thus more powerful in practice, even to those who could understand Sanskrit. It would also be more accessible to all. The way in which the Buddha taught all classes of society and both sexes also underlines this point.

A further aspect of the Buddha's teaching approach that shows its practicality is the very frequent use of similes or metaphors. This seems likely to be attributable to the Buddha's educative approach from the beginning. Some of the most well-known of these similes, such as the raft and the arrow, are very helpful to understanding the Middle Way, and will be discussed in more detail in section 3. Many of the other similes used in the *suttas* are less profound in their implications, but nevertheless provide a strong source of *meaning* for the reader or hearer.

Similes and metaphors can bring abstract doctrine to life because they are directly linked to bodily awareness through the right hemisphere of the brain. As Iain McGilchrist puts it, 'Metaphoric thinking is fundamental to our understanding of the world, because it is the *only* way in which understanding can reach outside the system of signs to life itself.'[2] Again, then, the Buddha's use of similes shows his wish to effectively move and inspire people to practice. The Buddha's resourcefulness in being able to create so many similes is also an indication of the development of his imagination, which is an aspect of his integration. I have written elsewhere about the relationship of the imagination to embodied meaning, and the way in which meaning can be integrated just as desire and belief can.[3]

However, the most central ways in which the Buddha's teaching methods reflect the Middle Way involve his attitude to authority, his ability to use dialectical or Socratic questioning, and (on occasion) his capacity to merely facilitate what we might now call discovery learning or student-centred learning. It is only possible for us to be aided by another in our engagement with the Middle Way if, to begin with, we recognise that we need to use our own judgement. We are thus allowed to make our own mistakes. There is no stronger demonstration than this of the universality of the Middle Way. A chemistry teacher can set up the experimental conditions for a student to find out for herself the universality of some general fact about the reaction between two substances (say, calcium and water). Similarly, the Buddha was able to help people discover the universality of the Middle Way from the fact that they could discover it for themselves rather than merely being told about it.

People are only able to discover for themselves if they are effectively free to make their own judgements. The *Kalama Sutta* is justly famous as the text in which the Buddha makes explicit not just the educative policy, but the epistemology of the path as one of autonomous judgement. The Kalamas of Kesaputta are a group of villagers who come to the Buddha in puzzlement, to ask how they should go about judging the rival claims of opposing religious teachers:

---

2 McGilchrist (2010) p. 115.
3 Ellis (2013b).

> 'There are, Lord, some ascetics and brahmins who come to Kesaputta. They explain and elucidate their own doctrines, but disparage, debunk, revile and vilify the doctrines of others. But then some other ascetics and brahmins come to Kesaputta, and they too...[do the same]. For us, Lord, there is perplexity and doubt as to which of these good ascetics speak truth and which speak falsehood.'
>
> 'It is fitting for you to be perplexed, O Kalamas.... Come, Kalamas. Do not go by oral tradition, by lineage of teaching, by hearsay, by a collection of scriptures, by logical reasoning, by inferential reasoning, by reflection on reasons, by the acceptance of a view after pondering it, by the seeming competence of a speaker, or because you think "The ascetic is our teacher." But when you know for yourselves, "These things are unwholesome, these things are blameable; these things are censured by the wise; these things, if undertaken and practised, lead to harm and suffering", then you should abandon them.... But when you know for yourselves, "These things are wholesome, these things are blameless; these things are praised by the wise; these things, if undertaken and practised, lead to welfare and happiness", then you should engage in them.'[4]

The Kalamas' position is writ even larger today, when global communication can give us access to an enormous range of voices and opinions. But the Buddha's response to it is remarkable by the standards of any age. It reflects scepticism and agnosticism as component elements of the Middle Way. This is sceptical because it refuses to accept any authoritative claims to 'knowledge'. It rejects a whole list of standard types of appeal by which religious teachers and others may claim to possess an absolute truth or reject an absolute falsehood. Some of these are the stock in trade of religious traditions, such as the appeal to tradition itself or to the sanctity of a canonical text. Some are more typical of philosophers, who may argue that because a claim is reasoned or 'rational' it must therefore be correct. But reasoning is only the method we use to link our prior assumptions into further conclusions, meaning that the conclusions have no more guarantee of truth than the starting assumptions. The final two elements of the list appeal to a speaker's status or the auditors' loyalty to her, but again, these offer no guarantee of the truth of what is being said. If competing teachers use rival appeals of this kind to claim their supremacy, it is then agnosticism that the Kalamas will need. They will then conclude not that some are right

---

4 *Kalama Sutta, Anguttara Nikaya* 3.65. Nyanaponika and Bodhi (1999) pp. 65–6.

and others wrong, or that all are right or that all are wrong, but rather they will hold all open for further examination.

The Buddha's list of objects of absolute appeal should remind us of the ones that he himself considered and went beyond in both the palace and the forest. The values of the palace might claim absolute authority because of (genetic) lineage, or because of the (political) competence of a speaker, or because of loyalty. However, it is these very absolute claims that created the problems that led Siddhartha to go forth. The values of the forest might be urged in particular groups by almost any of these appeals, but perhaps particularly by claims of competence (in meditative attainment), lineage, or scripture. As we have seen, the Buddha learned from both these sources, but at the same time he did not conclude that they were wholly correct. Similarly, there is no reason why the Kalamas cannot learn a good deal from the rival religious teachers – it is concluding that they are wholly right that is dangerous.

The advice to the Kalamas to 'know for yourselves' also reflects the Buddha's own experience in discovering the Middle Way. He could only do so by considering what he had learnt with critical awareness. With that he could discard the absolutisations and thus reach, not absolute knowledge, but *confidence* about the best judgement in the circumstances. 'The wise' are very likely to have an input into this, notwithstanding our need to make prior judgements about who is wise before we are able to consult them. However, the wise cannot have the final say, because they cannot be taken absolutely. Their path, in their body and their situation, may look different from yours even if you are both following the same Middle Way. Judgement, in the end, is made by creatures with bodies who 'know', in the sense of reaching a poised state of confidence that is adequate in the circumstances. It is not a set of verbal formulae that you can adopt from others by repeating them. Even the formulae mean something different when you say them from when they say them, so how could you simply accept the authority of what they say, even by repeating it word for word? It is a pretence and a delusion to even think you could do so.

The Buddha's epistemology, then, is one of autonomous judgement, but not in the sense of an isolated 'rational' self being able to figure everything out. Rather it is in the recognition that in practice our best chance of responding adequately to the circumstances is to allow as much reflective awareness as possible, to integrate as many perspectives as possible. To accept a teacher's words in their raw form, for any reason, is to short-circuit that necessary process. However, that does not prevent us *incrementally* paying close attention to a teacher's words in proportion to their *credibility*. Any of the factors on the Buddha's list might give us justification to give the teacher time and attention and reflect on what they say, without giving us justification to necessarily accept it.

The Buddha's epistemology is inextricable from his educational method. In addition to suggesting to the Kalamas how to deal with conflicting sources of information, he is suggesting how he himself should be interpreted. His personal authority, his reasoning, his charisma, and loyalty to him or to the Buddhist tradition might all provide reasons for paying him attention. To take the Buddha's words as perfect revelations of truth, however, would entirely conflict with the message of the *Kalama Sutta*. His words provide a context for us to work out the Middle Way for ourselves.

Predictably enough, given the extent to which the *Kalama Sutta* obviously challenges pretensions to absolute authority in Buddhism, it has met with defensive interpretations from traditionalists. Bhikkhu Bodhi, for example, objects to the way that

> On the basis of a single passage, quoted out of context, the Buddha has been made out to be a pragmatic empiricist who dismisses all doctrine and faith, and whose Dhamma is simply a freethinker's kit to truth which invites each one to accept and reject whatever he likes.[5]

This is fairly typical of the ways in which traditionalists who do not interpret the Buddha's teachings in terms of the Middle Way tend to straitjacket those teachings. They do this by putting them into the terms of a polarised debate between two kinds of absolutisation: in this case traditional Buddhist versus caricatured 'secular' beliefs. But absolute authority is not the only alternative to 'dismissal' of 'doctrine and faith'. Nor are the justified beliefs allowed by autonomous judgement arbitrary in the way Bodhi seems to assume.

Bodhi goes on to claim that the Buddha's approach here is an exceptional one determined by the circumstances. He claims that the Kalamas must have been people of 'refined moral sensitivity' for this advice not to be 'dangerous'. It's a fair enough point that

---

5 Bodhi (1998).

the gradual development of autonomous judgement requires the development of a corresponding degree of maturity, though that does not imply that it is not present at all for those in earlier stages. Bodhi also claims, moreover, that as the Kalamas

> had not yet come to accept the Buddha in terms of his unique mission, as the discloser of the liberating truth, it would not have been in place for him to expound to them the Dhamma unique to his own Dispensation: such teachings as the Four Noble Truths, the three characteristics, and the methods of contemplation based upon them. These teachings are specifically intended for those who have accepted the Buddha as their guide to deliverance....[6]

This is a clear example of one of the ways in which a message that is compatible with the Middle Way as a universal insight has been co-opted by Buddhist tradition and turned into a special revelation. Once the special revelation has been accepted, apparently the only way to develop offered by this tradition is to accept one's instructions on authority. One thus ceases the kind of autonomous enquiry the Buddha recommends. In terms of the wider Middle Way, however, this would be a regressive way of acting. The Buddhist tradition then simply becomes another stop in the forest rather than a promoter of further spiritual progress. When the Buddhist tradition merely offers another form of absolutisation, the Middle Way has been betrayed and the Buddha's message loses its universality.

The earlier our stage of learning, the more provisional structures the teacher will need to provide. However, there is no stage at which learning ceases to be autonomous, or where it ceases to involve the development of critical awareness. Critical awareness provisionalises the absolutised forms of previous stages of development so as to allow us to change.[7] The message of the *Kalama Sutta* is not incompatible with the use of provisional structures of all kinds, including considerable reliance on the Buddha's credibility. That can be one of the staging posts by which we gradually come to understand the Middle Way better. However, the Buddha's message in the *Kalama Sutta* needs to be interpreted in line with the Middle Way in general, as clearly avoiding absolutisation of any source of information at all stages. In the rest of this book I present evidence that this is not 'taken

---

6 Ibid.
7 This point is developed in relation to Piagetian and object-relations psychological models in Kegan (1982).

out of context' at all. If anything it is the traditionalists who insist on interpreting everything in the Pali Canon in terms of absolute beliefs that take it 'out of context'. They do so by interpreting the Buddha's message outside the context of the wider requirements for universal human development. They also ignore the use of the Middle Way in the Pali Canon as discussed throughout this book.

The Buddha's capacity to adjust his educative approach to the need of an individual for experiential learning is shown again and again in the *suttas*. A *sutta* typically involves an encounter and a discussion with someone – whether it is an enquirer or a critic. One of the most memorable examples of this is his encounter with Kisagotami, which I have developed myself into the starting point of a work of fiction called *Theme and Variations*.[8] This story actually originates in a commentary on the Canon.[9] A woman comes to the Buddha carrying her dead child and asking him to bring it back to life. The Buddha refrains from confronting her with the irreversibility of death in the abstract when he recognises that she is not ready to accept it. Instead, he asks her to fetch a grain of mustard seed from a house where there has been no death. Of course, she is unable to find one, and is thus jolted through her own activity into an acceptance of the death.

In the Kisagotami episode, the Middle Way is followed in the rejection of two opposed absolutes: that of merely confronting Kisagotami with her delusion and appealing to 'fact' on the one hand, or of playing along with that delusion in a way that prevents her from confronting it on the other. Whenever we encounter the delusions of others, we are likely to meet a similar dilemma. Their ability to overcome delusion depends on the psychological conditions of their maturity, education, and previous experience, not just on belief in an abstract statement that contradicts that delusion. In these circumstances, the goal of 'truth' is not served by belief in the 'truth'. Rather it's better served by following a path in which the conditions that gave rise to the delusion, as well as the 'truth', are practically recognised and integrated. Kisagotami was not ready for the 'truth', because our bodies require a return to the relative security of embodied experience to adjust to new conditions. This need for

---

8 Ellis (2011b).
9 *Therigatha* 10:1. Olendzki (2013).

embodiment in transition is often better served by completing a task for ourselves that applies our whole energies in activity, rather than accepting an abstract claim. Similarly, Siddhartha's recognition of the Middle Way was not achieved just by accepting the proposition that 'balanced health meeting the body's needs is required for effective practice', but rather by *feeling* that in the experience of the body itself.

What the Buddha expounded in theory to the Kalamas, then, is put into practice in the story of Kisagotami. She had to 'know' impermanence for herself, in the sense of finding it fully meaningful in experience. In practice, here, the Buddha does not privilege his own perspective over those of other teachers, but rather allows the learner to discover for herself which perspective addresses the conditions best.

2.d. The Buddha's Discourses

To fully understand the Buddha's educative approach we should not only consider the points in the previous chapter, but also look at the nature of the discussions in the *sutta*s of the Pali Canon. It is there that we can see how the Buddha responds to the great variety of people who approach him, whether with reverence or hostility, and channels their problems into helpful resolutions. In every case we can identify an absolutised assumption in the problem, and the Buddha responds to that assumption by leading the individual in the direction of the Middle Way.

The central technique is that also used by Socrates in the dialogues of Plato, which were composed in ancient Athens at a similar time in history. In the *sutta*s, as in Plato's dialogues, the teacher does not tend to approach a mistaken view by contradicting it and merely arguing for an alternative. That is most likely to simply spark an oppositional argument. It makes the interlocutor seek resources to defend the position he starts off identifying with, and thus become more entrenched in it. Instead, the teacher asks a series of questions that merely require acceptance or rejection from the interlocutor. These lead the interlocutor by degrees from an experiential position that he would take to be obviously correct to one that is contrary to the absolute position he initially took, but far more helpful. Another more modern version of this type of questioning may be employed in cognitive behavioural therapy.

As with a soldier trained to defuse live bombs, absolutisations need to be defused carefully before they are set off, and one does this by gradual adjustment that avoids sudden movements. In this way, the interlocutor continues to feel secure. The prefrontal cortex continues to offer a wider perspective to make any new challenges seem manageable, before the amygdala in the back of the brain triggers us into reaction. To defuse an absolutisation, we need to see it in a wider context, making more synaptic connections available to us. This can be done by practices that relax and broaden the mental state such as meditation, or that stimulate the imagination. However, for someone who has lost their motivation to engage in spiritual practice, or perhaps has not engaged in it effectively in the first place, it is beliefs that need to be examined. If we can convince somebody that their current beliefs actually imply more helpful ones than they are currently aware of, they may be able to gain a

The Middle Way in the Buddha's Ministry

better connection with the more integrated motivations associated with those beliefs.

As an example, let's start by looking at the *sutta* devoted to a discourse with Tissa in the *Samyutta Nikaya*.[1] This begins with Tissa, one of the Buddha's followers, complaining about what sounds like depression of some kind:

> 'My body seems as if it has been drugged, I have become disoriented, the teachings are no longer clear to me. Sloth and torpor persist obsessing my mind. I am leading the holy life dissatisfied, and I have doubt about the teachings.'

The Buddha then calls Tissa to him and asks him a series of questions.

> 'What do you think, Tissa, if one is not devoid of lust for form, not devoid of desire, affection, thirst, passion, and craving for it, then with the change and alteration of that form, do sorrow, pain, displeasure and despair arise within?'

In other words, as long as we remain dominated by obsessions, don't you think we're likely to get depressed? Don't you think how you're feeling is to be expected from time to time, given the teachings you've already understood and accepted?

Tissa assents to this, as he does to a whole list of other formulae for the 'lusts' we maintain. He is then asked the converse, namely whether we should expect such depression if we are free of those obsessions. Tissa says 'no' to this, as again he does for a whole list of such 'lusts'. The Buddha is simply reminding him of the theory, but also in the process that the theory is not just an abstraction, but that it is applicable to what he is experiencing.

The Buddha then asks him:

> 'What do you think, Tissa, is form permanent or impermanent?' – 'Impermanent, venerable sir.' ... 'Therefore...Seeing thus...He understands "there is no more for this state of being."'

Tissa knows that it is his obsessional states of mind that lead to his depression, but he is unable to actually recognise these at the moment. He feels too overwhelmed by those states of mind themselves. He absolutises this mental state because he believes it is all there is, and that there is no alternative to it. The recollection

---

1 *Samyutta Nikaya* 22:84. Bodhi (2000) pp. 929-31.

of impermanence, taken not as a cosmic truth but as a general statement prompting recognition of a changing mental state, gives Tissa just enough perspective to begin to see a way out.

The Buddha then offers an extended simile of one man showing another a physical path by pointing out the helpful turns to make at various points. He then likens this path to the spiritual path. He concludes: 'Rejoice Tissa! Rejoice, Tissa! I am here to exhort, I am here to assist, I am here to instruct!' The Buddha realises that it is partly just friendship and support that Tissa needs to help him find a way beyond the absolutisations that he has been locked into by his emotional state. Another person saying these things has more impact on him than merely thinking them in the abstract. We are not given any exaggerated indications of Tissa's response, but just told that 'Elated, the Venerable Tissa delighted in the Blessed One's statement.' There are no miraculous cures, but he has at least been given a boost for now.

For a contrasting example let us look at the *Sonadanda Sutta* from the *Digha Nikaya*.[2] Here, instead of support for a depressed friend, the Buddha is depicted as dealing with the dogmas of the religious elite of his day. Sonadanda is a brahmin, meaning a hereditary priest with prime social place at the top of the caste hierarchy. For him to have a discussion with the Buddha would be a bit like a bishop talking to a druid, or a hospital consultant talking to a new-age alternative healer. Nevertheless, Sonadanda has a sense that he has something to learn from the Buddha, even though he is also anxious about compromising his social status. The tension between these two impulses in Sonadanda creates a source of comedy in this *sutta*.

At first Sonadanda, resting on his verandah, sees other brahmins going to see the Buddha and, not to be outdone, resolves to go too. Other brahmins then advise him not to demean himself by going to see the Buddha, but to summon the Buddha to see him. However, Sonadanda responds by telling them all he has heard about the Buddha's qualities, and praising him as worthy of a visit. One gets the impression even at this stage of the uncertainty that arises at a time of changing paradigms. In some ways the dogmas of Brahminic superiority remain unquestioned, but in others, experience informs people of the spiritual achievements of the *shramana*s. Their experience is thus in conflict with their habitual thinking and vested

2   *Digha Nikaya* 4. Walshe (1995) pp. 125–32.

The Middle Way in the Buddha's Ministry 75

interests. Sonadanda is presumably an 'early adopter' – a relatively open-minded brahmin willing to respond to positive reports about this great *shramana* leader.

As Sonadanda actually sets out to see the Buddha, however, and even as he meets him, he is subject to lots of anxieties. The text portrays the closed feedback loop of his thoughts very well:

> But when Sonadanda had traversed the jungle-thickets, he thought: 'If I ask the ascetic Gotama a question he might say to me: "That, Brahmin, is not a fitting question, it is not at all a fitting question", and then the company might despise me, saying "Sonadanda is a fool, he has no sense, he can't put a proper question to the ascetic Gotama." And if anyone were despised by this company, his reputation would suffer, and then his income would suffer, for our income depends on the gaining of a reputation....'

Sonadanda continues caught up in the 'what ifs' of his anxiety, until finally he concludes to himself, 'If only the ascetic Gotama would ask me a question from my own field of the Three Vedas! Then I could give him an answer that would satisfy him!' The Buddha 'reading his mind' then asks Sonadanda:

> 'By how many qualities do the Brahmins recognise a Brahmin? How would one declare truthfully and without falling into falsehood: "I am a Brahmin"?'

This is often represented, of course, as indicating the Buddha's mind-reading powers, and/or his compassion. However, he would only need common empathetic observation to notice that Sonadanda was anxious. The Buddha's skill lies in the way he responds to that observation. Sonadanda's anxiety is indicative of his continuing attachment to Brahminical dogmas, which are closely interrelated with his status in the group. Thus if the Buddha were to challenge those dogmas, or even ask Sonadanda a question that presupposed the greater importance of alternative ways of thinking, there is a grave danger that Sonadanda would only respond defensively. The absolute oppositions would then continue, and no progress would be made from the conversation. So, the Buddha instead asked a question that was framed in terms of Sonadanda's own accustomed ways of thinking and speaking. This was a consummate example of the practice of the Middle Way. He neither imposed his own ideas nor completely capitulated to those of Brahminism, but nevertheless addressed the conditions of a context where Brahminism was still very influential.

At the same time, the Buddha offers further evidence of the universality and flexibility of the Middle Way. Just as the Middle Way can be expressed in the terms of different traditions today – for example Buddhist, Christian, and scientific – so could it be expressed in the time of the Buddha. The Middle Way begins from wherever you start, and if you're a brahmin then perhaps you follow a Brahminical Middle Way. From the fact that the Buddha was capable of speaking in this way, it also follows that he did not think of the Middle Way solely in one set of terms. He had developed the skills of synthetic thinking necessary to relate the concepts of one tradition with those of another. If he was alive in the West today, it is easy to imagine the Buddha teaching a Christian Middle Way, a Muslim Middle Way, a Scientific Middle Way, a New Age Middle Way, and so on with every tradition.

Sonadanda responds to the Buddha's question, giving five qualities of a brahmin: birth in the brahmin caste, scholarship, handsome appearance, virtue, and wisdom. In a fashion highly reminiscent of Socrates, the Buddha then goes on to question his interlocutor about which of these qualities are essential and which are dispensable for a 'true brahmin'. Sonadanda is ready to let go of the handsome appearance first as non-essential, then scholarship, then birth. Sonadanda meets opposition from the other brahmins when he suggests that birth is inessential. However, he tells them that he 'does not decry' these things, presumably meaning that he could still consider them important without considering them essential. When pushed on the essentiality of virtue and wisdom, however, Sonadanda argues that these are both essential because they are interdependent. When asked to explain what morality and wisdom are, however, he is at a loss, and hands over to the Buddha. The Buddha defines them in a characteristic way framed by moral practice, control of sense-inputs, the *jhanas*, insights, and the cessation of the taints.

The Buddha's amazing achievement here is to assist Sonadanda in letting go of his absolutist assumption that birth is an essential part of the status of a brahmin. This is astonishing, because it is the bedrock of the Brahminic claim on social and religious power at the head of the caste system. It is hardly surprising that Sonadanda's fellows objected to this, because it crosses a rubicon from an absolute position to one that is willing to prioritise on the basis of experience. As long as brahmins claim justified power on the basis of birth, (which is an absolute claim that cannot be incrementalised), they are absolutising. However, they do not have to shift to the opposite position of not valuing birth at all to start moving towards the Middle Way; they have only to recognise that birth is not *essential*. This opens the gates for *shramanas* such as the Buddha, or indeed anyone else, to become a 'true brahmin'. In the Buddha's adaptation of Brahminical language, a 'true brahmin' is just a good person, with the 'true' merely being a marker to separate him from a conventional brahmin. The basis of goodness is thus recognised as a mixture of qualities.

This is not merely 'skilful means' in the sense of a well-motivated manipulation to get someone in the 'wrong' tradition to start thinking in terms of the 'right' tradition. Instead we should see it more radically, as an indication that the Middle Way is independent of tradition, even though different traditions will recognise it to varying extents. It is not intrinsically less accurate to speak of a more integrated person as a 'true brahmin' (or indeed, a 'true Christian' or a 'true utilitarian') than as a 'true Buddhist'. Granted, the 'true' bit can be easily misinterpreted in terms of the very essentialising that I think the Buddha was trying to avoid, but in its context in the *Sonadanda Sutta*, it challenges essentialism. It also helps us recognise the plurality of moral paths that begin from different points. As an example of how to teach those whose thinking lies in a different framework from one's own tradition, it's difficult to surpass.

Given the limitations on further space I can give to the discourses, these two examples will have to stand for the wide range of other examples in the Pali Canon. The vast majority of them show a similar use of the Middle Way in teaching, avoiding either acceptance or simple contradiction of the absolute beliefs of interlocutors. In this way the Buddha can skilfully aid the interlocutors in engaging with the Middle Way. The sheer number of such discourses gives a weight of evidence of the Buddha's basic motivation, not towards absolutes of 'enlightenment', but towards integrative progress that avoids absolutes.

2.e. The Buddha's Politics

The political application of the Buddha's teachings creates one of the strongest arguments for their interpretation in terms of the Middle Way rather than in terms of an absolute Awakening. The key reason for this is the contrast between the *incrementality* that is a feature of the Middle Way and the *discontinuity* that is created by the absolutisation of the Buddha's experience. Politics is concerned with the use of power, including the threat of violence, for the benefit of society. Absolute Awakening, though, implies the prioritisation of a specific individual state traditionally said to be completely incompatible with violence or even with family life, let alone political power. This has led to the long-standing stereotype of Buddhism as an 'other-worldly' religion. This Buddhism is divided between pure monks seeking nirvana (*nibbana*), and lay-people – who are the ones obliged to soil their hands with political concerns (as well as killing, sex, and work) to keep society going. However, such discontinuity would be incompatible with the Middle Way as a universal path for all contexts. We also do not find it in the stories we have regarding the Buddha's attitude to politics.

The Buddha's political situation was, as Stephen Batchelor puts it, 'a delicate balancing act', and his ability to maintain that balancing act 'a tribute to his political instincts and social skills as much as his "enlightenment"'.[1] The Buddha had close contact with three states: Magadha (ruled by King Bimbisara until near the end of the Buddha's life, when Ajatasattu took over), Kosala (ruled by King Pasenadi), and the Vajjian Confederacy (which had a republican oligarchic type of government). All of these states are depicted as receptive to the Buddha's teaching, so that he gained high status there. However, they continued in rivalry, which erupted into war at the end, as Ajatasattu conquered both of the other states. The Buddha maintained friendship with both kings, and with the Vajjian nobility, without taking sides in their conflicts.

However, it seems to have been with King Pasenadi of Kosala that the Buddha had the closest relationship. This is reflected in the fact that an entire *samyutta* (collection of connected discourses), the *Kosalasamyutta*, is given over to the Buddha's discussions with Pasenadi. It is in one of these that the Buddha gives clear emphasis

---

1 Batchelor (2015) p. 109.

to the *experiential* basis of his political judgements (as all his other judgements), in a discussion of when to trust people. This discussion in many ways parallels that of the *Kalama Sutta*, beginning as it does with the Buddha questioning Pasenadi's assumptions about who could be known to be 'arahants or…entered on the path of arahantship' (i.e. Awakening).

> 'Great king, being a layman who enjoys sensual pleasures, swelling in a home crowded with children…, it is difficult for you to know: "These are arahants or these have entered upon the path to arahantship". It is by living together with someone, great king, that his virtue is to be known, and that after a long time, not after a short time; by one who is attentive, not by one who is inattentive; by one who is wise, not by a dullard. It is by dealing with someone, great king, that his honesty is to be known, and that after a long time…. It is in adversities, great king, that a person's fortitude is to be known, and that after a long time…. It is by discussion with someone, great king, that his wisdom is to be known, and that after a long time….'[2]

The key issue of all political discussion is that of power: in what circumstances is it permissible to wield it? We can ask that question in the abstract, but the results of doing so are likely to be inadequate to the complexities of a specific situation. If we ask it in the concrete complexity of a particular situation, then, it becomes primarily a question of whom to trust – as it was for the Kalamas. That is just as much a question for a king deciding to whom to delegate power, as it is for a citizen deciding whether to obey or resist a political power that is already set up. The Buddha here lays the emphasis on *integrated* judgement by discussing the time needed, the attention needed, and the wisdom needed to judge someone's trustworthiness. We need to follow the path ourselves in order to improve our ability to judge who else is following the path. We may then be able to see who is likely to make the most adequate judgements in the political realm as in every other.

Pasenadi then abruptly upsets the Buddha's exposition by revealing the crude realities of political power, and how far they are from this integrated basis of judgement:

> 'These, venerable sir, are my spies, undercover agents, coming back after spying out the country. First information is gathered by them and afterwards I make them disclose it. Now, venerable sir, when they have washed off the

---

2 *Samyutta Nikaya* 3.11.178–80. Bodhi (2000) pp. 173–4. Also given in more detail in *Anguttara Nikaya* 2.187.

dust and dirt and are freshly bathed and groomed, with their hair and beards trimmed, clad in white garments, they will enjoy themselves supplied and endowed with the five cords of sensual pleasure.'[3]

One has to assume that Pasenadi is referring to followers of the Buddha who are present, appearing as renunciants but actually about to go off and be treated by the king in reward (presumably) for their information about the Buddha's activities. At one and the same time this is a challenge to the Buddha's teaching – for it seems that he has not recognised this state of affairs – but also a confirmation of it. The Buddha has made no claims about exactly how long he himself needs to live with, deal with, and share adversities and discussions with a person to know them sufficiently, and his limitations are here made apparent.

Stephen Batchelor comments on this episode:

The king is playing a trick on Gotama to test him. He admits to him that all of these men are in fact his spies, who are disguised as wanderers and ascetics. Gotama remains equanimous. He does not criticise the king for trying to mislead him or others by disguising his spies as wanderers.... What emerges from this exchange is a glimpse of Gotama's skill in dealing with a fickle and powerful character.[4]

The Buddha is clearly subjected to political conditions, not only beyond the spiritual community that he founded, but even within it. He is not in control of those conditions, but has to deal even with nasty surprises. The practice of the Middle Way is exercised in constant interaction with these conditions, and involves always using the most integrated judgement available to him. That means avoiding the absolutisation of any belief – whether that is a belief about a person's trustworthiness, a political allegiance, or an ideology. But that practice does not make him omniscient.

Another example of the intrusion of political conditions on the Buddha's community occurs when the warlike king Ajatasattu, planning to attack the Vajjians, sends his minister to ask the Buddha for advice.[5] The Buddha, characteristically, does not offer direct advice either to attack the Vajjians or to refrain from doing so. Rather he asks his attendant Ananda if he has heard whether the Vajjians are following advice that he previously gave them to follow

3 *Samyutta Nikaya* 3.11.180. Bodhi (2000) p. 174.
4 Batchelor (2015) p. 96.
5 *Digha Nikaya* 16.1.6. Walshe (1995) pp. 231 ff.

The Middle Way in the Buddha's Ministry

'seven principles for preventing decline'. As long as the Vajjians are following these principles, the Buddha tells the minister, he would expect them to prosper and not decline. The minister interprets this to mean that the Vajjians should not be attacked directly, but 'only by means of propaganda' – though that interpretation is clearly his, perhaps created by his wish to have a clear response to take back to the king.

The seven principles for preventing decline are as follows:
1. Holding regular and frequent assemblies
2. Meeting in harmony, breaking up in harmony, and carrying on their business in harmony
3. Not authorising what has not been authorised already, not abolishing what has been authorised, but proceeding according to what has been authorised by their ancient tradition
4. Honouring, respecting, revering and saluting the elders amongst them, and considering them worth listening to
5. Not forcibly abducting others' wives and daughters
6. Honouring, respecting, revering and saluting the Vajjian shrines at home and abroad, not withdrawing the proper support made and given before
7. Making proper provision for the safety of *arahants*[6]

The continuity between these principles for the conduct of political life and those for the spiritual community is then immediately emphasised. The Buddha is depicted as calling the monks together and giving them a similar 'seven principles' for maintaining their community. The first four are identical to those given to the Vajjians; but for the fifth, sixth and seventh, not falling prey to desires, being devoted to forest-lodgings, and preserving personal mindfulness are respectively substituted.[7]

Given the universality of the Buddha's message, we need, as usual, not to get caught up in those features of his teachings and attitudes that merely reflect the circumstances. Instead we need to try to draw out from them the more general approaches that reflect the Middle Way – in this case as applied to political conduct. In the first two principles there is a clear emphasis on communication, enabling conflicts to be discussed and dealt with. The conditions for communication are maintained when people create

6 *Digha Nikaya* 16.1.4. Walshe (1995) pp. 231 ff.
7 *Digha Nikaya* 16.1.6. Walshe (1995) pp. 231 ff.

the conditions for it (regular and frequent assemblies) and when they give clear attention to resolving conflicts harmoniously, not allowing obsessions and anxieties to disrupt that communication. In the third, there seems to be a clear suggestion of maintaining a political constitution: that is, an agreed way of operating in the state that allocates responsibility and allows decisions to be made harmoniously. In the fourth, the Buddha perhaps assumes that there is a higher likelihood of wisdom amongst the elders, who have amassed more experience. They are not necessarily right, but they are worth listening to.

The fifth, sixth and seventh principles obviously deal with problems that are more specific to the context. However the version for the monastic community still has something in common with that for the Vajjians. Political bodies, as well as individuals, are maintained by the limitation of obsessive desires, the valuing of cultural resources as sources of meaning, and the maintenance of more integrated mental states (or at least of those who can teach and exemplify them). Forcible abduction of women is just one example of the results of obsession, and the maintenance of shrines just one example of a source of important cultural meaning.

These principles strongly suggest that the Buddha's advice on politics was simply an extension of the practice of the Middle Way and integrative practice that he advised for individuals. The maintenance of a context where individuals could practise was obviously part of his concern, but this is not entirely distinguishable from the political context itself as a field of practice. Just as conflicts within an individual can be worked with through integrative practice, so can those between individuals. Social conflicts are, after all, represented within the minds of all the individuals who participate in them, and individual conflicts can also be writ large as people project them onto the wider world. Why did Ajatasattu want to attack the Vajjians? The reasons are not just 'political', but would need to be found in Ajatasattu's psychological states and the conflicts to be found there.

The Buddha's avoidance of partisan advice-giving also tells us about a crucial kind of caution we need to adopt when making judgements about political matters. If we judge too hastily and wade into political conflicts between groups, we are very likely to start identifying with a particular group and adopt their biases, rather than maintaining the wider awareness that is required to resolve political conflict.

The Buddha has often been portrayed either as completely staying out of politics or as treating it only as a means to an end for the maintenance of support for the monastic community. However, when the Buddha refused to get drawn in, his most likely motive was not 'other-worldliness', but rather the wish to avoid feeding polarisation and conflict. Where he could make a difference by intervening, there is some indication that he did. For example, according to the commentary literature, he intervened to prevent violence erupting from a quarrel between his kinsmen, the Sakyans and the Koliyans, over water rights.[8] In this case, he was neither apolitical nor merely interested in his community – rather he wished to practice, apply, and spread the Middle Way in the political realm as everywhere else.

The Buddha shows little indication of a leaning towards any particular political ideology – although he lived in an age long before the explicit formulation of any such ideologies. However, I think we can be confident that he would not have simply identified with (for example) socialism, liberalism, or conservatism as providing all the answers, because the Middle Way would prevent one from absolutising political ideologies just as it would religious ones. If we look more closely at the values that underlie ideologies, however, it is possible to find indications of the way that the Buddha respected a whole range of these. Again, this is exactly what we would expect so as to avoid absolutisation in the political realm. Any value that addresses conditions can be appreciated and respected, but it can never be accepted as the final answer or as an end in itself. It is in the tension between differing values that we can find the most adequate ways forward.

The social psychologist Jonathan Haidt has provided a very helpful analysis of six basic political values (or 'moral foundations of politics') based on research of the common factors found in a variety of political beliefs in a variety of contexts.[9] These are:

1. Care, avoiding harm
2. Fairness, avoiding cheating
3. Liberty, avoiding oppression

---

8 *Dhammapada* Commentary 18. Burlingame and Khantipalo (2006).
9 Haidt (2012) chs. 7 and 8.

4. Loyalty, avoiding betrayal
5. Authority, avoiding subversion
6. Sanctity, avoiding degradation

Haidt found that those on the conservative end of the spectrum tended to draw on all of these values to some extent. Socialists (or 'liberals' in the American sense), on the other hand, put much more emphasis only on the first two and often rejected the last three. However, it can also be argued that we all need all of these values to be able to address a variety of conditions. It is the absolutisation of one or some values at the expense of all the others that reduces the capacity of political judgement to address conditions.[10] The Middle Way thus requires us to recognise and accept all these types of values as contributing helpfully to human life, but to avoid absolutising any of them. There seem to be plenty of indications that the Buddha indeed followed the Middle Way in the sense of recognising the value of all of them, as well as avoiding absolutisations.

That the Buddha *cared* for others at a personal level is clear from many examples, particularly from the episode when he upbraided some of his followers for not caring for a fellow community member with dysentery.[11] In this case it seems that some kind of quid pro quo was expected, so the monk was neglected by his fellows because he was unable to do anything for anyone else in exchange. However, the Buddha challenged this kind of absolutisation of fairness that would leave someone unattended when they were in dire need. That the Buddha also advocated care as a political principle can be seen in the *Kutadanta Sutta*, in which the Buddha advocates a series of 'true sacrifices' that should replace the formalistic and often violent sacrifices of Brahminism. The first of these involves an apparent burst of Keynesian welfare economics:

> 'To those in the kingdom who are engaged in cultivating crops and raising cattle, let your majesty distribute grain and fodder; to those in trade, give capital; to those in government service assign proper living wages. Then those people, being intent on their own occupations, will not harm the kingdom. Your majesty's revenues will be great, the land will be tranquil and not beset by thieves, and the people, with joy in their hearts, will play with their children, and will dwell in open houses.'[12]

---

10 I make this argument more fully in Ellis (2015a) ch. 4.h.
11 *Kucchivikara-Vatthu*, *Mahavagga* 8.26.1–8. Thanissaro (1997a).
12 *Digha Nikaya* 5.11. Walshe (1995) pp. 135–6.

It would be a mistake to conclude from this alone that the Buddha was an ideological socialist – not only would this be anachronistic, but it ignores the ways in which he also supports values more often associated with conservatism. What it does show is that he will support ways of addressing conditions that are used by socialists, even when these are unusual in the context.

That the Buddha supports fairness, in several possible senses of the term, is also evident. He supports the duty of kings to administer justice, as is shown when he agrees with Saccaka in his discourse with him that kings, as well as republics, should 'exercise the power in their own realm to execute those who should be executed, to fine those who should be fined, and to banish those who should be banished'.[13] That kings and other political rulers in turn should not be allowed to cheat is indicated by the idea of the social contract in the *Aggañña Sutta*. Here the institution of government is depicted as arising in a context of *mutual* duties of service between ruler and ruled.[14] Fairness in the sense of social equality is also supported, at least at a basic level, in the *Cakkavatti-Sihanada Sutta*, where the negative effects of 'not giving property to the needy' are shown as theft, murder, dishonesty, and sexual misconduct.[15] Again, it would not be fair to interpret this as showing that the Buddha believed all crime was solely caused by poverty, as that would involve absolutising one explanatory condition. However, it would be fair to conclude that he recognised the importance of avoiding gross inequality in society to a web of interacting political conditions.

The value of liberty in the Buddha's context is overwhelmingly understood in terms of going forth, which is the method by which the Buddha himself gained liberty from the constraints of palace life. Awakening is also often described in terms of liberation. The value of freedom also gains socio-political expression in the Buddha's rejection of the oppressive caste system, which prevented individuals from seeking any fulfilment beyond the limitations of the class they were born into. In the *Theragatha*, an outcaste sings of the way in which the Buddha's teaching enabled him to move

---

13 *Majjhima Nikaya* 35.12. Ñanamoli and Bodhi (1995) p. 325.
14 *Digha Nikaya* 27.20–1. Walshe (1995) p. 413.
15 *Digha Nikaya* 26.10–18. Walshe (1995) pp. 398–401.

beyond the degradation of his background.[16] One who has gone forth is said to have entered a casteless or classless condition.[17]

The value of loyalty for the Buddha is particularly shown by the store he sets on friendship. When Ananda suggests that friendship is half of the holy life, the Buddha wants to put it even more strongly:

> 'Not so, Ananda!... This is the entire holy life, Ananda, that is, good friendship, good companionship, good comradeship. When a bhikkhu has a good friend...it is to be expected that he will develop and cultivate the Noble Eightfold Path.'[18]

Friendship is particular. We give our attention to a few specific people with whom we associate rather than others, and maintain loyalty to them. This addresses the conditions of our embodied limitations. We cannot jump to a position of loving everybody equally, and if we focus too much on doing so then we are likely to merely absolutise that as a moral 'imperative', that has no actual moral effect. However, what we can realistically do is maintain our identifications with a few trusted people and gradually stretch them from there. Our loyalty to friends may also entail warning or challenging them, as is clear from the Buddha's discussion of speech ethics.[19] This has obvious political implications in terms of our maintaining relationships with those in positions of power, as the Buddha did with Bimbisara, Pasenadi, and Ajatasattu. The Buddha did not refuse to advise them, however much he may have disapproved of their policies on occasion, but was prepared to challenge them when he did so. Loyalty, then, is never absolute, but nevertheless a value recognised as important by the Buddha.

We have already seen the Buddha's willingness to use authority in his first address to the five ascetics (chapter 2.b). There he seems to be rather too willing to let his authority claim become absolute, but authority can also be used in the non-absolute form of incremental credibility.[20] As embodied beings, we have to decide how to bestow our limited energy and attention, so cannot give equal weight to everything. Indications of credibility such as reputation and expertise help us to decide the most justifiable way

---

16 *Theragatha* 12.2. Thanissaro (1994).
17 *Anguttara Nikaya* 10.48. Nyanaponika and Bodhi (1999) p. 249.
18 *Kosalasamyutta. Samyutta Nikaya* 3.18. Bodhi (2000) p. 180.
19 To Prince Abhaya, *Majjhima Nikaya* 58.8. Ñanamoli and Bodhi (1995) p. 500.
20 Explained more fully in Ellis (2015a) ch. 3.e.

The Middle Way in the Buddha's Ministry 87

to apply that energy and attention. There seems to be little doubt that the Buddha developed a formidable reputation in his context, which he obviously also made full use of. However, none of this justifies us in taking his authority absolutely.

We have also already had examples of the Buddha's respect for sanctity in the principles he gave to the Vajjians, which include respect for shrines and protection of *arahants* or *arhats*. It is easy to absolutise a sense of sanctity by being defensive about the purity of sacred people, places, or rituals, being over-sensitive to insults or desecration, and even fighting wars over them. However, as long as it doesn't dominate in a way that excludes other values, sanctity has an important place in the ecosystem of our values, because it allows sources of helpful values to be maintained and kept in mind.

We can thus see that the Buddha offers a model for inspiring political values that can be applied today. This is a model that puts learning from experience first, and avoids dogmatic ideology of all kinds. He recognised the value of government, and of a state containing a mixed economy of values that could address different conditions in different circumstances. Politics, for him, was not merely a means to an individualistic nirvanic end, but rather an incremental extension of individual practice to address wider conditions.

2.f. The Buddha's Death

Much more could be said about the Buddha's ministry and the ways that the Middle Way was practised and applied in that ministry. For example, I could examine the Buddha's relationship with close friends and followers such as Ananda, the way he responded to those who misunderstood and criticised his teaching, such as Sunakkhata, and the way he dealt even with threats to his life from his cousin Devadatta. There will always be scope for more detailed discussion of the Buddha's life (and I highly recommend Batchelor's work for such further discussion[1]), but space does not permit me to give it too much more attention here. I need to leave enough space for discussing the Buddha's teachings, and the wider issues of understanding the Middle Way that form the remainder of this book. However, before I leave the Buddha's life as a theme I want to say something about the way he left it.

For the tradition that had adopted an absolute interpretation of the Buddha's Awakening, there was always likely to be a problem with accounting for his death. If the Buddha has merely found an approach to conditions that enables us to respond to them as effectively as possible, death is clearly just another of those conditions that we need to adapt ourselves to. However, for those who believe the Buddha has *overcome* those conditions in some way, it would seem that the Buddha should have conquered death itself. In terms of the dogmatic framework of karma and rebirth commonly employed in the Buddhist tradition, it is believed that the Buddha achieved a distinctive type of death known as Parinirvana (*parinibbana*). This is a death in which, unlike most deaths, craving and delusion were absent and thus no more rebirth would ensue. From one absolute (*nibbana*), the Buddha is said to advance to another (*parinibbana*). Because life itself is believed to be a product of negative karmic effects, the tradition then rationalises the Buddha's life between *nibbana* and *parinibbana* as the result of residual karma from before his Awakening working itself through. From an embodied perspective, *parinibbana* sounds to us like the extinction of everything we value, all of which depends on life. To try to defend the absolutisation, the tradition has it remain mysterious whether the Buddha still 'exists' or 'does not exist' after

1   Batchelor (2015).

it,[2] so that we can regard *parinibbana* positively by giving it the benefit of the paradoxical doubt.

However, the mystery of *parinibbana* should come as no surprise to anyone who is trying to follow the Middle Way in their judgements. It is simply the mystery of death itself, minus the absolutist constructions imposed by rebirth belief. *Parinibbana*, when karma ceases and we do not know whether the self ceases, is indistinguishable in practice from agnosticism about both karma and the self. So the situation of the Buddha, living by the Middle Way, as he approached death, is remarkably similar to ours, if we are trying to follow the Middle Way in a context where afterlife beliefs are no longer assumed. We do not know what lies beyond death, but the Middle Way encourages us to question absolute beliefs about it. These include not only beliefs about the continuation of the self in rebirth after death, but also the denial of those beliefs as necessarily false, together with any other beliefs about our selves that do not fully face up to that cloud of uncertainty.

However, the story of the Buddha's Parinibbana as found in the *Mahaparinibbana Sutta* is inconsistent in the inspiration it can give us for practising the Middle Way in the face of death. This is due to the constant tension between the absolutised interpretation of the Buddha's position and the human portrait of a man facing death. There are miraculous elements, such the trees at either end of the Buddha's deathbed bursting into untimely blossom, and his death being accompanied by an earthquake, that we should be able to accept as poetic embellishments. However, there is also a jarring episode in which the Buddha reproves his attendant Ananda for not having taken the hint he dropped that he would have had the power to live to a hundred if he wanted, to then beg the Buddha to live on to a hundred.[3] This sounds like the expression of an early Buddhist difficulty in coming to terms with the idea that the absolutised Buddha had to die, leading to the use of Ananda as a scapegoat.

As far as the story shows, however, the Buddha himself had no particular difficulty in coming to terms with death. The particular type of practice of the Middle Way that many of us may face in relation to death, then, didn't seem to apply to him. That practice

---

2 *Majjhima Nikaya* 63.2. Ñanamoli and Bodhi (1995) p. 533.
3 The Buddha's Last Days, *Digha Nikaya* 16.3.40. Walshe (1995) p. 251.

consists in finding a way between the denial of our deaths on the one hand (believing that we will live for ever), and a merely abstract embrace of death on the other. In the latter case we may say that we have accepted 'impermanence', but remain in conflict with our repressed resistance to it. In the *Mahaparinibbana Sutta*, equanimity seems to rule the Buddha's approach to death throughout. There's a humour in the way he talks about it when he says 'Just as an old cart is made to go by being held together with straps, so the Tathagata's body is kept going by being strapped up.'[4] However, the Buddha's equanimity in relation to death itself doesn't mean that he doesn't encounter conflicts in relation to it. It's the dramatisation of these conflicts that offers one of the most interesting aspects of the *Mahaparinibbana Sutta*.

There seem to be two such conflicts. The first is about the timing of the Buddha's death. We have to take it for granted that the Buddha does have some degree of control over when he dies – but that also seems to be so in many other cases. There are thus two possible absolutisations that might distract him from finding the right time to die that addresses the conditions best. On the one hand there's an over-enthusiastic embrace of death as good that might lead him to go too soon, or on the other a tendency to put off death too long by seeing it as an evil. Linked to this is the second conflict, which concerns his legacy of teachings and community. On the one hand he can try to take control of that legacy and insist that it stands independently of him, so that he is entirely dispensable. On the other, he can recognise that he can't control the degree to which others will project his teachings onto him, and thus the way that his death will traumatically disrupt the teachings.

The first of these conflicts is dramatised by the appearances of Mara at various points in the *sutta*, tempting the Buddha to make an over-hasty departure. According to the Buddha's account, the first of these appearances goes back to shortly after his Awakening:

> *'Ananda, once I was staying at Uruvela on the bank of the River Neranjara, under the Goatherd's Banyan-tree, when I had just attained supreme enlightenment. And Mara the evil one came to me, stood on one side and said: "May the Blessed Lord now attain final Nibbana, may the Well-Farer now attain final Nibbana. Now is the time for the Blessed Lord's final Nibbana."'*[5]

---

4   *Digha Nikaya* 16.2.25. Walshe (1995) p. 245.
5   *Digha Nikaya* 16.3.34. Walshe (1995) p. 250.

Mara is associated with death as well as with absolute thinking, but in this case the two come together. Death no longer being a threat for the Buddha, it instead provides an over-neat solution that avoids all the messy inconvenience of having to teach unreceptive people. However, the Buddha replies:

> 'Evil One, I will not take final Nibbana till I have monks and disciples who are accomplished, trained, skilled, learned, knowers of the Dhamma.... I will not take final Nibbana until this holy life has been successfully established and flourishes, is widespread, well-known far and wide, well-proclaimed among mankind everywhere.'[6]

This response also contains a potential absolutisation, that seems rather like a hostage to fortune. How well-established do the monks and disciples have to be? How well-known does the holy life have to be? As the Buddha becomes older, however, Mara's visits recur, and now they urge the opposite extreme: 'All this has come about'[7] Mara claims in reference to the Buddha's requirements to enable death. The Buddha will have to compromise his absolute expectations on this point, and make an incremental judgement. The Buddha does not yield to this voice of absolutisation, but he does recognise that this voice draws attention to a condition that he needs to address. His death cannot be endlessly delayed in order to establish his teaching and community perfectly. 'You need not worry, Evil One. The Tathagata's passing will not be long delayed,'[8] he now responds to Mara.

The second conflict, regarding the Buddha's legacy, is expressed in his exhortations to his disciples to treat the Middle Way independently of him.

> 'You should live as islands unto yourselves, being your own refuge, with no-one else as your refuge, with the Dhamma as an island, with the Dhamma as your refuge, with no other refuge. And how does a monk live as an island unto himself...with no other refuge? And how does a monk live...with no other refuge? Here, Ananda, a monk abides contemplating the body as body, earnestly, clearly aware, mindful and having put away all hankering and fretting for the world....'[9]

---

6   *Digha Nikaya* 16.3.35. Walshe (1995) pp. 250–1.
7   *Digha Nikaya* 16.3.8. Walshe (1995) p. 247.
8   *Digha Nikaya* 16.3.9. Walshe (1995) p. 247.
9   *Digha Nikaya* 16.2.26. Walshe (1995) p. 245.

This is placed directly after the Buddha's acknowledgement to Ananda that age is catching up with him, so it is a direct response to the immediate implication that he will no longer be around to guide his followers. However, it is also one of the clearest statements of the priority and independence of a Middle Way founded on embodied experience. Dependent on him as they have become, his disciples are about to be pitched into this state of 'being their own refuge' whether they like it or not. It obviously does not mean that the Buddha's followers cannot trust or rely on others, but it does indicate that their *judgement* needs to be autonomous. We have already seen this autonomy articulated in the *Kalama Sutta*, and in the Buddha's words to Pasenadi about the grounds for trusting others.

However, the fact that the Buddha has articulated a path that his disciples need to follow after his death does not mean that they will be able to heed his words and follow that path. The transfer of identification from person to path may be very difficult for many people. This formulation of the Middle Way could itself become an absolutisation, then, in relation to the actual conditions for many of the Buddha's followers. The opposite absolutisation would be that the Buddha might conclude he does not control his legacy at all, or that there is nothing he can do to stop his death being a sudden loss of the path for many people. Between the extremes of insisting on his ultimate importance or unimportance, the Buddha simply treads the path of possibility within the limited scope of possible actions allowed by the state of his body as he approaches death.

On the one hand the Buddha makes clear the ways that he does not expect to be able to control things after his death.

> 'If there is anyone who thinks "I shall take charge of the order", or "The order should refer to me", let him make some statement about the order, but the Tathagata does not think in such terms.'[10]

He tells his disciples not to worry about the funeral arrangements, but also seems to be resigned to the fact that the lay-people will want to have an elaborate funeral and stupas to contain his remains.[11] On the other hand, though, he maintains the role of teacher right up to the end, consoling and praising Ananda when he

---

10 *Digha Nikaya* 16.2.25. Walshe (1995) p. 245.
11 *Digha Nikaya* 16.5.10. Walshe (1995) p. 264.

The Middle Way in the Buddha's Ministry

is distressed.¹² He teaches a wanderer named Subhadda even when on his deathbed. He also addresses the monks before death, to give them a last chance to address doubts or uncertainties.¹³

The Buddha's final words are concerned with facing up to conditions and the importance of the path: 'All conditioned things are of a nature to decay – strive on untiringly.'¹⁴ However, then, as soon as he dies, absolutising extremes become evident amongst his followers, with some followers 'who had not yet overcome their passions' weeping and tearing their hair, whilst 'those monks who were free from craving endured mindfully and clearly aware'.¹⁵ If we are not to believe the absolutisation that the latter were completely free from craving, it seems much more likely that they were repressing at least some of their grief. As soon as the great practitioner leaves, then, we are confronted with an immediate failure of Middle Way practice. This creates a social division between the stern grief-free followers and the apparently sentimental grief-filled followers.

The irony of division continues as the lay-people start to dispute over the Buddha's remains, with the Mallas claiming ownership of them against the claims of others. But fortunately a final application of the Middle Way prevails, as the brahmin Dona stands up and says:

> Forbearance is the Buddha's teaching.
> It is not right that strife should come
> From sharing out the best of men's remains.
> Let's all be joined in harmony and peace,
> In friendship sharing out portions eight....¹⁶

---

12 *Digha Nikaya* 16.5.13 ff. Walshe (1995) p. 265.
13 *Digha Nikaya* 16.6.5. Walshe (1995) p. 270.
14 *Digha Nikaya* 16.6.7. Walshe (1995) p. 270.
15 *Digha Nikaya* 16.6.10. Walshe (1995) p. 272.
16 *Digha Nikaya* 16.6.25 Walshe (1995) p. 276.

3. The Buddha's Metaphors

3.a. Beyond Allegory

In this section of the book I will be interpreting some of the key analogies used in the Pali Canon that offer insights into the nature of the Middle Way. These analogies obviously have great universality, because they can be applied easily beyond the specific context of the Buddha's life and teaching. They are all *metaphorical* in structure. For example, in the first analogy I shall discuss, the raft crossing a river is normally understood to *stand for* or *represent* the teachings of the Buddha. So that analogy is only supposed to be giving us an additional perspective that is really 'about' the teachings rather than about a raft. But this is a simplistic and misleading way to think about such a rich analogy. The raft, like all other powerful metaphors, relates to human experience much more universally, and has a wide range of possible connections with our everyday experience. To explain how some of the Buddha's analogies convey the Middle Way so powerfully, then, I will need to start with some points about metaphor in general.

The standard conventional account of metaphor tends to assume that our normal language is 'literal', in describing states of affairs directly. 'Metaphor', on the other hand, is supposed to provide a separate and merely auxiliary kind of addition to a literal account. In philosophical and linguistic terms, this approach is reflected in the *representationalism* that is still the most commonly assumed account of meaning. In representationalism, words gain their meaning from a relationship with an actual or hypothetical reality of some kind. It is claimed that I understand language only because it forms propositions or claims that could be true or false, and because I understand the circumstances in which they could be true or false. The most important meaning of language is judged to be *cognitive*, providing a possibility of knowledge stated in words. The other impacts that make language 'meaningful' to us are separated off as 'emotive' and thus as dispensable. 'Metaphor' in this model, is usually assumed to be such dispensable, auxiliary language and entirely separable from the meaning we gain from representations of the world.

The Middle Way challenges this model in the most basic fashion, with the implication that metaphor can no longer be so neatly divided from literal language. The standpoint of the palace or the forest assumes that the beliefs held in that context are final and certain. To assume that one's beliefs can be final and certain, though, requires further assumptions about the meaning of language. For that finality and certainty is only possible if the words used to represent human beliefs correspond to reality. The beliefs of the palace and of the forest may in some respects address some conditions. However, just by recognising that they are not final, the Buddha also questioned the relationship between the language used to represent them and the reality they were assumed to represent.

When the Buddha came to recognise the Middle Way, as already discussed, it was through the recollection of an *embodied* experience under the rose-apple tree. In the process, he recognised that the mere obsessive pursuit of representations in his mind that were taken to be true was not an adequate way to make progress in addressing conditions. By recognising that his embodied experience did provide a way forward, he was not only recognising the need for food to sustain him. Nor was he even just recognising the need for body-awareness to achieve *jhana*. He was also implicitly recognising the dependence of meaning on his body. The Buddha of course long pre-dated any explicit embodied meaning theory. However, the fact that he recognised bodily awareness as offering the potential to integrate conflicting beliefs must also mean that implicitly the meaningful materials out of which we form those beliefs are also embodied. Those meaningful materials are our sense of the meaning of language and other symbols – a sense that must be shared for belief to be shared. The way in which he used analogies in this teaching provides a further indication consistent with this.

Embodied meaning theory[1] (already mentioned in chapter 1.h) provides us with an explicit account of the relationship between embodied awareness and metaphor that can help us understand this link better. Meaning, on this account, is developed from early infancy through our neural association of bodily experiences with symbols or words of some kind.

---

1 See Lakoff (1987); Johnson (2007); Lakoff and Johnson (1980); Ellis (2013b).

To begin with, these associations take the form of *basic-level categories* or *schemas*. Basic-level categories are words for types of concrete object that we categorise in the most readily useful way at the time we are learning about them: words like tree, house, or cat. In most cases we have a whole set of active, embodied associations with these things that helps to build up our sense of their meaning. So 'cat' for a small child is not a scientifically defined carnivore but a rich experience of stroking, playing with, or annoying an animal.

Schemas operate similarly, but provide basic types of relationship by which we can understand words. As Mark Johnson explains:

> *In order for us to have meaningful, connected experiences that we can comprehend and reason about, there must be pattern and order to our actions, perceptions, and conceptions. A schema is a recurrent pattern, shape, and regularity in, or of, these ongoing ordering activities. These patterns emerge as meaningful structures for us chiefly at the level of our bodily movement through space, our manipulation of objects, and our perceptual interactions.*[2]

For example, the *container* schema can play a part in helping us to understand the meaning of words like field, basket, or box, with perhaps the most basic experience being of things inside or outside our bodies.

As we then grow up and need to understand more complex and abstract things around us, we use *metaphorical extension* of these basic categories and schemas. Thus we might come to understand what it meant to call a person 'feline', or for an academic to talk about her 'field'. We do this by extending the meaning of the basic category of 'cat' or the container schema we started with to include these ideas. By making these metaphorical extensions, we are not engaging in any special new kind of meaning, just extending the embodied meaning in ever more complex ways. Although the synaptic tracks in our brains and nervous systems that mark these meanings become ever more complex, they are still dependent on the same process of relationship to basic embodied experience.

The dependence of more abstract meaning on metaphorical extension can be readily seen by the use of metaphors in teaching and learning. When unsure of the meaning of a word, or of a more complex piece of language, we have not made a strong enough track to relate it to the more basic early experiences that would give

---

2 Johnson (1987) p. 29.

us an active impression of it, so we fall back to simpler or more basic metaphorical extensions. The teacher gives (or the student seeks) an analogy to help us grasp something.

Iain McGilchrist's work on brain lateralisation can provide a further insight into metaphor in relation to the way it is processed by the two halves of our brains.[3] The right hemisphere of the brain is the half that is open to new information from elsewhere. It is thus also the source of our understanding of metaphor, allowing us to connect different kinds of experience to each other. When this association starts to become handled by the language centres of the left hemisphere, however, they become merely another part of our closed system of signs that relate to one another, not to new stimuli from outside. We then lose our sense of the association being metaphorical at all – it becomes dead or 'literal'. Thus, for example, we no longer recognise that icing has anything to do with ice. Or we use cliched phrases like 'the lion's share' without imagining a male lion eating his fill of a dead zebra. Nevertheless, the meaning of these phrases still depends on their unacknowledged association, that originally occurred in the right hemisphere.

All of this implies that metaphor is not exceptional. Nearly all language is based on metaphor, because the meaning of all language depends on a process that relates meanings back either to basic concepts and schemas or to other metaphors. What we think of as 'literal language' is just complex language that makes use of a consistent cognitive model that enables us to express our beliefs. However, it is our beliefs about language that make it 'literal', not its meaning, and our beliefs remain dependent on meanings that are metaphorical. Language is only 'literal' because we have *forgotten* its metaphorical origins. In the context of the Buddha's teachings, then, there can be no such thing as a literal teaching that describes reality. Teachings such as those of the Four Noble Truths, karma, rebirth, and conditionality are heavily dependent on metaphor, even though they have been turned into beliefs.

In addition to such teachings, though, the Buddha gives a huge number of analogies or similes, which are found throughout the *Sutta Pitaka* of the Pali Canon. If we are to interpret these in terms of the embodied meaning of the Middle Way, then, these analogies are

---

3 McGilchrist (2010) pp. 115–18.

actually *more basic to our experience* than the formal teachings they are supposed to illustrate. Unlike the formal teachings, the analogies seem much more likely to communicate the Middle Way, because they are much harder to absolutise. Absolutised teachings present themselves as giving the final answers, solidifying a particular metaphor as the basis of a truth or a falsity. An analogy, on the other hand, immediately presents us with a new way of thinking about something that relates different concrete situations to one another. That linkage between concrete experiences can address more conditions by providing us with new resources for thinking.

The traditional way of interpreting the Buddha's similes, however, subjugates them to absolutised doctrine by turning them into *allegories*. An allegory is the interpretation of a metaphor in terms of one fixed meaning, showing what it 'really' represents: a story with a key. Well-known examples of allegories in Western literary tradition are *Aesop's Fables* and *The Pilgrim's Progress*. In *Aesop's Fables,* the story of the fox and the stork can be reduced to a clearly articulated moral about reciprocal consideration for others' needs. In *The Pilgrim's Progress,* 'Giant Despair' just stands for an *idea* of despair. Allegory has its place in the explanation of abstract material, but is unlikely to inspire our imaginations so that we ourselves make new links between situations and thus transform our response to them. All too often, allegory just makes a potentially threatening metaphor feel superficially safe, by tidying it up into conceptual equivalence.

The vast majority of the Buddha's similes in the Pali Canon are presented as allegories either in the text itself, or in common interpretation of that text. For example, a story is told of a man fleeing in terror, pursued by four vipers, five murderous enemies, and a sixth murderer. He seeks refuge in an empty village only to be told that 'village-attacking dacoits' are about to descend on it. He then reaches a river where he thinks the further shore would be safe, but he first has to construct a raft to cross this river. We are told at the end of this story exactly what each of these figures represents: the vipers are the four great elements, the five murderous enemies are the five aggregates, the sixth murderer represents delight and lust, the empty village is the six internal sense bases, and the dacoits are the agreeable and disagreeable phenomena that assail us through those senses. The further shore of the river is then Nirvana, and the raft is the Noble Eightfold Path.[4] One can see how, in ancient India, such an allegorisation would help people remember these formulae in relation to each other, but do they help us today in understanding and practising the Middle Way in experience? If by merely absorbing such a set of equivalences we think that we are making progress, then the reverse may well be the case. If we can reduce the metaphors to familiar dogmas, it may add to our certainty that we have found final answers rather than our capacity to investigate.

That this limited approach to the Buddha's similes is still influential today can be illustrated by Hellmuth Hecker's book on the Buddha's similes.[5] The book offers a range of similes from the Pali Canon, but entirely in the form of summaries followed by allegorical explanations. This limited approach takes us to the formal body of doctrine and then just leaves us there. It increases the impression that these doctrines offer final answers that will always directly aid us in our lives, with the similes being merely tributary to such answers. In effect, we adopt the most effective and immediate murder weapon for killing the metaphor. The possibility that these similes might have a meaning that goes *beyond* their formal equivalences in Buddhist doctrine is simply not considered.

In this section of this book, however, I intend to focus on some examples of those similes of the Buddha that offer universal application beyond the absolutisations of formal Buddhist doctrine. That means that they should speak to you and have relevance to your path, whether you are a Buddhist or not, and whether the formal doctrines they are often related to mean anything to you or not. They should be meaningful simply by virtue of your having a human body with a similarity of function and experience to other humans. These similes are thus about the Middle Way, not just about Buddhism, and I will interpret them in those terms. The fact that they are about the Middle Way also makes them symbolic rather than allegorical, offering a rich variety of associative connections with different situations in our experience.

4 *Samyutta Nikaya* 35.238. Bodhi (2000) pp. 1237–9.
5 Hecker (2009).

3.b. The Middle Way as Metaphor

Before I start looking at specific similes used by the Buddha, it's important to give some attention to the Middle Way itself in the same light. Of all metaphors in the Pali Canon, the Middle Way itself needs to be considered as the broadest and most striking. I have heard it dismissed as 'just a metaphor', but what a metaphor! It combines two crucial schemas that are basic to our early embodied experience – those of the path and of equilibrium. The path is identified by Lakoff and Johnson in the form of the 'source-path-goal' schema.[1] Our basic embodied experience from an early age includes moving from one place (the source) to another that we identify with reaching (the goal) along a route (the path). Equilibrium comes from our basic experience of balance, where there is danger in falling either on one side or the other.

As a metaphor, however, the Middle Way transposes our movement through time into a movement through space. This is a very common metaphor that can be graphically visualised as a timeline or as a decision tree. Just as when following a route we need to make many small adjustments to our direction to keep moving towards the goal, so in following the Middle Way we need to keep making new judgements about which direction to take. The equilibrium schema here refers not to a danger of falling or bashing into an obstacle, but to the danger of absolutisation. The embodied experience closely fits the metaphor here, because equilibrium is very much an experience of energy being gathered ready for use in adjustment. We don't know in advance what form the adjustment will take. This is very similar to the embodied experience of recognising and avoiding absolutisations.

If one assumes that a particular metaphor is a description of a final reality, then it can start to become an absolutisation, and the Middle Way itself is no exception to this. If we absolutise the path model, we may start to think that the best ways of understanding our human situations are always linear and informed by goals. However, openness to understanding systemic relationships not related to our goals may often be important. The recognition of this danger only requires extension of the way we are using the metaphor. We are never likely to give up having goals, because we

---

1 Lakoff and Johnson (1980).

are organic creatures with interests, and our left hemispheres are capable of linguistically representing those interests. So the best we can do is to sometimes recognise the limitations of those goals when they are placed in a larger context. The source-path-goal schema itself does not require that the goal will ever take a specific fixed form, only that we tend to move 'forward' with what may be a changing perception of why we are doing so and thus 'where' we are going.

We could also potentially absolutise the equilibrium element of the metaphor by assuming that a given judgement is justified by the experience of equilibrium alone. This would lead us into a fallacious appeal to moderation. Just because there is an element of balance or compromise in a judgement does not necessarily mean it is correct. Solomon's judgement, to divide a baby in half to satisfy a quarrel between two claimed mothers, is a classic example of this. The value of the Middle Way is only found by identifying the particular relevant absolutisations that we might fall into in a particular case, and this depends entirely on the beliefs and associated desires with which we encounter it. Again, then, problems that are created by absolutising the metaphor can be resolved by understanding it more fully.

There may also be some situations where at first sight the Middle Way appears not to offer the most appropriate framework for judgement. That may be because the person making the judgement is not yet capable of using it, or because absolutisation seems to be required in a desperate situation, to meet overriding goals such as survival. Again, though, these can be understood as compatible with the Middle Way in a wider sense. Even though we may not employ the Middle Way in our thinking in that situation, when we have the ability and awareness to reflect on it we can still conclude that conditions were most adequately met by that course of action. *Not* taking that course might also have reflected other kinds of tempting absolutisation. The important point is simply that when it can be applied, awareness that avoids absolutes still helps us better than unaware dependence on absolutes.

As we will see in the rest of this section, the Middle Way as a metaphor can be developed into a whole set of subsidiary metaphors offered by the Buddha. Each of these, in turn, tell us a little more both about what the Middle Way means and how it can be justified in experience.

3.c. Provisionality: The Raft and the Lute Strings

As discussed in chapter 1.f, provisionality is one of the elements into which one can analyse the Middle Way. It is a quality that combines the critical capacity to see the limitations of a current belief with the imaginative capacity to be aware of alternative options. Alternative options, like genetic adaptations or different tools in a toolbox, enable us to address new and unexpected conditions with appropriate adaptation. I'm going to look here at two outstanding similes of the Buddha that focus on provisionality.

The simile of the raft[1] is given by the Buddha in a discourse to some of his followers, to 'show you how the Dhamma is similar to a raft, being for the purpose of crossing over, not for the purpose of grasping'.

> *'Suppose a man in the course of a journey saw a great expanse of water, whose near shore was dangerous and fearful and whose further shore was safe and free from fear, but there was no ferryboat or bridge going to the far shore.... And then the man collected grass, twigs, branches, and leaves and bound them together into a raft, and supported by the raft and making an effort with his hands and feet, he got safely across to the far shore. Then...he might think thus: "This raft has been very helpful to me.... Suppose I were to hoist it on my head or load it on my shoulder, and then go wherever I want." ... By doing so, would that man be doing what should be done with that raft?'*
>
> *'No, venerable sir.'*
>
> *'By doing what would that man be doing what should be done with that raft? ... When that man got across and arrived at the far shore, he might think thus: "... Suppose I were to haul it onto the dry land or set it adrift in the water, and then go wherever I want." ... It is by so doing that that man would be doing what should be done with that raft.'*

The traditional Buddhist interpretation of this simile treats 'Dhamma' as 'Buddhist teaching' and shows the practical justification of that teaching. It is seen as merely for 'crossing over' – that is, for reaching Awakening. However, such an interpretation relies on a discontinuous understanding of 'Awakening': is it so clear *when* we have reached 'the other side'? It also underestimates the wide applicability of this metaphor, which makes a universal point about the need for provisionality in our beliefs. When a belief – any

---

1 *Majjhima Nikaya* 22:13–14. Ñanamoli and Bodhi (1995) pp. 228–9.

belief – has fulfilled its purpose in the particular conditions it was held, it is time to let go of it before it becomes a burden to us in new conditions. That this applies to the Buddhist teachings amongst other beliefs, however, is an indicator of their non-absolute nature, and also indicates that this metaphor is a Middle Way teaching.

The value of any analogy is that it obliges us to compare different situations that we might otherwise assume to be completely different. It is obvious how useful the raft is for getting across the river, and there is only a small degree of doubt that it would be an unnecessary burden after that crossing is completed. We could bring it along just in case there is another river – but for how long? However, it may be less obvious in the case of beliefs that we have become more deeply attached to: for example a religious teaching we have adhered to all our lives, a dying project or relationship, a misjudged investment, or patterns of speech and manners that cause unnecessary offence in a new country. All of these things are entered into because we have explicit or implicit beliefs about their value and benefit, but that value is also subject to uncertainty and change.

We may continue carrying the raft because of a lack of critical awareness of its ill-adaptedness for the new situation, but also perhaps because of a failure to imagine alternatives. When we arrive at the further bank, we need to be able to imagine ourselves managing without the raft. Perhaps, indeed, there are other items of equipment that would be far more valuable as replacements: a machete for the jungle we will then be entering, or a bag of food supplies. But to take these things we have to leave the raft. The anxiety we might feel about leaving it will need to be relaxed and set aside. Similarly, to be able to enter new territory in any other area of our lives we may have to gently set aside things that we have habitually regarded as indispensable up to that point: reputations, relationships, property, allegiances.

The provisionality of the raft metaphor is built on scepticism (as introduced in chapter 1.f), for we would not have the critical perspective to recognise the contingency of the raft if we regarded it as necessary or absolute. As we do not know which beliefs we will need to apply this critical perspective to in advance, it is practically important to maintain a general awareness of uncertainty, of the possibility of 'unknown unknowns'. We need this in relation to *all* our beliefs, however basic or embedded they seem to be, and whether they are positive or negative. When we arrive at the further bank we simply need the awareness to ask ourselves a question about whether we will need the raft any more (indicating awareness of its contingency) rather than to assume either that we will need it or that we will not. We may need to ask ourselves that question again and again in different circumstances. That same point is emphasised by a related analogy used in the Pali Canon that describes progress on the path as a sequence of relay chariots, each of which is only required to reach the starting point of the next.[2]

In relation to our cognitive processes, provisionality requires an open feedback loop rather than a closed one. In a closed feedback loop (also known as confirmation bias), we continue to interpret our experience as confirming a belief that then provides a basis for interpreting our experience. If our belief is about the value of the raft for us, that belief continues to be reinforced for us by our experience all the time we are crossing the river. On reaching the other side, however, we may be so habituated to that closed loop that we continue to interpret our environment in terms of the value of the raft. We may then compensate for the unconscious cognitive dissonance this creates by rationalising: 'Well, you never know, there could be another river soon, even though it's not marked on the map', or 'I need to take this raft because it might be abused by criminals'. We might focus on slight possibilities and amplify them, all the time reflecting our own anxiety rather than a sufficiently aware response to the conditions. In an open feedback loop, however, we allow new information from our senses to influence and modify our thinking to adapt to the new situation. Our experience continues to determine our beliefs, but our beliefs do not entirely determine our experience.

This ability to adapt to conditions may sound familiar to anyone who has studied evolution. Of course, evolutionary adaptations take place over a longer period of time and depend primarily on genetic rather than cognitive or behavioural modifications. Nevertheless, an organism that continues in its old habits and is not sufficiently open to developing new ones (for whatever reasons) is the one that is likely to die out, just as the man who carries the raft may exhaust himself in the jungle and expire before he finishes

---

2   *Majjhima Nikaya* 24.14–15. Ñanamoli and Bodhi (1995) pp. 243–4.

his journey. The relationship to evolution also does not imply that our provisionality is only made valuable by survival or reproduction. Having provisional options could help to fulfil any of a range of goals, which may involve the fulfilment of our needs at a variety of levels. For example, we may need to cross the river for social fulfilment, for intellectual fulfilment, or through a desire for integrative development.

Another key analogy of the Buddha's that is concerned with provisionality (though from a rather different angle) is that of the lute strings. This occurs in a conversation between the Buddha and a follower called Sona,[3] a solitary who has become frustrated by his failure to make progress in integrative practice. Sona, alone, starts to consider giving up the life of a *shramana*, and returning instead to the household life. However, according to the text the Buddha then magically teleports to his location to talk him out of it.

> *'Sona, weren't you now thinking of giving up the training and returning to lay life?'*
>
> *'Yes, Lord.'*
>
> *'Tell me, Sona, when in earlier days you lived at home, were you not skilled in playing the lute?'* – *'Yes, Lord.'*
>
> *'And, Sona, when the strings of your lute were too taut, was your lute well tuned and easy to play?'* – *'No, Lord.'*
>
> *'And when the strings of your lute were too loose, was your lute well tuned and easy to play?'* – *'No, Lord.'*
>
> *'But, Sona, when the strings of your lute were neither too taut nor too loose, but adjusted to an even pitch, was your lute then well tuned and easy to play?'* – *'Yes, Lord.'*
>
> *'Similarly, Sona, if energy is applied too forcefully it will lead to restlessness, and if energy is too lax it will lead to lassitude. Therefore, Sona, keep your energy in balance, penetrate to a balance of the spiritual faculties, and there seize your object.'*

According to the text, the Buddha then vanished, teleporting back to his previous location, and Sona, putting his advice into effect, rapidly attained Awakening.

---

3   *Anguttara Nikaya* 6.55. Nyanaponika and Bodhi (1999) p. 168.

The universal relevance of this simile, however, is again no more necessarily tied to the attainment of Awakening on the discontinuous traditional model than it is in the raft simile. As in the raft simile, there is indeed a goal in mind, but the analogy works just as well whatever the nature of that goal and in whatever circumstances it occurs. This time, however, the analogy is concerned less obviously with beliefs and more directly with our experience of effort. It is concerned with the way in which we focus energy to try to bring about the fulfilment of our goals. However, beliefs are still implicitly present, because they are assumed in whatever approaches we make to effort.

The string being too taut, which the Buddha associates with energy applied too forcefully, is often described as 'wilful effort'. In wilful effort, an absolutisation of the goal is leading us to focus on it too exclusively and to neglect surrounding conditions. The bodily tension that directly correlates to a taut string can be related to a closed feedback loop and narrow focus. These are typical of a person strongly affected by anxiety or obsessive desire coming from the amygdala or striatum at the back of the brain. The stress hormones may kick in, and our body tenses for 'fight or flight', even though this state actually interferes with our ability to reach the goals we are set on. We could be badly handicapped by such tension in many of the complex and challenging operations we may face in human society – playing a musical instrument in a concert, passing a job interview, meditating, opening up and expressing our feelings in conversation with a friend. Anxiety or obsession interferes with the wider awareness, the subtle simultaneous linking between many parts of the brain and nervous system, that is required for optimum performance. This is just as much an expression of our absolute (though often unconscious) beliefs about the situation as it is of our emotional state.

The string being too loose, on the other hand, is equivalent to a failure to focus energy when it is needed. This is likely to occur in reaction to the state of tension, when we are no longer able to sustain it and become exhausted. It is also the result of an absolutising belief – namely the negative belief that only an absolute effort is sufficient for our goals. Since we feel unable to produce such an absolute effort, we then feel we are failures. We thus lose confidence in our ability to reach our goals, creating the 'lassitude' mentioned by the Buddha – or in more modern terms, some level of depression.

This absolutisation of our goals also prevents us from thinking incrementally. It may well be that we cannot move immediately to a higher level of effort from such a state, but we can build it up by gradual engagement. However, if we are convinced that we cannot succeed before we begin, we do not even start this process.

This analogy is closely concerned with provisionality because of its theme of constant adjustment. We may find that we are adjusted to an even pitch for a short while, but the string of our effort gets too taut or too loose again. So there is a constant need for re-adjustment. Just as the man who reached the other side of the river in the metaphor of the raft needed to adjust to being on the other side of the river, the musician with the out-of-tune string needs to recognise that the conditions have changed. Each can then change his beliefs about how to respond to the present circumstances.

As well as provisionality, the lute strings analogy has a close relationship to the process of integration. Integration consists in the recognition of conflict (whether internal or external) followed by harmonisation that does not merely impose the beliefs of one side onto the other, but rather allows for both. Musical harmonisation provides a striking parallel to this process. When the string is too taut or too slack, it is not intrinsically bad, but rather out of harmony with the other strings. If this taut or loose string was in another context, perhaps when a different scale or musical tradition was being used, it might not be out of tune when giving out exactly the same note. However, the situation of being out of tune really does matter in the context. The same can be said for a desire that we have (with accompanying beliefs) that is out of harmony with the rest. The problem there is not that desire is intrinsically bad, but that the beliefs through which the desire seeks fulfilment are out of harmony with our other beliefs. For example, a smoker who is determined to give up for a whole host of reasons, and has managed to do so for two months, but one day has a relapse and smokes a cigarette, can be said to have an inharmonious desire: she needs to tauten or slacken the string a little. Integration is similar to harmony, in that it allows different parts of ourselves (or different parts of a wider group) to work together towards a common pattern that we can consistently and sustainably value.

You should be able to see from both of these examples that a sufficiently rich metaphor of the Middle Way can potentially touch on a whole array of related examples. It can thus be of considerable practical use to us in a wide range of situations if we can remain aware of the metaphor and continue to apply it. This universality is due to the metaphor's live relationship to the embodied schemas it is based on. I mentioned in the previous chapter that the Middle Way metaphor is built on schemas of source-path-goal and of equilibrium. These embodied schemas both have provisionality built in as a necessary aspect of the embodied situation. When we are pursuing a path, we have to keep adjusting both the way we think we can best reach the goal, and possibly also our conception of the goal itself. Equilibrium is also an immediate experience of constant adjustment to prevent us overbalancing in one direction or another. The raft and lute strings similes both apply these embodied schemas in different ways and thus dramatise the provisionality of the Middle Way in different ways. The raft focuses more on the flexible adjustment we need when following a path, whilst the lute strings focus more on the process of equilibrium. Reflecting on both of them can help us to begin to see the concrete universality of the Middle Way in turn.

3.d. Absolutisation: The Arrows

The flip side of the Middle Way is the things that it avoids, the evils of absolutisation. At the time of the Buddha it is hardly surprising that people would associate evil and suffering with a common form of weapon in that society – one that could strike unexpectedly, fatally, and at a distance: the arrow. The Buddha offered two especially important metaphors based on arrows: the poisoned arrow and the second arrow. Both have much to communicate about our immediate experience of absolutisation and of the circumstances it is likely to arise in. Both of them also illustrate a general (but contingent) link between absolutisation and suffering (what we may take to be 'evil' in the broadest sense).

The metaphor of the poisoned arrow occurs in the Shorter Discourse to Malunkyaputta.[1] Malunkyaputta is a follower of the Buddha who is evidently obsessed by metaphysical questions, and gets distracted in meditation thinking about them. He threatens that he will leave the holy life if the Buddha does not answer the metaphysical questions he has refused to answer: namely whether or not the world is eternal or infinite, whether or not the soul is the same as the body, and whether or not the Buddha continues to exist after death. This representative selection of metaphysical beliefs is the well-known basis of the Buddha's 'silence', and an important source on the Middle Way in Buddhism: I will be discussing this further in chapter 4.c. However, it is the Buddha's response to Malunkyaputta's obsession with answers to these questions that will be my focus here.

> 'Suppose, Malunkyaputta, a man were wounded by an arrow thickly smeared with poison, and his friends and companions, his kinsmen and relatives, brought a surgeon to treat him. The man would say, "I will not let the surgeon pull out this arrow until I know the name and clan of the man who wounded me;...until I know whether the man who wounded me was tall or short or middle height;...until I know whether the man who wounded me was dark or brown or golden-skinned;...until I know whether the man who wounded me lives in such a village or town or city;...until I know whether the bow that wounded me was a longbow or crossbow;...until I know whether the bowstring that wounded me was fibre or reed or sinew or hemp or bark;... until I know whether the shaft that wounded me was wild or cultivated;...

---

1 *Majjhima Nikaya* 63. Ñanamoli and Bodhi (1995) pp. 533–6.

> *until I know with what feathers the shaft that wounded me was fitted – whether those of a vulture or a crow or a hawk or a peacock or a stork; until I know with what kind of sinew the shaft that wounded me was bound – whether that of an ox or a buffalo or a lion or a monkey;...until I know what kind of arrow it was that wounded me – whether it was hoof-tipped or curved or barbed or calf-toothed or oleander."*
>
> *'All that would still not be known to that man and meanwhile he would die. So too, Malunkyaputta, if anyone should say thus: "I will not lead the holy life under the Blessed one until the Blessed One declares to me 'The world is eternal...[and all the other metaphysical issues listed]'"... that would still remain undeclared by the Tathagatha and meanwhile that person would die.'*[2]

This analogy superbly brings out the sheer silliness of absolute beliefs. Although they seem hugely important to those who are concerned with them, the answers, if they should ever be given, would make no practical difference to any immediate problem found in our experience. Our concern with these kinds of questions is formed in abstraction, not in concern for any real experience. It is self-feeding, proliferating, and excessive. Although it is tempting to abbreviate the list of things the man wanted to know, it is actually helpful to quote them in full, as I have above, so that one gets the full flavour of the excessiveness and proliferation that accompanies it. It is reminiscent of the conversational bore who goes on giving more and more repetitive detail about a single subject of no interest to his listeners, because he is more interested in his own closed feedback loop than he is with any observation of others' responses.

The particular form that the absolutising takes here is that of causal investigation. Although some degree of understanding of causes can be of great practical helpfulness (for example, in medicine), any enquiry about the causes of a particular event is potentially both infinite and endlessly disputable. Given that complex causal relationships ramify endlessly back in time, they can conceivably be surveyed in endless detail. Furthermore, no degree of detail in the enquiry will ever remove the basic uncertainty that accompanies our derivation of causal theories from observations. Taking causal enquiry as an end in itself is a trap for the sciences. There is always room for a variety of possible causal explanations for any given event, and people have often seemingly been bewitched by highly

---

2 *Majjhima Nikaya* 63.5–6. Ñanamoli and Bodhi (1995) pp. 534–5.

speculative causal theories (such as Freud's theories about the effects of infantile sexuality) when they are delivered with a sufficient air of authority.

The obsession of the man in the analogy could also be described as an information bias: the assumption that more information will always help us to make a more objective judgement. This ignores the limitations in our ability, as embodied creatures, to make meaningful use of data to draw conclusions. After a certain point, an excessive amount of data just becomes more 'noise' that interferes with our ability to use that data. Nassim Nicholas Taleb writes about this point forcefully:

> The more frequently you look at data, the more noise you are disproportionately likely to get (rather than the valuable part, called the signal); hence the higher the noise-to-signal ratio. Say that you look at information on a yearly basis, for stock prices, or the fertiliser sales in your father-in-law's factory, or inflation numbers in Vladivostok. Assume further that for what you are observing, at a yearly frequency, the ratio of signal to noise is about one to one (half noise, half signal) – this means that about half the changes are real improvements or degradations, the other half come from randomness. This ratio is what you get from yearly observations. But if you look at the very same data on a daily basis, the composition would change to 95 per cent noise, 5 per cent signal. If you observe data on an hourly basis, as people immersed in the news and market price variations do, the split becomes 99.5% noise to 0.5% signal.[3]

In other words, the more closely you look at the information, beyond a certain point of optimum balance that takes into account our limitations in using it, the less actual benefit you get from that information. Information is, as Taleb put it 'toxic in large quantities'. The man struck with an arrow is obsessed with gathering information about the arrow because of his absolute obsessions. One form that such absolutisation can take is the self-undermining belief in the value of all information.

However, the particular absolutising biases depicted in the analogy, as often in the Buddha's teachings, stand metonymically for any type of speculation that goes beyond experience – namely metaphysics or absolutisation. The *metonymic* relationship lets a part stand for the whole, and is typical of the Buddha's presentation of the Middle Way in general. He highlights the part of a more general

3   Taleb (2012) p. 126.

and universal insight that would be most relevant to his hearers in that context, rather than attempting to communicate the whole of it. More generally, such speculation can be distinguished by its always being absolute in form (never incremental), by its assuming an infallible source of information, by its assuming a representational basis of meaning, and by its forming opposed pairs of belief that are dualistically opposed. In section 4 I will discuss in more detail how these features can be identified as aspects of the Buddha's core insight about the extremes avoided by the Middle Way.

Malunkyaputta's specific concerns are more general than those of the man struck by an arrow, because he demands to know about the eternality and infinity of the world, the soul/body problem, and the Buddha's survival after death. These are still metaphysical concerns for some people today. Those who seek determinate answers about whether the world (i.e. universe) is eternal or infinite may turn to religious literalism about creation myths, or to science to offer such answers. In either case, though, the information available to us will always be insufficient to provide them. There may be relatively good evidence for the Big Bang Theory, but cosmologists are also likely to admit that this tells us nothing about what may or may not have happened before the Big Bang (however many speculations there may be). It is not enquiries into such far reaches of cosmic history that are necessarily fruitless, but rather the assumption that they can ever give us final answers on metaphysical questions. That assumption is a form of absolutisation, and the Buddha's analogy gives another example of absolutisation that we can compare to it. The similarities between the two despite the differences show that the points we need to take from it are general psychological ones about the unfruitful nature of absolutisation, not specific problems with the content of specific questions.

The Malunkyaputtas and men struck with arrows today are thus not a race apart, and are not limited to the most obvious examples like religious fundamentalists. They are representative of the absolutisations we can all enter into at any point. Further examples might include a stockbroker overconfident in his own skill, interpreting a random fluctuation in the market as a significant one and thus making an inadequate investment choice. It might also include a voter beguiled by 'dog-whistle' implicit racism from a candidate, voting for policies that she vaguely assumes will offer a solution to her financial problems by banishing immigrants. It might include a mother with strong beliefs about the unconditional nurture to be given to her child, but interpreting these in a way that fails to set boundaries to his behaviour, thus leading to continuing difficulties when he goes to school. None of us is exempt from such absolutisations, so if we ridicule the man with the poisoned arrow we must also accept that we ridicule ourselves.

More positively, though, there is also a way out of these circumstances, which is to (metaphorically) pluck the arrow out. I'm told that this is not always the best thing to do with an arrow, so such a straightforward action must thus stand for the more complex idea of doing the most adequate thing in a timely fashion. Perhaps we do need to find out a little about the arrow before we pull it out – but not too much. There will be a point of balance at which the most adequate action can be found – but the finding of that point of balance will be impeded if we get stuck in absolutisation. The finding of that point of balance is an aspect of provisionality, by which we continue to seek the best solution within a practicable framework. It will also involve the firm rejection of absolutisations that might impede us, which is also an aspect of agnosticism.

The other analogy I want to look at here is also concerned with pain or suffering and its relationship to absolutisation. This is the analogy sometimes known as 'the second arrow', though Bhikkhu Bodhi uses 'dart' rather than arrow. The discourse in which this occurs begins with the Buddha asking what difference integrative practice can really make. After all, however much practice you have done, you will still be subject to painful feelings, as well as pleasant and neutral ones.[4]

The Buddha then answers his own question thus:

> *'Bhikkhus, when the uninstructed worldling is being contacted by a painful feeling, he sorrows, grieves and laments; he weeps beating his breast and becomes distraught. He feels two feelings – a bodily one and a mental one. Suppose they were to strike a man with a dart, and then they would strike him immediately afterwards with a second dart, so that the man would feel a feeling caused by two darts. So, too,...he feels two feelings – a bodily one and a mental one.*
>
> *'Being contacted by that same painful feeling, he harbours aversion towards it.... If he feels a pleasant feeling, he feels it attached. If he feels a painful feeling, he feels it attached....*

4   *Samyutta Nikaya* 36.6. Bodhi (2000) p. 1263.

> '... *Suppose they were to strike a man with a dart, but they would not strike him immediately afterwards with a second dart, so that man would feel a feeling caused by one dart only. So too, when the instructed noble disciple is contacted by a painful feeling, he does not sorrow, grieve, or lament.... He feels one feeling – a bodily one, not a mental one.*'[5]

In many ways this is another version of the poisoned arrow example. Again, we have a basic experience of pain, and again, that pain is unnecessarily worsened by absolutisation. However, this example focuses not so much on developed conceptual beliefs as on our immediate assumptions, directly linked into our bodily responses. When we experience pain, our secondary distress and desire to make it go away may feel immediate and involuntary, but it is no less a result of absolutisation than our intellectual obsessions.

Absolutisation involves the maintenance of a closed loop in which obsession or anxiety produces highly goal-driven thoughts based on a rigid set of assumptions. But that rigid set of assumptions denies us the awareness of the wider context that we may need precisely to deal with the problem. This is just as much the case with the Islamist terrorist who obsessively believes that martyrdom when fighting the infidel will take him to paradise, as it is for the person in pain from an illness or injury who is tormented and restless. The former is unable to see the better alternative ways of addressing his anxiety and insecurity, and indeed finding the peace that he seeks in Allah, by treating his enemies as persons and engaging with them positively. Similarly the latter is unable to see that by relaxing the *conflict* with pain and accepting it as part of embodied conditions, they could actually reduce that pain substantially.

It is the contextualisation of pain that can prevent us assuming that pain is the whole story. This is the basis of mindfulness-based approaches to managing pain developed, particularly, by Jon Kabat-Zinn and his followers in recent decades.[6] Such employments of mindfulness meditation directly employ the second arrow simile, by using embodied processes of relaxation and the development of awareness to re-contextualise the first arrow. It is perhaps under-appreciated that Kabat-Zinn's approach is a direct application of the Middle Way. There are two ways of absolutising the first arrow so as to create the second. The first is to accept the second arrow

---

5 Ibid. p. 1264.
6 Kabat-Zinn (2013).

as an inevitable result of the first. However, there is also a second and opposite form of absolutisation which denies the first arrow on the grounds that the second can be eliminated. The Middle Way is always to put the unpleasant experience in a wider context, which even includes accepting our fears in relation to it rather than denying them.

The ideologies that have grown up in regard to pain can further illuminate that second extreme. Mary Baker Eddy, the founder of Christian Science, maintained the belief that we are all part of the one divine mind. Thus she believed that the body and its pain are delusory and can be annihilated by an understanding of the divine mind.[7] Rather than recognising the distinction between the two arrows, then, Eddy recognised the second and assumed that it was not distinct from the first. Buddhism is also not immune from idealist interpretations of this kind, which follow from the belief that pain, along with the other basic embodied conditions of our lives, is the result of karma. According to this way of thinking, the enlightened, having halted the process of karma, can eventually stop the first arrow as well as the second when they reach *parinibbana*. Such interpretations are obviously not consistent with the Middle Way as it appears in the second arrow simile. Rather they distract us from addressing conditions, by absolutising the belief that pain can be removed through the mind. In the process, they also deny our basic embodied experience.

The Buddha's broader insight in this simile applies to pleasure as well as pain. If we become obsessively attached to a pleasant stimulus, there is a second arrow there, too, but it is a painful arrow that involves insecurity regarding the loss of the pleasure. The attachment that creates the second arrow, once again, is absolutisation. Rather than appreciating the pleasure for what it is, in its context, we implicitly believe that it should provide us with final and absolute satisfaction, and/or that it will continue indefinitely. The result of this is frustration when we fail to get that absolute satisfaction from the pleasure. For example, the sexual relationship then loses its allure, as we realise that it is a complex relationship involving many trade-offs. Or the addiction to drugs or alcohol is redoubled as we seek a refuge from our sense of frustration and emptiness in another fix.

7   Eddy (1906).

The simile of the second arrow lies at the heart of a Middle Way interpretation of the first of the Four Noble Truths, which I will be returning to in chapter 6.b. However, we can also see it as a metaphorical expression of the Middle Way itself. First we have an experience, then we absolutise it – so the Middle Way involves just accepting that first experience as such and stopping there, with awareness of our responsibility for subsequent interpretation. The Buddha's teaching to Bahiya summarises the point well:

> 'In the seen will be merely what is seen; in the heard will be merely what is heard; in the sensed will be merely what is sensed; in the cognised will be merely what is cognised.... When, Bahiya, you are not "with that", then, Bahiya, you will not be "in that"; when, Bahiya, you are not "in that", then, Bahiya, you will be neither here nor beyond nor in between the two. Just this is the end of suffering.'[8]

---

8   *Udana* 1.10. Ireland (1990) p. 20.

3.e. Incrementality: The Ocean

Incrementality is a principle of the Middle Way because it is a very basic embodied experience. It's not so much an embodied schema as a feature of all embodied experience and indeed of all organic processes. An organism cannot instantaneously change from one state to a markedly different state, but has to change itself by gradual adjustment that enables it to continue operating effectively as it adjusts. Similarly, a change in our experience, marked as it will be by the development of new or strengthened synaptic links, cannot happen instantaneously. Some changes, of course, happen more quickly than others, but the most rapid changes also tend to be the least sustainable. If an unfit person with no training at all runs a marathon, they may well collapse and even die as a consequence. When a millenarian cult reaches the date when they expect a dramatic supernatural intervention and it fails to happen, the resulting cognitive dissonance is very likely to produce denial and rationalisation.[1] No instantaneous (as opposed to merely rapid) change to a completely different belief proves possible. As organic beings, we are incremental, and any progress we make is also unavoidably incremental. Where claims are made to the contrary, we have grounds for immediate suspicion of delusion.

Incrementality gets its most memorable treatment in the Buddha's teachings in one of a series of metaphorical comparisons between integrative development and the ocean:

> *'Just as the great ocean, bhikkhus, gradually shelves, slopes and inclines, and there is no sudden precipice, so also in this Dhamma and discipline there is a gradual training, a gradual course, a gradual progression, and there is no sudden penetration to final knowledge.'*[2]

The metaphor of the ocean is a rich one in many ways. It suggests fluidity, which can be associated with flexibility and provisionality. Clarity or murkiness in the water can be associated with that of mental states. The vastness of the ocean can also symbolise an openness of awareness – so much so that *jhana*-type states can be described as 'oceanic experiences'. However, this particular metaphor focuses more on the edge of the ocean, and indeed our

---

1 As demonstrated in Festinger et al. (1956).
2 *Udana* 5.5. Ireland (1990) p. 76.

experience on taking an individual path into the ocean. Of course, there can be precipitous cliffs by the ocean, but they are unlikely to provide our way into it. Rather we will look out for a gentle sandy beach where we can gradually adjust ourselves to the new conditions as we enter the water.

The incremental nature of 'this Dhamma and discipline' (i.e. integrative practice) is also emphasised in the Buddha's conversation with a brahmin called Ganaka Moggalana. There the Buddha compares 'gradual training, gradual practice, and gradual progress' to the building of a palace, the training of an archer, the training of an accountant, and the training of a horse.[3] A traditional verse used in Theravada Buddhist devotion, the *Ti Ratana Vandana*, also describes the Dhamma as *'ehipassiko opanayiko paccatam veditabbo'* – 'come and see', gradual, and to be understood individually. All of this emphasises the gradual nature of the path and its relationship to experience.

The reason for this need to stress incrementality lies in its contrast to the discontinuity that is associated with absolutisation. Discontinuity is a mark of absolutisation because when we impose a conceptual understanding on a situation, there will be a gap between that conceptual account and the conditions we are experiencing. For example, we may absolutise the category we place something or someone in ('he's a foreigner'), or the attributes we apply to them ('she's stupid'), or boundaries, whether literal or conceptual ('that's my area of concern, not yours'). Discontinuity is associated with a whole set of biases,[4] as we project certainty onto ambiguous information.

If we are thinking provisionally, that gap can be continually narrowed because we are able to keep modifying our conceptual account to reflect new experience. However, if we are thinking absolutely, our initial account of the situation must be the final one. All alternatives, if they are not appropriated into that absolute account, will thus be automatically rejected because they are regarded as negative rejections that threaten the absolute account. One thus either accepts a discontinuous, absolute belief or one rejects it, because incrementality is incompatible with it. This also has the effect of making the absolute belief *fragile*: it appears robust,

---

3 *Majjhima Nikaya* 107.2 ff. Ñanamoli and Bodhi (1995) p. 874.
4 See Ellis (2015a) section 3.

until it is entirely destroyed. The classic example of such absolute, discontinuous belief and its loss is dramatic religious conversion. At some point the conditions change in a way that makes an old absolute belief untenable, but then the incremental nature of the change is not acknowledged. Instead the opposite belief to the previous one is enthusiastically embraced. Thus it was when St Paul, former persecutor of Christians, fell off his horse, was temporarily blinded, and performed a complete and instantaneous volte-face in his attitude to Christianity.[5]

Of course people do have experiences of relatively rapid change, leading to a tipping point where they need to change their views. Conditions that call for rapid responses also involve a necessary discontinuity. It's thus helpful to distinguish three types of discontinuity:
1. Discontinuity of conditions
2. Practical discontinuity in provisional judgements
3. Absolutising discontinuity

Discontinuity of conditions is discontinuity that seems to occur in our experience. However, when we look more closely we always find that there is actually continuity in these conditions, but they just occur relatively quickly. For example, birth and death are both fairly quick and decisive, but nevertheless incremental, processes. Though we may need to distinguish a specific point of death for legal reasons, death is a process. Indeed, it is one that we are to some extent engaged in all the time we are alive.

Practical discontinuity reflects the way in which we have to assume the world is a certain way in order to act appropriately. To judge whether to eat food, I have to decide whether it is edible or inedible. To decide whether to apply for a job, I have to decide whether or not I meet the specifications sufficiently for it to be worth the time and effort of filling in the application. These discontinuities are a requirement for action, but we can remain aware that we are imposing them on an incremental experience. Maybe that food was getting a bit risky, and maybe the job is too much of a long shot – but I could quite reasonably have judged the other way given conditions that were only slightly different. Such judgements can remain provisional, because we can still re-examine whether they

---

5 Acts 9.

were the correct judgements in the light of subsequent experience, even if it is too late to change our actions.

It is absolutising discontinuity that is avoidable. Here we make a judgement about a situation in the unquestioning belief that it is the correct judgement, rather than just the best we can do according to the evidence in the circumstances. We are thus incapable of revising that judgement without overcoming an entrenched defensiveness, perhaps also feeling shame and humiliation. That's just how things are, we think. But by thinking in that way, we reduce our adequacy to new conditions.

That absolute beliefs about enlightenment or Awakening have this discontinuity should be clear. The Buddha's experience may have shown an apparent discontinuity of conditions, but like all such examples, it can be seen as incremental when looked at more closely. We may experience dramatic breakthroughs, just as the Buddha may have done. However, it is the imposition of the absolute concept of *nibbana* on that experience that introduces the discontinuity, connected to the ideas of the cessation of karma and of the taints. Interestingly enough, the text of the *Udana* as quoted above appears to agree that there is a contradiction between the 'gradual training' and enlightenment, stating that 'there is no sudden penetration to final knowledge'.

Wading into the sea may be cold and scary enough. Diving into it off a cliff is also possible, though dangerous. Neither of these activities, however, results in an instantaneous transformation into a fish. Incrementality is the lot of human experience, so let's stay consistently with it.

3.f. Agnosticism: The Elephant and the Snake

We may set out to make judgements in a provisional way, recognising incrementality and avoiding absolutisations. Nevertheless, maintaining that course is far from easy. For example, someone online starts to argue with you, making a lot of absolute assumptions as they go, together with false assumptions about you and your motives. You're keen to set them straight, first of all about your provisionality and next that their absolute assumptions are untenable. But the person sees you as an opponent and wants to win, and before you know it you're losing that additional awareness you would need to maintain provisionality. Without that awareness of alternatives, your position soon becomes just as absolute as his, and you want to win just as much.

To manage to avoid getting sucked into absolute thinking in that kind of situation, we stand little chance unless we have an awareness of the *opposing* dualistic dynamics that people set up. A dualistic dynamic frames the whole discussion of a particular question only in terms of one position and its opposite. To be able to think differently, you need to be able to recognise what is helpful on each side as well as what is unhelpful. You also need not to depend on the approval of the groups on either side. You also need to be bloody-mindedly determined not to be sucked into the dualistic system, and to maintain even-handedness. That is the practice of agnosticism. We have already seen the Buddha practising this in the conversation with Malunkyaputta in which he firmly avoids metaphysical beliefs *on both sides*.

There are two of the Buddha's similes that I think can further help us to appreciate the nature of agnosticism. The first, that of 'the blind people and the elephant', focuses on recognising the limitations of our view and encourages even-handedness. The second, the snake simile, focuses more on the negative consequences of getting hold of a view absolutely.

The simile of the blind people and the elephant is amongst the best-known of the Buddha's similes. It may well have pre-dated the Buddha, and is found in many other traditions subsequent to him. Its popularity is testament to the power and universality of the metaphor.

The account of the story in the *Udana*[1] begins with different brahmins and *shramanas* arguing with each other about the truth or falsity of the very same stock list of metaphysical beliefs used in the Malunkyaputta story. They argue about whether the world is eternal or infinite, whether the soul is separate from the body, and whether the Buddha exists after death. The story then goes on to depict the conflict created by these metaphysical beliefs:

> ... And they lived quarrelsome, disputatious and wrangling, wounding each other with verbal darts, saying 'Dhamma is like this, Dhamma is not like that! Dhamma is not like this, Dhamma is like that!'

Some followers of the Buddha then go and ask him about these disputatious sectarians. The Buddha says 'They do not know what is beneficial. They do not know what is harmful.' He then goes on to tell the story of a certain king, who commanded all the people in his country to be brought together who had been blind from birth. He then presented these blind people with an elephant. Each blind person was presented with a different part of the elephant: the head, the ear, a tusk, the trunk, and so on. The king then asked the blind people what an elephant is like.

> Those blind people who had been shown the head of the elephant replied, 'An elephant, your majesty, is like a water jar.' Those blind people who had been shown the ear of the elephant replied, 'An elephant, your majesty, is like a winnowing basket.'

Similarly, a tusk was thought to be a ploughshare, a trunk a ploughpole, the elephant's body a storeroom, its foot a post, its hindquarters a mortar, its tail a pestle, the tuft of its tail a broom. The blind people then fell to quarrelling and fighting, saying 'An elephant is like this, an elephant is not like that!' The Buddha compares the *shramanas* of various sects disputing over the Dhamma to these blind people quarrelling over what an elephant is.

The universal embodied experience that is being evoked here is that of limitation of the senses, with this being compared to limitation of belief. Restriction of alternatives due to lack of sensual capacity is compared to restriction of alternatives due to limiting assumptions. In some ways such a comparison does blind people a disservice, and those who object to it on those grounds are not merely being politically correct in a doctrinaire fashion – for blind people usually

---

[1] *Udana* 6.4. Ireland (1990) pp. 91 ff.

compensate for their lack of one sense by giving more attention to the others, and thus becoming *more* rather than less open when interpreting the information they receive. It is also unlikely that most blind people would rely so much on feeling only one part of the elephant, without using their hearing, smell, intuition, and touch of other parts of the elephant to compensate for limitations in their senses. The blind people in the story are much less aware of their limitations than most blind people would actually be.

To understand the power of the metaphor more positively, we need to focus not just on the fact that the people were blind, but on their limited response to that limitation, which fails to take it into account. The blindness is, of course, a device for showing us the limitations of our sense experience in a wider perspective. These limitations are simply part of our embodiment, just as the blind people in the story have been blind from birth. If we respond to those limitations with the same kind of delusion as these particular blind people, we will appear just as comically deficient. We will be so despite the fact that we have had genuine sense-experiences of a genuine object. It is the absolutisation that these particular blind people are subject to, not their disability, that makes them deluded.

The blind people could be scientists examining the universe and drawing absolute conclusions – for example, that all events in it are determined. How much of the universe have the scientists surveyed? Well, undoubtedly a great deal less, proportionately, than the blind people had of the elephant. Or the blind people could be meditators who have an intense integrative experience, but assume from this that they have achieved total integration: the 'elephant' here is the totality of their experience over their whole lives. How much of that have they integrated?

Werner Heisenberg reversed the parable in a telling joke:

> Six blind elephants were discussing what men were like. After arguing they decided to find one and determine what it was like by direct experience. The first blind elephant felt the man and declared, 'Men are flat.' After the other blind elephants felt the man, they agreed.[2]

Heisenberg's point, of course, is that in describing a thing from our point of view we are not only reliant on the limitations of that view, but that we also change it by observing it in the way we do.

---

2 Heisenberg (1958).

What is also intriguing about this story, however, is the way in which that active perspectivity results in agreement rather than further disagreement. The elephants are agreed because they have the same effect on the object of their observation, which in turn is due to a universality (among elephants) of certain functions and needs. Appeals to popularity offer us no certainty: the fact that the whole of society agrees about something does not mean it must be true. However, conflict between interpretations can be resolved through a similarity of function. If we are all fulfilling that function sufficiently adequately and are open to revising our view, we can reach harmony, just as humans can when using the Middle Way.

The Buddha's metaphor of the blind people and the elephant also has a positive implication that those who seek to justify absolute beliefs by partial experiences are nevertheless legitimately seeking meaning in their experience. All the objects that the blind people thought the elephant resembled (water jar, winnowing basket, ploughshare, etc.) would have been familiar items in the overwhelmingly agricultural society of the time. Thus, for the *meaning* of the elephant to be equivalent to one of those familiar items is at least a starting point for each of the blind people. Like them, we can start off with whatever meaning occurs to us from our experience (we need something to work with), as long as we don't jump to the conclusion that that meaning for us can justify a belief about how the elephant ultimately *is*. That meaning can be expanded, and provisional beliefs constructed from it can be considered, but it is the jump to an absolute belief that is unjustified.

In the case of God, enlightenment, or some other final or perfect concept, we can have a meaning for it that is acknowledged to be dependent on our own experience. However, agnosticism is the most appropriate response to *claims* about it (which can only ever be absolute claims). For example, people in different cultures may have what Buddhists would describe as a *jhana* experience – of energy, positive emotion, and insight coalescing in a peak experience. They may then describe it variously as an experience of God, as an experience of communion with nature, or as an excitation of the temporal lobe. To label that experience in those different ways is not intrinsically right or wrong – it is merely a starting point for relating a new experience to our existing framework of understanding. However, one can then continue to explore the beliefs one might have about that experience and its implications in different ways.

Either in an open and provisional way, or in a way that assumes that one label, within the base of metaphor and cognitive models that it assumes, is final. However profound that experience, the same point applies – that the absolute beliefs we may construct about it betray the significance of the experience itself. The blind people are not at fault for their limited descriptions, but they are at fault for disputing about them.

The other important metaphor concerning agnosticism in the Pali Canon is the simile of the snake, to be found in the same sutta as that of the raft.

> Suppose a man...wandering in search of a snake, saw a large snake and grasped its coils or its tail. It would turn back on him and bite his hand or his arm or one of his limbs, and because of that he would come to death or deadly suffering. Why is that? Because of his wrong grasp of the snake. So, too, here some misguided men learn the Dhamma...but, having learned the Dhamma, they do not examine the meaning of those teachings with wisdom.... They do not gain a reflective acceptance of them. Instead they learn the Dhamma only for the purpose of criticising others and winning in debates, and they do not experience the good for the sake of which they learned the Dhamma. Those teachings, being wrongly grasped by them, conduce to their harm and suffering for a long time.[3]

This 'wrong grasp of the snake' is then contrasted with a 'right grasp of the snake' by the neck using a cleft stick. Similarly a 'right grasp of the Dhamma' is said to conduce to 'their welfare and happiness for a long time' because its meaning is examined with wisdom and a reflective acceptance of it is reached.[4]

As with many of the other similes, traditional Buddhist authoritarianism has interpreted the 'Dhamma' as the teachings leading to enlightenment and solely controlled by the tradition. Thus a 'wrong grasp' of the Dhamma has become one that is contrary to those authorities. However, if 'Dhamma' is interpreted more helpfully and consistently as the Middle Way, a wrong grasp of it can be seen as one that slips into absolutisation. This is reinforced by the Buddha's account here of the nature of this 'wrong grasp'. It is said to be unreflective (so does not consider alternatives), only adopted so as to 'win' (suggesting narrow goal-driven motives), and lacking integration with the purpose for which it was originally learned. The

---

3 *Majjhima Nikaya* 22.10. Ñanamoli and Bodhi (1995) p. 227.
4 *Majjhima Nikaya* 22.11.

Middle Way can bite back if wrongly grasped, because it is grasped as another absolute. It thus leaves us in closed feedback loops that fail to address the conditions that led us to be interested in it.

The ways that the Middle Way can be metaphysically interpreted are legion, and here the Pali Canon is of little help to us. Although there is a detailed analysis of wrong views in the *Brahmajala Sutta*,[5] these are all overwhelmingly specific to the Buddha's time and context, consisting in numerous variations of the views debated by *shramana*s about the self and its existence after death. In my own experience, I have seen the Middle Way appropriated to every major metaphysical view, from Thomist Catholicism through to naturalistic atheism. Appropriation is a subtle process, to which the only antidote is a sufficient critical awareness. If you start off by merely engaging positively with a particular tradition or point of view, but then somehow find yourself assenting to absolutes, you will have gone past that point where a firm refusal to be led any further is needed.

As an example to represent many others, let's consider the appropriation of the Middle Way by naturalistic atheism. Many naturalistic atheists, if they do not dismiss the idea of the Middle Way altogether, will assume that naturalistic atheism already offers everything that anyone might seek in the Middle Way. They are likely to argue that scientific assessments are based on provisional use of evidence, and that scientific evidence cannot support belief in God or other supernatural entities. Some may concede that the non-existence of God cannot 'technically' be proven, but dispute whether there is any practical distinction between failing to believe in God and belief in the non-existence of God. The use of terms like 'negative atheism' to blur the distinction between atheism and agnosticism extends this appropriation of the argument further by controlling the vocabulary. What this whole way of thinking does is to impose a dualistic structure on the discussion (theist v atheist, naturalist v supernaturalist) rather than a dialectical one that seeks to learn from the opposed position. At various points along the way, the Middle Way is likely to be turned from a practical process of movement and equilibrium to a rigid position. The 'provisionality' of scientific method may become merely a reason for accepting

---

5   *Digha Nikaya* 1. Walshe (1995) pp. 67 ff.

scientific findings rather than a practice. The practical limitations and possible social biases of formal, organised science may be forgotten. The possibility that 'natural' as well as 'supernatural' could become an absolutisation may be equally forgotten. So might the practical difference in attitude between someone who accepts and explores the meaning of a God they may avoid believing in, and those who sweep the meaning aside with the belief. There is a possibility that, in some cases, the distinctions blurred by these appropriations may turn out not to be practically significant, but there is also a great likelihood that in many cases we have failed to anticipate, they may indeed turn out to be.

Getting hold of the wrong end of the snake, then, often involves the formal adherence to dualistic or oppositional structures. These are implicitly maintained when people think they have 'got' the Middle Way or its equivalent. They may believe they are addressing conditions, have found an 'objective' standpoint, have a secure source of information, or a transcendent intuition. The Middle Way then simply becomes a term that develops or extends this basic standpoint rather than one that challenges it. In the process, the very sources of delusion that they sought to avoid bend back and bite them, once again injecting the poison of absolutism into their veins.

There are no completely secure ways of avoiding the snake's bite. Even the practised snake-catcher may at times fail as he brings the cleft stick down to try to trap the snake's head. The snake may wriggle free, and a familiar form of anxiety or obsession may take hold in, at best, a slightly new form. The wrong hold of the snake, then, is not confined to the ignorant and inexperienced, but becomes only gradually less probable for those who try to apply the principles of the Middle Way. Scepticism is perhaps the most crucial of these principles to recall, so that we do not forget the basic uncertainty that attends even the most familiar beliefs. But a degree of individual integration will also be required to give us the confidence to defy both the opposing groups when necessary. A helping of agnostic courage will also be needed to remain in the Middle when the going gets tough.

The snake is a deep-rooted symbol with great ambiguity. Our embodied relationship to snakes from an early age is likely to be instinctive fear: with good reason given how deadly some species of snake can be. However, the majority of snakes are not so deadly, just as the majority of absolutisations are only mildly harmful. In the later Buddhist tradition, the nagas (serpents), who dwell in the depths, are a symbol of wisdom, and for Jung, the snake was often an embodiment of his soul, meaning his unconscious insights. This may reflect the ways in which overcoming our fear can connect us to the insights offered by wider experience, or the ways in which snakes can confound our expectations. The right hold of the snake needs to accept that ambiguity, maintaining the wariness that attends that fear but no longer being dominated by it. With sufficient awareness, the cleft stick can be applied with skill.

3.g. Integration: The Wet Piece of Wood

The elements of the Middle Way that I have discussed here so far all put the emphasis on our judgement at a particular time. But of course we cannot assume that we have the ability to simply choose how we judge, regardless of the conditions that have directed us in one way rather than another. For example, those with limited self-esteem due to a childhood full of violence and deprivation may find their judgements habitually hijacked by anxiety. Injunctions to provisionality and agnosticism really may not mean much until that basic anxiety has been soothed. Even those of us with more fortunate backgrounds may find it hard enough to maintain the equanimity we need to remain aware at crucial points of judgement. It is longer-term work on ourselves and our habitual states that is needed to create the conditions for better judgement. This is the practice that is emphasised by the Buddha' teachings on the Eightfold Path, which I will discuss in section 5.

If we ask what that Eightfold Path tries to achieve, however, and we are to answer that question in the continuous terms of the Middle Way rather than the discontinuous terms of enlightenment, the answer must be integration. Integration is the effective and long-term resolution of conflict between different desires and beliefs. Conflict is resolved, not by one prevailing over another, but by each taking into account the conditions addressed by the other and modifying or re-framing beliefs to fit those conditions. For example, suppose you've already had one ice-cream and part of you wants another one. The part of you that recognises that this will not actually address the longer-term condition of your embodied desire and its fulfilment is the part that addresses conditions better. Rather than repressing that desire, if you subject it to sufficient awareness in the light of alternatives, the value of the more adequate belief will become clear. The energy that was going into the less adequate belief can then be redirected into the more adequate one through a re-framing of assumptions. In this way practice can transform judgement.

The best metaphor for integration that I've come across does not come from the Buddha, but from a poster used by Quaker peace campaigners: the two mules. Here two mules are depicted as tied together, but start off by straining against each other to reach separate piles of hay. Neither can get what they want because they are in opposition. However, after a while they get frustrated with this and pause for reflection. At this point a little more awareness arises in the mules and they start to eat one pile of hay together, followed by the other. Here the two mules are embodiments of our opposing desires with associated beliefs, and of the way that beliefs can become more adequate through a process of awareness and reflection.

In the Pali Canon, however, there is one metaphor for integration that focuses on quite different aspects of it from the two mules – the damp piece of wood. This example is perhaps rather easy to overlook, because it might at first seem rather unappealing. However, its lack of immediate appeal is perhaps part of its value, since the process of integration may well include reconsidering what does not at first seem very appealing but finding value in it. This simile (or metaphor) appears at two different points in the *Majjhima Nikaya* with differing interpretations. In both of them, the contrast is between a wet piece of wood that cannot catch fire and a dry one that can. In one version, though, the fire is positively associated with spiritual progress, whilst in the other the fire is negatively associated with craving. The wetness of the piece of wood thus entirely changes its significance in the two instances, from being a protection against absolutisation to being an impediment to awareness.

The more positive use of the wet piece of wood occurs in a *sutta* that is concerned with mindfulness of the body:

> 'Suppose there were a dry sapless piece of wood, and a man came with a fire-stick, thinking, "I shall light a fire, I shall produce heat." What do you think, bhikkhus? Could the man light a fire and produce heat by rubbing the dry sapless piece of wood with an upper fire-stick?' – 'Yes, venerable sir.' – 'So too, bhikkhus, when anyone has not developed and cultivated mindfulness of the body, Mara finds an opportunity and a support in him.'[1]

> 'Suppose there were a wet sappy piece of wood, and a man came with an upper fire-stick, thinking: "I shall light a fire, I shall produce heat." What do you think, bhikkhus? Could the man light a fire and produce heat by taking an upper fire-stick and rubbing it against the wet sappy piece of wood?' – 'No, venerable sir.' – 'So too, bhikkhus, when anyone has developed and cultivated mindfulness of the body, Mara cannot find an opportunity or a support in him.'[2]

1 *Majjhima Nikaya* 119.24. Ñanamoli and Bodhi (1995) p. 955.
2 *Majjhima Nikaya* 119.27.

The piece of wood in each case can be associated with our bodies, and the wetness of the wood with our integration. The body is (or seems) solid, and what is solid is associated with rigidity, but water is associated with fluidity and flexibility. By imbuing the solid with the fluid, then, we make it flexible, and make both communication and reformation easier. Without that flexibility created by awareness, though, the wood is liable to combustion by fire. Fire here is Mara, the obsessive desires and anxieties that often assail us from the striatum and amygdala at the back of the brain. The more we can attain an integrated, mindful state based in awareness of the body, the harder it is for those obsessive states to make an impression on us. Our wider awareness will see them in a bigger perspective (understanding that they do not tell the whole story) and avoid transmitting the combustion of absolutisation.

In the alternative, reversed, version of this simile, the comparison is inserted into an account of the Buddha's early life, just before he begins the practice of asceticism.[3] The dry piece of wood can be ignited with spiritual awareness, but this point is accompanied by messages about the irrelevance of asceticism and about the intermediate value of withdrawal for practice. Here the piece of wood has three states: lying in water, wet but on dry land, and dry on dry land. The wood lying in water is said to represent 'those recluses and brahmins who still do not live bodily and mentally withdrawn from sensual pleasures'. The wood lying on land but still wet represents those who have withdrawn but whose craving 'has not yet been fully abandoned' – in other words, they are still obsessed with the objects of their craving and anxiety, even if they are not in immediate contact with them. The dry wood lying far from water, though, represents those who have both withdrawn from the sources of craving and overcome craving itself.

This version of the simile, then, stresses the value of withdrawal as a necessary but not sufficient element of integrative practice. If you want to heal conflicts, you have to move away from contexts where those conflicts are so pressing that you will be constantly caught up in closed feedback loops that maintain the conflict. Instead you need to put yourself in conditions where more awareness can be developed. Some kind of 'space', created by at least temporary withdrawal for

---

3 *Majjhima Nikaya* 36.17-19. Ñanamoli and Bodhi (1995) pp. 335–7.

meditation, reflection, or retreat, will be necessary for this, but this does not have to mean a lifelong career as a *shramana*. As we all find out when we enter such a space for practice, it does not guarantee progress, but merely offers one of the necessary conditions for it. It's quite possible to sit in meditation in idyllic conditions with your mind still racing around a hamster-wheel of anxieties.

At the same time, it points out the irrelevance of asceticism both for those who are withdrawn but still subject to craving, and those who are withdrawn and have overcome craving. 'Even if those good recluses and brahmins feel painful, racking, piercing feelings due to exertion,' we are told, this makes no difference as to whether they are able to deal with their craving. This relates to the expectation that wilful effort and repression are what brings about integration and that 'practice' is about wilfulness. That this is mistaken becomes all the clearer when we interpret these similes in terms of integration. That's because what we are trying to do is not then modelled as 'beating' craving but rather as reconciling conflicting desires, none of which are intrinsically bad apart from their conflict.

Despite these nuances, however, to me the reversal of the simile is far less effective. It loses the relationship between the body and the piece of wood that provides a schema on which the first version can relate to our experience. We don't want our body to be burnt up, but rather maintained. The body's suffusion by water as a symbol of flexibility and change can be related to many other symbolic uses of water, including baptism in the Christian tradition. The metaphor of fire for obsession is also famously used in the Buddha's 'Fire Sermon',[4] re-used by T.S. Eliot in his poem 'The Waste Land'. Fire can be both destructive and helpful to us, but its potential destructiveness probably lies deeper in our unconscious experience. It also provides a basic association with the uncontrolled and fast-spreading destructiveness of absolutisation.

The concept of integration is more flexible, wieldy, and universal than that of Awakening, for a number of positive reasons. It is incremental (though more or less rapid), being a matter of gradual progress 'with no sudden penetration to final knowledge', as we saw in relation to the Ocean simile in a previous chapter. We do not need to understand integration in relation to any state of 'total integration', whether such a state exists or not, but only as a process.

---

4 *Samyutta Nikaya* 35.28. Bodhi (2000) p. 1143.

It can readily help us to understand the value of a range of practices, both of an immediate experiential kind (such as meditation) and a more conceptually-based kind (such as critical thinking). However, it is not confined to the individual level, but makes just as much sense at a socio-political level. There we can see conflicts between the desires and beliefs of different people integrated by the same process of awareness and re-framing (which is often built into mediation techniques).

The concept of integration can also help us make sense of the inconsistencies and asymmetries that we find in the supposedly enlightened, including the Buddha. For the Buddha is not only not omniscient, but does not always seem to have the most optimally-adapted responses entirely free of absolutisation. When he gives a group of monks some teachings on the foulness of the body, then goes away on retreat, he comes back to find that thirty of them have committed suicide, being 'repelled, humiliated and disgusted with this body'.[5] Now, if one monk had committed suicide, we could perhaps put this down to a mere lack of omniscience, but thirty looks rather like carelessness! Also, when Devadatta tries to take leadership of the community from him, the Buddha abuses him as a 'lick-spittle'.[6] These are all the kinds of mistakes, even if they are very serious, that we might expect to be made by a fallible human being, but not by a completely integrated person, let alone an 'enlightened' one.

The concept of integration, however, is open to an asymmetrical form. There is no reason why we cannot understand it as applying to a person more in some circumstances than others, in relation to certain kinds of stimuli rather than others. One person may be very integrated when it comes to reasoning, but hopelessly unaware in their emotional life, or vice-versa. The cognitive bias of domain dependence also indicates that people can learn an advanced skill in one area but completely fail to apply it in another: some marriage guidance counsellors cannot hold their own relationship together and some decision theorists make terrible personal decisions.[7] The Buddha, then, may have been much more integrated in some respects than others: but this recognition is consistent with the

---

5   *Samyutta Nikaya* 54.9. Bodhi (2000) p. 1773.
6   *Cullavagga* 7. Horner (1952).
7   Ellis (2015a) ch. 4.3.i.

concept of integration in a way in which it is not consistent with discontinuous enlightenment.

If we look more carefully in the Pali Canon we can find, not the Buddha who is instantaneously consumed by the fire of enlightenment, but rather a Buddha who is a human with a human body, gradually suffused by integration just as a log is soaked in water. Buddhists have always insisted that we, too, can be like the Buddha. To make that a genuine possibility, though, we need a much more human-compatible model of what he achieved, and of what we can achieve through practice.

4. Issues in the Buddhist Interpretation of the Middle Way

4.a. The Misunderstanding of Scepticism

I can now no longer put off engaging with the way in which Buddhist tradition has interpreted the Middle Way, and offering some kind of account of both its strengths and its limitations. This section of the book will thus be more orientated towards conceptual criticism than the previous ones. The basis of judgement, though, will remain the same: a thoroughly practical one that begins with questions of how embodied human beings can make better judgements in their lives.

I will, in due course, be looking at the expressions of the Middle Way that might be more familiar to Buddhists: the positions of 'eternalism' and 'nihilism', the emptiness teachings, and the Buddhist preference for 'eternalism' over 'nihilism'. There will be much to challenge both in the assumptions with which these doctrines often have been formed by the Buddhist tradition, and in the idea that they are practically helpful today in those forms. However, in order to understand the basis of my critique of the way Buddhism has often treated the Middle Way, it is necessary to start with some basic philosophical issues.

These issues are, first, how we understand the implications of scepticism, and second, how we have traditionally been obsessed by ontological ways of thinking (i.e. ways of thinking that are concerned with how things *are*). I shall contend that there are basic mistakes of approach that have distorted the conventional understanding of the Middle Way in both cases. These are not 'East' versus 'West' issues, but rather unjustifiable assumptions that have been widely made in both Asian and Western contexts, as far as I can ascertain. Whether the Buddha himself was subject to them to any extent is almost impossible to ascertain with any degree of justification, because of the ambiguity of the records.

We need to begin with scepticism, which I have already identified as one of the five principles of the Middle Way. The practice of the

Middle Way involves the avoidance of absolutes on either side, because the sceptical recognition of uncertainty is incompatible with such absolutes. Yet doubtless this will have been a matter of surprise and controversy to many Buddhists, who, in common with most Westerners, tend to regard scepticism as an 'extreme'. For most people, scepticism is an arcane pursuit, limited to cloistered philosophers who are without practical goals or concerns, beyond making an impression on academic peers through abstract controversy. This view of scepticism has been aided by Western philosophers. Descartes vainly tried to defeat scepticism by finding certainty. Hume thought that a sceptic couldn't really live their scepticism. Wittgenstein was obsessed with defeating scepticism by showing it to be using an aberrant form of language.[1]

The reputation of scepticism amongst many Buddhists has fared no better, due to the negative depiction of 'sceptics' or 'eel wrigglers' who were followers of Sanjaya Bellatthaputta at the time of the Buddha. King Ajatasattu is portrayed as having visited a series of *shramana* leaders to ask them about the benefits of spiritual life, but being most unimpressed by Sanjaya:

> *'Sanjaya Bellatthaputta, on being asked about the fruits of the homeless life, replied by evasion. Just as if on being asked about a mango he were to describe a breadfruit-tree.... And I thought "Of all those ascetics and brahmins, Sanjaya Bellatthaputta is the most stupid and confused."'*[2]

We should perhaps here note a possible manifestation of the general ideological tendency for the nearest doctrines to one's own ideology to be treated as the biggest threat. As here, the strongest condemnation is thus reserved for the leader who gives responses that most resemble the Buddha's. But Sanjaya's responses to metaphysical questions posed by Ajatasattu are pretty much identical to those given by the Buddha to Malunkyaputta previously discussed.[3] They both refuse to answer these questions. In the case of Sanjaya, for some reason his motive for doing so is assumed to be impracticality or indecisiveness of a kind that is not attributed to the Buddha. This is similar to the assumption made about scepticism

---

1 See Ellis (2012) ch. 1.b for a more detailed account of why these Western philosophical objections to scepticism fail.
2 *Digha Nikaya* 2.33. Walshe (1995) p. 97.
3 *Majjhima Nikaya* 63. Ñanamoli and Bodhi (1995) pp. 533 ff.

by David Hume two thousand years later, who concluded that in practice sceptical arguments are 'cold, and strained, and ridiculous'.[4]

Scepticism is most often assumed to be impractical because it offers arguments that point out the uncertainty of every possible claim. Yet, if we are to begin with an acknowledgement of our embodied experience, this uncertainty should be no surprise at all. It should hardly be necessary for sceptics to point out that we do not know for certain that we are not making an error in our judgement at any moment. Nor should it be news that we might possibly be dreaming or under an illusion right now. It should, indeed, be obvious that our senses cannot give us information that is not already formatted by our position, sensual capacities, conceptual limits, assumptions, and expectations.[5] Given our embodied situation, it is certainty that would be surprising rather than uncertainty. It appears to be only a habit of over-certainty due to the over-dominance of the goal-driven and linguistic centres of the left hemisphere (otherwise known as confirmation bias), that makes many of us unable to appreciate this point.[6]

The confusion in many ways seems to be a basic logical one, because it is only about what is or is not a necessary implication of sceptical argument. To point out a lack of certainty (i.e. to refuse to affirm an absolute) is not in any sense to deny, yet we have an ingrained tendency to regard every refusal to accept our favoured positive position in the same light. 'No' can mean either a mere failure to affirm or a denial, yet the mere failure to affirm is far too often interpreted in the light of a denial. It can hardly be overstressed that *scepticism denies nothing*. Its recognition of uncertainty, indeed, applies just as much to negative positions as to positive ones, so it no more favours or disfavours those negative positions than it does the positive ones. For that reason the implications of sceptical arguments alone make scepticism a two-sided argument: every time a particular claim is challenged, its direct opposite must be equally challenged. Scepticism thus, by the momentum of its own arguments, requires the balance of the Middle Way.

---

4 Hume (1978) p. 269.
5 For a more detailed account of these basic sceptical arguments see Ellis (2012) ch. 1.a.
6 McGilchrist (2010).

Added to this common logical confusion is a confusion about the relationship of uncertainty to practical judgement. When we make a practical judgement, we do have to make assumptions, both about how things are and about what our goals should be. I cannot even bite into a sandwich without assuming it is nutritious rather than poisonous, and acting on the basis of my hunger. However, that practical constraint does not remove the value of scepticism in supporting provisionality during the reflective phase *before* that judgement is finalised. A sceptic *can* live her scepticism, and she does so by considering as many alternatives *as possible* before making a particular judgement, and thus making her judgement more adequate. 'As possible' of course still creates a practical limitation in the number of options we can actually consider, but the extension of our options nevertheless improves the probabilities of making a better judgement. When the consideration of further options starts to impact negatively on the quality of the judgement, we still have to limit the options considered in order to address the conditions. However, if, instead, we had assumed one option to be absolute, those additional alternatives would never have been considered. Scepticism reminds us that no option has an absolute justification, even though, in the end, one option must be chosen on the basis of the balance of justification.

Nor does scepticism necessarily require an impractical duration to that reflection on alternatives. Every judgement is time-framed because it occurs in an embodied life in which certain desires and relationships are already underway, with all of them time-framed. I can't put off eating the sandwich for ever. An adequate judgement of how to respond to that embodied context includes a respect for the need to make a judgement within a certain time-frame. No sceptic has reason to be frozen in ineffectual contemplation just because they recognise uncertainty. Rather, the belief that it is justified to wait indefinitely is subject to balanced sceptical doubt like any other.

To act in a timely way, we don't require freedom from all uncertainty, but rather the *confidence* to act in a particular context. Such confidence is a product of the integration of our energies and is thus an embodied state, not a purely mental result of abstract beliefs. In Buddhism the term *saddha*, which can be translated as 'confidence' or 'faith' and is one of the five spiritual faculties, can most helpfully be interpreted as such a confidence, though it is also unhelpfully conflated with absolute belief in the Buddha and his revelations (see 6.h). Opposed to *saddha* is *vicikiccha* (disabling doubt), which is often unhelpfully translated as 'sceptical doubt' or 'uncertainty'. This is a kind of doubt that consists in a conflict in our energies and can, for example, emerge as a hindrance to disrupt meditation. In the Pali Canon, the role of this hindrance (together with the others) in splitting energy is made vivid through the image of channels being dug to lead water away from a flowing river.[7]

This kind of 'doubt' is created by absolutisation that represses alternatives, not by the recognition of alternatives that enables a more adequate range of options to be considered. Scepticism, in the sense of the use of sceptical arguments to recognise uncertainty, is the best way to remedy 'doubt' in this sense. Such scepticism, far from being the diversion of water in the canals, could be said to be looking out for diggers who are planning to illicitly start canals to divert the water.

Since scepticism only reminds us of uncertainty, it is no threat at all to provisional beliefs that take that uncertainty into account. However, it is a threat to absolute beliefs, because they seek to exclude awareness of it. Scepticism thus requires the Middle Way, because it implies the avoidance of both positive and negative absolute beliefs. The Middle Way also requires scepticism, because when we are seeking more adequate beliefs we can only do so by distinguishing provisional beliefs from absolute ones.

The mistake often made by Western philosophers and Buddhists alike seems to have been to respond to scepticism in a purely philosophical way – that is, a way that tries to assess it as a belief according to its contents. Scepticism is worryingly elusive if you insist on looking at it in that way, because it doesn't assert any contents. It is just a method or a way of arguing. Its positive significance and value in practice does not depend on a represented content, but rather on the psychological states that must accompany it. If we recognise the uncertainty attaching to one view, we open ourselves to alternatives. If we are also able to imagine actual positive alternatives, we are then able to arrive at more helpful and adaptive beliefs at every stage.

It is by only dealing with scepticism philosophically that people have arrived at the assumption that scepticism is, or can be 'extreme'. Of course there is no guarantee that scepticism may

---

7 *Avarana Sutta, Anguttara Nikaya* 5.51. Thanissaro (2003).

not lead us to extremes according to the conventions of a particular group, but in general scepticism is the only position that *cannot* be extreme. There is thus no contrast between 'extreme scepticism' and 'mitigated scepticism'. You can either recognise uncertainty in every judgement, or you can be selective about it. If you're selective, you are still subject to absolutism and its effects in the judgements that remain absolute. There is no practical necessity to be selective, because the beliefs we need to live and thrive do not have to be absolute. Scepticism offers no threat to your provisional belief that your food will nourish you or your friends support you, only to your failure to recognise that sometimes they may not.

The response to scepticism in Buddhist tradition, too, has often been to 'mitigate' it when it did not need mitigating, making the scepticism selective rather than applying it even-handedly. Selective scepticism has meant, for example, accepting some applications of the Middle Way but not others. It has meant maintaining scepticism about metaphysics believed in by other groups whilst turning a blind eye to absolutisations in the Buddhist tradition itself (such as absolute enlightenment, karma, and rebirth). Even when scepticism has appeared to be consistent in theory across the board (as in the Mahayana perfection of wisdom and emptiness literature), it has not been consistent in practice. Rather it has been made compatible with authoritarian power-structures and a class division between monk and lay. This power-imbalance driving the ideology meant that the emptiness teachings got very selective application, and some sources of belief were in practice taken to be unquestionable.

It may be objected that many people are not ready to understand, let alone face up to, uncertainty, and thus that Buddhist selectivity has had a practical justification as a skilful means of teaching. However, there is a further issue here that stems from another misunderstanding of the practical implications of scepticism. It is not that facing up to scepticism about everything makes Buddhist practice too hard, but rather that the assumption that scepticism applies to *everything in the universe* rather than to *our judgements about everything we encounter* makes it unnecessarily hard. Once scepticism is recognised as being concerned with *our judgements* it becomes, not easy, but incrementally possible. The mistake of thinking that scepticism is about everything in the universe is what I call the *ontological obsession*.

4.b. The Ontological Obsession

Ontology is the study of how things ultimately are, and is a fruitless metaphysical activity given that we can only ever have access to how things appear. Normal talk about how things *are* 'really' is a convenient shortcut for talking about how they consistently appear and thus how we can interact with them. For example, to say that John is *really* in Paris implies that I thought he was somewhere else, and that I could go to Paris to meet him or contact him there. However, I could both talk about and assume John's presence in Paris in a more ultimate or ontological way by failing to accept the possibility of alternatives. For example, I could try to contact him in Paris and be excessively distressed about his failure to return my call, because I fail to consider the possibility that the information I have about him *really* being in Paris is mistaken. Ontology is a form of absolutisation, because if we really believe things *are* a certain way, we rule out all alternatives (though sometimes philosophers [mis]use the term 'ontology' when they are really interested in analysis: which means what an idea implies on closer examination, not its ultimate reality).

Buddhist talk about emptiness, non-substantiality, and delusion often implies a recognition that ontological claims cannot be justified, because they require a certainty that we can't have (though there is also some debate amongst Buddhist schools on this point – which I am not going to get into). However, an obsession with 'how things are' also often continues even when this recognition is present, because 'how things are' remains the focus of attention and the assumed basis of a meaningful discussion on the topic. 'How things are' as a focus of attention can be contrasted with 'how we judge things' as an alternative focus of attention. For example, one can say 'the self is empty' or one can say 'absolute claims about the self are unjustified': the former puts the emphasis on what is or is not the case about the self, the latter on how we judge it.

The ontological obsession has a major effect on the way the Middle Way is presented throughout Buddhist scriptures and literature. The alternative to the two extremes is constantly presented as conditioned arising or conditionality, itself a description of how things are rather than of how we judge them. Yet a belief in conditionality as the state of how things normally are, whilst avoiding any belief in unconditioned things, is unjustifiable. From our limited, embodied standpoint, we cannot be sure that everything is conditioned. I will be returning to the subject of conditionality for a fuller examination in chapter 6.a.

The continuation of the ontological obsession even in the face of theoretical disavowals of ontological claims is not surprising if we think about the operation of meaning for human beings. If you read 'don't think of an elephant', you are likely to immediately disobey that instruction, and 'don't think of vomit' is likely to arouse at least a faint feeling of disgust. Mere negation has little effect on meaning, because the meaning of terms like 'elephant' and 'vomit' is embodied. It is overwhelmingly the effect of immediate associations rather than the more abstract cognitive modelling that a sentence involving negation puts us in. In order to practise the Middle Way in the sense of actually avoiding both poles of an absolute and its contrary, it is not enough just to change our view of abstract beliefs about the lack of truth to be accorded to absolute statements. We need to change what we find most meaningful, and thus what will engage our attention.

Buddhist practice shows some recognition of this point insofar as it promotes analysis and reflection on doctrinal beliefs about emptiness and non-substantiality. For example, the Madhyamaka school offers a meditation on emptiness involving systematic reflection on levels of emptiness. However, even here the emphasis remains on accepting the truth of one abstract formula and the falsity of others, with reflection and analysis as tools to achieve this abstract acceptance or non-acceptance. The ontological obsession continues, because attention is still focused on having the right views of objects, rather than on making the right sorts of judgements.

For some practitioners, this basic limitation in the way Buddhist tradition has framed the Middle Way may not seem to matter too much. The way things are and our judgements about them may seem to be different sides of the same coin, with one being a proxy for the other. Buddhist practitioners continue to make progress using this proxy method. However, I want to argue that in many respects it creates an unnecessary obstacle for the practice of the Middle Way.

The reason for this can be encapsulated by a famous metaphor from the Mahayana text, the *Bodhicaryavatara*:

> Where is there hide to cover the whole world? The wide world can be covered with hide enough for a pair of shoes alone. In the same way, since I cannot control external events, I will control my own mind.[1]

This analogy most obviously points to the economy of effort, as well as much greater likelihood of success, involved in focusing on changing one's own mind rather than the world. That doesn't imply that we should not try to change the world at all. Rather it means that we might do so much more successfully by working with our minds so as to make more adequate judgements that address the conditions of the world. A very similar point can be made, however, about changing our view of the world as a whole, as opposed to changing our response at the crucial points of judgement where we interact with it. It is one thing to believe that everything in the phenomenal world is empty in a general sense. It is quite another, and much more important, to avoid absolutising the essential identity you assume for particular people or things (such as your father, your car, or your theory) when it would in some way address conditions better to get beyond the identity you have assumed.

As I have argued throughout this book, the Middle Way is a method. That method is shown at certain points of crucial judgement in the Buddha's life. The Buddha probably applied that method in a great many other situations that we do not know about. Even so, however, the use of that method did not entirely require him to change his physical constitution as a human being, nor to dwell uninterruptedly in states of transformed consciousness. The Buddha's ability to access temporary states of enhanced integration such as *jhana* was probably of great value to him, as was the virtue of his habitual ways of thinking and acting. However, it was when these states or tendencies were put to the test in judgement that they counted most. Judgement sets a course for our subsequent beliefs, inspires actions and omissions, and affects others both directly and by example. It is judgement that also, by freezing an assumed set of conditions to act in, creates a kind of portal for interaction between experience and conditions ('subject' and 'object'). But if it is judgement that we need to change, it is judgement that needs to be our primary focus. Only secondarily can we consider the conditions in ourselves and the world that are affected by those judgements.

1 Shantideva (1995) section 5.13.

The ontological obsession also creates a great many unnecessary difficulties. Not only does thinking of judgement 'by proxy' through objects of judgement create a greater danger of appropriation by absolutising beliefs, but it also makes it harder to maintain a clear theoretical understanding of the Middle Way itself. The appropriation by absolutising beliefs can be seen throughout the history of Buddhism. Different schools of thought started to enter into disagreement precisely because they were focusing, not on method, but on ontology. For example, the Pudgalavadins disagreed with the other schools by claiming that there is a real 'person' separate from the aggregates. The Sarvastivadins also claimed that there were really existent atomic phenomena called 'dharmas' whilst the Madhyamaka asserted instead that all 'dharmas' are empty, and the Yogachara that they were ultimately 'mind only'. It is not necessary to enter into the (irrelevant) technical details of these metaphysical controversies to get an impression of how much of a completely unnecessary distraction from genuine practice they were, given that they did not focus on judgement but rather on ontology.

The ontological obsession also makes it more difficult for people to understand or practise the integration of opposing views. That's because of a constant tendency to focus on the *content* of those views in absolute form (i.e. the supposedly substantial beliefs in supposedly substantial things we are referring to) rather than an experiential form that takes account of their psychological function. With experiential beliefs, such as a belief about the best quantity of oil to put into a cake recipe, it is relatively easy to resolve disagreements in relation to the objects of experience. We can do this through observation and experiment. We can taste and compare the results of cakes with different quantities of oil. However, when it comes to absolute beliefs about final entities, there are no possible resolutions between disputing beliefs as long as they are framed absolutely: for example, either the self exists in some form or it doesn't. It is only by re-framing the question so that it actually becomes a question about experience (and thus incremental) that we can resolve the dispute.

This re-framing generally does not occur in traditional Buddhist discourse. Instead we get different approaches in the Pali Canon and in the Mahayana. In the Pali Canon and Theravada tradition, an authoritative answer is often given: we are usually simply given words that stand for the idea of a resolution. In the Mahayana, we instead often get endless 'flips' and paradoxes. Each of these can provide a *substitute* for the resolution of the conflict, and may thus tend to distract us from actually engaging in its resolution by practising the Middle Way when all we have done is substitute one idea for another. Attribute substitution of this kind is a recognised phenomenon of cognitive bias, in which we substitute a simpler answer that we can access more quickly for the more complex and difficult one that is needed to meet the conditions. Thus, for example, in a psychological study, students were asked how many dates they had recently just before being asked how happy they were. They tended to substitute the answer to the date question as an easy way of avoiding the potential complexity of the happiness question.[2] In the same way, Buddhist texts tend to substitute a formula or a paradox for an actual application of Middle Way method.

Let me offer some examples of each of these types of Buddhist response. Let me stress that in doing so I am pointing out limitations in what they do, but at the same time not denying that they go a certain distance in pointing people roughly in the direction of the Middle Way, and are thus helpful up to a point.

As an example of the first kind of response let's take the *Honeyball Sutta*.[3] Here, the Buddha starts off by proclaiming to a lay enquirer that his teaching 'does not quarrel with anyone in the world'. The Buddha then goes on to explain that his teaching avoids conflict, because conflict is caused by mental proliferation. If 'nothing is found there to delight in and hold to, this is the end of the underlying tendency to lust', along with doubt, conceit, being, and ignorance. The loss of these underlying tendencies puts an end to 'resorting to rods and weapons…quarrels, brawls, disputes, recrimination, malice and false speech'.[4] Although Maha Kaccana (one of the foremost disciples of the Buddha) then goes on to explain this in more detail, little is really added to this by his explanation.

Here we have, then, an explanation of absolutisation as proliferation (which is descriptive of the way its closed feedback loop dominates the mental state). It's also made clear that we could get rid of conflict by getting rid of absolutised desires and beliefs. What we're not told, however, is how to move an absolutised belief into a provisional one in which the conflict can be resolved. Of

---

2 Kahneman (2011) pp. 101–3; Ellis (2015a) ch. 3.d.
3 *Majjhima Nikaya* 18. Ñanamoli and Bodhi (1995) pp. 201 ff.
4 *Majjhima Nikaya* 18.8. Ñanamoli and Bodhi (1995) p. 202.

course, we might follow the practices of the Eightfold Path and, becoming gradually more integrated in our judgements, work it out for ourselves in relation to the specific absolutisations we become aware of in our own minds. However, the *sutta* would be a lot more effective in communicating how the Middle Way can help us avoid conflict if it illustrated some kind of re-framing process. An apparently intractable problem needs to be reconceived in incremental or experiential terms that can then be agreed upon by both sides. Instead, we are only left with certain highly formalised ways of labelling or pointing to that process that fit a certain 'correct' way of understanding conditions.

As an example of the second kind, let's take an extract from the *Diamond Sutra*:

> Buddha replied to Subhuti: Good men and good women seeking the Consummation of Incomparable Enlightenment must create this resolved attitude of mind: I must liberate all living beings, yet when all have been liberated, verily not any one is liberated. Wherefore? If a Bodhisattva cherishes the idea of an ego-entity, a personality, a being, or a separated individuality, he is consequently not a Bodhisattva, Subhuti. This is because in reality there is no formula which gives rise to the Consummation of Incomparable Enlightenment.[5]

This is very typical of a lot of material in the 'Perfection of Wisdom' (*Prajnaparamita*) and other related Mahayana literature. On the face of it, it may seem like the Middle Way, because each absolute position is contradicted by the other, but all the text presents us with is a flip between two absolute perspectives. The contradiction between the two perspectives confronts us with a paradox, and the assumption seems to be that discussion of the issue in language can move no closer to the Middle Way than this. However, the paradox is unnecessary, because the contradiction can always be resolved by re-framing one's understanding of the concepts so that they are no longer absolute. *Incrementality* is the key to this. The paradox in this quotation only occurs because of an absolute view of 'liberation', but in practice the incremental liberation (i.e. integration) of one person is interdependent with all the others. Socio-political integration supports individual integration and vice-versa. The ideas of the bodhisattva and of a formula that produces enlightenment are also

---

5   Price and Mou-Lam (1969) section 17, p. 52.

unhelpfully absolutised. No bodhisattva who has a body is going to be free of ego, but it does not follow from this that she is unable to help other beings make progress. The fact that there is no absolute formula for enlightenment also does not mean that there are no helpful expressions in words.

The ontological obsession has resulted in the effective obscuring, or perhaps even betrayal, of the Middle Way in a great deal of Buddhist literature and thought. All of this is due to the assumption that the Middle Way was best understood and described in terms that were focused on how things are or are not. The assumption throughout is that the meaning of our language is necessarily based on the representation of ontologies, rather than the associative impact of symbols on our bodies, and thus that language is intrinsically inadequate for spiritual purposes. Language does indeed have limitations, but, like any tool, those limitations depend on the skill with which it is wielded. Merely taking refuge in paradox does nothing to refine our skill with language.

We are now in a position to move on from this and to understand the Middle Way as a method of judgement. For the Middle Way, language can always be better or worse used, and 'to be' is just a piece of shortcut language.

4.c. The Range of Absolutes

Earlier Buddhist treatments of the Middle Way are often typified by unnecessary limitation in the range of absolutes that it is taken to avoid. This limitation is largely corrected by later (particularly Mahayana) treatments, but Buddhist understanding of the Middle Way may still often be limited by these earlier treatments. This can be seen when the Middle Way is taken to apply *only* to certain kinds of views and not others, whether this is asceticism and self-indulgence, 'eternalism' and 'nihilism', or existence and nonexistence. It is thus important for Buddhists to recognise the full range of absolutes if they are to have an adequate understanding of the Middle Way for practice.

Let me begin with a quick survey of the ways that the Middle Way is presented in the Pali Canon. Although not as generalised as the Mahayana, even these present a wider appreciation of different kinds of absolutes on either side than is often recognised. The pairs of opposites to be avoided include hedonism versus asceticism, the belief in versus rejection of the fixed self, accepting or denying the eternality and infinity of the universe, belief that the Buddha does or does not exist after death, and existence versus nonexistence.

The Middle Way between asceticism and self-indulgence has long been clear enough from the story of the Buddha's early life. It is more formally expressed in a conversation with Rasiya the headman:

> 'There are, headman, these two extremes which should not be cultivated by one who has gone forth into homelessness: the pursuit of sensual happiness in sensual pleasures, which is low, vulgar, the way of worldlings, ignoble, unbeneficial; and the pursuit of self-mortification, which is painful, ignoble, unbeneficial. Without veering towards either of these extremes, the Tathagata has awakened to the middle way, which gives rise to vision, which gives rise to knowledge, which leads to peace, to direct knowledge, to enlightenment, to Nibbana. And what is that middle way awakened to by the Tathagata...? It is this Noble Eightfold Path....[1]

It should be noted that there is nothing here that *limits* the Middle Way to the avoidance of only these particular two poles. The relationship between the Middle Way and the Eightfold Path

---

1 *Samyutta Nikaya* 42.12. Bodhi (2000) p. 1350. For further references to absolute self views in the *Samyutta Nikaya*, see also 12.35, 22.1, 22.81, and 24.3-5.

also suggests a wider applicability involving all the elements of the Eightfold Path (those involving views, aspirations, and mindfulness as well as effort and action). The interdependence between our views of pleasure, on the one hand, and our views of ourselves, the world, and the categories we use to describe it, on the other, can hardly be separated. For example, if I have a self-indulgent practice of overeating, that also implies an absolute view of myself as gaining ultimate satisfaction from food, of the food as providing ultimate satisfaction, and of myself and the food as wholly separate. 'Without veering towards either of these extremes' also suggests the even-handedness I will discuss in chapter 4.e.

There are a great many discussions in the Pali Canon that are concerned with views of the self. The challenge to belief in a fixed and eternal self is otherwise expressed as the *anatta* or 'no self' doctrine, which is one of the three marks of conditioned existence (see chapter 6.b). However, it's also clear that this doctrine needs to be interpreted as a Middle Way avoidance of either belief that the fixed and eternal self exists, or the contrary that it does not. We have already seen this mentioned in the *Malunkyasutta*, along with other metaphysical polarities avoided by the Buddha. Here is another instance:

> 'Kassapa, [if one thinks,] "The one who acts is the same as the one who experiences [the result]," [then one asserts] with reference to one existing from the beginning: "Suffering is created by oneself." When one asserts thus, this amounts to eternalism. But, Kassapa, [if one thinks,] "The one who acts is one, the one who experiences the result is another," then one asserts with reference to one stricken by feeling: "Suffering is created by another." When one asserts thus, this amounts to annihilationism.[2]

This links a number of different types of absolutisation together: beliefs about the self continuing to exist in a fixed and eternal form are linked to beliefs about responsibility. If the self exists eternally, and the law of karma is also assumed, then the actions of the self will affect that self in the future, and one is wholly responsible for one's fate. If, on the other hand, the self continually changes, even if the law of karma does apply, it's assumed there is no responsibility for the way in which one is affected by conditions. The absolutes here, then, also suggest beliefs in free will and determinism as they are applied to the issue of moral responsibility.

2   *Nidanasamyutta, Samyutta Nikaya* 12.17. Bodhi (2000) pp. 546-7.

In discussing the arrow simile above (chapter 3.d), we have already seen the Buddha's avoidance of the belief in or denial of the eternality and infinity of the universe, and belief in or denial of the Buddha's existence after death, as well as the affirmation or denial of the fixed self. This same standard set of alternative absolutes is also discussed in the discourse with Vacchagotta. There Vacchagotta asks what danger the Buddha sees in these views. The Buddha replies:

> 'Vaccha, the speculative view that the world is eternal [repeated subsequently for all the other metaphysical views] is a thicket of views, a wilderness of views, a contortion of views, a vacillation of views, a fetter of views. It is beset by suffering, by vexation, by despair, and by fever, and it does not lead to disenchantment, to dispassion, to cessation, to peace, to direct knowledge, to enlightenment, to Nibbana.'[3]

Many of the processes of absolutisation are metaphorically suggested here. A thicket (or a fetter) suggests being caught up or trapped, as in the closed feedback loop associated with absolutisation. A wilderness suggests aridity – the aridity of recycled dead metaphors and unquestioned assumptions. Contortion suggests the defensive rationalisations into which people will enter to defend their metaphysical views. Vacillation suggests the 'flipping' process of people going directly from one absolute position to its opposite without being able to re-frame the issue. It would be rather strange here if the specific views listed were rejected because they had these effects, but other views that demonstrably had similar effects (because of their psychological resemblance to the specific views listed), were not to be rejected for the same reasons.

In both of these contexts, as well as others where this set of metaphysical views are mentioned, not just two opposed views but four alternatives are listed: positive, negative, both positive and negative, or neither positive nor negative. These alternatives suited the logical categories assumed in that context, but are not very relevant in the modern West, where such a logic of four alternatives is not widely accepted. However, it makes little difference which logical possibilities are considered, since the Buddha's key point is a rejection of the current framing of the problem. If we are

---

3 To Vacchagotta on Fire, *Majjhima Nikaya* 72.14. Ñanamoli and Bodhi (1995) p. 591.

re-framing a problem that has been seen absolutely so that it can be resolved incrementally, the 'both' and 'neither' options of the old framing are no longer relevant. For example, if we re-frame the problem of the eternality of the universe into one that we can be experientially concerned with, such as whether observations could be made of phenomena from a time prior to the Big Bang, this is not an assertion that the universe is both eternal and not, nor that it is neither eternal nor not eternal. Rather it is putting the question in terms that avoid such speculative beliefs entirely.

However, the broadest of the absolutes to be avoided given in the Pali Canon is that suggested in a brief discourse with Kaccanagotta:

> '"All exists": Kaccana, this is one extreme. "All does not exist": this is the second extreme. Without veering towards either of these extremes, the Tathagata teaches the Dhamma by the middle....'[4]

It is what Western tradition has known philosophically as realism (all exists, being physical) and idealism (all does not exist, being only mental) that are clearly rejected here, whether you interpret these two positions as opposed to each other on the matter of 'existence', or united in asserting it, but merely conceptualising it differently. This suggests a need to avoid the ontological obsession in which claims are made about what exists or does not exist. At the same time, there is a recognition of the need to distinguish what we assume to exist or not exist for practical purposes.

> 'This world, Kaccana, for the most part depends upon a duality – upon the notion of existence and the notion of nonexistence. But for one who sees the origin of the world as it really is with correct wisdom, there is no notion of nonexistence in regard to the world. And for one who sees the cessation of the world as it really is with correct wisdom, there is no notion of existence in regard to the world.'[5]

It would be contradictory for the Buddha to at one and the same time be claiming that he does not apply notions of existence and nonexistence, and yet claiming to know the world 'as it really is'. It is much more helpful here to interpret the Buddha as referring to the phenomenal world that we might experience and develop provisional beliefs about. Such provisional beliefs have an uncertain original justification and may be supplanted by better

4 *Nidanasamyutta, Samyutta Nikaya* 12.15. Bodhi (2000) p. 544.
5 Ibid.

alternatives at any point, so we should thus avoid the assumptions that any such beliefs about 'existence' or 'nonexistence' are final. Our role in making judgements in this world depends on a merely practical duality, not a different type of 'truth'. We do not need to create a 'two truths' doctrine. The distinction between the need to avoid premature duality in our reflections and the need to apply duality in practical judgements is simply a separation of elements of judgement over time.

This passage alone, let alone the others discussed so far in this chapter, should be enough to show that even in terms of the text of the Pali Canon, the Middle Way can be readily seen not as a mere avoidance of a few specific absolutes, but rather of absolutes in general. Nevertheless, there seems to be a general Buddhist failure to update the Middle Way to take into account all that we have learnt since the Buddha's time about forms of absolutisation. We need to do this to see the Middle Way as offering an approach that can guide every single judgement in Buddhist practice.

This can be related to a tendency not to take the Middle Way seriously at all, and not to emphasise it in expositions of Buddhist doctrine. I once made a survey of 60 books about Buddhism from my bookshelves. Given my long-standing interest in the Middle Way, you would expect this selection to reflect more on Buddhist interest in the Middle Way than average, yet only 25 out of the 60 books even mentioned the term 'Middle Way' (or any equivalent such as 'Middle Path') in their indexes. Of those 25, about 50 per cent mentioned it only once or twice, usually to state that the Middle Way was equivalent to the Eightfold Path. It would thus be fair to state that probably less than a fifth of books about Buddhism take the Middle Way seriously as a topic worth any discussion. If writers do not even mention the Middle Way, it is hard to distinguish why they have not done so. However, one reason may well be that they understand it only in relation to a few specific metaphysical issues, and do not see it as having relevance beyond these. These metaphysical issues, in turn, may be perceived as peripheral to Buddhist practice, when they are actually vital to every single judgement we make in practice.

To appreciate this more fully, it might help to offer a fuller list of the range of types of absolutisation. I have undertaken this task much more fully in *Middle Way Philosophy 4: The Integration of Belief*. There I have also related every type of absolutisation to the cognitive biases recognised by psychology and also to many metaphysical positions and informal fallacies recognised in Western philosophy. I am not going to offer anything like that detailed analysis here, but offer a list of types of absolutisation that may at least boost awareness of the range of what we are talking about:

- Source (e.g. assumption that anything said by a particular source must be true or false)
- Subject (e.g. assumption that fixed self exists or not)
- Agency (belief in free will or determinism)
- Object (e.g. belief in the ultimate existence or nonexistence of material or abstract objects)
- Cause (belief in 'real' causes, or that a particular cause is sole, ultimately sufficient, ultimately necessary, etc.)
- Probability (assuming that the increments involved in probability are absolutes – e.g. treating a small risk as a certainty)
- A priori beliefs (e.g. in the essential nature of a subject or object, or the 'reality' of numbers or the laws of geometry)
- Person (e.g. that a person has an essential quality or category)
- Value (e.g. that there's an absolute source of moral value in certain principles, goals, or virtues)
- Boundaries (that we have correctly identified what is 'really' part of one thing and what is not)
- Time (e.g. absolute beliefs about the value of past, present, or future events because of their position in time, including biases like the sunk costs fallacy, status quo bias, and neomania)
- Meaning (e.g. representationalism that assumes words can completely represent objects or experiences)

Many of our judgements are subject to absolutisation in several of these categories at once. For example, if I become unduly anxious about my daughter being out very late when she had not phoned me, I might be making absolute assumptions about the sole *cause* of her not phoning being a threat to her, about a low *probability* of danger that I treat as a reality, about the absolute nature of *boundaries* of behaviour that are ambiguous, and about the *meaning* of thoughts created by anxiety as representing realities. Any of these judgements can be treated provisionally as well as absolutely, but when they become absolute they do so 'emotionally' as well as 'rationally'. Careful reflection is needed on our everyday judgements to distinguish the different assumptions present, as absolutes can be found in the most trivial judgements.

All of these categories of absolute judgement are at least implied by the Pali Canon treatment of the Buddha's Middle Way. The absolutisation of sources and representations is avoided in the Buddha's instruction before his death, already quoted in chapter 2.f: 'You should live as islands unto yourselves, being your own refuge....'[6] As we have seen, avoidance of absolute beliefs about the self also implies avoidance of such beliefs about agency and about other persons. Avoidance of beliefs about existence and nonexistence applies to objects, causes, probabilities, a priori beliefs, boundaries, and representations. It is the absolutisation of beliefs about the essence or boundaries of an object, and the absolutisation of the abstractions that we take to be equivalent to the object, that are most at stake when we claim to know about things. All objects also have a temporal dimension, which cannot be absolutised either, and the extension of Buddhist teaching over the three times is also made clear in Buddhist ideas about the succession of Buddhas from past, present, and future.

Perhaps it is the Buddha's avoidance of the absolutisation of values that might not seem so obvious from the foregoing. Fuller exploration of this will have to wait until the discussion of ethical practice in chapter 5.c. However, it is clear that the Buddha avoided the abstract formulation of absolute moral rules, and that very specific monastic rules we might find bewildering today (like the prohibition of high or wide beds) were probably formulated to meet very specific circumstances for which they were relevant. If we are to adopt an embodied understanding of ethical beliefs, such beliefs cannot possibly be absolutely justified, but nor are they lacking justification as long as they are relevant to experience.

In general, then, the Buddha's Middle Way should be taken as avoiding all absolutes in all situations of judgement. That does not imply that, practically speaking, we are necessarily capable of banishing all absolutes, but it does imply that all absolutes are in question as the source of evil. In every case, the Middle Way consists of the avoidance of both positive and negative absolutes. If we cannot identify both extremes we should remain in practical doubt as to whether we are applying the Middle Way.

'All absolutes' is a term that also encompasses 'all metaphysical beliefs', and in some of my writings I have referred throughout to

---

6 The Buddha's Last Days, *Digha Nikaya* 16.2.26. Walshe (1995) p. 245.

absolutes as 'metaphysics'. I'm aware that this runs against a whole set of habits both in established Buddhist and in associated academic discourse. For some reason, most Buddhist scholars do not consider the term 'Buddhist metaphysics' to be an oxymoron. Of course, if we are trying to describe the beliefs actually held by the Buddhist tradition, many of these are indeed metaphysical. As I hope I have demonstrated, though, there is a prescriptive basis in the Buddha's helpful teachings for taking these to be mistaken. The most common way in which the Buddha's objections to metaphysical beliefs are reconciled with 'Buddhist metaphysics' involve selective scepticism, based on common assumptions to which I objected in chapter 4.a above. It is assumed that the Buddha cannot possibly be referring to *all* metaphysics, because it's considered impossible to avoid all metaphysical positions.

In the standard discussions found in analytic philosophy, metaphysics tends to be conflated with basic or foundational assumptions. It might be claimed that I must absolutely assume, for example, that the world exists, and that the things in it exist in time and space. However, the fact that I *generally* assume these things, and that they form part of the embodied reliances of which I am habitually confident, does not mean that I couldn't doubt them and consider alternatives if I had a particular reason to do so. It may be difficult even to imagine the world not existing, but if someone were to confront me with evidence that suggested a viable alternative, then I would see no reason not to consider it. My belief would turn out to be provisional if I was open to such alternatives, but absolute if I was not. The basicness of our reliance on particular beliefs should not be confused with absoluteness of assumption.

However, if you ask most scholars to engage with the idea, clearly suggested by the Buddha at least on some reasonable interpretations, that we should avoid all metaphysics, the trouble they have with it seems to be rather similar to someone suggesting that the world might not exist. Even T.R.V. Murti, one of the most influential of scholars who have discussed the interpretation of the Madhyamika ('Middle Way') school of the Mahayana, states early on in his study that 'We cannot have a way of life that does not imply a philosophy, an appraisal of reality.'[7] The idea that the whole point of the Buddha's approach might be to refrain from offering an

---

7   Murti (1955) p. 37.

'appraisal of reality', and that this, indeed, might be the basis of a Middle Way Philosophy, just doesn't seem to figure as a possibility on the academic map. It is not contradictory to offer a philosophical account based on thoroughgoing and balanced scepticism: rather it is an expression of provisionality.

If we were to be selective in our scepticism about metaphysical beliefs, indeed, on what basis could we possibly select? If we adopt a particular set of conventions, or just maintain the metaphysical beliefs we think we already have, there is still no escaping the uncertainty that attaches to those assumptions as soon as they are considered. If we claim that some metaphysical beliefs (such as the belief that the Buddha was enlightened) have practical value, we immediately have to turn those beliefs into something less than an absolute in order to explain that practical value. That the Buddha reached a standpoint from which human experience can be better understood, due to a high level of integration and insight into conditions, is a belief that could inspire us to emulate him. But turning this into the abstraction of 'full and perfect enlightenment' achieves nothing except the basis for absolute appeals to authority.

'Buddhist metaphysics' has particularly included two kinds of claims that have done a lot to obscure Buddhist understanding of the Middle Way. One of these is the belief that all opposed absolutisations are aspects of one essential opposed pair ('eternalism' and 'nihilism'). This I will unpick in the next chapter. The other, that some metaphysical beliefs are better than others (specifically, that eternalism is better than nihilism) will be the subject of the final chapter of this section.

4.d. The Clustering of Absolutes: 'Eternalism' and 'Nihilism'

So far we have been examining the idea in Buddhism that there is a Middle Way between any two given opposing absolutes. However, there is nothing about that idea that necessarily implies the *clustering* of absolutes, that is, the view that one type of absolute necessarily implies another. This view, however, is a widespread assumption in traditional Buddhist treatments of the Middle Way. Not only are absolutes taken to be clustered into necessary relationship, they are also polarised into two necessary positions. These are normally referred to as 'eternalism' (*sassatavada*) on the one hand, and either 'nihilism' or 'annihilationism' (*ucchedavada*) on the other. If this was correct, then every instance of the Middle Way would be a navigation between these two essentialised extremes.

At the core of these beliefs about clustering of absolutes are two associations. One is between views of the self and practical motivations for ethics or other practice. The other is between views of the self and ontological views of existence. 'Eternalism', then, often means absolute views about the fixed self that also imply belief in the essential nature of objects in the universe, linked to asceticism in pursuit of karmic reward. 'Nihilism', on the other hand, clusters as absolute beliefs about the nonexistence of the self, together with the nonexistence of essential objects and a rejection of moral motivation.

The first of these links, between views of the self and moral or spiritual motivation, is given trenchant exposition by Sangharakshita:

> How absolute is the dependence of the Middle Path in ethics upon the Middle Path in metaphysics and in psychology, and how indispensable comprehension of the latter to understanding of the former, should now be apparent. The belief that behind the bitter-sweet of human life yawn only the all-devouring jaws of a gigantic Nothingness will inevitably reduce man to his body and his body to its sensations; pleasure will be set up as the whole object of human endeavour, self-indulgence lauded to the skies, abstinence contemned, and the voluptuary honoured as the best and wisest of mankind. Similarly, the contrary belief that the macrocosm is grounded upon absolute Being, whether personal or impersonal, is automatically adumbrated in the sphere of psychology as the belief that above or behind the microcosm, the little world of human personality, there exists a soul or self which is on the one hand related to absolute Being...and which is on the other hand quite different from, and independent of, the physical body. In this case matter

will be considered illusory or evil or both, and the body regarded as the principal cause of man's non-realization of his identity with or dependence on the Divine. The object of the spiritual life will be held to consist in effecting a complete disassociation between spirit and matter, the real and the unreal, God and the world, the temporal and the eternal; whence follows self-mortification in its extremest and most repulsive forms.[1]

Sangharakshita's account may not represent that of all Buddhists, but it is influential, and its assumptions are striking. He quite explicitly claims that the relationships between the clustering metaphysical beliefs on each side are absolute, meaning that there can be no exceptions to the correlations between them. This creates a very strong and sweeping set of claims that only require the production of counter-examples to be disproved. It is easy to produce such counter-examples: for example, there are many examples of materialistic scientists who do not believe that there is anything beyond the physical, but who are not thereby self-indulgent. They may thereby be quite ascetically devoted to their scientific work. There are also religious believers who believe in both God and the soul but who do not thereby adopt asceticism: Trollope's novels of comfortable and somewhat indulgent clergymen in the nineteenth century could furnish lots of examples. What seems to have happened here is that a set of correspondences of belief that were typical at the time of the Buddha have been absolutised. It is assumed that those correspondences *must* apply universally, without much critical thought about the exceptions when they are applied to the modern context.

At the same time Sangharakshita also imports into this passage almost Platonic attitudes to the body, with the assumption that focusing on the body's sensations is associated with hedonistic attitudes. This is mistaken in a more profound way that is not just the confusion of contingent associations with necessary ones. Hedonism is an absolutisation of pleasure which takes us *away* from the actual experience of pleasure. Adequate engagement with bodily experience is the starting point, instead, for scepticism and provisionality.

The second of these links, between beliefs about the self and beliefs about essential existence (*svabhava*), is perhaps suggested in

---

1   Sangharakshita (1987) pp. 162–3.

the discourse with Kaccanagotta quoted in the previous chapter. It is put more clearly in Nagarjuna:

> *To say 'it is' is to grasp for permanence.*
> *To say 'it is not' is to adopt the view of nihilism.*
> *Therefore a wise person*
> *Does not say 'exists' or 'does not exist.'*
>
> *'Whatever exists through its essence*
> *Cannot be nonexistent' is eternalism.*
> *'It existed before but doesn't now'*
> *Entails the error of nihilism.*[2]

Here again, the association has a consistency in a certain context, particularly when applied to the continuing existence of the self. However, once again a contingent relationship seems to be being taken to be a necessary one. Pradeep Gokhale comments on a conflation of essential existence with eternal existence:

> *Even if existence is treated as svabhava, existence need not be eternal. Svabhava of a thing, simply because it is svabhava, need not be eternal. Burning is svabhava of fire in the sense that fire cannot cease to burn in so far as it exists as fire; not in the sense that burning (because it is svabhava) must continue even if fire ceases to exist.*[3]

Not only does the essential existence of an object not necessarily imply its eternity, as pointed out here, but one could also add that the eternity of a subject (the self) doesn't necessarily imply that of all objects. As Gokhale goes on to point out, Nagarjuna's ontological Middle Way doesn't necessarily imply an ethical Middle Way.

It is perhaps this basic incoherence in Buddhist claims about the extremes avoided by the Middle Way that has discouraged many scholars or reflective Buddhists from trying to understand it as a consistent doctrine. They may agree that the Middle Way appears to be the best policy in a particular case, yet not connect it to other such cases because they have no clear basis of generalisation with which to think about it. If the Buddhist tradition stakes its claims about the Middle Way on the philosophical coherence of 'eternalism' and 'nihilism' as beliefs to be avoided, it is onto a loser.

I came to appreciate this point myself in the work I did for my PhD thesis[4] (the beginning of the development of my Middle Way

2   Nagarjuna, *Mulamadhyamakakarika* 15.10–11. Garfield (1995) p. 40.
3   Gokhale (1996).
4   Ellis (2001).

Philosophy). This attempted to find a basis of incremental moral objectivity in the Middle Way, and argued its case primarily by contrast with the failures of the 'eternalism' and 'nihilism' of Western thought. Yet in categorising Western thinkers in this way, I was obliged, like Nagarjuna, to isolate one particular type of absolutisation to be the defining one – in my case the one I alighted on was moral absolutism as opposed to moral relativism. I found all sorts of patterns in the clusters of metaphysical assumptions that supported absolutist and relativist positions. Nevertheless, I remained troubled by the lengths I had to go to in order to categorise every single thinker in this way. Marx is a particularly good example of a philosopher who crosses the aisle and is difficult to categorise as either 'eternalist' or 'nihilist'. There's a considerable danger of ad hoc argument (interpreting the evidence tendentiously to fit the theory) when one has such a grand theory to consistently maintain, without an immediate practical requirement to check it against. It is this experience of trying hard to make sense of 'eternalism' and 'nihilism', but in the end failing, that has led me to abandon any belief in the *necessary* clustering of metaphysical absolutes into two essential positions. In the end I also realised that this clustering was irrelevant to the practical functioning of Middle Way Philosophy.

That there is no *necessary* clustering does not imply that there is not a great deal of clustering between absolute positions, and that some are more likely to be used to support each other. For example, in classic theism, belief in God's existence tends to cluster with belief in his revelations, which tends to cluster with moral absolutism, which tends to cluster with belief in free will. However, there are potential exceptions to all of these links. You might potentially believe in God's existence but not that he gives revelations, or that he gives revelations but, due to the uncertainty of our interpretation of them, moral absolutism does not follow. Some theists are moral situationists. Even those who are moral absolutists may also not believe in free will, but instead be predestinarians. Similar arguments can be made about any traditional cluster of metaphysical beliefs, whether positive or negative.

Metaphysical beliefs support each other primarily because they are believed within an absolute framework. In such a framework, it is assumed that the language gains its meaning from a potential relationship with reality. The role of embodied categories and schema, metaphors, and cognitive models built on them is ignored, because it is assumed that a given cognitive model offers a true way of referring to the world. Many of the metaphysical beliefs recognised in Western philosophy – such as naturalism and supernaturalism, moral relativism and absolutism, theism and atheism, free will and determinism – share a single elaborated cognitive model, based on interlinked dead metaphors, that philosophers take to be a basis of truth.[5] That cognitive model may entrench disagreement as well as agreement.

To understand the metaphysical beliefs of the time of the Buddha, we must similarly appreciate that there was a cognitive model that was taken for granted by the Buddha's contemporaries. This included karma, rebirth, a cyclic cosmology, and the possibility of liberation from rebirth. Most of the arguments between different schools in the Buddha's context involved mere movements between different positions within this cognitive model. The *meanings* of these positions continued to support each other even where beliefs differed. Those of the Buddha's contemporaries who were sceptical enough not to believe in karma, for example, were almost inevitably portrayed only negatively in terms of that dominant model. The clusterings of 'eternalism' and 'nihilism', which take attitudes to karma as their point of departure, only make sense within this cognitive model. The implications of the Middle Way, however, take us far beyond it, to the embodied experience of humans prior to such models.

To give too much significance to clustering as a basis of understanding the Middle Way would involve giving too much significance to the *content* of absolute claims. The habit of those who maintain absolute claims, though, in the mental state in which they maintain them, is to constantly emphasise the content of their claim. They believe it must be true for x, y, or z reasons, all involving selective scepticism, confirmation bias, and representationalism. This emphasis on the content of the claim distracts our attention from the psychological function of the claim and the wider context of assumptions in which it is made. However, because of its irrelevance to experience, the content of an absolute or metaphysical claim is insignificant, operating merely as a badge of which group you belong to.

---

5   For more details of this see Lakoff and Johnson (1999) ch. 21.

There are many claims that are ambiguous, being potentially absolute or potentially provisional, and require interpretation. If, when interpreted, though, the only meaning of a sentence as a whole (as opposed to its parts) is absolute, that sentence meaning only has an absolutising function. Its relationship to other absolutising functions is of no particular practical relevance except as an indicator of group allegiance. For example, let's take the sentence, 'Barack Obama was not born in the US.' Of course, the terms 'Barack Obama', 'born', and 'US' have meanings in themselves. However, given its lack of relationship to evidence, its lack of incrementality or provisionality, and its context in the 'Birther' movement, all the sentence as a whole signifies is absolute allegiance to the group opposed to Barack Obama. Is this sentence eternalist or nihilist? It's hard to say, but it sure doesn't hit the Middle Way.

In the absence of necessary clustering, we simply have to understand the Middle Way as a principle of judgement navigating between *any opposed pair* of positive and negative absolutes. This may be in any context where they may arise. Since the Middle Way is not a metaphysical position, it does not need to be metaphysically defined in relation to metaphysical positions. It only needs to be practically defined in relation to absolute positions as we encounter them in experience. It would be inconsistent with the Middle Way itself to understand it in terms that were dictated by the content of metaphysical beliefs.

4.e. Even-handedness and the Preference for Eternalism

In addition to the Buddhist view that there is a coherent cluster of absolute views called eternalism and nihilism, there is also a skew towards one of these clusters rather than the other: a belief that eternalism is preferable to nihilism. For example, a commentary on the *Dighanakha Sutta* says:

> *The eternalists know that there is a present life and an after-life. They know there are pleasant and unpleasant effects of wholesome and unwholesome deeds. They engage themselves in meritorious actions. They recoil from doing evil deeds. However, they relish and take delight in pleasures which could give rise to fresh existences. Even when they get to the presence of the Blessed One or his disciples, they find it hard to abandon their belief immediately. So it may be said of the eternalist belief that although its faults are not grave, it is hard to discard.*
>
> *On the other hand, annihilationists do not know that there is passage to the human world from other existences and there is an after-life. They do not know there are pleasant and unpleasant effects of wholesome and unwholesome deeds. They do not engage in meritorious actions, and have no fear of unwholesome deeds. They do not relish and take delight in wholesome deeds, which could give rise to fresh existences, because they do not believe in an after-life. However, when they get to the presence of the Blessed One or his disciples they can abandon their belief immediately. Thus with regard to the annihilationists' belief, it may be said, that its faults are grave but it is easy to be discarded.*[1]

The eternalist belief is said to be *saggavarana*, meaning that it is conducive to better rebirths, though not *maggavarana*, conducive to the path to nirvana.[2] Thus, at least in the Pali commentarial literature and later interpretation, the view has become widespread that the Middle Way is by no means an even one, but rather a first preference between three options where there is also a clear second preference.

The effects of this second option can be seen in the traditional Buddhist distinction between monastic and lay Buddhism. The goal of the monastic is nirvana, but the goal of the lay practitioner (especially in the Theravada) is usually only to gain a better rebirth so as to be able to seek nirvana in a future life. The lay Buddhist is

---

1 Pesala (2013).
2 *Saratthapakasini*: Buddhaghosa's commentary on *Samyutta Nikaya* 22.1 (not translated into English).

expected to concentrate on basic moral conduct, such as following the five precepts, and to be generous in supporting monastics. The lay Buddhist, then, is apparently not expected to follow the Middle Way at all, but rather to be an eternalist, following a systematic and unquestioned ideology that provides a moral framework of merit.

This view contrasts with the view of the Middle Way I have been offering so far, including the five principles outlined in chapter 1.f and elaborated in section 3. Agnosticism, as one of these principles, involves even-handedness as a key aspect. If we are even-handed we do not treat one absolute view as preferable to another, nor do we make any distinction between positive and negative absolute views. We recognise each to be equally unhelpful. The universality of the Middle Way as I have approached it also implies that the removal of the Middle Way for lay Buddhists is completely unacceptable. It is a result of discontinuity in thinking about a path that is incremental.

In the previous chapter I have already explained how eternalism and nihilism as necessary clusters of absolutes are not coherent ideas. However, to defend the priority of eternalism, it could conceivably be weakened to a preference for any positive absolute over any negative. This would be foolish for the simple reason that the labels 'positive' and 'negative' are entirely conventional, and can often simply be swapped round in substitution for one another. If I believe in free will, for example, this is contradicted by determinism. So does that make determinism negative? If I consider determinism as a positive position, though, the denial of determinism by indeterminism appears negative. Even theism and atheism could be re-described so that atheism is a 'positive' 'belief in the nonexistence of God' and theism is a 'negative' 'non-belief in the nonexistence of God'. What is 'positive' and what 'negative' is an accident of description depending only on the conventions one adopts, with the only necessary element (at least in the context of the Middle Way) being that they are opposed to each other.

If we are thinking in terms of clusters of absolutes, positives and negatives can quite easily be promiscuously combined. There is no necessity for positive absolutes to be combined with other positives or negatives with negatives. Orthodox Marxism, for example, combines a 'positive' absolute belief in the socio-economic determinism of history and a 'positive' view of the value of the ultimate Communist society with a 'negative' view that propounds the nonexistence of God and a presumably 'negative' view suggesting the necessary ultimate self-destructiveness of capitalism. There is simply no reason, generally speaking, to prefer positives to negatives, whether we are thinking in terms of single absolutes or clusters of absolutes. The functions of absolutes remain the same in all cases.

However, let us look more closely at the reasons that might be offered for the preference for eternalism. The preference, it may be argued, is merely practical. Not everyone can be a monastic, not only because the monastic support-system would then disappear, but also because most lay-people are not ready to be monastics. Such arguments depend on assumptions about the monastic and lay communities that may or may not be generally correct. However, the wider point that not everyone is ready to practise the Middle Way explicitly, on which it depends, is well worth considering.

Once again, Robert Kegan's work on psychological stages,[3] which combines a range of earlier models and considerations of both cognitive and moral maturity, can be of great help. According to his approach, psychological development can be analysed into five identifiable stages, with each new stage offering a new stable level of awareness. At each of these, that which was taken for granted in the previous stage becomes an object. Thus, at stage 1 we become aware of an objective phenomenal world apart from ourselves. At stage 2 we become aware of separate people and objects within this world. At stage 3 we become aware of ourselves in relation to this world and thus adopt interpersonal, communal values. At stage 4, we become systematic and ideological, seeing the world in terms of consistent facts and moral principles that may override our interpersonal loyalties in some cases. At stage 5, we recognise the role of our own judgement in forming these facts and moral principles, and, thus, gain the capacity to be provisional in their use.

The vast majority of the adult population fall into stages 3 and 4, with apparently only 1 per cent of the population reaching stage 5.[4] Yet the full practice of the Middle Way appears at first sight to apply only to those at or transitioning to stage 5. It is only in stage 5 that we seek to avoid the final level of absolutisation, in the form of absolute ideological beliefs that we recognise as insufficiently adequate to changing conditions. Is there a case for compromising

3 Kegan (1982).
4 Figure quoted in Morad (2017).

the Middle Way on pragmatic grounds for those at earlier stages of development? That might seem necessary for those still working to establish a consistent ideological view that they identify as their own (stage 4), or those even still working to see themselves as part of a mutually supportive community (stage 3). On the face of it, eternalism as traditionally formulated resembles a stage 4 ideological view, in which one has a consistent view of the world and the values one should prioritise within it.

However, we also need to recall here the ways in which the Buddha's earlier development reflected a gradual engagement with the Middle Way. When he left the palace, he had not yet discovered the Middle Way, but was nevertheless moving on because of the dawn of a new critical awareness. In terms of Kegan's stages, the 'Going Forth' probably represents a move from stage 3, where values depend on interpersonal relationships, to stage 4, where a personal ideology is developed. Stage 4 provides a necessary starting point for stage 5, which involves the explicit discovery of the Middle Way, so a move to stage 4 can also be seen as a move *towards* stage 5.

Whilst Kegan's scheme provides a valuable orientation in human development, the stages are obviously not entirely discontinuous. Nor does a higher stage offer a greater justification than the previous one without the implicit possibility of the next. From the viewpoint of stage 5, stage 4 is no more justified than stage 3, since both tend to absolutise limited perspectives. The move to stage 4 emphasises separation, whilst the move to stage 5 re-emphasises connection and thus in a sense reconnects with the strengths of stage 3 (as represented by the rose-apple tree episode). Stage 3 is, on average, a stage that women are more likely to get stuck at, whilst men are more likely to get stuck on stage 4[5] – a further consideration that the staged development should not be understood as a simple hierarchy.

There is thus a case, which echoes the practical justifications that can be given for the priority of eternalism, that a lop-sided movement from one set of associated absolutes to their opposites is a necessary part of human development. It's only thus that we develop a basis for a later explicit appreciation and practice of the Middle Way. However, this does not undermine the importance

5 Kegan (1982) pp. 210–15.

of even-handedness, since the value of this lopsided move is only evident from the later point where even-handedness can be achieved. Each transition from one stage to another also demands a practice of the Middle Way at a more detailed level. With each transition we need to embrace a new way of thinking sustainably, but not leave behind the old level prematurely whilst we are still dependent on it. Even a five-year-old transitioning to stage 2, becoming aware of herself as amongst objects in the world, cannot absolutise that new perspective by moving instantaneously to it, but needs to navigate for a while between attachment to the old perspective and the allure of the new one. To be able to engage with new conditions at any level we need the Middle Way, though applied in a way that is adapted to that level, and not necessarily fully explicit.

This psychological case also differs from the traditional Buddhist prioritisation of eternalism in important ways. It recognises that the transitional ideology adopted in stage 4 can take a wide variety of forms, most likely including negative absolutisations as well as positive ones. It also needs to be understood in terms of its psychological function rather its ideological content. It does not involve any affirmation of the justification of metaphysical claims themselves, but only of the increased level of awareness that may accompany a transition from one set of metaphysical beliefs to another, for which provisionality itself is needed.

Most importantly, it is not tied to the monastic-lay division and accompanying absolutisation of Awakening, which effectively make the prioritisation of eternalism part of a social power structure. On the least charitable interpretation, eternalistic ideology is a distraction given to the lay-people so that they can continue to maintain the monks in the style to which they have become accustomed, without too many complaints. This criticism ignores the ways in which monastics contribute positively to lay life by providing an important source of inspiration and wisdom. Nevertheless, the continuation of the belief amongst monastics that lay-people should believe in an absolute ideology that they have surpassed themselves can offer a breeding ground for miscommunication, hypocrisy, and corruption.[6]

---

6 See Sangharakshita (1993) for evidence from his personal experience of Theravada monasticism.

The issue can hardly be separated from that of karma, which will be discussed in more detail in chapter 6.d. Amongst the bad Buddhist arguments for belief in absolute karma is a pragmatic moral one – that belief in karma enables people to be moral because they believe there will be negative consequences to their negative actions and positive consequences to their positive actions. What this argument does is to mistake the accompanying philosophical rationalisations for the more basic psychological awareness that forms the basis of moral practice in stages 3 and 4. As recognised by Piaget and Kohlberg in research that preceded and contributed to Kegan's,[7] people entering stage 3 make advances in their moral practice by first recognising the value of others' perspectives in interpersonal relationship with one's own, and then those entering stage 4 recognise the value of rationally consistent moral beliefs.

The crucial conditions for such moral awareness are thus not specific doctrines about moral consequences. Rather they are the consistent moral perspective of a community, together with the developed capacity of the individual to accept that moral perspective as a basis on which to interpret their own moral experience. It's only possible to be stimulated into moral awareness by reflection on karmic consequences because one is ready to reflect in that consistent ideological way. Other consistent moral ideologies (for example, utilitarianism) could do exactly the same job. The belief in karma thus forms an *example* of the kind of consistent moral perspective a community can offer to those entering stage 4. However, it is not itself constitutive of the meaning of stage 4, because it is not universal. The need for people to pass through Kegan's stages does not imply that the beliefs adopted in each stage have to take the form required by traditional Buddhism.

Indeed, there are not necessarily any intrinsic advantages in accepting the positions normally seen as 'eternalist' over those seen as 'nihilist' as a basis of moral judgement. Either can offer socially-sanctioned moral rules that may generally address certain predictable conditions within the context of that community, but due to their absolutisation may also fail to do so when they present rigidity in response to new conditions. Let's take the example of sexual ethics. A stereotypical traditional (male) lay Buddhist will refrain from rape, abduction, and adultery on the grounds that this

---

7   Kegan (1982) ch. 2.

is a traditionally prescribed interpretation in Theravada countries of the third lay precept (which proscribes 'sexual misconduct'). However, it is in Western countries, where 'nihilist' values of disbelief in karma and extinction at death are common, that social and legal disapproval of more subtle forms of sexual misconduct, such as sexual harassment, has become common. In many cases, then, 'nihilism' seems to offer more adequate moral prescriptions than 'eternalism'. In both cases, though, the crucial factor in finding these forms of sexual misconduct unacceptable is social pressure (accepted at stage 3) and social ideology (accepted at stage 4). If we ever find more traditional Buddhist societies relatively wanting in moral awareness when compared to more modern ones, we can plausibly blame the priority of eternalism.

In general, then, we can find a similar picture in the priority given to eternalism as that in many other areas of Buddhist teaching. A form of the teaching that probably had a helpful function and helped to address conditions in the Buddha's context, by giving a particular cultural expression to more universal psychological needs for staged development, has become absolutised. As a result, Buddhists have maintained these teachings as ends in themselves, rather than prioritising the Middle Way with its potentially more universal perspective. An application of the Middle Way that served a purpose in one context, and indeed contributed to an understanding of how the Middle Way itself worked, has become mistaken for the whole. Instead, Buddhists need a metonymic view that sees the parts in their tradition as instances of a whole that can also be applied in different ways. In this wider perspective, even-handedness is a key element of the practice of the Middle Way.

5. Interpreting the Eightfold Path

5.a. The Eightfold Path and Integration

As we have already seen in chapter 2.b, the Buddha equated the Middle Way to the Noble Eightfold Path in his First Address. This equation has provided an easy excuse for those Buddhists who prefer to ignore the Middle Way, as they can choose to discuss the Eightfold Path instead. But the relationship is one of interdependency rather than substitution. The Eightfold Path, as I shall explain throughout this section, provides us with a variety of methods for developing integration. Integration provides a key condition for developing and maintaining the awareness needed to recognise alternatives to absolutisation. However, to develop integration using the Eightfold Path also requires us to interpret it in a way that avoids absolutisation. The Eightfold Path is not just another set of absolute moral or ritual instructions, but a set of methods for working with our embodied experience that will be undermined if it is absolutised. The Eightfold Path needs the Middle Way, just as the Middle Way needs the Eightfold Path.

The Eightfold Path can be analysed in terms of the Threefold Path of morality (right action, right speech, and right livelihood), meditation (right effort, right mindfulness, and right concentration), and wisdom (right view and right aspiration). Each of these is primarily concerned with different aspects of integration: morality with socio-political integration, meditation with integration of individual desires, and wisdom with integration of belief. In each case, conflict is maintained by absolute belief of some kind, which excludes other alternatives, and thus stops conditions from being addressed. Such conflicts can be resolved through the relaxation of assumptions, so that new frames allowing other possibilities can be considered. Such a relaxation of absolute assumptions can be achieved by working directly with the body and mental states, or through a more critical, discursive approach, or both.

However, the interrelationship between all these different types of integrative practice also needs to be appreciated. One needs some degree of individual integration to be able to work effectively to overcome conflict at the socio-political level. The socio-political also creates the wider environment in which the conditions for individual integration become possible. Integration of belief changes our longer-term responses to our environment rather than merely changing our immediate states of mind, but changes in our immediate states of mind can also be very helpful in developing the capacity for provisionality. Integration of belief is also vital to socio-political integration, because groups of people and society as a whole need to be able to investigate and address conditions collectively. On the other hand, society also creates the conditions for integration of belief through education (in the broadest sense of the term).

A method can be absolutised if it is *solely* relied upon to the exclusion of the other interdependent methods (so that we implicitly hold the belief that one method solves all our problems). The Eightfold Path avoids this, and thus encourages the Middle Way by highlighting the way that different methods interact so as to produce lasting integration. Its eight 'limbs' are sometimes depicted as sequential, but are obviously not so, though of course we might concentrate on some aspects more than others at different times.

However, the Buddhist tradition also absolutises the Eightfold Path by separating it into 'mundane' and 'supramundane' versions[1] corresponding to the goals of lay and monastic Buddhism. The 'supramundane' version is said be the 'true' Eightfold Path, with a perfect view that then needs to be fully recognised through practice, with the 'mundane' version being a mere preparation for this. This Platonic type of interpretation takes an intellectual formulation of the goal of the path to be the norm and the path as a means to reach the goal, rather than recognising that the path is found in experience together with the goals. Since many people can't engage with a 'supramundane' goal, it also creates an unnecessary discontinuity in the path. For equivalence with the Middle Way, then, the Eightfold Path needs to be interpreted incrementally rather than as a pursuit of absolutised enlightenment.

---

1   Bodhi (1999).

The precise analysis of integration offered in the Noble Eightfold Path is also contingent. The cake could be cut differently. Why is mindfulness separate from concentration and why is livelihood separated from action? Why is there no separate mention of compassion, or of the development of the imagination? Like other aspects of Buddhist doctrine, these are probably products of the particular circumstances of the Buddha's context. We need to be able to generalise from this specific analysis to a more general understanding of the path to be able to apply it in different circumstances. Nevertheless, the Eightfold Path as taught by the Buddhist tradition has a high level of universality compared to some other teachings, provided we interpret it in conjunction with the Middle Way.

5.b. The Middle Way in Meditation

Most Buddhist expositions of the Eightfold Path begin with Right View: an approach that reinforces the tendency to understand Buddhism in top-down ways framed by absolute belief. If, however, our aim is to understand more fully how important the Middle Way is to the Eightfold Path, it is probably better to start with meditation. A common pattern for those getting involved with Buddhism in the Western world is to first try meditation, often as a way of addressing unsustainable feelings of stress or anxiety. Apart from addressing such sources of anguish, however, meditation can confront one very directly and experientially with why the Middle Way is necessary. Only then might the need for ethical practice and the cultivation of wisdom to supplement meditation become clearer.

'Meditation' in the context of the Eightfold Path refers to an overall practice of mental (and physical) cultivation, not just to a formal practice of sitting in meditation. It includes three limbs: right mindfulness, right concentration, and right effort. These are three interdependent aspects of the integration process, together creating awareness. The process of working with all three of them is the Middle Way, as already discussed in the lute strings analogy (chapter 3.c). As the Buddha puts it there, 'If energy is applied too forcefully it will lead to restlessness, and if energy is too lax it will lead to lassitude.'[1] Working in mindfulness, concentration and effort is concerned with the modulation of that energy, steered by our beliefs about it.

Awareness, in general, requires energy flowing through our synaptic connections and nervous system. If that energy is set too rigidly to flow in one particular pattern, dictated by some brain processes rather than others, it may, on the one hand, be concentrated but also unsustainable, or, at the other extreme, sustainable but not concentrated. At some point the other processes in the body and brain will reassert their importance to the whole organism. This is where a balance between concentration and mindfulness is needed.

In neurological terms, the development of concentration is identified with the *task positive network*. This consists of a correlated set of areas of the brain that appear to be stimulated when we

---

1 *Anguttara Nikaya* 6.55. Nyanaponika and Bodhi (1999) p. 168.

focus our attention. This network tends to alternate, in waking experience, with the *default mode network*, a different linked set of parts of the brain that are more likely to be activated when the mind is not closely focused.[2] It has been suggested by scientific studies that mindfulness, on the other hand, stimulates modifications to the insula and the anterior cingulate cortex of a kind that change the relationship between the task positive and default mode networks – in other words, our *ways* of being concentrated.[3]

Concentration without mindfulness is energy applied too forcefully: it is what happens when our attention is compelled by an external stimulus (such as an examination or performing an operation). The Buddha was said *not* to have praised every kind of concentration as necessarily good.[4] Mindfulness without concentration, on the other hand, could be too slack and lead to lassitude. Right effort involves constant awareness and monitoring of both concentration and mindfulness.

Some Buddhist meditation practices focus on concentration relatively more than mindfulness: for example, the kasina practices in which meditators re-create the image of a coloured disc in the mind's eye. Concentration requires both applied and sustained thought, in which our attention is first drawn to an object and then sticks with it.[5]

Education, and many forms of intensive work or other activities, place considerable demands on our concentration. As long as our goals and an obvious sensory object that furthers those goals are connected, we will concentrate on that object, until some other goal or object intervenes. Our body may remind us that it has other needs – that it has run out of glucose or that it needs a change of activity due to discomfort – or the external stimulus may change to make the goal less important compared to others – for example, work has finished and our goals shift to getting home and relaxing. Our capacity for temporarily suppressing other needs or stimuli when necessary, though, can be developed, especially by removing external stimuli and focusing on simple and cognitively undemanding internal objects, as we do in meditation.

---

2   Fox et al. (2005).
3   Fox et al. (2014).
4   *Majjhima Nikaya* 108.26. Ñanamoli and Bodhi (1995) p. 885.
5   Gunaratna (1995).

However, the ubiquity of mobile phones and social media is now creating a worldwide crisis of concentration,[6] with many people checking their phones every few minutes, unable to properly concentrate on any other activity. Without that concentration, our energies cannot be effectively applied to understanding or responding adequately to complex experiences. Deeply worn synaptic channels convey craving and anxiety from the striatum and amygdala at the back of the brain, constantly calling us back from any deeper engagement. We do this not because we get much satisfaction from the trivial rewards or trivial alleviation of anxiety that little hits of positive feedback on social media or games will give us, but because we have sought those little hits so often that it has reconfigured the architecture of our brains. For those old enough to have been brought up before mobile phones, perhaps the damage is limited, but for young people who have never developed the capacity for sustained concentration, the effects may be profound. The destruction of attention impacts our aesthetic experience, our attention to others and hence our relationships, and our capacity for sustained reading, writing, reflection, or thought. It is potentially a disaster for the human capacity for integration, and can only be resolved by sufficient awareness of the longer-term effects of constant attention to phones.

Mindfulness, in contrast to concentration, is not concerned with the goal-driven attention, but rather with our capacity to maintain wider awareness of background experience, and to maintain that awareness over time. Mindfulness is closely related to awareness of the body. The chief sutta of the Pali Canon that explains the practice of mindfulness, the *Satipatthana Sutta*, gives four foundations of mindfulness in the contemplation of body, feelings, mind, and mind-objects.[7] In accordance with embodied meaning, then, mindfulness is built up from bodily experience, using practices such as the mindfulness of breathing, mindful walking, and awareness of the different parts of the body (now generally called body-scanning). Since feelings are felt in the body, awareness of pleasurable and painful sensations follows from that, but wider body awareness should stop us being caught up in absolutisation of those pleasures

---

6 Twenge (2017).
7 *Majjhima Nikaya* 10. Ñanamoli and Bodhi (1995) pp. 145 ff. Also *Digha Nikaya* 22. Walshe (1995) pp. 335 ff.

and pains. Similarly when becoming aware of the mind and its objects, the practitioner can have a wider context in which to place craving, hatred, and delusion.

Mindfulness has a crucial role in integration, because without that wider awareness we cannot access any alternative ways of understanding a particular experience. We can be relentlessly concentrated, and have a highly coherent understanding of what we are experiencing, but completely miss aspects of it because our attention is so goal-driven. The goal-driven nature of our normal attention is well illustrated by the famous 'invisible gorilla' experiment.[8] Here subjects were asked to count the number of passes made in a basketball game, but most of them completely missed a man in a gorilla suit walking into the middle of it. Mindfulness, when maintained in tension with concentration, can make us more peripherally aware, and hence more creative in response to what we experience, as well as more resilient to stress.[9] It is not merely an aesthetic state to be experienced in meditation, but, as Ellen Langer has made clear, just as much a cognitive state affecting our judgement.[10]

The analysis of mindfulness into two parts in Buddhist tradition[11] reveals two aspects of this integrative potentiality. *Sati* is our breadth of awareness at a particular time, including our awareness of our bodies, our mental state, our environment, and others. It is *sati* that Zen masters have traditionally tested by asking disciples which side the door handle was on as one entered the room, or which shoe one had taken off first. The other aspect, though, *sampajana*, is just as important. *Sampajana* is the sustenance of awareness over time, sometimes translated as 'continuity of attention'. It is *sampajana* that might bring us up short when we are falling prey to addictive or compulsive activities, having forgotten our resolve to, for example, only check our phone every hour, or stop eating chocolate. It's at the point when you are about to do these things mindlessly that the wider awareness needs to kick in, together with a wider confidence that connects you to a feeling of well-being that would be broken up by indulgence in the compulsion.

8   Chabris (2011).
9   Haase et al. (2015).
10 Langer (2014).
11 See Nyanaponika (1962) ch. 2 for further traditional analysis.

Sati and *sampajana* are interdependent, but we need both together to be able to avoid absolutisations. We become mindful when we recognise that there are *alternatives* to the belief about something that we are taking for granted. We then don't need to be dominated by a particular goal-driven abstract conception. Concentration by itself can consist only in goal-driven obsession with a particular goal, even though within the framework that it creates some degree of integration is also possible. For example, supposing that I am reading a book, but start to get bored and impatient, constantly leafing forward through it and wishing it was over: this disrupts my concentration, and recollection of my goals in reading it may be enough to get me back on track. I may just force myself to keep reading, suppressing the disruptive feelings so as to reach my goals. However, if I do this I will probably not have dealt with the recurrent reasons why I am feeling bored and impatient. For this I will need mindfulness which is not just focused on the goals of my activity, but also enables me to be aware of my feelings and the conditions that produced them.

Concentration and mindfulness, then, are different features of mental states that need to be held in tension, without one or the other being absolutised as a total solution. We can ensure more adequate awareness and the avoidance of absolutisation in our thinking through mindfulness. However, we also need our mindfulness to be accompanied by goal-driven concentration if it is to be adequate. Although mindfulness creates the potential for integration, without concentration there would be nothing much there to integrate. In order to develop both mindfulness and concentration and hold them in balance, we also need right effort.

Many people associate 'effort' solely with what meditators tend to call *wilful effort*, namely forcing yourself to concentrate in a particular way for particular ends. Wilful effort can also be associated with striving for an idealised view of what we seek, whether in meditation or any other activity. This in turn involves an absolutised representation of the 'right' state of affairs that focuses on this to the exclusion of the actual state of affairs. Wilful effort can thus quickly become self-undermining in meditation, because it leads you to focus exclusively on your goals and neglect the conditions that need to be addressed to reach those goals. In meditation, reaching your goals involves not focusing too narrowly on them, so you are forced to broaden them and gain wider awareness in the process of meditating. Having no goal at all, however (and thus no concentration), is equally lethal to meditation: you are likely to just sit down and drift in a way that involves a mere outward pretence of meditation.

So the lute-strings have to be tuned. One does this, in the process of meditating, by constantly catching oneself slipping into one absolutisation or another. All the hindrances to meditation recognised in the Buddhist tradition[12] involve absolutisations: the belief that I'll be satisfied by sense-desire, the belief that I'll be satisfied by indulging hatred, the belief that anxiety can be allayed by indulging it, the belief that the meditation is not worth focusing my energy on, and the belief that I can't really do meditation (known as 'doubt'). The meditation practice creates a dedicated space for failing to meditate, and then recognising the assumptions that cause one to fail. Thus from each recognition of failure one becomes a little more aware, creating an open rather than a closed feedback loop. On recognising my lapse I can return to the more open middle zone: the zone of awareness with goals held proportionately in relation to each other rather than with one overwhelmingly dominant.

The traditional Buddhist framework of the Four Exertions can also provide an analysis of how that process of using wider awareness to correct your course can extend over time. I have written in more detail elsewhere about how these can be updated so as to be understood as avoiding unintegrated desires, and developing and maintaining integrated ones.[13] Right Effort is very much an application of *sampajana* (as well as wider wisdom). To get a sense of how much effort it is appropriate to apply at a particular time, we also need to be able to anticipate to some extent how far a particular hindrance to our concentration and mindfulness is likely to be disruptive.

In meditation you have to constantly navigate through narrow straits. Through the strait with 'I know how to do this, it's easy' on one side, and 'I can't do this' on the other. Or with 'Just do the practice' on the one side, and 'Be open to your experience, man' on the other. Or with 'I'm not putting up with this nonsense any longer' on one side, and 'Relax and accept this, it's all part of you' on the other. In meditation you find out how anxious you are,

---

12 Thanissaro (2003).
13 Ellis (2013a) ch. 4.a.

how addicted and compulsive your mental states, and how much craving and hatred you have within you. But if you experience all of this as being merely part of your containing body-awareness, not in abstraction as some world-shattering catastrophe, you'll be fine. There is no better direct way to appreciate what the Middle Way is about, and why it needs to be practised at every point of judgement.

Through a regular practice of meditation, it is possible to develop a more regular habit of coming back to the Middle Way, and of maintaining that wider perspective on things. It won't always be there, but the more regularly you practise and the longer you keep doing it, the more reliably that habit is likely to build up. You may (or may not) also develop temporarily integrated states such as *jhana*, which will help to boost your awareness and confidence for the moment, and may also be invested for longer-term benefit. Meditation by itself may not change your wider view on things in the way it needs to be changed to become more adequate, but it can certainly help create important conditions for doing so. When that wider awareness helps your longer-term beliefs to also change, a process of longer-term integration will be well under way.

Meditation, then, like the other elements of the Path, needs the Middle Way to be helpfully understood. We cannot understand what '*right* concentration', '*right* mindfulness', and '*right* effort' are without considering their relationship to each other and also to all the rest of the Path. Meditation is not an end in itself, but it does have a unique immediacy, directness, and power over experience, which makes it probably the best place to start in the practice of the Middle Way. Without an immediate and experiential sense of that balancing process, it is all too easy to absolutise ethics and wisdom.

5.c. The Middle Way in Ethical Practice

In the broad sense of ethical practice (and the starting point for its justification), the Middle Way as a whole is ethical practice. The best way to judge is what will best address the conditions and overcome absolutising delusions. The meditation and wisdom elements of the path are just as much part of that better judgement as the more explicit practice of ethics. I have argued this wider point about the nature of good more fully elsewhere.[1] That the Middle Way is good (and absolutisation evil)[2] in my view represents the universal aspect of Buddhist teaching, once we have avoided the appeal to absolute enlightenment and its effects.

However, there is also a narrower sense of 'ethics' which focuses more explicitly on our behaviour, especially but not exclusively as it affects others, rather than on our mental states, attitudes, or inner judgements. Sangharakshita fairly catches this point when discussing the place of ethics in the Buddhist path:

> The term ethics can be used in two senses, a broader and a narrower. Ethics in the broad sense is the art or science of human conduct and character as possessing value in relation to a standard or ideal.... As such, ethics is more or less identical with religion in its more practical aspect. Ethics in the narrow sense is concerned with external, bodily and vocal behaviour....[3]

There is an interdependence between this narrower sense and broader sense. The narrower sense focuses on the impact of the individual on socio-political integration, whereas the broad sense is also concerned with individual integration. At every stage the conflicts in an individual (and their resolution) and those in society represent and reflect each other: for the 'enemy' in society is represented within the mind of the person who hates, and it is hatred in individuals that creates enmity in society. Our 'enemy' who frustrates our desires is not another person, but the desires of that person insofar as they are contrary to the desires we have at present.

The Eightfold Path in relation to ethics in the narrower sense consists of right action, right speech, and right livelihood, these moral priorities also being analysed in the Five Lay Precepts and

---

1 Ellis (2012) ch. 3.i (and also section 7).
2 Ellis (2015a) ch. 3.n.
3 Sangharakshita (1989) p. 48.

the Ten Precepts. All of these in some ways address conflict by inducing us to follow principles that *generally* reduce or avoid that conflict. The *generally* is importantly distinct from *absolutely*, and to understand Buddhist ethics helpfully we need to leave behind the assumption that ethical principles are necessarily absolute. As Stephen Batchelor writes of the Buddha's ethics:

> *Today we would call it 'situational'. This is an ethics that starts by recognising the complexity and uniqueness of every moral situation and recognising, too, that no Torah-like book of rules is capable of providing a definitive, a priori solution. In facing a moral dilemma, one does not ask 'What is the right thing to do?' as though the answer to the question already exists in an ideal metaphysical space, but rather 'What is the most wise and loving thing to do in this specific instance?'*[4]

The Middle Way is required to interpret each moral principle. On the one hand this avoids the assumption that the principle is an absolute rule. On the other it avoids the negative assumption that there are thereby no morally better actions that could be generally or approximately described by principles. The challenge is to live with the messiness of recognising a small edge of uncertainty even in the case of the biggest moral outrages. In Buddhist tradition, the idea of a precept involves a general rule that one adopts for oneself as an implication of one's commitment to spiritual development. Insofar as it is dependent on that commitment, though, a precept is not an absolute rule.

Right action, as analysed in the Five and the Ten Precepts,[5] involves abstinence from taking life, from taking the not-given, and from sexual misconduct. Positive correlates for each of these can also be offered in the promotion of loving-kindness, generosity, and contentment. The ways in which each of these actions generally avoid conflict and integrate desires, both between and within individuals, should be fairly obvious (except that we so rarely think of conflict as being between desires rather than being between people). If I kill another person, if I harm them physically or mentally, if I steal their property or anything else they value, or if I use power to impose myself on them for sexual gratification, then I am obviously likely to

---

4   Batchelor (2015) p. 223.
5   The Ten Precepts seem to have only been widely used in the Triratna Buddhist Order, but are based on sources in the Pali Canon: see Sangharakshita (1989) pp. 19–30; also *Digha Nikaya* 5.16 and *Majjhima Nikaya* 114.

produce a negative reaction in which I become an object of hatred. I also produce a negative reaction of guilt within myself, for I have overridden my intuitive response to others as worthy of respect.

To recognise others as intuitively worthy of respect is an aspect of our normal embodied experience as human beings. We recognise other persons, and also other living creatures, as distinct from inanimate objects from an early age, using a gestalt process in the right hemisphere of our brains.[6] We are only capable of overriding this intuitive basis of respect for others through the over-dominance of our goal-driven left hemisphere. Military training has to overcome a basic reluctance to kill other persons in order to be successful, but nevertheless some studies have shown that only 15–20 per cent of soldiers on the battlefield actually fire at the enemy.[7]

So it is only through repression of our awareness of others as persons that we are able to kill, harm, steal, and rape. If we can avoid doing so, even if initially only through social motivations, we avoid a potent blockage to integration in the form of guilt. Buddhist tradition helpfully identifies two forms of helpful guilt that are likely to follow if we harm others, called *hiri* ('shame') *and ottappa* ('fear of wrongdoing'): the former involves not living up to one's own expectations, and the latter other people's.[8] By acting in ways that repress our awareness of others as persons, especially without moral awareness or justification, we put ourselves into conflict with our own better inclinations as well as the voices of others within ourselves. In this way we make integration, and thus Middle Way judgement, far more difficult. We are likely to be subject to fragile feelings either of remorse or of overconfidence that continues to repress that remorse.

If on the other hand we can get in touch with our feelings of loving-kindness, empathy, and generosity (and in the process relax the inappropriate use of our competitive instincts) we will support the development of integration. The Buddhist tradition encourages this through the four meditation practices known as the *brahmaviharas* ('abodes of the Gods'): these are the cultivation of loving-kindness (*metta-bhavana*), compassion, sympathetic joy for another's success, and equanimity. In each case we begin by connecting with

---

6 McGilchrist (2010) pp. 54–58.
7 Grossman (1995).
8 *Majjhima Nikaya* 39.3. Ñanamoli and Bodhi (1995) p. 362 and note 416.

kindly feelings towards ourselves and gradually extend them to include neutral people, enemies, and all others. The cultivation of such feelings can get all the parts of ourselves on the same side and thus improve our judgement, as well as more directly helping us to relate to others on an emotionally positive basis.

Right speech on the Eightfold Path involves a similar recognition of others and avoidance of unnecessary conflict. In the Five Lay Precepts, only abstinence from false speech is mentioned, but in the Ten Precepts, three other speech precepts are added: abstinence from harsh, useless, and slanderous speech. The ways in which all these types of speech are generally likely to create conflict with others should be obvious. Sometimes these types of speech may be engaged in with others' approval in some contexts. Nevertheless, they are likely to create conflict in the longer term with those who are lied to, spoken to harshly, gossiped about, or had their time wasted. Those who are affected by unethical speech in this way are likely to conflict externally with the speaker. Beyond this, though, they also have representations within the speaker that give rise to conflict through guilt.

The importance of avoiding 'false' speech raises the question of how we judge what we are saying to be 'true' or 'false' given scepticism. Again, however, 'truth' and 'falsehood' do not need to be interpreted absolutely, and the problems created by 'false' speech are basically ones of conflict. 'False' speech is speech that most other people, and indeed oneself under normal circumstances, are likely to regard as untrue because it does not accord with the 'facts' that they generally accept. Speech is not made 'false' in this way because it is subject to uncertainty, but rather because we have not subjected our statements to a demand for justification. We may also have chosen to ignore the likelihood of very different interpretations because of some narrowed motive. If we are to act in harmony with other people we need to establish a shared basis of assumed beliefs in order to do so, and that basis is disrupted by false speech. Speech that maintains a motive of adequacy is likely to strike a Middle Way between the absolutisations involved in maintaining 'truth'. There will be over-certainty on the one hand, and giving up on the value of justification on the other.

The prioritisation between avoiding false, harsh, useless, and slanderous speech is an issue that is discussed by the Buddha in the *Prince Abhaya Sutta*. Here, though he disavows any speech that is false or useless, the Buddha makes clear that he is prepared to use his own judgement as to when speech that others might interpret as harsh can be justified:

> *'Such speech as the Tathagata [Buddha] knows to be true, correct and beneficial, but which is unwelcome and disagreeable to others: The Tathagata knows the time to make such speech.'*[9]

The simile that the Buddha uses to justify this is one of removing an obstruction from the throat of a choking child.[10] In such circumstances, we can be confident that unwelcome and disagreeable action will actually be beneficial. However, in the case of speech one needs to judge how willing another person is to listen to a point that challenges their view. If there is no possibility of disagreeable speech being helpful then perhaps silence is a better option. Such judgements about the prioritisation of moral principles in speech, then, again need the Middle Way to be interpreted. Just as we can't be certain of the 'truth' of our speech, neither we can absolutely prohibit 'harsh' speech. Nor we can indulge in it indiscriminately.

Judgements as to when speech is beneficial also require a Middle Way judgement, but this time one that is dependent on our judgement of consequences. We might judge that it is beneficial, for example, to speak out about corruption in a workplace. As we don't have a full understanding of the conditions, though, it's also easy to make a mistake about positive or negative consequences. If we blow the whistle, but the judicial system is corrupt and more employees get victimised, our courageous speech may turn out to be in vain. A judgement about how well we understand the conditions also needs to be part of a judgement about speech. We need to avoid an absolute commitment to what might superficially seem to be beneficial speech if it might actually make things worse.

The third limb of the Eightfold Path relating to ethics in the narrow sense is right livelihood. In the Buddha's time, the emphasis in the exposition of right livelihood was on the avoidance of occupations that caused harm (such as trading in weapons or slaves)[11] or that involved other breaches of the Five Precepts. However, right livelihood is also absolutised in the Pali Canon in the superior form

---

9 *Majjhima Nikaya* 58.8. Ñanamoli and Bodhi (1995) p. 500.
10 *Majjhima Nikaya* 58.7, Ñanamoli and Bodhi (1995) p. 499.
11 *Anguttara Nikaya* 5.177. Nyanaponika and Bodhi (1999) p. 142.

of 'supramundane' right livelihood which is not affected by any taints: that is, monastic life.[12] It is evidently only monks who can fully avoid causing harm in their livelihood. Since monks (at least in the Theravada and Early Buddhist model) rely on lay-people to support them, though, this creates an asymmetry that interferes with social integration. In the context of the complexity of modern economies, too, the avoidance of harm or of any other breach of the precepts is no longer an easy criterion to apply. We can try to *minimise* harm, but this may not be the only relevant value to use in judging our livelihoods. If the harm is just done somewhere else down the chain of exchanges, little has been gained.

However, the highlighting of right livelihood in Buddhism shows a recognition of the importance of economic conditions. We cannot just separate economic conditions as an assumed background before we judge our actions. This involves an avoidance of absolute assumptions of free will or determinism in relation to economic activity. We cannot justify any assumption either that we are totally responsible for the economic conditions we operate in, or that we are not responsible for the livelihood we choose. In some circumstances, the options may seem narrow: for example, you might have to choose between an exploitative job in a clothing factory and being unable to feed your children. However, we still make choices within the constraints that we are landed with, even when this is only a choice between evils. To say we 'make a choice' is to recognise that we are aware of different options and have an experience of choosing between them.

Any choices we make about our livelihood are also of great importance to us, because they will greatly condition our habits and development. A job in which no choices and judgements can be made, and thus where there is no sense of responsibility (such as working on a factory production line), can be very stressful, because we are constantly having to repress our wider awareness of other possibilities. This is the alienating effect of much capitalist labour identified by Marx,[13] and such alienation clearly interferes with our integrative development. On the other hand, a creative job involving lots of choices and judgements (such as being an artist or a teacher, or perhaps running one's own business) helps

12 *Majjhima Nikaya* 117.28–33. Ñanamoli and Bodhi (1995) p. 938.
13 'Economic and Political Manuscripts' from Marx (1977) pp. 77 ff.

us to potentially develop greater integration. In such a job our judgements constantly create feedback which gives us an incentive to reflect on those judgements and their adequacy. To some extent, though, simple physical labour can offer similar feedback potential for development when practised mindfully in deliberate avoidance of alienation.

Of course, our choice of livelihood also has a big effect on conflicts in society, beyond that recognised by the Buddha as creating harm. For example, writing for a newspaper (such as the *Daily Mail*) or a website (such as Breitbart), that purveys highly selective or even fake news for manipulative political ends, is probably wrong livelihood. It can only have the effect of exacerbating conflicts in society between groups that assume different starting points and are given no incentive to further investigate the justification of the claims that are being made. In many ways, it would be better to sell simple, physical poison that can be readily identified as dangerous (though disapproved in the Pali Canon) than to sell this kind of metaphorical poison, and if it was done by a monk it would be no better. The avoidance of absolutisations (including biases) that cause conflict gives a much more adequate guide to right livelihood in the modern context than a mere prohibition of certain harmful occupations.

Choices about livelihood, then, involve the complex balancing of various factors. How much does the livelihood encourage absolutisations in myself or in society, whether directly through harm or indirectly through other means? How much does it positively help myself and others to develop greater integration? Taking it seriously as a criterion involves the questioning of economic norms in capitalist society. It is too easy to claim that we 'have no option' but to do a morally dubious or soul-destroying job, and accept the wielding of economic power over our mental states without criticism. The Buddha's Middle Way when used to help interpret right livelihood can prod us to wake up to these pressing issues, alongside other moral issues, that are so important in our everyday environment.

5.d. The Middle Way of Wisdom

The final two 'limbs' of the Noble Eightfold Path to be considered are right view and right aspiration. The translations of both of these limbs are highly varied, in ways that illustrate the difficulties of interpretation. *Samma ditthi* has been translated as 'right vision', 'right view', or 'right understanding'. *Samma sankappa* has been rendered as 'right emotion', 'right aspiration', 'right intention', or 'right resolve'. In the first, the metaphor of sight for many has a strong association with knowledge of abstract doctrine, but that may be misleading. If you understand right view as entirely abstracted, this may have the further effect of starving right aspiration of cognitive elements, as though it was just about doing an emotional 'catch up' with a definitive intellectual understanding of how things should be. In practice, though, right view and right aspiration are interdependent, indeed scarcely distinguishable, in the same way that 'reason' and 'emotion' are in practice scarcely distinguishable. Both are ways of labelling responses to experience that in turn go on to shape that experience further, and both can be relatively more or less wise and more or less deluded, as judged by a standard of adequacy to conditions.

Though right view is often explained in terms of knowing and accepting a set of Buddhist doctrines,[1] such an emphasis on 'knowledge' may in many cases support absolute interpretation. It may thus interfere with integrative practice. It is also theoretically believed that the enlightened have 'no view',[2] but the appeal to this perspective can very easily be used in a selective, ad hoc fashion to oppose only those views one disagrees with. The whole idea of an ultimate 'no view' seems to be the result of the discontinuity imposed by belief in absolutised enlightenment, so that it is assumed all views are absolute. It's only if all views are absolute that anyone going beyond those absolutisations must have no view at all. But going beyond absolutisation is an everyday occurrence, whenever we consider alternatives that we did not previously consider.

The Buddha in practice obviously had views about all sorts of things. Much better sense can be made of the concept of right view by interpreting it as *provisional view* and the *avoidance of absolute view*,

---

1 *Majjhima Nikaya* 9. Ñanamoli and Bodhi (1995) pp. 132 ff.
2 *Sutta Nipata* 5.3. Saddhatissa (1985) p. 92.

in other words the Middle Way. Everybody who is embodied has a view, but if we are to maintain our view in acknowledgement of the fact of that embodiment, we must do so along with a recognition of possible alternatives. However, the fact that the Middle Way never seems to be even mentioned in most Buddhist expositions of right view suggests how little this point is appreciated.

The Buddha's discourse with Kaccanagotta may offer a glimpse of a Middle Way focused understanding of right view:

> 'This world, Kaccana, is for the most part shackled by engagement, clinging, and adherence. But this one [with right view] does not become engaged and cling through that engagement and clinging, mental standpoint, adherence, underlying tendency; he does not take a stand about "my self".'[3]

Here the Pali terms translated as 'mental standpoint', 'adherence', and 'underlying tendency' (explored by Bodhi in a footnote) can be readily understood as combining desire and belief in entrenched synaptic paths that lead us to think only in certain well-worn terms. It is thus crucial for anyone cultivating right view to do so by involving wider awareness that stimulates the right hemisphere as well as the cognitive centres of the left.

Sangharakshita makes a similar point with reference to right view:

> I have found that students of Buddhism often think that Right Understanding...means making a study of the whole of Buddhist thought.... But really it is not like that at all.... It is a vision, and as such something direct and immediate, and more of the nature of a spiritual experience than an intellectual understanding. Of course the experience, the insight, can be expressed intellectually, in terms of doctrinal concepts...but it is not identical with these.[4]

However, Sangharakshita's account could equally give us an impression of an overwhelming 'commissioning' experience that sets us out on the path. It is not a question of having a single experience that can be unambiguously understood to reveal the truth of the path to enlightenment. Nor is it a question of 'understanding' a list of traditional formulations. Rather, right view involves a combination of intuitive, cognitive, and emotive engagement with the Middle Way as a method and direction. We get enough of a

---

3 *Samyutta Nikaya* 12.15. Bodhi (2000) p. 544.
4 Sangharakshita (1990a) p. 22.

sense of that method for it to inspire confidence and thus to set out on the path, and this confidence is then often given further support by subsequent experience. Incrementality needs to be a key part of the way we understand and communicate right view.

'Right view', then, cannot possibly consist of simply absorbing a set of traditional Buddhist doctrines, as it is normally presented. The right view consists in the most adequate set of beliefs in any given situation, even amongst those who have never heard of formal Buddhism or its doctrines. The most adequate set of beliefs is the one that allows us to consider the largest possible range of alternatives that are compatible with a situation (with our psychological capacities, as well as the externalities, recognised as aspects of the situation). This ensures that we are not limited by absolutising our current set of assumptions. It is the provisionality of the view that makes it 'right' rather than its content. Thus a scientist considering alternatives to a cherished theory, a husband reconsidering the irrational jealousy he has had towards his wife, or even a Buddhist reconsidering her understanding of the doctrines she identifies with so much – all can have right view simply by avoiding absolutised view and allowing a certain messiness into the frame. In some circumstances a traditionally Buddhist 'right view' may be a wrong view, because it has been absolutised.

In other circumstances, though, the Buddhist doctrines may indeed help someone to identify right view. For example, reflecting on impermanence may make someone aware that their assumption that another person or thing would always be fixed in their present form was inadequate. I will be saying more about the interpretation of impermanence, together with that of other traditional Buddhist doctrines, in chapter 6.b. With all such doctrinal 'views', however, their helpfulness depends on using the Middle Way to interpret them, rather than using some absolute version of them to interpret the Middle Way. Right view puts the Middle Way first by constantly applying its method.

The relationship between right view and right aspiration is like that between belief and desire: each always implies the other. We articulate our desires in terms of beliefs about desirable objects and the conditions of their attainment, and we hold beliefs because it accords with our desires to do so. In between, mediating the two, is meaning – that is, the associative links we have available to consider alternative, possible beliefs. Provisionality depends on having a range of meaning available to us in any given situation, so that various possible alternative beliefs might be constructed. Enough energy needs to be given to the imagination, which explores those alternatives, rather than only flowing down the accustomed channels of belief. We aspire rightly when we value those imaginative alternatives, and can maintain a view that helps us keep them open.

Remaining *inspired* in following the path depends not just on having 'beliefs' about the true path that we then have to find 'emotional equivalents' for.[5] Rather it's a matter of the most integrative beliefs being also attached to new meanings that are also attached to new desires. The practical value of Buddhist beliefs does not consist in an abstract relationship to 'truth', but rather in the ways that they can stimulate provisionality and thus integration. Provisionality consists of the availability of new meanings, and if we can gain access to those new meanings, hitherto repressed or neglected, we are likely to find that they bring emotional energy with them.

Buddhists often recommend the cultivation of 'right aspiration' or 'right emotion' through the use of the *brahma-vihara* meditations (which cultivate positive emotion) and of devotional practices.[6] What is interesting about both of these, when more closely examined, is that they both consist (when effective) of bringing our experience into contact with new and wider meaning, and they do not depend on specific culturally Buddhist content.

The *brahma-vihara* meditations involve the cultivation of the positive emotions of loving-kindness (*metta*), compassion, sympathetic joy, and equanimity in a systematic way in meditation through the bringing of awareness to the positive emotion we find in experience. The technique is generally to begin by focusing attention on people we can easily feel positive towards (such as ourselves or a good friend), and then to gradually expand this feeling to be directed towards everyone else, including those one regards as enemies.[7] This type of meditation is often seen as working with emotion, which it is, but it is also simultaneously working with the *meaning* of each person in our experience. It opens up that meaning from a narrow set of assumptions to a wider one. For example, if

---

5   Ibid. p. 36.
6   Ibid. pp. 46–58.
7   Details are given in the *Visuddhimagga*. Ñanamoli (1991) ch. 9.

I recognise that my hated boss, who is also a family man, is kind to his children, the meaning of my boss is expanded in a way that may allow me to judge him differently in future. Is this a 'cognitive' process or an 'emotional' one? It is obviously both, and its significance consists not in that categorisation, but in the way in which it encourages provisionality in our basic responses to others. It is this breadth of meaning that might also *inspire* me to practise differently in my relation to these people.

Devotional practice is another area that is often seen as 'emotional'. Again, though, its positive significance is not best seen by dividing 'doctrine' from 'worship' and seeing the latter as helping us somehow finding an 'emotional equivalent' for the former. Devotional activities may inspire us by reminding us of symbols that we strongly associate with that inspiration. It also strengthens those associations through bodily activities such as singing, reciting, bowing, or making offerings. But what is it that leads us to associate those symbols with that inspiration? Only associative experience that needs to be developed through embodied meaning and metaphor can give the Buddha, or whatever other symbol we are using, that kind of power. The outward forms that we come to associate with are contingent: it could be a Buddha that stirs us, or it could be a tree, or sunlight reflected in a puddle. But such associations will have a particular power to inspire us if they fulfil our psychological needs in particular ways.

It is here that the concept of archetype can come into its own. An archetype is a symbolic function, rooted into a particular relationship with our bodily energies through a set of associations that are boosted by that function.[8] The function of the Middle Way, which is that of opening up alternatives, is the one that is labelled by Jung as the Self or God Archetype, though in Buddhist terms it could just as well be called the Awakening or Enlightenment Archetype. This archetype is not a supernatural entity in the universe, but rather a glimpse of a potential greater integration with vaguely realised wider perspectives in our own experience. Sometimes, through what might be labelled religious experience, meditative experience, or flashes of insight, we recognise that we could be a lot bigger than we are. With that recognition often comes a flash of energy, and a sense of the potential greater meaningfulness of

---

8 For a more detailed discussion, see Ellis (2013b) section 4.

the world we experience. Whatever symbols we use to embody that archetype may serve, through association, to inspire us with a wider awareness of that potentiality.

Right aspiration or right emotion, then, can indeed be cultivated by devotional practice, as it can by a range of other practices. However, that devotional practice does not have an essential form, and does not have to be culturally Buddhist. Association with the archetype might just as well come from an association through another religious tradition such as Christianity, or from art, or from what we often call 'the natural world' – i.e. a sense of awe that we associate with landscapes, plants, and animals. Again, the method is best practised by not absolutising its specific application in Buddhist tradition, but by recognising that method as a universal one that can be instantiated in particular Buddhist contexts.

As we have seen with the rest of the Eightfold Path, then, it is indeed the Middle Way. Every single limb of the path needs to be interpreted in terms of the Middle Way and gains its value in those terms. Given the universality of the Middle Way, the Eightfold Path also needs to be interpreted with a similar universality. Every single application of it is contingent, so by taking such applications to be necessary or sufficient, we betray the path itself. Nevertheless, if a particular traditional Buddhist application of the path is understood in these thoroughly universal terms, there is nothing wrong with the use of traditional forms themselves. These forms have often helped to preserve a more universal implicit sense through the ages.

6. Interpreting Buddhist Teachings

6.a. Conditionality

There have already been a number of mentions of my suggestions for the interpretation of traditional Buddhist teachings. In this section, though, I will aim to clarify and consolidate them, addressing traditional Buddhist concerns. In some respects, my message is simple throughout: that Buddhist teachings are helpful insofar as they are interpreted in accordance with the Middle Way, and unhelpful if they are not. Conditionality, the Four Noble Truths, the Three Marks of Conditioned Existence, the Eightfold Path, karma and rebirth, Going for Refuge and the institution of monasticism can all be interpreted in this way. That is why I have begun with the Middle Way and not with other teachings that Buddhists more commonly cite as starting points. It may be that, after reading this section, you disagree with my particular conclusions about how to prioritise the Middle Way. But the bigger point is simply that it should be prioritised, because our understanding of the method precedes that of its application, however you understand that it should be done.

Conditionality (*paticcasamuppada* – also translated as 'conditioned co-production', or 'dependent co-arising', or 'dependent origination') is often said to be the most basic insight of the Buddha, and is often given as the basis of the Middle Way. It is said that we can accept neither the self-existence of objects, nor their nonexistence, because their existence is dependent on all other phenomena. For example, when asked questions about the ultimate nature of the self or the universe, the Buddha 'teaches the Dhamma by the middle' by instead pointing to these things as conditioned.[1]

As I have already argued in chapter 4.b, this emphasis on the conditionality of objects rather than the limitations of our judgements seems to be a product of the ontological obsession.

---

1 *Samyutta Nikaya* 12.35 and 12.48. Bodhi (2000) pp. 574, 584–5.

There is no necessity to offer any claims about the nature of all possible phenomena in order to practise the Middle Way. It is difficult to see how claims about the conditionality of all phenomena are more justified than other metaphysical claims that the Buddha avoided. After all, we are no more in a position to determine whether everything we might possibly encounter in the universe is conditioned than we are to ascertain whether or not it has a first cause or an end-point in space. It is also difficult to see how holding beliefs about the conditionality of all phenomena has any practical value that the practice of provisionality in relation to each judgement about them does not. But why have so many Buddhists through the ages apparently found the doctrine of conditionality so helpful and insightful? This can be readily explained by seeing conditionality as a placeholder for provisionality, where some of the features of provisionality are associated with the idea of conditionality. Beliefs about conditionality have the potential to be useful, but only insofar as they actually impact our judgements.

The Buddha's famous words to Ananda about conditionality can cut both ways:

> The Venerable Ananda came to the Lord...and said 'It is wonderful, Lord, it is marvellous how profound this dependent origination is, and how profound it appears! And yet it appears to me as clear as clear!'

> 'Do not say that, Ananda, do not say that! This dependent origination is profound and appears profound. It is through not understanding, not penetrating this doctrine that this generation has become like a tangled ball of string, covered as with a blight, tangled like coarse grass, unable to pass beyond states of woe, the ill destiny, ruin and the round of birth-and-death.'[2]

I have often had this passage quoted to me by Buddhists, with an assumed appeal to authority and tradition, whenever I dared to question any traditional assumption about conditionality. But it may not just be those who question Buddhist tradition who are in Ananda's position. It may also be Buddhist tradition itself that assumes it has got it clear, but has instead turned it into a tangled ball of string. If the doctrine is practical in intention, it needs to be consistent with the sceptical recognition that our knowledge of any specific relationships between conditions is limited. Generalisations about such conditional relationships also need to be such as take

---

2   *Digha Nikaya* 15.1. Walshe (1995) p. 223.

into account our degree of ignorance. Yes, there do seem to be conditions, or 'facts' out there that impact on us in unexpected ways. However, any attempt to generalise about them that leaves out our own role in understanding and assessing those conditions is liable to grave misunderstanding.

For our understanding and judgement are part of the conditions, and are the first things whose conditionality we need to take into account. In many ways Buddhist teachings emphasise this. The five aggregates (*skandha*s)[3] that give us the impression of a self also give us the impression of an object: form, feeling, perception, volitional formation, and consciousness are all aspects of our experience. They are all also conditioned in ways that prevent any of them offering a necessary representation of reality. In the classic list of twelve *nidana*s (links of conditionality) used on the outer ring of the Wheel of Samsara, the first nine emphasise the conditional relationships between different elements that give rise to our judgements: ignorance, volitional formations, consciousness, name and form, the senses, contact, feeling, craving, and grasping.[4] For example, my belief that my neighbour is contemptible is conditioned by the limitations of my own view, my previous judgements that have tended in that direction, my slight headache, the way the neighbour appears and is labelled, the limited ways my sight and hearing have been able to perceive him, the limited contact I've had with him, the ways in which I've found those experiences unpleasant, my desire not to have to engage with him (hatred), and the steps I've taken to avoid doing so. My judgement is, to put it mildly, not merely a 'truth' about something I've just perceived that is 'really there'.

Buddhist teachings about conditionality can thus contribute towards scepticism, and so towards provisionality, by helping to make us aware of the specific conditions that affect our judgement. They also make us aware of the conditions that may have affected the object we are judging, so as to discourage us from absolutising our view of it. They also provide resources to help us reflect on the limitations of the conceptual boundaries that we impose, thus encouraging incrementality. Reflecting on the conditioned relationship between supposed opposites, and the ways in which they actually depend on each other, can similarly be helpful in

---

3 *Samyutta Nikaya* 22.48. Bodhi (2000) p. 886.
4 *Samyutta Nikaya* 12.65. Bodhi (2000) p. 601.

supporting agnosticism and integration. So, there is indeed a close link between the practice of the Middle Way and reflections on aspects of conditionality. However, that the Middle Way is not simply conditionality itself can be readily seen from the ways that the concept of conditionality can be absolutised, and thus become contrary to the Middle Way.

One way in which it can be absolutised, which I have already mentioned, is to take conditionality as a theory about the universe. In its most general form it is expressed thus:

> *This being, that is; from the arising of this, that arises; this not being, that is not; from the cessation of this, that ceases.*[5]

What this effectively asserts is that every phenomenal object is necessarily dependent (at least in the form we understand it) on other objects. But we have no knowledge of the basis on which to claim this as *necessary* rather than just to offer it as a provisional theory.

Another way that conditionality can be absolutised is to adopt specific instances of it as general truths, which is what seems to have occurred with the twelve *nidanas* (ignorance, volitional formations, consciousness, name and form, the senses, contact, feeling, craving, grasping, becoming, birth, and death). These twelve links have become the basis of the standard Buddhist doctrine of conditionality, even though there are many other versions at different points in the Pali Canon with different numbers of links.[6] The traditional interpretation of these links is authoritatively stated in Buddhaghosa's *Path of Purification*.[7] It divides the links up into two sets of causal and resultant phases, with ignorance and volitional formations as causes in this life, resulting in the effects of consciousness, name and form, the senses, contact, and feeling in this life. These then give rise to the causes of craving, grasping, and becoming in this life, which karmically result in birth and death in future lives. This absolutises in several ways. It rigidifies an account of interdependent conditions into a single prescribed order and form of explanation. It brings rebirth in as a necessary part of the account (see chapter 6.e below). It also rigidifies the causal phases as necessarily prior

---

5   *Udana* 1.3. Ireland (1990) p. 13.
6   Jones (2011) p. 62. *Samyutta Nikaya* 12. *Digha Nikaya* 15.
7   Ñanamoli (1991) ch. 17.

to judgement (and thus determined once past judgement has been made) and the resultant phases as necessarily after it (and thus a matter of responsibility).

Recognition of the final problem was one of the most striking contributions to Buddhist thought made by Ñanavira Thera, an English Theravada monk living in Sri Lanka who questioned the traditional model of the twelve *nidanas*. Ñanavira criticised the rigidity of the distinction between feeling and craving, according to which we must be unable to influence the pleasant or unpleasant nature of our feelings in the present:

> To hold the view that whatever a man experiences, pleasant, unpleasant, or neutral, is due to past acts, is to adopt a form of determinism making present action futile – one is a killer on account of past acts, a thief on account of past acts, and so on.... If...the pleasant feeling that I experience when I indulge in lustful thoughts is the vipaka [result] of some past kamma [karma], then I have no present responsibility in the matter and can now do nothing about it. But I know from my own experience that this is not so; if I choose to enjoy pleasure by thinking lustful thoughts I can do so, and I can also choose (if I see good reason) to refrain from thinking such thoughts.[8]

In effect Ñanavira is pointing out that craving conditions feeling just as feeling conditions craving, even though this would involve reversing the traditional order. Such a recognition also puts into question the traditional belief that the opportunity to prevent another round of conditionality lies between feeling and craving. Often it does: if I can feel a desire or an aversion that's in danger of becoming obsessive, but manage to hold it in a wider awareness so that it is not absolutised, that is where practice starts to make an impression. However, our level of awareness might also make a difference to what we attend to (contact), how it feels, or whether we act on our craving by grasping. Judgement may be required at any of these points, and we cannot assume the traditional analysis to be the last word.

The problem should by now be becoming a familiar one. A universal insight that concerns the way in which we make judgements is recognised by the Buddha, but expressed in a specific way, relevant to the conditions of the time, in early Buddhism. One specific way of expressing the insight then becomes rigidified: it becomes 'Buddhist doctrine'. In the case of the twelve *nidanas*, it is

---

8   Ñanavira (1987) p. 18.

also reinforced by its use in the Wheel of Samsara pictures, which are used as models of instruction. The specific teaching then gets mistaken for the universal insight. When Buddhism encounters very different conditions (in the West, or in the modern world generally) it is then no longer in the most helpful form. Even those Western teachers who are prepared to make some changes in the way they present Buddhist doctrine to suit modern audiences do not go so far as to identify the underlying insight in its most universal form. Thus they do not completely separate it from the specific doctrines that are now a major stumbling-block to understanding the insight. Instead, they may assume that the specific doctrines only have to be understood correctly by a little more effort on the part of those corrupted by the modern world.

Amongst such Western teachers, Sangharakshita can be distinguished for having identified and promoted the *positive nidanas* or 'spiral path'. These offer a formulation of the recognition that conditionality can also be turned to positive effect. The twelve positive links are prompted initially by the recognition of *dukkha* (frustration), which turns the closed feedback loop of the wheel of conditionality into an open one. When we recognise that there is a problem with the self-feeding, obsessive cycle by which our absolutisations create the conditions for their own perpetuation, there is a window of opportunity. Wider conditions can then be allowed to help modify our closed loop. The twelve positive links that then follow are given as faith, gladness, rapture, tranquillity, happiness, concentration, knowledge and vision of things as they really are, revulsion, dispassion, liberation, and destruction of the taints.[9]

It is helpful to point out that conditionality has positive as well as negative effects. However, the sequence of twelve positive links is no more a necessary description of a process of spiritual development than the sequence of twelve negative links is a necessary description of the closed process of absolutisation. The links do identify some of the signs of progress (with the exception of the dubious metaphysics of 'knowledge and vision of things as they really are'). Integrated energies create positive emotion, and awareness of former limited perspectives leads us to distance ourselves from them. However, those signs do not have to occur in this order, nor to condition each

---

9   *Samyutta Nikaya* 12.23. Bodhi (2000) pp. 553–6. Also see Jones (2011) ch. 4 and Sangharakshita (1987) pp. 135–42.

other anything like as neatly as this scheme suggests. If we were to place any value on this scheme, it should only be as an indicator of one out of many possible ways of thinking about the way that recognition of wider conditions can impact us helpfully.

When we are already thinking in provisional terms, reflections on conditionality offer a helpful way of exploring the phenomenal relationships between apparent objects in the world we have constructed. Conditionality can point to interdependence, and if our models take into account interdependence more fully, they can be more adequate. Such reflections on interdependence have a fruitful link with systems theory and complexity theory, as explored by Joanna Macy[10] (see chapter 7.f). However, all too often it seems that awareness of conditionality in Buddhism has been a placeholder or partial substitute for provisionality. Western Buddhists, perhaps taking the provisionality of Western education and science for granted, have either projected it onto Buddhist conditionality, or replaced it by specific formulations of conditionality that then become dogmas.

Appealing to conditionality as a universal 'truth' of the universe will not help us when we are caught up in the confirmation bias of a restricted view. When we are not taking into account conditions that we really need to face up to, such abstractions do not help. Only the recognition of the limitations of our view, and a recognition of possible alternatives, will help us then, not adherence to traditional formulae. To make sure that conditionality is not interpreted in this way, it is clear that Buddhists need to practise the Middle Way as a prior condition of its interpretation. The leading emphasis also needs to be on the conditioning effects of their embodied limitations on their own beliefs.

10 Macy (1991).

6.b. The Three Marks of Conditioned Existence

The next few chapters will be concerned with the first three of the Four Noble Truths, or Four Tasks, that have already been discussed in chapter 2.b in relation to the Buddha's First Address. Here is the traditional form of the Four Noble Truths as given in the First Address, in Bodhi's translation:

1. *The noble truth of suffering...the five aggregates subject to clinging are suffering.*
2. *The noble truth of the origin of suffering: it is this craving which leads to renewed existence....*
3. *The noble truth of the cessation of suffering...it is the remainderless falling away and cessation of that same craving.*
4. *The noble truth of the way leading to the cessation of suffering: it is this Noble Eightfold Path....*[1]

However, the Four Tasks as I would prefer to paraphrase them would be something like this:

1. Recognise the inadequacy that results from closed feedback loops in our experience.
2. Avoid the absolutisations that create these closed loops.
3. Realise the possibility of greater adequacy through alternatives.
4. Develop integrative practices that help to cultivate that greater adequacy.

It is the gap between these accounts of the Four Tasks that will be my theme. The fourth one has already been discussed in section 5, but it remains to look more closely at how the traditional Buddhist account of the first three needs to be reinterpreted.

In all four of them, to maintain congruence with the Middle Way we should not talk about general 'truths' that could be easily mistaken for absolutes. Rather we should make generalisations about the ways in which we understand and respond to our experience as human beings. Those responses are not 'true' or 'false', because they always need to be under review so can never be presumed to be either. Rather they are incrementally adequate or inadequate according to how far they are capable of responding to new conditions that we experience.

In the first 'task', it is not *dukkha* as a generalised 'suffering' that is the problem to be addressed. Rather it is closed feedback loops with

---

1 *Samyutta Nikaya* 56.11. Bodhi (2000) p. 1844.

their tendency to produce inadequately fixed patterns of judgement despite changing conditions. In the second 'task', if we describe the cause of the problem as 'craving', there is much danger of damning desire itself: but it is absolutisation that distinguishes craving (and aversion) from sustainable desire. In the third 'task', we do not need a complete cessation of such absolutisation to get greater adequacy, but only to be able to consider alternatives that may break the closed feedback loops. Thus the path needs to help us gain greater adequacy through provisionality and integration, not to necessarily result in 'cessation'.

To investigate the first of these tasks more fully in this chapter, then, we need to look at the interpretation of the three marks of conditioned existence. In traditional Buddhist teaching these offer an analysis of the First Noble Truth. These three marks are *dukkha* (suffering/frustration/inadequacy), *anicca* (impermanence), and *anatta* (no-self/non-substantiality). The Buddhist tradition tends to interpret these marks as cosmic laws, when they can be much more helpfully seen as features of the closed feedback loops we encounter in our experience.

As suggested already in chapter 2.b, *dukkha* is a term that captures the general effects of absolutisation. Because Buddhists so often present it as something about 'existence' itself being bad or at least unsatisfactory, it puzzled me for a long time from my earliest acquaintance with Buddhism. Why should we see everything as intrinsically bad, I thought, as opposed to seeing it as intrinsically good? In order to even make sense of some things as being bad or unsatisfactory, others need to be good by contrast. If we consult our experience, it also obviously contains a mixture of good and bad, of satisfaction and dissatisfaction. To emphasise the negative as the essential feature of that experience would be a failure of even-handedness and thus a betrayal of the Middle Way. We could only imagine the phenomenal world to be intrinsically bad by having an unrealistic expectation that it would be perfectly good in the first place – and thus that there was something 'wrong' with the presence of any suffering or unsatisfactoriness. This would be an example of what is known as the 'nirvana fallacy': an unnecessarily negative view of something because it fails to live up to standards of perfection.

However, the concept of *dukkha* does not have to be interpreted in this way, and there are indications even within the tradition that it should not be. The term has been associated by some commentators with 'a badly fitting chariot wheel':

> Su *and* dus *are prefixes indicating good or bad. The word* kha, *in later Sanskrit meaning 'sky,' 'ether,' or 'space,' was originally the word for 'hole,' particularly an axle hole of one of the Aryan's vehicles. Thus* sukha...*meant, originally, 'having a good axle hole,' while* duhkha *meant 'having a poor axle hole,' leading to discomfort.*[2]

In these terms, *dukkha* thus turns out to be a traceable metaphor originating from a specific type of unsatisfactory experience, which occurs in relation to specific goals. Those goals could be widened, as long as they are not absolutised, so that *dukkha* means a tendency to interfere with the attainment of goals: in other words, inadequacy. A badly fitting chariot wheel is an inadequate chariot wheel, just as an absolute belief – such as that eating will always make me feel better if I feel upset – is inadequate. Such inadequacy has an entirely contingent relationship with 'suffering', because suffering may or may not be an indication of inadequacy (like disease, it may just be a sign of other conditions). Nor will I always find inadequacy unpleasant: for example, sexual misconduct may feel very pleasant at the time, but it is problematic because it is inadequate to the wider conditions such as my longer-term relationships. The inadequacy, and thus the 'suffering', may only emerge over time, or be evident in a repressed sense of guilt at the decisive moment.

The confusion of this kind of inadequacy with a cosmic law is probably due to the need to reconcile it with karma and rebirth beliefs in the time of the Buddha. The Buddha's explanation of *dukkha* in the First Address emphasises it being part of a cosmic system in which our very existence is the result of it: 'Birth is suffering, ageing is suffering, illness is suffering...'[3] etc. However, anyone who has experienced or studied birth, ageing, or illness will be aware that whether these phenomena are unpleasant, or even unsatisfactory, to us, depends entirely on the entrenched assumptions we make about them. They amount to new conditions that *could* cause us suffering, in the literal sense, if we fail to adapt to them. Ellen Langer, for example, has completed studies that show how much the negative effects of ageing can be allayed by 'mindfulness' – in her wider

---

2   Sargeant (2009) p. 303.
3   *Samyutta Nikaya* 56.11. Bodhi (2000) p. 1844.

sense of being able to make novel distinctions and choices rather than being caught in closed feedback loops of thinking.[4]

A more fruitful element of the Buddha's account of *dukkha* is that 'the five aggregates subject to clinging are suffering'. This makes it clearer that the First Noble Truth can only be properly understood in necessary relationship to the second. If we take any aspect of our experience of ourselves (or of objects) and absolutise it, then we will experience a conflict or disjunction that is due to inadequacy. Once again, though, we need to make decisive use of the Middle Way to help us critically sort the doctrine as traditionally presented.

The associated concept of *anicca* (impermanence) needs similarly careful interpretation. It is very often interpreted as a cosmic truth, but we have no way of knowing whether or not all phenomena are impermanent. Whether an object is permanent or impermanent for practical purposes in relation to our experience also tends to depend on how we analyse it. An oft-cited example comes from the pre-Socratic philosopher Heraclitus, who claimed that a river shows essential impermanence because new waters are always flowing in.[5] But this depends on where we place our attention in relation to the river: is it to the atoms and molecules of water that are changing in a particular spot, or to the fact that water of some kind continues? Do we turn our attention to the banks that define the river, or the content between the banks? Parmenides, who made the opposite argument that impermanence is illusory,[6] offers an equally speculative metaphysical argument that takes contingent features of our categorisation and assumes they must define some sort of reality. For him the *idea* of the 'river' is real, even if the experience is not.

A more persuasive practical argument for impermanence is suggested by the discussions of it in the Pali Canon. For example take the following:

> *When a monk often entertains the perception of impermanence, his mind shrinks away from gain, honour and praise, turns back from them...and either equanimity or revulsion towards them is established in him.... It is for this reason that it was said 'The perception of impermanence, when developed and cultivated, is of great fruit and benefit....'*[7]

4 Langer (2010).
5 Plato, *Cratylus* 402a. Reeve (1998).
6 Parmenides, *On Nature*. Curd (2011).
7 *Anguttara Nikaya* 7.46 (5). Nyanaponika and Bodhi (1999) p. 182.

Here we are *not* told that impermanence is a metaphysical truth. Instead we are told that if we train ourselves into noticing it (as opposed to assuming permanence) then we are less likely to develop absolutising attachments to our achievements. For example, I might feel satisfaction at the social affirmation involved in having my book praised by someone whose opinion I value. The reflection that this praise is likely to be succeeded in my changing experience by negative criticism or indifference might then help me to put it into a wider perspective of awareness. The praise does not cease to be valuable as praise, but it does need to be put into perspective.

However, it is this perspective that is the valuable element here, the element that may make reflections on impermanence useful to us. What is helpful is a bigger temporal perspective, of the kind that may be employed to try to avoid a range of temporal biases in which we focus on past, present, or future to the exclusion of a wider awareness of time.[8] For example, status quo bias involves resistance to change and attachment to the past at the expense of the present and future. Neomania (such as obsession with buying the latest gadgets) involves attachment to a conception of the future without the perspective offered by the past (where there is a history of once-new gadgets quickly becoming obsolete). A bigger temporal perspective may often involve an awareness of impermanence, leading us to pan out into a bigger time-frame. However, there are also some occasions when it may involve awareness of relative permanence as opposed to relative impermanence. For example, if I am impatient to change a situation such as listening to a bore or being stuck in traffic, what I need to do to adapt to the conditions is to become more accepting of the inescapable *persistence* of those conditions.

The third mark of conditioned existence is *anatta*, most commonly translated as not-self, but probably better rendered as non-substantiality, given its implications for objects as well as the subject. The Pali Canon accounts make it clear that the Buddha's teaching is not just to deny the existence of an ultimate self, but rather not to affirm either an ultimate self or its absence.[9] The purpose of the five aggregates formula is to wean us off belief in a self, given that none of the aggregates – form, feeling, perception,

8 See Ellis (2015a) ch. 3.j for more detailed discussion.
9 *Samyutta Nikaya* 44.10. Bodhi (2000) pp. 1393–5.

volitional formations, or consciousness – should be identified with the self.[10] However, since each of these aggregates is also the focus of belief in a given ultimate object, it also seems clear that *anatta* should apply to objects just as much. A 'thing' is not a piece of matter, or an object of feeling, perception, choice, or consciousness. Rather a 'thing' needs to be recognised as our own construction, selected from the complexity of conditions for our own purposes.

The doctrine of *anatta* is a clear application of agnosticism to metaphysical claims, and thus of the Middle Way. It is only if we continue to misunderstand the implications of scepticism (see chapter 4.a), that we could possibly turn it into a denial of anything, or argue that it is potentially 'nihilistic'. Unlike *dukkha* and *anicca*, it is balanced in its whole conception. Thus any Buddhist who claims to take *anatta* seriously should take the Middle Way seriously, as all the absolutisations avoided by the Middle Way are also recognised as avoidable in the doctrine of *anatta*.

As with any belief that we can justify through experience, though, beliefs about the self can take provisional or absolute forms. I can have a view of myself that is open to revision because it consists in incremental qualities, and I can thus adjust that view of myself in the light of new experience. To take a simple example, I might have a deluded view of myself as highly intelligent, but then take an IQ test and find that it shows me to be not as intelligent as I thought. If I'm capable of responding to that new evidence, at least by reflecting and investigating further, then my view of myself will have shown itself to be provisional in that respect. If, however, I immediately assume that the IQ test must be wrong, it is more likely that the self-view I am working on is absolute (and thus ultimate and metaphysical). The implication of *anatta*, like that of the Middle Way in general, then, is not that we should not have any beliefs about the self, only that those views should be provisional. For them to be provisional, they need to be justifiable by experience rather than formed on the basis of absolutisations.

In contrast, Buddhists seem to have spent a long time arguing about matters that entirely miss the point behind *anatta*, such as whether the Buddha intended that there is no self, or whether there is a true self that can be reached by avoiding the false self,

---

10 *Samyutta Nikaya* 22.1. Bodhi (2000) pp. 854–6.

as in various Hindu schools.[11] Once again, we need to interpret the doctrine on the basis of the Middle Way rather than putting some other version of it first and interpreting the Middle Way in its terms. From an embodied perspective, the self is not a disembodied abstraction, but an experience of inhabiting a complete human body. That experience is gradually differentiated by a unique set of meanings as we make billions of associative connections.

It's worth recognising that for some other groups (such as Jungians) 'self' can actually mean a highly integrated standpoint. For them it can be a way of talking about a glimpsed end-point in which the different parts of ourselves have integrated by recognising the limitations of their attached assumptions. In these contexts, 'self' is an archetype (see chapter 6.e below), and such archetypes can be discussed in a provisional way. However, any such talk will fall foul of the spirit of *anatta*, and of the Middle Way, as soon as it slips into an assumption that we have sufficient access to such a self to 'know' its perspective. That would be an appropriation and projection of the self-archetype.

Anatta is primarily a recognition that we *do not know* the self or its absence. Incrementally speaking we do get a better understanding of it the more integrated we become, because the absolutisations that blocked our accurate self-view can thus be integrated. Some kinds of self-view are obviously absolute and also problematic, such as narcissism at one extreme, or lack of basic self-esteem at the other. Other kinds of self-view may depend on almost any other absolutisation, because our view about, say, God's existence, or determinism, gets so closely identified with our fragile sense of self-worth. Views about responsibility are a particularly morally relevant type of absolutisation, by which our absolute assumptions about ourselves get conceptually meshed with absolute views about responsibility or its absence.

Rather than as instances of conditionality, then, the three marks of conditioned existence have their main value as prompts to provisionality. By being reminded of alternatives outside our usual loops of assumption, we can engage in a process of integration. However, they are only the starting point – the first task. Next we need to look more closely at what drives the process of absolutisation.

---

11 Thanissaro (2013).

6.c. Craving and Absolutisation

The Second Noble Truth traditionally tells us that the cause of *dukkha* is craving or 'thirst' (*tanha*), and the Third Noble Truth that this craving can be ended. Craving is said to be of three types: craving for existence (*bhava-tanha*), craving for non-existence (*vibhava-tanha*), and craving for sense-objects (*kama-tanha*). Thus not only our desires for food, sex, possessions, etc., but also our very desire for life, causing rebirth, is said to be part of it. The breadth of what appears to be meant by craving has created a problem of interpretation in the Buddhist attitude to desire, since we cannot live without desire. We also cannot make any progress along the path without desiring to do so. We have to crave to be free of craving. How, then, can we reconcile our basic experience of the ubiquity of desire with its apparent denigration on the Buddhist path?

One widely-accepted explanation of this is that there are actually two different types of desire, wholesome and unwholesome. Here the terminology varies slightly in different sources. Some suggest that there are wholesome and unwholesome types of *tanha*.[1] Others use the alternative term *chanda* to represent a wider form of desire which can include both skilful and unskilful forms.[2] Either way, the outcome is that there are two types of desire, one accompanied by awareness that enables progress towards nirvana, whilst the other continues the unenlightened round in delusion. This may sound acceptable if only viewed in the abstract, but the practical problem here is that of how we could identify these forms of desire other than by their outcomes. There seems to be nothing other than the outcomes (which we may not ever experience) to distinguish them in at least some cases. For example, is my desire to buy another book about Buddhism a matter of good desire or bad desire? My motives are likely to be ambiguous, and my rationalisations debatable. On the one hand it could provide useful reference, even insight, but on the other it could add another burdensome possession along with all my other books. To tell me that it is good desire if it leads to enlightenment is of no practical help in such a case. It gives me no basis of judgement that is meaningful in terms of my embodied experience within a reasonable time-frame. The discontinuity between good

---

1 Morrison (1997). *Nettippakarana* 87. Ñanamoli (1962).
2 Payutto (1994).

and bad desires of this kind also breaks the principle of incrementality. I need to be able to take appropriate account of the amount of ambiguity in my experience of desire, rather than imposing absolutising concepts onto it.

An alternative approach to this problem in Buddhism is to assume that there is only one kind of desire, and that although craving takes us to enlightenment, we will have destroyed it by the time we get there. You could see this as a 'purgative' explanation of desire: although purgatives are taken in like other food, they nevertheless have the effect of making us vomit out the food. Similarly there are some types of desire which have the beneficial effect of removing other (harmful) desires, even though we have to have desire for them in the same way to begin with.[3] This approach is reflected in a discourse in the *Anguttara Nikaya* in which Ananda, the Buddha's attendant, is asked to visit a nun who pretends to be sick, presumably with the intention of seducing him. Ananda gives her a stern talking-to on the subject of craving, including:

> 'It has been said: "Sister, this body has come into being through craving; yet based on craving, craving can be abandoned." With reference to what was this said? In this case, a monk hears it said: "They say that a monk of such-and-such a name, by the destruction of the taints, in this very life enters and dwells in the taintless liberation of mind, liberation of wisdom, having realised it for himself by direct knowledge." Then he thinks "Oh, when shall I too realise the taintless liberation of mind, liberation by wisdom?" Then some time later, based on that craving, he abandons craving.'[4]

There seems to be some implicit acknowledgement of the ambiguity of our motives here. A monk might make genuine progress through being motivated to new efforts, even though at least part of his initial motivation was envy. Thus, it is perhaps also implied, the embarrassed nun could also learn to make progress with her craving, whatever her initial motives, by learning from her mistakes. Only having one type of craving rather than two could leave us more able to accept incremental variations in it, but on the other hand it could also lead us to see all craving as intrinsically bad. We thus find it impossible to imagine a state that is liberated from craving but is also human.

---

3   This is an adapted simile of Pyrrhonist origins: Sextus Empiricus, *Against the Logicians* 8.480. Bett (2005).

4   *Anguttara Nikaya* 4.162. Nyanaponika and Bodhi (1999) pp. 110 ff.

All of these problems are created by the absolutisation of enlightenment, rather than interpreting Buddhist insights in terms of the Middle Way. The absolutisation of the assumptions being made also seem to involve alienation from the body. Desire is a basic function of the body, and as a result there is a big discrepancy between the theory of craving and actual Buddhist practice developed in experience. Middle Way practice involves becoming aware of our desires when they are narrow and destructive, and understanding them in a bigger context in which they are no longer over-dominant. So it is this process of awareness and integration that should be the basis of our theoretical understanding of craving too. No successful practitioner, including the Buddha as far as we can tell, ever *eliminated* desire: the Buddha kept on wanting to eat, teach, walk, etc., or he would not have done these things. So we should not even think theoretically in terms of *eliminating* desire, nor in terms of eliminating 'bad' desire that is in practice impossible to distinguish from 'good'. Instead we should think consistently in terms of *integrating* desire.

If we stick to an integration model, there is no such thing as 'bad' desire. Desires can no more be 'bad' than other features of our bodies can be. They are just a way of talking about the energy that flows through our synaptic connections when we make a judgement and act on it. They are the basis of our motives and our values. However, *absolutised* desire is destructive in all the ways that Buddhist tradition identifies as 'craving'. Here it is not the desire itself that is destructive, but its association with an absolute belief that assumes its own ultimacy or finality, and that comes into conflict with other such absolute beliefs. 'Craving', then, should be distinguished from other desire, not because of any feature of the desire itself, but rather of the accompanying beliefs (whether those beliefs are implicit or explicit).

That this is actually a completely feasible interpretation of the Pali literature on craving is suggested by Robert Morrison's interesting paper on *tanha*. Morrison points out that *tanha* is not a 'distinctive affect' (i.e. a distinctive type of desire), but rather a way of talking about an interdependent relationship with delusion (*avijja*):

> In the sutta dealing with ta.nhaa it is said that ta.nhaa is 'nourished' by avijjaa, which in turn is nourished by the 'five hindrances', which are nourished by 'the three wrong ways of practice', and so on, whereas in the sutta dealing with avijjaa, it is said that avijjaa is nourished by 'the five

hindrances', which are nourished by 'the three wrong ways of practice', and so on, making ta.nhaa more fundamental than even avijjaa. However, both are said to be conditionally dependent, implying that we can understand ta.nhaa and avijjaa as the affective and cognitive aspects of the one state. In other words, there is a conditional interdependence between affective state and perceived world which cannot be experientially separated.[5]

In an associated footnote, Morrison also gives further evidence that *'avijjaa is not simply a lack of knowledge, but thinking one has knowledge when one has not'.*[6] 'Delusion' (*avijja*) in Buddhism can thus be readily seen as absolutisation, and craving as a distinctive form of desire only in the sense of its interdependence with that absolutisation.

There is thus only one sort of desire, namely energy flowing through our brain and nervous system. However, when the beliefs that format this desire are absolutised, they reflect the dominant activity of a closed feedback loop. This is one that we can visualise, or schematise, as a loop between the linguistic and goal centres of the left prefrontal cortex, in cyclic combination with the motivational signals coming from the older parts of the brain, such as cortisol and dopamine. It is the looped channels through which the desire flows that make it subject to delusion. However, with enough connection to the right hemisphere of the brain providing wider embodied awareness – experienced via the parts of the 'interoceptive' parts of the brain, such as the insula, that are associated with mindfulness[7] – that closed feedback loop can be opened up. Our desires then serve better-adapted purposes, and start to address the conditions we find ourselves in more flexibly.

If craving is understood as desire associated with absolutisation, this understanding can be applied equally to the three types of craving identified in Buddhist analysis – namely craving for being (*bhava-tanha*), craving for non-being (*vibhava-tanha*), and craving for sense-desires (*kama-tanha*). The craving for being is associated with the traditional motive for rebirth, and is associated with 'eternalism', while the craving for non-being is associated with 'nihilism'. However, the incoherence of the belief that the different absolutisations associated with 'eternalism' and 'nihilism'

---

5 Morrison (1997), referring to *Anguttara Nikaya* 5.116.
6 Ibid. note 18.
7 Fox et al. (2014).

are necessarily connected has already been dealt with in chapter 4.d. Any further association of these clusters with specific kinds of desire is equally unnecessary, and counter-examples can be easily offered. Materialistic scientists may strongly desire to live for ever, intent on a cure for ageing, thus combining craving for being with 'nihilism'. Or a Catholic who believes in the eternal soul may also be in despair and wish to commit suicide.

More broadly, though, craving for being applies to any absolutised state that one may crave. For example, one may crave to *be* secure, or to *be* beautiful in the sense of having these states as our essential nature, as opposed to recognising the incrementality whereby we will only ever be secure or beautiful to some degree. The same would apply to *having* something that we regard as having a similar essential nature, such as the ultimate car or the perfect wife. At the same time we might crave *not to be* insecure or ugly, or *not to have* a 'crap' car or wife (an expletive of this kind is a very common means of communicating absolutised rejection). The craving to be can be distinguished from the craving of sense-desire only roughly by the latter's immediacy. Rather than idealising or demonising the object of my craving by developing abstract beliefs about it (craving to be), a mere unreflective craving for the object of my desire just prioritises it absolutely without any further rationalisation (sense-desire). All craving reflects absolutisation (in a way that ordinary human desire may not), but the distinctions between types of craving may help us to identify different ways that absolutisation can appear.

Craving for being, then, does not have to be associated with rebirth, any more than belief in an eternal soul has to be associated with belief in God. Maintaining a human body could conceivably be something we crave, but only if we abstract it as an alienated idea. It's far more likely to be just a basic human desire emerging from our acknowledgement of our bodies. Having a body cannot be assumed to be a result of bad previous actions – it is the root of our human experience. On the face of it, far from helping to release us from craving, belief in rebirth may help to enmesh us in it further by providing new absolutisations that take us away from our basic experience of that embodied root. However, further exploration of this point should wait until the next chapter, in relation to a wider discussion of karma and rebirth.

6.d. Karma and Rebirth

The belief in karma and rebirth is perhaps the most obvious source of absolutisation in Buddhist tradition, and for that reason has been the first target for those who want to make Buddhism compatible with scientific findings. It is the 'supernatural beliefs' involved in the acceptance of rebirth that are, for fairly obvious reasons, difficult to accept: we do not know what happens after death, and there is no evidence for rebirth that cannot be readily interpreted in other ways. Traditional Buddhist beliefs about karma are also more absolutised than might at first appear from those modern Buddhists who present them as merely 'actions having consequences'. Yet both karma and rebirth, like other Buddhist teachings, are not fixed in interpretation, and can be understood in terms compatible with the Middle Way. They offer one way of approaching the question: 'What are the *effects* of absolutisation on the one hand, or of practising the Middle Way on the other?'

Any general claims we may make about the consequences of better or worse judgements need to be provisional in nature. Whatever intuitions we may have on the subject, they do not justify us in ever making claims about what will *necessarily* happen in the event of a certain type of judgement or action. Causal relationships are complex, and they depend on our relating different categories of event to each other: for example that if I raise my hand whilst holding a ball and then let go of it, it will fall. But there may always be assumptions in our understanding of those categories and relationships that we have not taken account of. The statement 'If I raise my hand whilst holding a ball and then let go of it, it will fall' may seem 'true', but not if the ball was made of something lighter than the surrounding atmosphere, or if there was no gravitational field. The examination of such claims is the business of science. Science follows a method compatible with the Middle Way, making theoretical claims only of a provisional kind, that remain open to examination. Neither scientific method nor the Middle Way can justify us in making causal claims from an absolute and universal dogma about causal relationships.

On the face of it, though, the Buddhist view of karma seems to be just such a dogma. Though there is some variation in its interpretation, all schools agree that the karmic effect (*kamma-vipaka*) of an action (including a mental action such as a judgement) must be morally proportionate to the action,[1] that this effect may occur across lives, and that it is completely inevitable.[2] Since the effects of our actions depend on a range of conditions *apart* from our own judgement, the only way this could occur is through a cosmic law of some kind that guarantees the precise way those conditions will *always* operate: one that can only be asserted to be operating universally through absolutising dogma.

Some traditional schools (such as the Yogachara) also insist, in addition to this, that *all the conditions* we experience are karmic ones, so that we necessarily deserve whatever happens to us. This, however, is clearly not supported by the Pali Canon. The Buddha points out that 'some feelings...arise...from bile disorders', or wind disorders, or changes of climate, or assault:[3] in other words, that there are biological causes, and actions of others, which contribute to the conditions we encounter as well as the results of our own actions. Elsewhere he also points out that we do not know whether we existed in the past, whether we did evil actions in the past, or what our precise balance of karma is:[4] thus it cannot be concluded that all feeling is karmic.

However, this helpful recognition that karmic effects cannot be traced retrospectively, and that we cannot know precisely how karma operates, does nothing to remove the remaining dogmatic assumption. That is the belief that all our actions will inevitably produce karmic effects. Our experience of the *likely* effects of absolutising judgement is sufficient to offer a well-justified *general* warning. However, the distinction between the absolute and the general is crucial if we are to avoid developing new absolutisations in our very attempt to deter people from them.

Perhaps the key point here is concerned with the comparison of karmic beliefs to scientific ones. If we maintain an edge of scepticism in our attitudes to scientific findings, and thus insist on provisionality even whilst acknowledging the justification of substantial confidence in such findings, we should be able to take a similar

---

1 *Majjhima Nikaya* 41. Ñanamoli and Bodhi (1995) pp. 379–85.
2 *Samyutta Nikaya* 42.6. Bodhi (2000) pp. 1336–8 (as commonly interpreted – but see below).
3 *Samyutta Nikaya* 36.21. Bodhi (2000) p. 1279.
4 *Majjhima Nikaya* 101.4. Ñanamoli and Bodhi (1995) pp. 827–8.

attitude to generalisations about the effects of absolutisation. The Buddha dramatises this point in a comparison with a boulder:

> 'Suppose, headman, a person would hurl a huge boulder into a deep pool of water. Then a great crowd of people...would send up prayers..., saying "Emerge, good boulder! Rise up, good boulder...." What do you think, headman? Because of the prayers...would that boulder emerge...?'
>
> 'No, venerable sir.'
>
> 'So too, headman, if a person is one who destroys life...after death, that person will be reborn in a state of misery....'[5]

Traditionally, this has been read as asserting that karmic effects are *inevitable*. However, the very use of the Buddha's metaphor does not assert such absolute inevitability in the abstract, but rather places the likelihood of negative effects from an overwhelmingly disintegrative action into the same level of confidence that we place in commonly observed 'natural' causal relationships. It is not *inevitable* that a boulder will sink rather than rise up when thrown into a pool of water, just highly likely. We do not have to go into very fantastical scenarios to imagine the circumstances where the boulder might float, since there is some stone on earth that floats in some circumstances – pumice. Similarly, we should overwhelmingly expect that killing will result in negative effects (leaving aside the rebirth element for the moment). This is not *inevitable*, just so highly likely that we should place a good deal of practical confidence in it. It is exactly the same type of confidence that we should place on scientific findings that are consistent with all the evidence so far, such as anthropogenic climate change: namely, a strong but provisional confidence, in which the possibility of alternatives continues to be open, but practical reliance is nevertheless placed on the overwhelmingly likely explanation.

How might a *general* law of karmic effects be understood today? The impact of our judgements on the brain is an obvious way to understand it. By judging in one way, we create new synaptic connections, or strengthen existing ones, in a fashion that makes similar judgements a more likely option to be considered in the future. A frequently repeated judgement, such as the addict's judgement that getting her fix takes overwhelming precedence over all other considerations, sets up deeply entrenched ruts that

---

5   *Samyutta Nikaya* 42.6. Bodhi (2000) p. 1337.

it gets harder and harder to get out of. Absolutising judgements have negative effects, because they consist in such frequently repeated judgements, caught in a closed feedback loop. Provisional judgements have generally positive effects, however. They leave open alternative options that can help us to maintain mental states in which we have a variety of options in future.

However, the negative effects of absolutisation are not necessarily negative in the sense that they produce suffering. They are negative in the sense that our reliance on rigid and thus potentially maladapted patterns of judgement becomes greater. Whether rigidity causes you to suffer also depends on luck – the luck of changing conditions around you for which your rigid attitudes may or may not be adapted. The belief in a just world, a recognised cognitive bias[6] of which absolutised belief in karma is often one manifestation, involves a deluded tendency to ignore that element of luck and regard all effects as just. The remedy to this is not to regard it instead as unjust, but to find a Middle Way in which both luck and the effects of our judgements are recognised as contributory.[7]

The overwhelming motive for belief in rebirth, however, is to make karmic law absolutely consistent. If our actions do not have observable effects of moral equivalence in this life, we can nevertheless apparently be assured that they will operate in a future one. This commitment to absolute moral recompense is taken to override the evidence that during our lives all judgement and other experience depends on the specific living brain (in connection with the rest of the body) in which it occurs. Of course, mysteries are possible, but we have no positive evidence that a connected capacity for judgement can survive the death of an individual brain. Nor do we have evidence that it can operate in a different brain, with quite different synaptic connections, to the one it began in. If we were to question our confidence in the general dependence of judgement and experience on the living brain, we would need a strong weight of counter-evidence to do so. Instead of such counter-evidence, however, we have only an absolutising belief.

It is thus clear that belief in rebirth conflicts with the Middle Way. I am not here going to enter into any detailed discussion of

6 See Lerner (1980).
7 See Ellis (2015a) ch. 4.g.

the evidence that some Buddhists have offered for rebirth (such as child prodigies, child memories of 'when I was big', or memories accessed under hypnosis).[8] Such evidence may point to mysteries and limitations in our understanding of human memory and personality. However, I have yet to come across any case of such evidence where rebirth was the only probable explanation. More importantly, if we are to follow Hume's advice to match our judgement to the weight of the evidence, we need to set these alleged pieces of evidence alongside the overwhelming weight of evidence on the other side of the scale. That would lead us to conclude that it is far more likely that those who believe they support belief in rebirth are mistaken than otherwise. Such a conclusion can also be supported by the high likelihood of confirmation bias, given that those who use such evidence for belief in rebirth are doing so in support of an absolute belief rather than a provisional one.

The 'evidence' is far less important than the motives for wanting to believe in rebirth. Even amongst those Western Buddhists who say they are agnostic about rebirth, there remains a tendency to see it as desirable to believe in it. Given the way in which such beliefs can scarcely avoid being absolutisations, introduced so as to maintain absolutisation of karma, this seems an obvious misapprehension. There may also be confusion here between the *meaningfulness* of rebirth as a symbol and the value of maintaining belief in it. As with other metaphysical beliefs, we can draw their sting if we separate out the meaning from the belief and develop a positive understanding of that meaning.

For the meaning of rebirth, we have to look at what kinds of experiences it can be metaphorically related to. This must surely be the experience of closed feedback loops itself, as is underlined by the Wheel of Samsara. The Wheel of Samsara depicts the cycle represented by the twelve *nidana*s, beginning with ignorance (absolutisation) and continuing through karmic formations, consciousness, name and form, the senses, feeling, craving, and grasping to becoming, birth, and death. Although, as noted in chapter 6.a above, this shows a possible conditioning process, it does not show a *necessary* analysis in a *necessary* order. Rebirth can be a meaningful element of this process by showing the recursion

---

8   E.g. Govinda (1966) pp. 120–51; academic arguments also come from works like Stevenson (1974).

involved. Rebirth symbolises the very fact that we go through the same sort of process over and over again without awareness that we are doing so.

Every time a smoker takes out another cigarette, every time a fundamentalist goes over the same obsessive and falsely comforting certainties, every time a commitment-phobic person backs out of a relationship at the same threatening point, every time the computer gamer eliminates another little electronic threat or obtains another little electronic reward – each time another 'rebirth' occurs. Unaware of the bigger or longer-term picture, we continue with our little fulfilments for the moment and constantly reinforce the neural pathways on which we've come to depend. Every time we go down those pathways yet again, we experience rebirth.

To avoid that rebirth, though, we do not need to stop the round altogether by achieving absolutised enlightenment. Instead, every moment of awareness in which we can experience alternative options offers a mitigation of that rebirth. As a result, it's not only a few exceptional buddhas, arhats, or bodhisattvas who can avoid rebirth. We all can, incrementally. By interpreting the Second Task in genuinely universal terms, then, we can also lay the groundwork for a universal understanding of the Third Task.

6.e. The Buddha's Authority and Status

The Third Task, as mentioned in chapter 6.b, is to realise the possibility of greater adequacy through alternatives. This is an incremental version of the recognition of absolute enlightenment that is traditionally stated as the Third Noble Truth. We do not have to *believe* in absolute enlightenment or its historical attainment to realise the possibility of progress. Nevertheless, enlightenment or Awakening as *meaning* may still be very helpful, in a Buddhist context, for us to talk about the directionality of the Middle Way. The meaning of Awakening in the context of Buddhism is overwhelmingly associated with the figure of the Buddha himself – as a source of authority and as an archetypal inspiration.

The specific historical individual, Siddhartha Gautama, is distinguishable from the universal and symbolic Buddha in a similar way to that in which Jesus can be distinguished from Christ. As a historical figure the Buddha has a certain authority within the Buddhist tradition, but it is important to clarify what that 'authority' means. In accordance with the Middle Way, that authority should not be absolute.

Authority in general is one of the values that shapes our lives. We have justification for *respecting* the authority of parents and the state because of our organic relationship with them. There are also advantages to society of allowing those with more experience or awareness to most strongly influence relevant social judgements. In a modern democratic society, however, no authority is absolute. Even highly integrated individuals can make serious mistakes that might be corrected by the perspective of others participating in decision-making. This aspect of democratic culture is very much in accordance with the Middle Way, because if we are to avoid absolutisation we need to avoid the absolutisation of any one type of value over others. In Jonathan Haidt's very useful research into foundational social values (already mentioned in chapter 2.e), authority came out as only one of the six types of value that people commonly appeal to: authority, sanctity, loyalty, fairness, care, and freedom.[1] These different values can address conditions in differing ways. I've argued elsewhere for the ways in which a Middle Way approach to social and political judgement needs to be open to all of

---

1 Haidt (2012) ch. 7.

these types of value, rather than absolutising one or more of them at the expense of the others.[2]

However, Buddhist tradition has for most of its history been practised in traditional Asian societies, in which authority (frequently accompanied by the other traditional values of loyalty and sanctity) is often absolutised. We can see this in the monarchical political systems, the hierarchy and patriarchy of traditional social systems, and also, of course, in religion. In traditional religious contexts, perceived truth is passed on primarily through the acceptance of the authority of either a God or a past master. This is mediated through the social structure of an equally authoritative religious leadership, who often also appeal to texts or traditions that convey the authority of the past masters. In traditional Buddhism, of course, this means that the authority of the Buddha is appealed to as the source of the scriptures and traditions, and these are interpreted by the monastic hierarchy. In this social context, it is hardly surprising that the Buddha's authority is absolutised. The use and implication of provisional judgement through the Middle Way has been obscured by many centuries of one-sided interpretation that maintained vested interests. The absolutisation of enlightenment is very much a tool for this maintenance of religious power.

To adopt a view of the Buddha's authority that follows the Middle Way rather than this tradition, we do not have to reject that authority altogether. After all, authority can be very helpful to us in the religious sphere as in any other. Traditionally-minded Buddhists are likely to argue that our escape from delusion requires that we subordinate ourselves to an authority. The guru has wisdom from direct experience that goes beyond that delusion. If we do not thus subordinate ourselves, we are likely to merely rationalise our current beliefs in various defensive ways that stop us from progressing. Thus, they will argue, we must accept a guru or authoritative teacher if we are not to remain deluded. This argument shows an appreciation of our own delusion. However, it takes insufficient account of the delusions that may still be maintained by those believed to be enlightened teachers. It also ignores the ways in which their disciples are likely to unhelpfully project authority onto what may be a misinterpretation of the teacher's intentions. Modern media culture is increasingly shining a light into the widespread

---

2   Ellis (2015a) ch. 4.h.

hypocrisies and corruptions of those who have been given the status of gurus. This shows fairly conclusively that an assumption of absolute authority given to any spiritual teacher is misplaced. That's not because all gurus are bad, but because we have no justification, in a world of embodied uncertainty, for assuming that they are all perfect.

Much the same points, then, apply to the authority of the historical Buddha. Here, though, we are also dealing with the additional uncertainty created by his antiquity, and the limited sources of information we have about him. He lived about 2,500 years ago. There are no contemporary written records about him. Our only sources are documents that were compiled by the Buddhist tradition with all its vested interests, and only written down 500 years later. We thus have plenty of reasons to be cautious about anything the Buddha is alleged to have said. *In addition*, though, there is also the possibility that the Buddha may have been wrong in what he said, or that it may have been misinterpreted, even if it was recorded accurately.

The historical Buddha still has *credibility*, in the sense that his sayings are worth our attention. That's especially so if we have a personal relationship with the Buddhist tradition and are thus likely to gain understanding of the Middle Way from it. His authority extends to prima facie credibility.[3] However, what he is alleged to have said can never be justifiably assumed to be correct or helpful without further investigation, and comparison to other perspectives.

As I have already argued earlier in this book, our reason for accepting the Middle Way is neither necessarily nor sufficiently based on the Buddha's authority. The Middle Way is not helpful because the Buddha taught it, but because (or to the extent that) it describes a generally helpful way of making judgements about our experience. We may provisionally accept it for all sorts of possible motives, which for Buddhists may include trust of the Buddha's authority. Nevertheless, we will need to be continually open in practice to challenges to that perspective, and to hold it because we also appreciate other values than authority. The Middle Way can also be understood from a variety of other sources, as my final section in this book will aim to show. It is not necessary to be

---

3 For more on the distinction between credibility and absolute authority see Ellis (2015a) ch. 3.e.

Buddhist, or even to pay much attention to the Buddha, in order to follow the Middle Way.

However, the Buddha has another sort of status that has no necessary connection with the specific teachings attributed to the historical Buddha. The figure of the Buddha, as represented in art and sculpture, or even in the mythologised way he is presented in Mahayana sutras, is not a portrait of a historical figure, but a representation of an *archetype*. An archetype (a term first used by Jung) here means a universal pattern of meaning created by similarities in human function. The model of integration (discussed in chapter 3.g) can help to explain the ways in which archetypes reflect key human functions. The Middle Way can also be readily applied to our treatment of archetypes so as to avoid *projection* of archetypes, which is a form of absolutisation.

Archetypes can be seen as developed metaphors which enable certain symbols to have universally similar associative power. They are linked in a similar way to basic schemas etched into our brains from infancy, with the importance of those schemas being genetically similar. One such archetype that has already been mentioned (in chapter 1.g) is the Shadow, which is represented by the figure of Mara in the period leading up to the Buddha's Awakening. The Shadow represents everything that we reject, hate, and repress. Though we may project it onto 'external' objects of hatred, whether natural or supernatural, the hatred lies within us and is created by a conflict in our own experience. That does not mean that people or things in the world may not be harmful to us, but even if they are, it does not imply that we have to hate them, or that hatred would be the best response to them. Our hatred results in unreflective negative responses that simplify a complex person's behaviour into one negative quality that we wrongly take to be their essence. In a similar way we can project repressed attractive traits onto others from the archetype that Jung called the anima or animus, and heroic traits onto someone we imagine as having success that we crave ourselves according to the Hero archetype. Sangharakshita finds these archetypes also present in some versions of the story of the Buddha's Awakening: the hero as Muchalinda the serpent (who spreads his hood over the Buddha to protect him) and the anima as the Earth Goddess (who bears witness to the Buddha's achievement to avoid disabling doubt).[4]

4 Sangharakshita (1990b) pp. 33 ff.

Though the early life of the Buddha may seem like that of a hero, the more basic universal archetype represented by the Buddha figure (or by other representations of enlightenment in Buddhism such as the mandala or stupa) is that which gives us a glimpse or foretaste of complete integration. This archetype was called the 'Self' or the 'God' archetype by Jung. Given that integration is a unification of energies that already exist in us, it is not surprising that we should experience at least partial foretastes of such unification. We may do so either in temporary states of integration such as *jhana*, or perhaps from some external stimulus that jolts us into a momentary openness of awareness far beyond the usual. 'Religious experience' is a momentary connection with that archetype, and is likely to be accompanied by experiences of insight, energy, awe, ecstasy, compassion, profound contentment, and equanimity – all resulting from the temporary dissolution of the conflicts that normally divide our energies.

The Self or God Archetype also unites the other three primary archetypes by resolving conflict between them. Thus the heroic, the feminine (or masculine for women), and the Shadow all contribute their energies to a greater whole. In each case our own untapped potential, which up to that point has been projected and assumed to lie in something other than ourselves, is recognised as in a sense our own. The 'Self' that they become part of, though, is also much wider than the ego we normally identify with. To become integrated, we should no longer alienate our wisdom as hatred, our compassion as sexual possessiveness, or our profound aspiration as narrow ambition. The more we can become integrated in this way, the closer we will get to the state symbolised by the Buddha image.

The account I'm suggesting here of the archetypal significance of the Buddha figure gives him a parallel meaning and function to the archetype of God. This is not to skate over the large doctrinal differences between the Buddha and God, and the differences between the respective traditions in which they are embedded. Rather it is to point out that when we look at the potentially integrative *function* of each figure in the experience of those who respond to the symbol, those functions are parallel. In each case the figure can offer inspiration through association between our experiences of glimpses of integration on the one hand, and our commitment to working to create it in a more stable actual form on the other. When Buddhists engage in devotional acts before the

Buddha figure, they can thus be seen as evoking and revivifying that association so as to inspire further effort on the path. I have argued Christians may also be seen as doing this when they worship God.[5]

In both cases, too, there is also a projection of the archetypal figure that is an absolutisation. The projection of God as a supernatural entity is obviously extremely common in Christianity and other theistic traditions: so common as to be considered the norm. The projection of the Buddha as an entity separate from the devotional individual is also debatably common in Buddhist tradition. The Adi-Buddha or 'Primordial Buddha' of some schools of the Vajrayana seems to have been conceived in a form very similar to God.[6] The role of Amitabha in the Pure Land Schools is to bring worshippers, who cannot save themselves, to the Pure Land where it becomes easier to gain enlightenment.[7] Even in Theravadin Southeast Asia, popular belief externalises the Buddha figure as a separate agency. In discussing the offerings made to Buddha images, Donald K. Swearer remarks:

> Although we do an injustice to the tradition to minimise the claim that such offerings honour the memory of the teacher-founder, the expectation of receiving some sort of boon or benefit reflects the belief that the image itself has a special power to grant the wishes of the devotee. A similar dynamic lies behind all merit-making rituals. By making an offering, especially a lavish and costly one, the donor hopes to effect a reciprocal response from the power infused into the Buddha image.[8]

Although the projection of the archetype may be less prevalent in Buddhism than it is in Christianity, the underlying issue is the same. The Buddha, like God, can be absolutised by being projected, and thus the Middle Way betrayed. If we recognise the Buddha as symbolising our own potential integration, and thus maintain some awareness both of our conflicts and of their potential resolution in our response to the Buddha as a symbol, the Middle Way is maintained. If, however, we see the Buddha as in some way offering a shortcut to the fulfilment of our desires or the relief of our anxieties, we will have gone through a process of what psychologists call attribute substitution.[9] This means substituting an easier

5   Ellis (2018) ch. 8.a.
6   Conze (1951) pp. 190–1.
7   Williams (1989) pp. 256–76.
8   Swearer (1995) p. 31.
9   See Kahneman (2011) pp. 97–104.

problem for a harder one, and thus failing to address the conditions of the harder problem that actually affects us. This is a form of absolutisation involving an appeal to an authority to substitute for experience that can be observed as reducing moral adequacy.[10] If we imagine a Thai student making an offering to the Buddha in order to pass an exam, this is more likely to induce a brittle absolute belief that he will pass than the type of engaged confidence that will actually support his revision.

To ensure that we are devoting ourselves to the right object – one that will remind us not of a remote idealised goal, but of a path and its method – we can also alter our interpretation of the meaning of the Buddha figure. In my book on Christianity, I suggested that although God represents the archetype of complete integration, Christ, with his dual human and divine nature, is more an archetype of the Middle Way.[11] The Buddha, on the other hand, can serve both as an archetype of complete integration (insofar as he represents enlightenment) and as an archetype of the Middle Way. The two archetypes differ insofar as the latter must constantly remind us of the method, its edginess and incompleteness and imperfection. The path towards completeness may not be best served by too much dwelling on images of completeness, because the Middle Way may deliberately prefer incompleteness so as to avoid idealisation. Thus in addition to the archetype of enlightenment, we also need to be equally inspired by images of incompleteness and creative disruption, and by images of balance.

All the resources are present in Buddhism to start treating the Middle Way itself as an archetypal figure. Some images in the Mahayana, such as the wrathful deities, already make the point that enlightenment also means facing up to the Shadow. Others, such as Padmasambhava with his fierce smile, already symbolise the dialectic of apparently contrary elements. The spatial organisation of the mandala, as recognised by Jung, is an image of integrating different elements of the psyche.[12]

If the Middle Way is actually the Buddha's greatest insight, as I contend, then informed and helpful Buddhist devotion and ritual should emphasise this point, rather than the absolutisation

---

10 Sunstein (2005); Ellis (2015a) ch. 3.d (2).
11 Ellis (2018) ch. 6.a.
12 See Ellis (forthcoming) ch. 5.

of enlightened status that is too often its theme. The most central liturgies could be about the early life or the discovery of the Middle Way. The rose-apple tree could replace the bodhi tree as the one most significant to the Buddha's insight. As suggested in chapter 1.f, the ritual eating of rice porridge could offer a reminder of the Buddha's key point of recognition. Buddha figures could have a new mudra (hand position) to visually represent the Middle Way. The discovery of the Middle Way could be the basis of a festival.

One of the biggest barriers to the wider recognition of the importance of the Middle Way is the false assumption that it cannot be inspiring – but is in some way safe and mediocre, despite the courage required to follow it. Nobody, not even most Buddhists, currently seem to perceive the Middle Way as itself something inspiring: yet there is no necessary reason why this should be the case. Buddhism is full of cultural resources from millennia of practitioners who have tried to interpret, symbolise, and apply the Middle Way. All that is required is a slight shift of focus in the interpretation and celebration of the Buddha and his legacy to make Buddhism much more genuinely universal. Middle Way Buddhists could have the satisfaction of developing a distinctive strand of Buddhist tradition, yet having no basis of doctrinal disagreement with Middle Way Christians, Middle Way Marxists, or anyone else committed to interpreting their tradition in the most helpful way possible.

6.f. The Meaning of 'Dharma'

The term 'dharma' (or *dhamma*) is the one commonly used in Buddhism (as well as Hinduism, Jainism, and Sikhism) to refer to the truth, to the path, and to the teachings of the religion. It derives from roots meaning 'to hold', and can have a wide range of related meanings including 'that which is established or firm, steadfast decree, statute, law, practice, custom, duty, right, justice, virtue, morality, ethics, religion, religious merit, good works, the law or doctrine of Buddhism, the ethical precepts of Buddhism'.[1] 'The Dharma' is also one of the three jewels to which Buddhists commit themselves when going for refuge (see below), so its centrality and importance as a concept can hardly be underestimated.

However, its ambiguity is rather problematic. All language is ambiguous to some extent. The appreciation and acceptance of ambiguity usually helps us address conditions by recognising that the sharpness of category boundaries is created by our own concepts rather than being part of the world. For example, being relaxed about racial ambiguity, or ambiguity of gender or sexual orientation, is an excellent liberal habit. However, ambiguity becomes unhelpful when it obscures the distinction between absolute and provisional beliefs. That's because it confuses people when they are trying to avoid absolute beliefs, and are not sure of their status, which then may lead them to absolutise without being aware that they are doing so. When the Middle Way is appropriated and turned into a metaphysical concept, then similarly unhelpful ambiguity occurs. When the reverse happens, though, and concepts that are often understood metaphysically start to be consciously interpreted in ways that are provisional and experiential, ambiguity is being used helpfully. It's all a question of the practical effect. In the case of 'dharma', however, the ambiguity can cut both ways.

There are three particular senses of 'dharma' whose confusion can have a very negative effect:
1. Ultimate knowledge of reality
2. The most helpful way of responding to conditions
3. The teachings of the Buddha according to the Buddhist tradition

Using the same word for something (unless it's a well-known homonym, like the two senses of 'bank') often tends to make people

---

1 Monier-Williams (2008).

assume that they are the same thing. For example, using the word 'sport' for the slaughter of animals as well as harmless physical recreations like tennis and swimming can make people assume that the former is a matter for equal light-heartedness, and they may thus dismiss any misgivings they might have about it. With 'dharma', the use of the same word for the first and the second senses listed above tends to make people assume that the most helpful way of practising is one that knows the truth. A more helpful view, though, is to realise that one *does not* know the truth. The use of the same word for the first and third senses may make people assume that the Buddha's teachings are always ultimately true, and thus not investigate them critically. The use of the same word for the second and third may make people assume that Buddhist teachings are always the most helpful, and thus again discourage critical examination.

All of these potential effects are absolutisations. Absolutisations, though, are rather like ghouls that need real flesh-and-blood provisional beliefs to feed on so that they can keep going. They readily appropriate areas of provisional belief so that they can claim that all the achievements of provisional action are 'really' their achievements – as we must know through the appeal to authority (or the a priori abstract reasoning) that is used to demonstrate the essentiality of absolutisations. The ghouls have been feeding on 'the dharma' for rather a long time, with the expressed permission of the authorities, and as a result it has become rather contaminated. Some Buddhists have become concerned about this, and have brought in Emptiness to try to clear out the ghouls (as discussed in chapter 4.b), but the ghouls are quite happy to welcome Emptiness to the feast, given how readily it can turn into another ghoul. No, the only way to maintain the provisionality of 'the dharma' is to decisively identify the ghouls and reunite them with the bodies they sprang from.

You can see this book as an exercise in trying to clear the ghouls out, by making it clear that the first sense is quite different from the second, and doing some critical sorting in the third sense. The second sense of 'dharma' is the Middle Way, whereas the third sense contains a mixture of the Middle Way and absolutisation that need to be distinguished. The second sense is universal, which means that it may be found anywhere, not just in Buddhism. The third sense, however, is exclusive. I have tried to engage with the third sense in this book by engaging with the Pali sources and the traditional Buddhist form of the teachings, but these are contingent and peripheral to the second sense.

It is because of this unhelpful ambiguity that I do not use the term 'dharma' anywhere else in this book, despite the habitual way in which most Buddhists use the term. The only occasion on which I might use it might be when addressing Buddhists, but then much qualification is necessary. One could, for example, try to avoid the ambiguity by only talking about the 'absolute dharma', 'the universal dharma', and the 'dharma of the Buddhist tradition' – but even this is very likely to be misunderstood. How many Buddhists will assume that the universal dharma must be absolute to be universal, instead of the opposite? Or that the opposite to the 'absolute dharma' is the 'relative dharma' (which is another form of absolute dharma – just negatively so)? Our terminology is so unhelpfully confused on this point that I really recommend letting go of the term 'dharma' altogether.

Instead of 'the dharma', I use the terms 'Middle Way' for universally helpful practical beliefs, and 'Buddhism' or 'the Buddhist tradition' for Buddhist teachings. However, whichever set of terms you adopt, I suggest that the key requirement is that you have a practical rationale for doing so. That means not simply an adoption of tradition, nor an assumption of the 'essential' meaning of a term. Our use of language, like our use of Buddhist tradition generally, is a matter of interpretative responsibility.

6.g. The Community and Monastic Tradition

The ideal of a supportive community on the path – the Sangha – has been a central one since the Buddha gathered his first five followers at Sarnath. Yet we need to ask how much the Buddhist Sangha supports its members in treading the path of the Middle Way. Or, how much does it maintain a presumption of absolutised enlightenment which may often distract from that path? Human beings are social animals, and our relationship with others is built into the whole emotional regulatory system of a human body. Thus the role of the community is crucial in encouraging or discouraging the Middle Way. As we shall see, that role can hardly be said to be as helpful as it could have been, due at least partly to the absolutisations entrenched in the monastic basis of the Sangha in most schools of Buddhism.

However, before looking at the institution of the Sangha it is helpful to consider more generally the role of groups in the practice of the Middle Way. A set of recognised cognitive biases – in-group bias, social proof, groupthink, and false consensus – often operate to absolutise the accepted view of a group and repress any contrary thinking from any individual within that group. In-group bias leads us to treat members of our own group and their views more favourably.[1] Social proof is our tendency to accept the view of the surrounding group even when it contradicts evidence that we have observed for ourselves.[2] Groupthink is the tendency to prioritise harmony within the group over critical thinking in group-based decision making.[3] False consensus is the tendency of those within groups to overestimate the ubiquity of the group's views and treat them as normative for everyone.[4] All of these biases clearly involve absolutisation of the group's view. They use the shortcut of group view to prevent individuals from making autonomous judgements (social proof). If autonomous judgements are made it prevents them being considered (in-group bias) or taken into account in practical decision-making (groupthink). False consensus even prevents the existence of alternative views being recognised at all.[5] It is from

1 Taylor and Doria (1981).
2 Asch (1956).
3 Janis (1982).
4 Ross, Greene, and House (1977).
5 For a more detailed discussion of the implications of the biases see Ellis (2015a) ch. 3.e.

these biases, amongst others, that the Buddha was fleeing when he left the palace and the two religious groups.

Groups are often instruments of power, and it takes considerable psychological development and maturity to challenge a group in which you are embedded. In Robert Kegan's scheme of psychological development,[6] we start to do so usually only at a post-adolescent stage of development, when we start to think more systematically (stage 4). But even then, although our systematic thinking may start to challenge our parents and friends, it is still likely to depend on a wider group whose system we have adopted – whether that is the systematic thinking assumed by an education system, a religion, or a profession. We remain very much subject to the power of groups until the final, and rarely achieved, stage of psychological development (stage 5). It is probably only at that stage that we are able to start practising the Middle Way fully and explicitly by freeing ourselves from group biases.

Unfortunately, if we try to free ourselves from a group too dramatically and prematurely, we are only likely to swing to the opposite form of absolutisation. This will in turn be supported by a counter-group with a counter-culture. The 'dropout' society of the *shramanas* in the Buddha's time offered such a culture, which the Buddha was able to use as a stepping stone after he left the palace. Sangharakshita has analysed individuality in similar terms within Buddhism by talking of the contrast between the group and 'individualism', which is part of the counter-group. The 'true individual' needs to follow a middle way which involves taking the best features from both the initial group and the counter-group, in the process 'no longer limited by group consciousness'.[7]

So how can the group be a help rather than a hindrance to an individual following the Middle Way? It must obviously try to offer support without using power, implicitly or explicitly, against the non-conforming individual. It will need a shared basis of operation that makes use of the Middle Way by not absolutising its own values, and supporting individuals in developing provisionality and integration. It needs to have the development of individual integration as part of its shared expectation. It needs to allow the individual to escape its expectations and encounter alternatives to

---

6 Kegan (1982). See chapter 4.e above.
7 Sangharakshita (1990c) pp. 40–1.

aid the development of provisionality. It also needs to be organised in such a way that its own assumed values can be challenged and modified. Thus the group as a whole, too, needs to be going through a process of integration with other groups that oppose it. A group organised in such a way at least stands a chance of nurturing genuine individuality, and thus also being a more adaptable and successful group in the long-term.

The Buddha's Sangha initially meant the community of *shramanas* following him, and later came to mean the monastic community and the wider lay community. In many ways that initial community was advanced for its time in developing the helpful features of a group that nurtures individuals. For one thing, it avoided the use of power as much as possible. Followers were free to join (as long as they were not fleeing from lay responsibilities such as conscription or debt)[8] and leave. Mixed motives were expected and worked with. The community welcomed people of any background.[9] Those who broke important monastic rules, for example by killing or having sex, were said to place themselves beyond the monastic community through their own actions rather than being 'punished'.[10]

The discourses also give plenty of evidence that the early community participated in a culture of critical enquiry, and that individuals were encouraged to evaluate and probe the Buddha's teachings to reach their own conclusions. People were evidently in a position to compare the beliefs of different schools, as the *Kalama Sutta* (discussed in chapter 2.c) testifies. The practice of solitary meditation and reflection was also encouraged in those who were ready for it, and celebrated in some well-known passages of the Pali Canon such as the 'Rhinoceros Horn' verses.[11] This shows the ways in which practitioners were encouraged to get an individual perspective beyond the group.

However, despite all these positive features, the seeds of absolutisation that could undermine Middle Way practice were also already there from the beginning. The gap between *shramanas* who had 'gone forth' and lay-people who had not was one of them, growing later into the full monastic-lay division. The discontinuity of that division

---

8 Wijayaratna (1990) pp. 15–16, 117–21.
9 Ibid. pp. 12–13.
10 Ibid. p. 144.
11 *Sutta Nipata* 1.3. Saddhatissa (1985) pp. 4–8.

is inconsistent with the principle of incrementality, as explained in chapter 3.e above. Whenever we impose a big conceptual discontinuity on our social arrangements, we are at risk of forcing people to repress those aspects of themselves that are on the wrong side of the divide. This creates both internal conflict for those affected, and external conflict between the differing interests of the social castes we have created. In the case of monks and lay-people there is an absolute material dependency on one side and an absolute spiritual dependency on the other, which incentivises the monks to maintain pretences to make sure their needs are met,[12] and disincentivises most lay-people to follow the path with much seriousness.

The monk-lay division is also a result of the absolutisation of enlightenment, the effect of which is to separate off that goal from the lesser goal of merit-making for lay-people. I have already discussed the relationship between this and the belief in 'eternalism' as a second-best option in chapter 4.e. As I argued there, this division between first- and second-class Buddhists is not a necessary response to the need for people to pass through earlier psychological stages before they can fully engage with the Middle Way. The Middle Way is also required in the negotiation of the transitions between the earlier stages, and to provide an overall justification to the direction of the path. If we don't absolutise enlightenment, but instead say that all Buddhists are following the incremental Middle Way, their progression can then be much more flexibly aligned to their conditions. The burden of material support can also be more justly shared. Though the path may in practice have discernible stages like those recognised by Kegan, those stages do not have to be unduly formalised or delimited.

The gap between monks and lay-people is only slightly softened by limited institutional provisionality. There is the initial minor ordination, which creates a period of probation before the major one. There are 'lay' ordinations such as the *upasaka* ordination, and there is the recent development of lay activity in Buddhist countries.[13] Such patches on a system founded on a dualism are not sufficient to remove the dualism, but in many ways reinforce it by keeping it going so that some of the conditions are addressed despite the dualism. Whilst they contribute to practical adaptation, they do not

---

12 As documented by Sangharakshita (1993), previously mentioned.
13 Swearer (1995) pp. 141 ff.

provide any justification for maintaining the dualism when it is not necessary to do so.

A further seed of absolutisation in the early Sangha lay in its dependency on the Buddha as an individual, and the lack of comparable figures to replace him on his death. The Buddha instructed his followers to 'be islands unto yourselves' and to rely on the teachings (see chapter 2.f above), but most people were not yet at a point of psychological development to enable them to do that. The result, instead, was the development of inflexible sets of rules and procedures to substitute for the great teacher: monastic rules, memorisation of verbal formulae, and study eclipsing meditation. It is not surprising, in these circumstances, that provisionality did not generally continue to be nurtured, and instead absolutisations became an ever-tempting shortcut for preserving the teachings.

Fortunately provisionality was not wholly lost, but became a mere means to an end practised only within a limited sphere. Tibetan monastic 'debates' are a wonderful exemplification of this: they appear on the surface to involve genuine debate, but are actually staged events with a fixed result.[14] 'Reflection' as taught in Buddhist tradition also aims to absorb the teachings for ourselves in order to internalise the traditional doctrines, not to offer alternatives or to modify the teachings.[15]

The more distant the inflexible 'truths' became from the context of their origination, the greater their fragility. The Buddhist community showed a great capacity to renew itself in the development of the Mahayana and Vajrayana in the lands north of the Himalaya. However, it was then destroyed in India by a combination of Hindu appropriation and Muslim destruction, ethnicised and relativised in China and Japan, then practically finished off throughout the Buddhist world by a combination of Marxism, Christianity, and capitalism. If the Buddhist community was really focused on addressing the variety of conditions, one would have thought it would have a generally better track-record in dealing with them. Instead, though, it has remained set in a basic form that is focused on a past set of conditions, endlessly reasserting doctrines that were helpful for people in a different past world. In that world, belief in rebirth was vital to social ethics, states were generally ruled by

---

14 Perdue (1992).
15 E.g. in Ratnaguna (2010).

authoritarian methods, there was no understanding of scientific method, very little formal education in the population, and much lower levels of contact with very different views. We no longer live in those conditions.

However, it is the teachings compatible with provisionality that have been preserved in Asian Buddhism which have attracted most interest in the West – meditation and mindfulness techniques, archetypal imagery, and sceptical philosophy. Provisionality has been stimulated because new alternatives have become available in both East and West. Yet at the same time, many Buddhist teachers have felt obliged to offer only traditional Buddhist models as the basis on which the Buddhist community could be organised. Thai monks can be seen incongruously going on their alms rounds in English villages, whilst Tibetan gurus abuse their female disciples under cover of the system of Tantric initiation.[16]

It is quite possible to develop a Buddhist community that is not divided between lay and monastic practitioners. Such a community can also be open to modification from outside, genuinely universal rather than over-dependent on a specific cultural interpretation of Buddhism, and encouraging of integrative practice equally at every stage of development. The key, of course, is to work on the basis of the Middle Way and its five elements. The authority of the Buddha and loyalty to Buddhism can be recognised as values that are important to any Buddhist, but not as absolute values that should always determine our judgements. The greater likelihood of better judgement by the more integrated can be recognised along with the likely asymmetry in those judgements. Thus experienced practitioners and teachers can be appreciated as having credibility, but nevertheless always subject to scrutiny. Openness to a wide variety of ideas beyond Buddhist tradition can be recognised as central to the continuing evolution of helpful Buddhist beliefs.

Buddhist social organisation should evolve just as Buddhism itself does, but my strongest suggestion for its reform is that it should no longer be monastic, nor based on any discontinuous model of ordination. The society or the association is a more appropriate model than the monastery. That's not because monasteries cannot be reformed, or do not offer important strengths as institutions where serious and devoted practice can take place. Rather

---

16 Whitaker (2017).

it's because an associative structure can incorporate democratic elements that assist it in remaining provisional. In an associative structure, responsibilities can be matched to capabilities on an individual basis, rather than a whole class of people being given an intrinsically superior status. Accountability to wider society can also be ensured through an associative structure, all of which aids the practice of provisionality.

But what about depth? What about commitment? Isn't there a danger that a Buddhism based on associative 'lay' structures would just be superficial and conventional, rather than encouraging depth of integrative practice? To answer that question, it is first important to turn to the wider question of faith in Buddhism, and what Buddhists are committing themselves to.

6.h. Faith and Going for Refuge

'Faith' is a term that is often used in the West as a euphemism for 'absolute religious belief', although it also has another set of associations with experienced confidence and trust that give it a potentially much richer meaning. I have argued for the value of treating 'faith' in that sense, and for rejecting absolute belief, in my recent book on Christianity.[1] In Buddhism, the same contestable range of meaning stretching from absolute to experiential can be applied to the term *saddha*, which has been translated as 'faith', 'conviction', 'confidence', and 'confidence-trust'. 'Faith' in one mouth can mean absolute belief in the Buddha's Awakening, but in another confidence in the Middle Way. As with the term 'dharma', the ambiguity means that non-absolute interpretations of it can easily become the means of appropriation for absolute interpretations. However, the reverse can also be the case, and there are strong practical arguments for standing up for an experiential sense when by doing so we can contribute to turning religious thinking of all kinds in helpful directions.

Embodied confidence arises from our accustomed relationships to the world around us, through which certain experiences can become highly meaningful and certain assumptions justified, even though they are fallible. I'm confident in riding a bicycle because I know from lots of previous experience that I won't fall over, not because I believe in a revelation from God telling me that I am capable of riding a bicycle. But of course it's still possible that I might fall over. 'Faith' in the Middle Way is a similar kind of experience. The more I place reliance on it offering the best course, the more it generally works to address conditions better. That's not despite but partly *because of* my recognition that my interpretation of it is fallible and needs constant adjustment. Because I am making the best judgement I can as an embodied human being, and taking that situation fully into account, my judgement is then as justified as it can be. To be experiential, however, faith must also be incremental. The further ahead I place my reliance that things will be roughly as I have experienced them, the less justified that reliance becomes by that experience. This kind of faith thus justifies a *direction*, with

---

[1] Ellis (2018) section 2.

its accompanying short- and medium-term goals, but it does not justify any projection of a final destination.

In contrast, however, most traditional accounts of faith in Buddhism downplay this element of confidence in the Middle Way and insist on identifying it with a belief that the Buddha was enlightened:

> What is the treasure of conviction [saddha]? There is the case where a disciple of the noble ones has conviction, is convinced of the Tathagata's Awakening: 'Indeed, the Blessed One is worthy and rightly self-awakened, consummate in knowledge & conduct, well-gone, an expert with regard to the world, unexcelled as a trainer for those people fit to be tamed, the Teacher of divine & human beings, awakened, blessed.'[2]

Sangharakshita, similarly, defines Buddhist faith as

> The act (expressed by 'taking refuge') or state...of acknowledging unquestioningly that the man Gautama...is in possession of Full Enlightenment.[3]

As I have argued from the beginning of this book, however, whether the man Gautama was in possession of full enlightenment is a complete irrelevance to our confidence on the path. One simple argument appears to seal this point. If it was unexpectedly revealed by conclusive historical evidence that the historical Buddha had been a complete hoax, would this make the slightest difference to your confidence in practising the Middle Way? If your confidence was in the content of the insights that the Buddha offered as to how to overcome delusion as a human being, then the answer would obviously be 'no'. It is only if you had confidence only in historical claims that have no necessary relationship to this that your faith would be in the least shaken. Thus this description of 'faith' in the tradition of Buddhism seems to be built on a most unfortunate confusion – one that has evidently developed from the absolutisation of enlightenment.

The formal expression of faith in the Buddhist tradition is the act of going for refuge to the Three Jewels: the commitment that defines a Buddhist. This consists in the recitation 'I go for refuge to the Buddha. I go for refuge to the Dharma. I go for refuge to the Sangha', but also in the sense of commitment that this represents. The practical necessity of commitment in order to make progress

2   *Anguttara Nikaya* 7.6. Thanissaro (1997b).
3   Sangharakshita (1987) p. 312.

on the path should be obvious. In the absence of integration we are likely to experience a variety of motives, some of which drag us away from the path. Commitment can bring us back through conscience (mentioned already in chapter 5.c) in its two forms: the expectations we have set for ourselves and those we have set up with others. Having some sort of formal statement of commitment can remind us of our earlier, more integrated intentions. If this statement is made in public, it brings other people in to help by enlisting their witness of our intentions. Going for Refuge can thus be seen as an expression of genuine, embodied faith that seeks to create formal reminders of that faith in future.

The objects of refuge, if carefully and responsibly interpreted, can offer a similar basis of commitment to the practice of the Middle Way. The Buddha can represent the archetype of integration, as discussed in chapter 6.e above, and thus the potential for integration within ourselves. To look at a Buddha image and go for refuge to it can thus be a way of kindling aspiration in ourselves. The Dharma, despite the unhelpful ambiguities discussed in chapter 6.f above, can be interpreted as the universal understanding of the Middle Way as it develops in our personal understanding. The Sangha can represent the ways in which others can help us maintain and develop our aspiration to follow the Middle Way, and indeed the potential integration we can develop in relation to their desires and beliefs as well as our own.

However, such an experiential understanding of the Refuges is a very long way from most Buddhist accounts of them. These focus on a person who has attained absolutised enlightenment, the revealed teachings of the absolutely enlightened, and the community of those who have followed those teachings to attain near-enlightenment in turn. As Sangharakshita trenchantly puts it:

> *The Buddha has attained the Transcendental,...the Dharma is the means to the Transcendental,...and the members of the Sangha, by which is meant in this context the Arya Sangha, have gained the Transcendental Path.... One who denies, or even seriously doubts, the existence of such a state as Nirvana, or even the possibility or desirability of its attainment, is naturally precluded from taking refuge in any of them.*[4]

That rules me out, then, and presumably also the Buddha, who in the *Diamond Sutra* says

4   Sangharakshita (1987) p. 446.

Subhuti, the basis of Tathagata's attainment of the Consummation of Incomparable Enlightenment is wholly beyond; it is neither real nor unreal.[5]

On Sangharakshita's account, which reflects that of all traditional Buddhist teachers, it seems that nobody with any sense of integrity who wished to practise the Middle Way could possibly take refuge. However, there is no justification for always taking those who give the most dogmatic expression to a complex tradition at their word. Even for such teachers, there is a rich human experience behind such absolutisations that could be given more appropriate expression.

There is a further problem, also, with the use of 'refuge' as a metaphor. A refuge implies that there is something we are fleeing or seeking shelter from, which in this case is *dukkha* or 'suffering'. Bhikkhu Bodhi argues that 'a refuge must be itself beyond danger and distress.... Only what is beyond fear and danger can be confidently relied upon for protection.'[6] The idea that the Refuges are 'beyond fear and danger' however, involves another absolutisation. There's also a false assumption that something absolutely secure is needed as the basis of commitment. Again, this fundamentally misunderstands the nature of the Buddha's insight, in which our desire for security always needs to be challenged and given a wider context. It is not helpful to deny that desire for safety and security, and to some extent we need to follow it in order to work with it practically. Nevertheless, should we really make a metaphor that involves hiding from and evading conditions the basis of our commitment to facing up to them? The security of the womb arguably provides a psychological basis for all our subsequent confidence, but nevertheless, practice involves moving on from that security so as to balance our need for it with other conditions.

To me there seems to be something incongruous about the relationship between the embodied associations on which that metaphor is based, and the wider meaning it is supposed to have for us as a pledge of spiritual commitment. The institution of Going for Refuge and the prominence given to that metaphor seems to be a product only of the commentarial tradition.[7] It is not found in the Pali Canon, which is not surprising given how poorly it fits many of

---

5 Diamond Sutra 17. Price and Mou-Lam (1969) p. 53.
6 Bodhi (1994).
7 *Khuddakapatha Atthakatha* (Paramatthajotika), *Dighanikaya Atthakatha* (Sumangalavilasini), and *Majjhimanikaya Atthakatha* (Papañcasudani).

the most helpful teachings of the Pali Canon. Going for Refuge has been emphasised, not because of the importance of the metaphor, but because of the need for commitment to a spiritual path.

As with the Four Noble Truths, then, it seems that a re-phrasing of the Three Refuges is required to bring out their most helpful meaning. They are not refuges, because if anything they make us go out into the rain, but they are commitments.

I commit myself to the integrative potential symbolised by the Buddha archetype.

I commit myself to the universal Middle Way.

I commit myself to the support of the practising community, and to integration with the wider community.

The two sections of this revised third refuge seem to be necessary because of the exclusivity of the way the traditional Sangha Refuge is interpreted. Formally speaking the Sangha Refuge consists in the Arya-Sangha, i.e. the community of those who have obtained stream-entry, meaning that they are nearing enlightenment and are irreversibly set for it. In our fruitless search for absolute reliability, we are effectively being told here that ordinary imperfect spiritual friends are not good enough to rely on, and we should not commit ourselves to them. Again, this substitutes an absolutisation for an act of commitment by an embodied person who recognises their limitations and the limitations of those around them. We can never in fact be certain that we have found a single stream-entrant (even if the idea of a stream-entrant makes any sense), let alone committing ourselves to 'belief' in stream-entrants. However, the need for interaction with other members of a community to help us on the path is very much part of our embodied experience, as is the need for integration with all others in human society.

It is helpful to recognise both of those elements in a revised Sangha Refuge, then, because both are equally important. On the one hand we only make progress as individuals because of our relationship with others. We need to accept their support, encouragement, inspiration, and possibly advice, and offer the same in return to others. The giving and receiving of such support is not dependent on a formal status in a hierarchy of integration or spiritual attainment. Due to integrative asymmetry we cannot rely on those who are generally more advanced always being right, nor on those who are generally less advanced always being wrong. We can learn from everyone, though not equally.

On the other hand, the community of practitioners (however you conceive its boundaries) also works within a wider community of people, on which it is dependent. The integration of each individual within a practitioner community is to some extent dependent on the integration of that narrower community. However, the integration of the narrower community is also dependent on that of the wider community. Without the effects of democracy, scientific provisionality, and globalisation, for example, it is hard to imagine Western Buddhism making anything like the progress it has so far. The revised Sangha Refuge should thus involve a commitment not just to how the individual can be helped with their individual progress, but also to integration *in* the wider community. That implies, of course, that we cannot ignore politics.

That wider commitment would capture the helpful spirit behind those great developments of Mahayana Buddhism, the bodhisattva ideal and the bodhisattva's vow. Formally speaking, the bodhisattva is someone who has put off final enlightenment to save all sentient beings, and in her altruistic vow pledges to bring all sentient beings to enlightenment before taking it herself. In some ways this is a patch: a reaction to the limitations and absurdities of the idea of absolute enlightenment for one individual that fails to take into account the social embedding of each individual. In practice, the bodhisattva's vow means that the practitioner helps others to become more integrated and to follow the Middle Way *in addition to* herself, seeing her own and others' development as interdependent and inseparable. Thus it is entirely appropriate for a revised Sangha Refuge to take into account the way in which individual integration and socio-political integration are mutually dependent.

Both faith and commitment, then, should have an important place in Buddhism as they are part of an adequate response to the conditions around us. Commitment is the basis of both depth and breadth of practice. However, faith and commitment in Buddhist tradition have far too often eclipsed provisionality, and they have been able to do so because they have assumed an absolutised form. If we are more conscious of these absolutised forms and the need to take an explicitly agnostic stance towards them, it may be possible to find more consistently helpful interpretations of Buddhism.

7. Alternative Sources of the Middle Way

7.a. The Blind People and the Elephant Again

This final section of the book will offer a brief account of a number of alternative sources of the Middle Way. These will not be alternative Middle Ways, but rather corroborations of the Buddha's Middle Way achieved in different times and places. They offer further indications that we are dealing with a universal feature of human experience here, not the freak occurrence of one person's unique revelation.

The main problem with these alternative sources seems to be that they remain unrecognised by the majority of Buddhists and academics alike. Thus my task will be simply to point out the ways in which they reproduce the Middle Way. The effect of over-specialisation in scientific thinking is often like that of the blind people and the elephant discussed in chapter 3.f: there is so much emphasis on analysis and the use of evidence, that synthetic links are simply not made a lot of the time. If we are not to make the same mistake, we should not complain about the view of the Middle Way offered by the following sources being partial. That will always be the case with such general principles as the Middle Way. As I wrote in the earlier chapter, it was not the blind people's disability that created the problem in the parable, but their assumption that they had a complete view.

The following feels of the elephant are by necessity going to be brief, and will do little more than try to raise awareness of the connection. Some of them have already been mentioned earlier in the book, but will be listed for the sake of completeness. For a fuller explanation of any of them you will need to follow up the references. I'm aware of the dangers in such brief summaries: specialists may object disproportionately to details, rather than thinking syntheti-cally about the relationships between the approaches I'm going to discuss. If you do that I'm afraid you will have missed the point of what I'm aiming to communicate about the Middle Way, as I'm sure that there are lots of ways in which details can be challenged. In the present section, then, I strongly suggest that you reflect on the connections between all the brief chapters before too firmly formulating your objections to any specific one.

Nor is the account of alternative sources of the Middle Way that follows by any means necessarily complete. I shall be concentrating on Western sources, but there are potentially many non-Western ones. Chinese thought, particularly the Neo-Confucianism of the Song period, offers one of these. The complexities of Hindu schools such as Vedanta and Samkhya also need more attention, as do the Sufi tradition in Islam and the Rabbinic and Kabbalistic traditions in Judaism. I do not feel sufficiently knowledgeable about these traditions to yet venture any judgement about how far they engage with the Middle Way in general. It is important not to superficially assume that labels like 'non-dualism' or 'mysticism' necessarily point to a genuine Middle Way perspective. However, it seems very likely that, at least for those with an existing cultural relationship with them, these traditions are well worth a process of critical exploration linked with charitable interpretation.

There is also relatively little discussion here of various Western philosophical sources that some may wish to identify as potential sources of the Middle Way. It would divert me too much here to discuss the pros and cons of, for instance, Aristotle, Nietzsche, and Heidegger.[1] My general view of these figures is that their absolutising assumptions (positive or negative) are often insufficiently acknowledged by their advocates, and that to engage with the Middle Way adequately, a more practical emphasis is required than they tend to offer.

---

1 These and many other Western philosophers are discussed in Ellis (2001).

7.b. Pyrrhonian Scepticism

The earliest Western 'sceptics' were Pyrrhonists, of the school founded by Pyrrho of Elis (c. 360 – c. 270 BCE). Though Pyrrho wrote nothing that survives, it is clear from the writings of his followers that he was a balanced sceptic with practical goals. He was thus completely unlike the caricature of scepticism as negative that has become the norm in Western popular thinking (see chapter 4.a). Pyrrho is said to have travelled to India with Alexander's armies, and to have learnt much from Indian thinkers. This provides a historical explanation for the striking similarities between his teachings and the Buddha's Middle Way.[1] Our main source of information about Pyrrhonism in the West, though, is the writings of Sextus Empiricus, his second-century Roman disciple.

Sextus' definition of scepticism is strikingly reminiscent of the Middle Way:

> *The Sceptic way is a disposition to oppose phenomena and noumena to one another in any way whatever, with the result that owing to the equipollence among the things and statements thus opposed, we are brought first to epoché [suspension of judgement] and then to ataraxia [freedom from mental disturbance].*[2]

Equipollence involves weighing up both positive and negative claims in order to recognise that they are equally unjustified. By doing this we are able to suspend judgement rather than getting dragged into absolutisations. There is a general relationship here (though it may be debatable in detail) between epoché and provisionality (though the consideration of alternatives is not explicit) and between ataraxia and integration. If, as with enlightenment, we can avoid an absolute interpretation of ataraxia, we can read it as the overcoming of psychological conflicts that are due to absolutisation.

That Pyrrho sought to avoid absolutisations can be readily seen from his three characteristics of things – which are very similar to the three marks of conditioned existence in Buddhism. He argued that things were *adiaphora* (without self-identity), *astathmeta* (unstable), and *anepikrita* (indeterminable).[3] This suggests strongly that it is metaphysical beliefs about how things ultimately are that

---

1 Flintoff (1980); Kuzminski (2008); Beckwith (2015).
2 Sextus Empiricus, *Outlines of Pyrrhonism* I.8. Mates (1996).
3 Beckwith (2015) pp. 25-33.

he wishes to avoid. As long as we interpret these in a similar fashion to the Buddhist three marks (see chapter 6.b), we can use them as stimuli to provisionality rather than new metaphysical principles. Sextus offered a 'purgative' account of the value of Sceptical beliefs (already mentioned in chapter 6.c) as flushing themselves away with their critical targets.[4] However, it is not necessary to remove beliefs altogether to make them provisional.

Pyrrho is recorded as saying that we should be *adoxastous* (without views),[5] but it is also clear that this is for practical ends rather than being an end in itself. This suggests that our judgements about what qualifies as a 'view' should ultimately be practical ones. He also seemed to value even-handedness (*aklineis*) and rigorous agnosticism (*akradantous*) of the kind discussed above in chapter 3.f. In short, of the elements of the Middle Way, all seem to be present to some extent (scepticism, provisionality, agnosticism, integration) apart from incrementality.

The practical advice for cultivating integration may seem thin in Pyrrhonism. It is also perhaps over-dominated by a therapeutic metaphor in which the purpose of philosophy is merely to restore us to conventional health and avoid any stress. But we should perhaps bear in mind that Pyrrhonism shared many of its spiritual practices with other Hellenistic philosophies – particularly Stoicism and Epicureanism. The extent of the practical resources offered by all three major Hellenistic philosophies has been strikingly explored by such writers as Martha Nussbaum and Pierre Hadot.[6]

One of the key limitations of Pyrrhonism as an account of the Middle Way seems to be a limitation of ambition, contrasting with the greater ambition to change our lives helpfully that is found in Buddhist sources. This can result in a lack of positive engagement with the value of provisional beliefs in Pyrrhonist responses both to science and to ethics. This limitation of ambition seems to be due to a reliance on conventionality. In the absence of 'truths', the Pyrrhonist response is to go along with appearances, without any recognition of the ways that 'appearances' in the experience of an individual are formed by culturally dominant metaphors, cognitive models, and conventional beliefs. In classical Pyrrhonism there is

---

4   Sextus Empiricus, *Outlines of Pyrrhonism* I.206–8. Mates (1996).
5   Beckwith (2015) pp. 36–7.
6   Nussbaum (1994); Hadot (1995).

thus no developed concept of provisionality involving the critical questioning of one view through the awareness of alternatives. This affects its compatibility with scientific method as well as provisionality in ethical enquiry.

The extent of this problem depends to some extent on the disagreement between two schools of interpretation: 'rustic' and 'urbane' Pyrrhonism. According to the more dominant 'rustic' interpretation, the Pyrrhonist avoids any and all beliefs, and accepts only 'appearances', which are believed to be products of psychological states that are determined and involuntary. The contradictions in this position are evident from the implicit assumption of determinism that accompanies its view of involuntary psychological states. The 'urbane' interpretation, on the other hand, allows the sceptic to distinguish between dogmatic beliefs on the one hand (ones that take appearance to be reality) and 'ordinary' beliefs accepted through practical necessity on the other.[7] This does allow the distinction between dogmatic and non-dogmatic beliefs that I have argued is necessary to the Middle Way and should guide our interpretation of the Buddha's version. However, it does not address the problem of the conventionality of non-dogmatic beliefs, and fails to identify absolutisation as the distinguishing feature of dogmatic beliefs.

As in Buddhism, then, the helpfulness of modern interpretation of Pyrrhonism as a source of the Middle Way depends on a principle of interpretative responsibility. We can find many features of the Middle Way there, but a critical process applying practical criteria is necessary to distinguish the Middle Way elements from absolutisations that have also become part of the tradition. In contrast to the situation in the Buddhist tradition, where those absolutisations are generally positive ones involving an appeal to absolute enlightenment as a source of epistemological guarantees, the absolutisations in Pyrrhonism tend to involve the negative absolutisations of relativism. These assume that the perspectives of a specific context offer the only justifiable story for those in that context.

---

7   Bruzina (2002).

7.c. Christian Incarnation

There is little doubt that the vast majority of Christian thinking is absolutist in nature, appealing to God's existence, God's revelation, God's saving grace, and God's creation of nature as sources of absolute authority. Yet there is also a Christian Middle Way that can, through the careful critical process attempted in my recent book,[1] be distinguished from those absolutisations. That Christian Middle Way is one that I find especially in a strand of the teachings of Jesus, in the mystical tradition, and particularly in the role of the archetypal Christ in the Christian psyche. As with the Buddha, I make no claims that the Middle Way is 'true' or 'original' Christianity, only that it is *helpful* Christianity. At all costs, Buddhists should avoid the simplistic and triumphalist assumption that their religion has the Middle Way correctly and completely and others do not: in all cases it is a matter of degree, and our judgement about it involves a discerning critical process.

In Middle Way Christianity, God needs to be understood as a living experience rather than an abstracted absolutisation, the focus of faith (as discussed in chapter 6.h) rather than belief. The archetypal function of that experience is the same as that of enlightenment and the Buddha figure, as discussed in chapter 6.e: namely a forward glimpse of complete integration. Just as the Buddha can represent the Middle Way as well as complete integration, though, Christ can represent the functional archetype of the Middle Way. Being both wholly human and wholly divine, the Christ archetype represents the dialectic between a glimpsed perfection or finality on the one hand, and the ragged imperfection of human experience on the other. The perfect and the imperfect each offers the potential to break the closed feedback loops of the other, and find a Middle Way between impossible divine standards and morally relative worldly assumptions.

Since the absolute beliefs in each case depend on closed feedback loops of obsessive or anxious motive, it is disruption creating an open feedback loop that can address this situation and allow actual gradual change for humans inspired by God. The crucifixion is the symbolically disruptive event that forces the self-feeding cycle of beliefs to be re-considered, thus allowing new integration to take

---

1   Ellis (2018).

place and more adequate beliefs to be developed. The crucifixion, then, is a symbol of the loss involved in moving from certainty to provisionality. The utterly unexpected positivity of that new perspective, following the painful disruption of the crucifixion, is also symbolised by the resurrection.[2]

The big difference between the ways that the Middle Way is treated in Buddhism and in Christianity, then, is that in Buddhism Siddhartha *discovers* the Middle Way, whereas in Christianity Christ *embodies* the Middle Way. There are both advantages and disadvantages to each of these types of approach, with the Christian approach providing us with powerful symbology even though it offers less by way of practical integrative teaching. Christ as an archetype of the Middle Way is above all *personal*. The sense of total loss and overwhelming suffering associated with the crucifixion is how humans often experience necessary adjustments of their values in a changing set of conditions, and the resurrection how humans experience unexpected breakthroughs. That symbolism potentially has a depth of resonance with the depths of human experience that the Buddha's more positively-driven quest may lack.

That doesn't mean that there are not also many Middle Way elements to be found in the teachings of Jesus. Jesus synthesises moral and religious perspectives, 'completes' (integrates) the law with human experience, offers sceptical challenges to the ideologies of the powerful and dogmatic, leads people to think the previously unthinkable (promoting provisionality), emphasises the integrative emotion of love that breaks down rigid views of others, and leaves us in a position of uncomfortable, indeterminate balance between values.[3]

That there are also absolutisations in the gospel accounts of Jesus' actions and teachings is a prompt, once again, for interpretative responsibility. For instance, Jesus' relationship to God can be interpreted very much as one of embodied faith and confidence, rather than the insistence on certain propositional beliefs.[4] The same applies to the faith of individuals who were healed by Jesus. If we let go, either positively or negatively, of the question of whether miraculous events are historical, we can be more open to finding

---

2 Ibid. pp. 134 ff.
3 Ibid. pp. 92 ff.
4 Ibid. ch. 5.d.

other kinds of significance in them: for example, that the crowds in the feeding of the five thousand received 'all they wanted',[5] suggesting a balancing shift in their appetites which may or may not have been accompanied by the multiplication of food supplies.[6]

The Christian mystical tradition can be a major source of inspiration in seeking out Middle Way interpretations of Christian faith, despite the fact that its proponents throughout history have had to compromise their direct *experienced* relationship with God with the doctrines of the Church. Its *via negativa*, particularly, offers an agnostic approach to God in the sense that it recognises God to be unknown. The inconsistency in the best known expositor of the *via negativa*, Pseudo-Dionysius, is that he simultaneously believed in divine revelation.[7] Mystics have typically cultivated increasingly integrated states, and sought to combine love and wisdom. Meister Eckhart and Hildegard of Bingen went some way towards recognising the archetypal nature of God by identifying God or Christ with the Self.[8]

Christian tradition, then, has at times cultivated integration. It has recognised agnosticism at least in some areas. It has also been stimulated by the humanity of Christ to incremental, compassionate approaches. In the recorded teachings of Jesus, quite a radical scepticism and provisionality can also be discerned at times. None of this should lead us to avoid recognition of the power of absolutisation that has also developed in Christianity, resulting in dogmatism, repression, intolerance, and conflict. The arguments of the 'New Atheists' have done much to spread awareness of these negative effects of Christian absolutisation,[9] but much less to help us develop a balanced awareness of the Christian tradition as simultaneously offering resources to challenge that absolutisation.

Similar arguments to these can be made about other religious traditions, and indeed other kinds of tradition (philosophical, political, artistic, etc.). It is not that all traditions have the same message: taken as a whole they do not, and their absolutisations conflict with each other. However, every tradition addresses conditions through human experience in some way, as well as

5   John 6:11-12.
6   Ellis (2018) ch. 5.e.
7   Pseudo-Dionysius (1924) Caput V.
8   Ellis (2018) p. 171.
9   For example, Harris (2007).

lapsing into absolutisation in others. It is naïve universalism that asserts all religions to always be saying the same thing. A much more adequate *critical* universalism suggests that there are always some elements compatible with the Middle Way to be found in every tradition, once they are sorted from the absolutisations. Once we find those Middle Way elements, we have also found the basis of compatibility and harmony between traditions.

7.d. Jungian Individuation

The work of Carl Jung (1875–1961) has already been mentioned a number of times in this book. It is Jungian thinking that is at the base of the concept of integration as used here. It is Jung who first recognised the diversity of voices within us, and the psychological and moral value of unifying those voices. The process of integration within an individual he called 'individuation'. Jung is also the originator of the concept of archetypes, which can help us distinguish the meaning and inspirational value of our images of Gods, Buddha, and others from our beliefs about them. The value of the Middle Way as it is discoverable in Jung's work is dependent on these core ideas and the insight into universal human functions that they reveal. It doesn't depend on more debatable features like the effectiveness of his psychoanalytic work, or even the philosophical consistency of his outlook.

The Middle Way is mentioned explicitly at a number of points in Jung's *Red Book*,[1] a rich record of Jung's personal visions and reflections that has only been published long after his death. It is this early and less formal work that gives a much more vivid expression to the Jungian Middle Way than his later work.[2]

> *Divinity and humanity should remain preserved, if man should remain before the God, and the God remain before man. The high-blazing flame is the middle way: whose luminous course runs between the human and the divine.*[3]

Here 'divinity' is an archetype of completeness or perfection, and 'humanity' the opposing of that archetype with an insistence on imperfection. Yet both have their role as meaning that can contribute to the development of more adequate beliefs, if they are not prematurely absolutised with the dismissal of the other. 'Man remains before the God' in the sense that imperfection is always challenged by perfection, and 'the God remains before man' in the sense that perfection remains a challenging idea that can inspire the incremental beliefs of human experience, even though that experience never achieves perfection. The Middle Way is then a source of inspiration that can arise within the ambiguous space between the ideas of perfect and imperfect.

---

1 Jung (2009).
2 The case for this is made in Ellis (forthcoming).
3 Jung (2009) p. 289.

In the *Red Book*, the Middle Way is directly recognised in a number of encounters with archetypal figures who represent differing values inside Jung himself. He uses it to navigate between their demands without taking any of them absolutely. For example, in his memorable encounter in a vision with the Bull-God Izdubar, Jung manages to navigate between maintaining respect and empathy for the Bull-God's greatness and pride, whilst also recognising that he is a creation of his own mind and thus that he is flexible. When the Bull-God is badly injured by the 'poison' of rationality, Jung manages to rescue him by carrying him home and smuggling him through the door in his pocket. The God has become as light and small as Jung needs him to be.[4]

Given that an archetype is a basic function found in human experience, expressing profound and universal human needs and aspirations, the recognition and cultivation of the archetypes is vital. However, much of the time we do not recognise the archetypes as our own functions. We identify with the hero without recognising that he is our own ego, or we worship God as a supernatural being without recognising that he reflects our own integrated energies. The process of projecting archetypes onto something separate from our experience (whether 'externally' or 'internally') is equivalent to that of absolutisation, and provides a different standpoint from which to understand absolutisation. One way of describing the Middle Way, then, both in the depths of our imagination and in our everyday relationships, is the avoidance of the projection of emotions like identification, hatred, cupidity, and awe onto others. At the same time we should not deny those emotions and their place in our personal psyche.

Jung's approach to meaning and language also implicitly recognises its embodied basis. Many of the encounters in the *Red Book* reflect his frustration with representationalism, and he sees the barriers to integration dependent on his interior characters' assumption that words can represent truth or falsity. Jung's inspiration is 'The Spirit of the Depths', which represents an embodied and intuitive sense of meaning, in contrast to the narrowly cognitive.[5] In another vision, he meets its antithesis, the

---

4 Jung (2009) pp. 277–314, Ellis (forthcoming) ch. 1.
5 Ellis (forthcoming) ch. 9.

dry-as-dust scholar whose castle hides a daughter symbolic of the scholar's repressed emotional experience:

> Perhaps you think that a man who consecrates his life to research leads a spiritual life and that his soul lives in larger measure than anyone else's. But such a life is also external, just as external as the life of a man who lives for outer things. To be sure, such a scholar does not live for outer things but for outer thoughts – not for himself, but for his object. If you say of a man that he has totally lost himself to the outer and wasted his years in excess, you must also say the same of this old man. He has thrown himself away in all the books and thoughts of others. Consequently his soul is in great need, it must humiliate itself and run into every stranger's room to beg for the recognition that he fails to give her.[6]

To live for 'outer thoughts' I take here to be narrowly conceived representations: things that we assume to be substantially present in accordance with our categorisations and assumptions. In the process of obsessively pursuing beliefs about these 'outer things', we neglect the ways in which our own embodied experience helps to form these representations. Not only does this result in narrow-minded literalism in which intuition, metaphor, and emotion are neglected, but also a fragility and unhappiness that cannot be acknowledged.

On the other elements of the Middle Way – its scepticism, provisionality, incrementality, and agnosticism – Jung is less consistent, despite the scepticism that implicitly shapes his refusal to adopt the absolute perspectives of his inner figures. Jung was tempted by the monist metaphysics of Gnosticism and by Platonic accounts of archetypes, but he continued to insist, nevertheless, that his work was empirical and scientific rather than metaphysical. He was also influenced by some of the sceptical approaches in philosophers like Kant and Nietzsche. Some of his early statements on philosophical themes (most closely corresponding to the time of the writing of the *Red Book*) reflect sceptical perspectives in line with his practice, such as this one:

> The only true basis for philosophy is what we experience ourselves, and through ourselves, of our world around us. Every a priori structure that converts our experience into an abstraction must inevitably lead us to erroneous conclusions.[7]

---

6 Jung (2009) p. 29.
7 Jung (1898).

In general, the Jungian Middle Way is one founded on the development of integration and the avoidance of projection, but the explicit philosophy that Jung assumes is not always consistent with this. As Jung scholar Renos Papadopoulos writes:

> It is important to appreciate that there are two Jungs – the one with an open epistemology and Socratic ignorance, and the other Jung who, following Gnostic epistemology, was, in fact, essentialist and universalist.[8]

As with Buddhism and Christianity, the Middle Way in Jung and Jungianism needs a critical process to be picked out, and a sense of responsibility in interpretation. However, once one starts to read Jung in that way, his work offers an unparalleled intuitive depth of inspiration and symbolism for the Middle Way.

---

8   Papadopoulos (2006) p. 48.

7.e. Scientific Falsificationism

It may be argued by many that scientific method encapsulates the value of provisionality, requiring our beliefs to be constantly re-examined in the light of new evidence. However, where science is understood in verificationist and naturalist terms (i.e. where it is assumed that observations can provide us with natural 'truths'), that provisionality is limited, because the power of confirmation bias is not sufficiently taken into account. Confirmation bias is our tendency to only perceive what we are looking for, and only conceptualise what will fit our pre-existing models. In naturalistically interpreted science, the projections we make in the limited cave of our selective interpretations are mistaken for 'facts' about 'nature'. It is only with the development of falsificationist theories of science that the weaknesses in this model began to be addressed.

It is Karl Popper who first put forward such a view of scientific progress, seeing it as *subtractive*. We develop theories, test them against observation or experiment, and, if we find them wanting, we learn something about what is *not* the case.[1] Popper also distinguished between open and closed feedback loops, identifying that it is in open feedback loops, where a theory is modified by being negated in the light of observation, that it can then be modified. This is a model of *adequacy* rather than *truth* in science that is central to provisionality as a principle of the Middle Way, following the experimental approach of the Buddha's early life. Popper identified this process as operating in evolutionary progress as well as in scientific investigation.[2] In order to follow such an approach, we also need to remain sceptical about any claims to have reached a finally true position, and agnostic in maintaining a middle space where we reject both absolute and relative interpretations. We thus investigate confidently despite continuing uncertainty.

Popperian progress does not occur by discovering absolute falsifications, any more than by discovering absolute verifications. However, the insight it offers is that we can nevertheless justify rejecting and modifying a theory that has been 'falsified' in our terms on practical grounds. By modifying theory we enter a dialectical process with the conditions, whereby we maintain the aspects of

---

1   Popper (1959).
2   Popper (1994) ch. 3.

our theory that seem to be adequate, but reject those that do not meet the conditions. This gives us the best sort of objectivity we can manage (for the moment) as embodied beings having limited senses and concepts.

Popper persisted in rejecting any psychological basis for the justification of falsifications, but it seems clear from the use of open feedback loops in scientific falsificationism that they are due to openness in the psychological state of investigating scientists, who are able to modify their view by taking into account new information rather than selectively seeking out information that confirms their view. It is this openness of psychological state that enables the comparison of alternative views, and thus a form of justification that is distinct from naturalistic 'proof'.

For example, if we take the discovery by Galileo of craters and mountains on the surface of the moon, this discovery created a basis for falsifying the Aristotelian belief that the moon must be a perfect sphere. One of Galileo's contemporaries offered an ad hoc hypothesis to make Galileo's observations compatible with Aristotle: namely that the craters and the spaces between the mountains on the moon must be filled with a transparent substance.[3] The opponent was sceptically correct in effectively pointing out that Galileo's disproof of Aristotle's theory was not absolute, as the transparent substance hypothesis could not be proved wrong. However, the obviously circular nature of the opponent's proposal is what makes it unjustifiable. It is a manifestation of a closed feedback loop motivated by defensive absolutisation of Aristotle's theory.

Popper's approach was refined by his follower Imre Lakatos, who used information from the history of science in practice to make the theory more adequate. He concluded that the process of falsificatory refinement actually occurs to smaller sub-theories within a wider 'research programme'[4] (which Kuhn more influentially called a 'paradigm'). Both Lakatos and Kuhn[5] traced scientific paradigms as being dependent on confidence in their basic assumptions, which could gradually ebb away as that paradigm proved less fruitful in giving rise to new tests. Crucial to the objectivity *of character* in scientists, then, is the integration of the desire to maintain a

3 Drake (1978) p. 168.
4 Lakatos (1974).
5 Kuhn (1996).

favoured theory, on the one hand, and the desire to acknowledge new information, on the other. This will also require the Middle Way in the avoidance of both positive and negative absolutisation: positive absolutisation of the paradigm as opposed to negative absolutisation that assumes the paradigm is immediately and totally destroyed by any apparent counter-evidence.

Science, when understood on this type of model rather than naturalistically as a source of 'natural laws' or other absolutised results, can thus contribute importantly to the practice of the Middle Way in modern society. Its limitation is that it is practised in socially-organised contexts according to a traditional, socially prescribed, set of procedures, and thus often has surprisingly little effect on the integration of individuals, even including scientists themselves. Science is often badly handicapped by dogmatic naturalism in its teaching traditions, and thus also by the widespread belief that values need to be (or indeed can be) excluded from scientific work. This means that not only personal integration, but also agnosticism and incrementality, are often insufficiently addressed in scientific thinking. A much greater emphasis on the philosophy and psychology of science as part of scientific training is needed to redress this.

There is a scientific Middle Way, but science is also a tradition. To distinguish that Middle Way in scientific tradition, as with every other tradition, we need to look critically at its limiting assumptions as well as the successful ways that it has addressed conditions. The perspective offered by other traditions (that may be offered by education in the humanities) provides a vital support to the provisionality of science. We are only able to be genuinely provisional if we can consider alternatives.

7.f. Systems Theory and Biology

When science is conducted in a provisional way, the very way it categorises its objects of study is affected. As I argued in chapter 6.a, the traditional Buddhist emphasis on the conditionality of subject and object can be a placeholder for provisionality. In turn, conditionality is also a likely implication of provisional ways of understanding. One reason for this is that selecting particular categorisations as essentially correct, as well as ascribing rigid boundaries to those categorisations, are forms of absolutisation. For the same reason, then, that recognition of conditionality in Buddhism, which questions assumptions about essences and boundaries, can offer an approach to the Middle Way, similarly its counterpart in science can do so. Systems theory (together with the related complexity theory and network theory) is a recent cross-disciplinary development in science that can offer further evidence of the universality of the Middle Way.

A systems view of the world avoids the rigid identification of simple objects relating to each other, but instead talks about systems nesting within other systems. Each system consists of a balance of interacting conditions that has attained a degree of stability and distinctness, even though no system is completely independent. For example, a human being is a system, which interacts with the wider systems of the environment and human society, as well as the narrower system of cells within the body. Instead of the classical model of linear causality, in which one event causes another, systems thinking also tries to do more justice to complexity by conceptualising causality as mutual relationships between systems. This involves a diachronic perspective, as mutually causal relationships occur over time rather than at one point in time: for instance the interdependent relationship between foxes and rabbits rather than a specific fox killing a specific rabbit. Such thinking gives us a resource for the Middle Way by re-framing and resolving absolutisations that are created by normal substantive and linear thinking.

There is a particularly interesting application of systems theory in the work of Humberto Maturana and Francisco Varela. These are biologists who have developed a new view of 'knowledge' (what I would prefer to call adequate or justified judgement) in terms of living systems.[1] They coined the term *autopoiesis* for the

---

1 Maturana and Varela (1992).

self-regulating and adaptive activity of living systems. Autopoiesis requires closed feedback loops which maintain boundaries between a given organism and its environment and serve the interests of the organism behind those boundaries, but on the other hand, open feedback loops are also required for an organism to adapt to its environment. Thus organisms always need to find a point of balance between response to their environment and maintenance of their autonomous system. 'Knowledge' Maturana and Varela define as autopoietic activity – in other words the implicit strategy adopted for sustainably maintaining the organism distinct from its environment. A balanced and stable relationship between systems is known as *homeostasis*.

It is this approach that can provide an understanding of the biological basis of the Middle Way. It is important not to confuse the Middle Way with homeostasis itself, because homeostasis, although based on balance between systems, involves complete stability in the relationship between systems (even though it may contain conflict and change at a lower level). However, the closer we can get to homeostasis in our relationship with our environment, the more sustainable it will be. The Middle Way is probably best described as a *movement in the direction* of homeostasis. Our autopoiesis as human beings means that our continued existence, both as individuals and groups, is the central value for us. We are capable of inflicting massive changes on our environment to help maintain ourselves. That leads to a massive instability in the system, as anyone familiar with current environmental issues will know. We cannot assume that we will ever reach complete homeostasis in relation to our environment, because modification of our environment is so much part of our basic operation. However, we can move in the direction of that stability by reducing the closed feedback loops through which we uncompromisingly impose our own intentions on the environment. In the process of reducing those closed feedback loops and increasing open ones, we can at least reduce conflict and make our lives more sustainable than they would otherwise have been.

This relationship between the Middle Way and homeostasis has striking parallels with that between the Middle Way and enlightenment in Buddhist tradition. Buddhism traditionally claims that enlightenment is unconditioned or uncompounded, meaning that it is no longer subject to change and must thus involve a completely stable, homeostatic relationship between the individual and the environment. We do not know whether such a state is possible, so in practice our understanding of how to move towards it is of much more practical importance. Maturana and Varela understand the Middle Way as a 'via media' applied in scientific 'knowledge'[2] and also in ethics,[3] running between representationalism and solipsism. The representationalist impulse to find out about the world and represent it has the virtue of trying to address conditions, whilst what they call the 'solipsist' impulse tries to find certainty through withdrawal into individual experience as the sole reality, thus at least facing up to our inability to represent the world.

The same 'via media' identified by Maturana and Varela can also be traced psychologically in the development of individual humans, as in the work of Robert Kegan[4] already discussed in chapters 4.e and 6.g. At each new stage of development in Kegan's scheme, a person has to find a new balance (a temporary, partial homeostasis) in relation to new conditions. This obliges them to revise their basic assumptions about themselves and their relationship to the world. As they do so, they are developing new physical capacities (new synaptic connections), but those capacities are also increasingly adequate beliefs about the world. The transitions at each stage can only occur because neither the previous stage nor the next stage are absolutised, thus requiring provisionality, incrementality, and agnosticism. At each stage, also, greater integration is developed, as previous conflicts with the environment are overcome.

Systemic approaches, which try to take into account the bigger picture in both space and time, and prioritise thinking about relationships as opposed to linear processes, can also be found in a great many other fields. A recent textbook created by Fritjof Capra and Pier Luigi Luisi very usefully synthesises the great range of such systemic work in different areas.[5] These approaches can all be counted as 'Middle Way' in the sense that they avoid the absolutisations involved in assuming that beliefs formed in a more limited way drawing on a limited context of research are the whole story – or indeed at the other extreme that they tell us nothing. Scepticism and agnosticism about such absolutised linear beliefs will also

---

2 Ibid. p. 241.
3 Ibid. p. 245.
4 Kegan (1982).
5 Capra and Luisi (2014).

follow from this, although accounts of systems theory sometimes need to give more emphasis to the way in which systemic beliefs are also subject to sceptical limitations. Systems theory should thus not be interpreted naturalistically or cosmologically.

Provisionality also follows from the conditionality that is emphasised in systems theory. Changes in living systems are also described in terms of *process*, which makes the recognition of incrementality also a crucial requirement for systems theory. As Capra and Luisi put this:

> From the very beginning of biology, the understanding of living structure has been inseparable from the understanding of metabolic and developmental processes. This striking feature of living systems suggests process as a third perspective [together with organisation and structure] for a comprehensive description of the nature of life. The process of life is the activity involved in the continual embodiment of the system's pattern of organisation.[6]

These developmental processes are a very basic condition for anything human, so we ignore them at our peril in any discussion of human concepts or activities. Life may do relatively rapid change, but it does not do discontinuity – so nor should our thinking.

Integration, as the remaining principle of the Middle Way, is crucial to the development of living systems, and to the adaptation of living systems to the wider systems in which they are placed (such as the human adaptation to Gaia). Whilst it is recognised in systems theory that living systems require closed feedback loops to maintain themselves, it is open feedback loops that enable *integration* with initially conflicting desires, meanings, and beliefs in the wider system. It is only by accepting information from beyond our current bounds of assumption and taking it into account that we can begin to modify our own patterns of judgement and thus reduce conflict. Systems theory crucially applies this recognition to the human place in the wider environment so as to offer the potential for addressing the eco-crises that currently threaten to engulf human civilisation.

---

6   Ibid. p. 302.

7.g. Embodied Meaning

Our understanding of how human beings can gain that increasingly adequate relationship to their environment has also been greatly boosted by the development of the embodied meaning theory of George Lakoff and Mark Johnson[1] (already mentioned in chapters 1.h, 3.a, and 3.b). Working from evidence in linguistics, cognitive science, and philosophy, these thinkers have transformed our view of the nature of meaning and language. The traditional theory of representationalism (that still dominates much linguistics and philosophy) takes meaning to be a static relationship between propositions (claims about the world written in sentences) and their truth or falsity in the world. Embodied meaning theory has shown that, instead, meaning must be understood dynamically as part of our development. Whenever we absolutise, we effectively deny that dynamic meaning. Embodied meaning theory is often referred to as 'cognitive linguistics' – but for a variety of reasons I think this is a misleading label for it. It is not just cognitive, but puts 'cognition' in a far bigger context of human meaning that is just as much emotional. It also has implications that go far beyond linguistics.

Meaning is part of the development of every organism, because it consists of associative links made in the synaptic and nervous system in relation to particular sorts of stimuli. The 'cognitive' and 'emotive' aspects of such links can never be separated, but are always inter-dependent. A human child starts to make such links as soon as it can differentiate objects or types of relationship and relate them to specific sounds or other stimuli. In chapter 3.a it was explained how these basic associations can develop into the most complex and abstract language, through basic categories and schemas that are extended through metaphor and the development of cognitive models. This explanation of linguistic meaning is also entirely consistent with the meaningfulness of visual or other sensual symbols, such as those of art and music. Indeed the associative meaning of any object: a tune, a sculpture, or a favourite tree all gain their meaning in the same basic associative way as words.

Embodied meaning theory provides the basis of a whole new angle on the Middle Way, which depends on an understanding of absolutisation as entrenched representationalism. Whenever

---

1   Lakoff and Johnson (1980); Lakoff (1987); Johnson (2007).

we absolutise, we assume that a particular proposition or set of propositions is true or false as a description or representation of reality. This in turn involves the assumption that language is meaningful in a way that allows it to *represent* truth or falsity. This involves a deluded set of implicit assumptions about meaning that are completely out of harmony with the way in which meaning is developed in our bodily experience. Instead, a cognitive model (which is a consistent set of assumptions based on a dead metaphor) is assumed to be a potential representation of reality, and meaning is said to be dependent on belief rather than the other way round.

In relation to systems theory, embodied meaning is systemic, because it regards meaning as a set of connections or relationships within the network that is a human body. That meaning-network also interacts with the wider network of social communication that determines the forms of shared words and symbols, but cannot be reduced to purely communicative terms. In contrast, representationalism is linear, assuming a line of conditionality from hypothetical reality to language that represents that reality. As a view of meaning, this may work in its own context of assumptions, but it neglects a whole wider set of conditions.

To follow the Middle Way, we need to recognise the basis of our beliefs in meaning, and the basis of that meaning in embodied and associative experience. Meaning can be *fragmented* by absolutisation because our beliefs about another perspective (or another group, person, or even part of ourselves) can block our ability to find their symbols meaningful.[2] When we fail to understand the meaning of another perspective, it is impossible to then develop more adequate shared beliefs, because such beliefs would depend on shared meanings.

Thus the use of the imagination becomes an important aspect of provisionality, enabling us to consider the meaning that forms the basis of alternative beliefs before we engage with them fully on the level of belief. The practice of the arts, or any other practice that involves the imagination, can help us to extend the meaning available to us and to play with alternative sources of meaning, in a way that can only help our beliefs to become more adequate (the integration of meaning).[3] That openness to new sources of meaning needs to be combined with scepticism towards absolutising beliefs

2 Ellis (2013b) section 2.
3 Ibid. sections 5 and 6.

that seek to block our access to new meaning.[4] For example, think of the way that totalitarian regimes repress the arts, because the arts can help people to think in new ways that might potentially threaten that totalitarian power.

Embodied meaning also provides a further justification for incrementality as a basic feature of human meaning. From an embodied point of view, a particular symbol, word, or piece of language will have a *degree* of meaning for a specific person. Representationalism, on the other hand, is associated with discontinuous beliefs about the meaningfulness or meaninglessness of language. Perhaps the most extreme instance of this was the logical positivist philosophy of figures like A.J. Ayer, who rejected all ethical and religious language as 'strictly meaningless' because it could not be absolutely verified[5] (completely ignoring the sceptical recognition that scientific, or any other, belief also cannot be absolutely verified!). However, a similar set of implicit assumptions about meaningfulness is adopted by every sneering analyst who dismisses ideas that they don't relate to as 'meaningless'. We can only apply discontinuous criteria of meaningfulness or meaninglessness by neglecting the conditionality for meaning in the incremental activity of neural connections, as well as the complex interdependency and mutual resonance of those connections. Even in the most extreme and obvious case of 'meaninglessness', where I encounter a passage in Chinese characters that I do not 'understand' in the conventional sense, I recognise it as a passage in Chinese characters, and may also be able to guess other basic aspects of its meaning from the context.

Embodied meaning thus has several important implications for helping us understand the Middle Way from new standpoints. It gives us a new reason for recognising that absolutisation is mistaken, its assumed representationalism being out of harmony with our embodied experience in a basic way. This supports scepticism as the basic recognition of the uncertainty of beliefs, and agnosticism about absolute claims. It supports incrementality by helping us recognise that meaningfulness is a matter of degree. It helps to provide an explanation of the role of the arts or any other meaning-making in supporting provisionality. It also provides the basis of another form of integration, the integration of meaning, as a prior condition for integration of belief.

4   Ibid. section 3.
5   Ayer (1946).

7.h. Brain Lateralisation and Absolutisation

One of the most important events in the recent history of ideas has been the publication in 2010 of *The Master and His Emissary* – Iain McGilchrist's multidisciplinary book on brain lateralisation and its impact on human culture and history.[1] McGilchrist's account of the two halves of the brain is based on a great deal of evidence, and a sophisticated view of the roles of the two hemispheres that overtakes previous over-simplifications of the subject. Nevertheless, he is able to point out the major effects of the differing specialisations of the two hemispheres: the left being goal-orientated and maintaining linguistic representations, the right open to stimuli from the senses, body, empathy, and metaphor. It must be stressed that to account for our mental processes in terms of the brain is *not* necessarily reductionist. Rather than claiming that the mind is *only* the brain, McGilchrist offers an additional wealth of insights into the mind we experience from within, that reinforce the need for provisionality at whatever level of description we use.

McGilchrist's account is also about the Middle Way, because the over-dominant left hemisphere is very clearly the source of absolutisation. Though we all use both hemispheres continually, it is the effectiveness of the connection between them that is crucial. The left hemisphere, which handles our explicit, linguistically expressed, beliefs, can adopt an assumed self-sufficiency, taking itself to have the whole story, when it is over-dominant and insufficiently moderated by awareness from the right hemisphere.[2] Closed feedback loops between the left prefrontal cortex and the limbic system provide constant reinforcement for the supposed self-sufficiency of the left hemisphere, which is objectifying, manipulative, and rationalising.

Although the left hemisphere can make our beliefs *logically* consistent, it is the assumptions that it makes before beginning a process of reasoning that are more significant for the adequacy of its beliefs. It is only some connection with the right hemisphere, bringing in new information or a new metaphorical framework, that can shift those assumptions, whether they are formally positive

---

1 McGilchrist (2010). Also see my summary and extended review at Ellis (2011c).
2 McGilchrist (2010), pp. 37 ff.

or negative. It is the right hemisphere that is *embodied* in the sense of being linked to awareness of the whole body in a way that the left is not. Thus embodied meaning can be seen as basically processed through the right hemisphere when we connect McGilchrist's work to embodied meaning theory.

The differing approaches to time in the two hemispheres are also a crucial aspect of McGilchrist's account.[3] Only the right hemisphere can experience duration as such, by being aware of time passing. The left hemisphere has ideas about time and duration, and uses measurements of time as concepts, but cannot directly experience the passing of time or be directly aware of itself as having different states at different points in time. That means that it is the left hemisphere that is the source of our impatience: rather than being content with an experience of duration, it wants its goals to be fulfilled instantly. One of the crucial links between absolutisation and the prevention of integration is thus revealed. Integration involves the awareness (*sampajana* in Buddhism) that we have different states at different times, but that these states are all part of a wider experience. However, the absolutising left hemisphere can block this with its implicit certainty that this moment is the whole story.

The Middle Way as we can understand it in relation to brain lateralisation, then, is *not* a middle way between right and left hemispheres. Rather it is the Middle Way between different opposing absolutisations produced by the left hemisphere. To experience that Middle Way and judge differently, we need sufficient shared awareness linking the specific judgements of the left hemisphere, isolated in time, with the right, that places them in a wider temporal context. The right hemisphere provides that linking, integrating awareness, but without the left hemisphere there would be nothing to integrate. It is only with sufficient input from the right hemisphere, with its ability to challenge the left's self-sufficiency from wider experience and re-frame through imaginative awareness of alternatives, that the left hemisphere can judge provisionally.

If we link this account of brain lateralisation to the approaches to the Middle Way discussed earlier in this section, it offers further insights and corroborations. Systemic forms of thinking can be

3 Ibid. pp. 75–7.

generally associated with those that draw on the right hemisphere sufficiently to broaden our awareness of the network of conditions beyond the linear models that the left hemisphere tends to construct in isolation. Embodied meaning can be interpreted as an account of meaning that pays sufficient attention to the role of bodily awareness and metaphor in creating our experience of meaning – all dependent on the right hemisphere rather than the dominance of the left alone. Falsificationism can be understood as an approach to scientific method that makes sufficient allowance for the ways in which all discovery requires new information to disrupt existing theory: again, allowing the right hemisphere a sufficient connected role rather than depending on the left in isolation.

All the principles of the Middle Way suggest challenges to over-dependence on the isolated left hemisphere. Scepticism is a challenge to the certainty that the over-dominant left hemisphere tends to adopt. Agnosticism is a challenge both to that certainty and to the dualism that the left hemisphere can fall into when it models contrary views only as negations to its existing views, excluding alternatives from active consideration. It's only through the right hemisphere that we become aware of third alternatives, and it's the capacity to become aware of them that offers the basis of provisionality.

Incrementality, already noted as a feature of organic processes, is likewise a feature of the embodied awareness of the right hemisphere in contrast to the abstracted discontinuity typical of the left. This point is directly illustrated by Zeno's Paradoxes, discussed by McGilchrist as directly reflecting the hemispheric split.[4] For instance, according to Zeno's Paradox, an arrow flying towards a target will never reach that target, because the intervening space and the time taken can both be infinitely divided. Logically this will be the case – but only on the basis of incorporeal left hemisphere assumptions as opposed to actual experience of things (including our bodies) moving through time and space regardless of their divisibility. The right hemisphere, in contrast, experiences things in time and space as *gestalts* – as indivisible wholes grasped at once rather than in terms of divisible measurements.

Integration can also thus only be possible because of the interaction of the right and left hemispheres. Where the left

---

4   Ibid. pp. 138–9.

hemisphere creates conflict through the illusion of separateness and the imposition of closed feedback loops in the service of rigid goals, the right hemisphere offers the possibility of reconciling those goals with each other through open feedback loops and adaptation. The conflicts of the left hemisphere are not with the right, but with itself at different times, as due to lack of linking awareness over time the left hemisphere can flip or swing between one goal and its contrary (think of an irresolute slimmer or smoking quitter). Of course, conflict also has a social aspect that consists in the left hemispheres of different persons or groups having incompatible goals, but their mediation nevertheless depends on right hemisphere awareness to enable re-framing of the terms of the conflict.

7.i. Cognitive Bias and Absolutisation

A further approach to the Middle Way can be glimpsed in the massive development of cognitive psychology by a range of figures in recent decades. This has particularly taken the form of the identification of cognitive biases that have been shown to have universal effects in restricting our thinking. Whilst a great many people have contributed to this, the figure of Daniel Kahneman stands out as the populariser of the crucial concepts of fast and slow thinking.[1] 'Fast' thinking is the automatic thinking that we employ much of the time for practical ends, because it involves less cognitive effort and less energy. 'Slow' thinking, on the other hand, involves working through the connections explicitly and taking the time that is necessary to properly justify one's judgement. Kahneman's main model for 'slow' thinking is explicit reasoning, but I see no reason why the imaginative consideration of alternatives should not be another form of it, because that also takes time. Both explicit reasoning and exercise of the imagination are short-circuited by the hasty and habitual use of 'fast' thinking.

It is our use of 'fast' thinking when 'slow' thinking would be more appropriate and effective that produces cognitive biases. There are a very wide range of these, which I have surveyed elsewhere.[2] For example they might include confirmation bias, where we only consider evidence that fits our prior view; sunk cost fallacy, where we continue with a useless project because of the previous effort we have put into it; and actor-observer bias, where we judge others as having much more responsibility for negative events than we do in the case of ourselves. In each of these cases, we employ 'fast' thinking that might be appropriate in some past contexts but that makes our responses to current ones far less adequate. This employment of 'fast' thinking when 'slow' thinking is required is another term for absolutisation.[3] That's not to say that 'fast' thinking isn't often appropriate, but it's our assumption that it needs no further investigation at points where we *could* practically engage in such further investigation that creates absolutisation.

Kahneman also documents a substitution process that helps to defend fast thinking: by substituting an easy problem for a harder

1 Kahneman (2011).
2 Ellis (2015a) section 3.
3 See Ellis (2015b).

one, we make an absolute answer permissible. This is one reason why people make mistakes in complex calculations when they are overconfident that their familiar methods will work. Kahnemann also offers some provocative substitutions of the kind we may use for complex or difficult questions. For instance, instead of asking 'How much would you contribute to save an endangered species?' one implicitly substitutes 'How much emotion do I feel when I think of dying dolphins?' and instead of 'How should financial advisers who prey on the elderly be punished?' one implicitly substitutes 'How much anger do I feel when I think of financial predators?'[4] This again helps to identify a key feature of absolutisation, involving the substitution of an existing abstract concept or conceptual belief (even when this is based on an emotional impression) for the greater work of examining a wider range of experiences or concepts.

Often we can effectively do nothing about cognitive biases, because they are part of our embodied situation, probably produced by genetic inheritance. However, there is an area of cognitive bias that can be addressed by action of a long-term, integrative type. Because researchers such as Kahneman have usually focused on faults in reasoning, and thus expected resolutions to be the result of applying 'rationality' in the context where the bias occurs, they have often underplayed our capacity to address biases.[5] But logical reasoning is only one small possible component of a more adequate approach to cognitive biases: one that employs the whole Eightfold Path to develop a more integrated basis for judgement. It is *awareness* that can prompt us to slow down when necessary, and that awareness comes from sufficient connection with the right hemisphere, not merely more rigorous 'processing' in the left. It also involves development *over time* of a kind that the 'rational' left hemisphere may not recognise as 'its' development at all: an openness to unknown unknowns.

A 'cognitive' bias is thus not merely cognitive, but just as much 'emotional'. It simultaneously applies shortcuts based in the representational linguistic centre of the prefrontal cortex, ignores the wider embodied context of our judgement, operates a closed rather than open feedback loop in relation to the environment, and substitutes a linear for a more adequate systemic standpoint. Each

---

4 Kahneman (2011) pp. 98-9.
5 Ibid. pp. 417 ff.

bias needs to be seen, not just in isolation, but also in relation to the other biases and to the overall psychology of absolutisation. Over-dominance of the left hemisphere, representationalism, confirmation bias, projection of archetypes, delusion, dogma, and Mara are all different ways of talking about the same phenomena from different points of view. It is only the blind people feeling the elephant who are unwilling to draw the synthetic conclusions that are demanded when considering these overlapping problems.

The development of a general practice to work with cognitive biases and overcome their negative effects is still in its infancy. Cognitive behavioural therapy provides approaches that are mainly used in a medicalised context for those with diagnosed mental health problems, where a consensus about problematic forms of thinking is easier to reach. Yet these approaches are generally not used in the mainstream in the places where they could make the most difference. For instance, there is virtually no discussion of how cognitive biases affect political viewpoints when politics is discussed in the media. There is also no widespread discussion of the ways that traditional institutional viewpoints (such as the doctrines of religious groups) are products of absolutising bias. In *Thinking Fast and Slow*, Kahneman talks about his past work in Israel – but with no mention of the obvious cognitive biases in common Israeli political attitudes. Not only do a great many synthetic links need to be made (against the grain of cautious, over-specialised academia) to make our insights into cognitive bias effective, but they also need to be far more courageously applied in a much wider range of contexts. Recognising their relationship to the Middle Way could be one important step in that process of synthesis and application.

7.j. Ellen Langer's 'Mindfulness'

Ellen Langer has already been mentioned in this book (chapters 5.b and 6.b), because of her huge contribution to our understanding of 'mindfulness'. I have put the word in quotation marks, not to cast suspicion over it, but only to point out the ways that Langer's sense of the term 'mindfulness' is a little wider than that employed in Buddhism. Whilst she includes broadened awareness and attention of the kind found in Buddhist mindfulness, Langer gives a lot more attention to the cognitive realm. 'Mindfulness' for her is a quality we apply to our judgements, very similar to 'provisionality' as I have been using it in describing the Buddha's Middle Way. It involves the awareness of alternatives, in the form of what Langer often calls 'novel distinctions', or the awareness of new relationships that can be made through analogy.[1]

Langer's work is very much concerned with the Middle Way, because it is focused on avoiding absolutisation of all kinds, and with making more adequate judgements in an entirely flexible way. Absolutisation is what Langer calls 'mindlessness'. She describes this mindlessness in terms of many different cognitive biases, particularly those that involve absolutising particular framing, particular categories, or particular associations.[2] Mindlessness is the maintenance of a rigid mindset in changing conditions. She also sees mindlessness as absolutisation in the process of learning, as a specific learning shortcut we have used that may work in one context but does not actually prepare us for another. Rote learning for a test is a classic example of this. When we learn by rote (as Buddhist monks have traditionally done) we completely neglect the context that is required to make an answer 'right' in any meaningful sense.[3] Such learning also assumes that 'facts', or certain set skills, have an absolute value that is independent of our ability to actually use them subsequently.[4]

This approach is compatible with many of the ones mentioned in the earlier part of this section. It is a systemic approach in the sense of identifying the kind of synthetic learning that is required to

---

1 Langer (2014) pp. 127-8.
2 Ibid. part 1.
3 Langer (1997) ch. 4.
4 Ibid. ch. 7.

focus on relationships in a wider set of conditions, whilst 'mindless' learning is unexamined linear learning. The narrow focus on specific represented goals in mindless learning, as opposed to the ability to engage with new ideas in a mindful approach, also makes it clear that this mindfulness involves effective use of right-hemisphere functions in co-ordination with left. Whilst Langer often talks about 'novel distinctions' and distinctions are the speciality of the left hemisphere, their 'novelty' requires sufficient connection with the right hemisphere. It is the wider awareness of mindfulness, too, that gives us the best practical strategy for becoming aware of cognitive biases.

Langer's way of approaching mindfulness is also subtractive in the same fashion as Popper's falsificatory approach in science, and she is careful to point out the differences between her scientific approaches to it and a traditional religious approach that may begin with dogmatic positive claims.

> My work on mindfulness has been conducted almost entirely within the Western scientific perspective. Initially, my focus was on mindlessness and its prevalence in daily life.... The notion of mindfulness develops gradually by looking at aspects of mindlessness and then at the other side of the coin.[5]

In this respect her provisionality of approach seems to be preferable to the top-down linear teaching approach often found in traditional Buddhism, and more expressive of the Middle Way.

Apart from the value of provisionality through awareness of multiple perspectives, Langer shows awareness of the value of incrementality in writing about experiments in conditional learning: students who were taught a new task using conditional language (suggesting that this might be the best way of doing it) were better able to apply the skills to a new context than those taught it using absolute language.[6] Conditional language of this kind is also incremental language, because it is implied that there is a degree of justification for using it according to the context. She also points out the relationship between mindlessness and a focus on outcomes as opposed to process.

On entirely practical grounds, Langer draws attention to the dangers of dualism in our treatment of the mind and body, which

---

5 Langer (2014) p. 79.
6 Langer (1997) pp. 15–22.

provides an example of scepticism and agnosticism that could be extended to other absolutised topics. In the process she implicitly acknowledges the embodied basis of meaning by discussing the power of context on the body that unconsciously processes the meaning of that context.[7]

Langer seems generally willing to leave others to explore the relationship between her account of mindfulness and that found in Buddhism. However, where she does enter into that relationship there seem to be some misunderstandings of Buddhist meditation:

> As an example of the semantic and philosophical tangles that arise if we try to compare Eastern and Western views of the mindful state, consider the activity of creating new categories. While this is a form of mindfulness in my definition, it appears to be in direct opposition to what one does during meditation. In meditation, the mind becomes quieter and active thought is discouraged. In some forms of meditation, thoughts and images that come to mind are considered unimportant and are relinquished as soon as one discerns their presence. At the same time, in many Eastern views, the proper meditation techniques are said to result in a state that has been called de-automatization. In this state, old categories break down and the individual is no longer trapped by stereotypes.[8]

Surprisingly, she still seems to be subject to the utterly misleading non-meditator's impression of mindfulness meditation as 'emptying your mind'. It's not surprising that she finds a contradiction between such a practice and one that supports creativity and awareness in the cognitive sphere as elsewhere. This false contradiction seems to result from the use of a rigidified metaphor of the mind as a container that has thoughts, ideas, and knowledge inside it, implying that if we no longer experience those 'contents' in meditation then we must have 'emptied' the mind. But rather than this metaphor, mindfulness meditation is better understood using an integration metaphor. If we experience unwanted thoughts during meditation (just as during any other activity requiring concentration – see chapter 5.b) this is a result of conflict between implicit goals that need harmonising through a process of re-framing. Meditation places all thoughts within a larger context so that they no longer cause disruption, but it is an unsustainable approach to meditation to simply repress disruptive thoughts.

---

7   Langer (2014) ch. 10.
8   Ibid. p. 80.

Leaving this misunderstanding aside, Langer's use and development of the term 'mindfulness' is highly complementary to the Buddhist approach, provided it is interpreted in terms of the Middle Way. Like all the other alternative modern approaches to the Middle Way discussed so far, it is not particularly influenced by Buddhism, but has developed in the broad context of Western psychological thought. In this case, though, there is also a creative coincidence of the central vocabulary used.

7.k. The Authentic Individual

Finally, it is important to recognise the implicit Middle Way found in Western views of the individual as they have developed in both politics and philosophy during the last few centuries. Whilst the development of liberal democracy has placed the individual in a greater position of social responsibility than ever before, it has also been in danger of idealising the individual by not allowing for the instability and conflict that forms many individuals' judgements. Out of the ongoing ideological disputes that have followed, the idea of the *authentic* and *autonomous* individual has emerged from time to time both in liberal thought and in existentialist thought.

The authentic individual provides some indications of the Middle Way, because her incremental development involves an acknowledged engagement with the other (i.e. with viewpoints that were previously unknown or unvalued). Provisionality is always required to make that engagement with other views helpful, and integration is often implicit in the understanding of how the individual develops so as to benefit from recognition of new viewpoints. However, the authentic individual can also often be idealised as a 'rational' individual in a way that puts too much emphasis on left-hemisphere-based logical consistency, and takes too little account of the continuing conflicts within us that lead us into inconsistent or inadequate assumptions.

The idea of the authentic individual could easily form the basis of a book in itself. I am just going to mention three key thinkers (out of many who could be discussed), who contributed to it in rather different ways.

John Stuart Mill (1806–73) first argued forcefully for the social benefits of provisionality as part of his influential argument for political freedom, *On Liberty*.[1] The individual who is able to question established norms of thinking, he wrote, potentially benefits everyone, because it is only by considering new alternatives that society is able to advance from old ones. Even if society does know 'the truth' already, considering alternatives enables it to understand that truth in a more lively and effective way.

Mill is best known for his utilitarian thinking, but his insights into the value of provisionality and of individual autonomy can be

---

1   Mill (1972).

separated from the necessity of a solely utilitarian moral framework. As long as we are prepared to allow benefits (in the widest sense of the term) a role in stimulating moral awareness, we can accept Mill's liberal arguments that society is best organised when it enables alternative views to be considered and individuals to make free decisions about them in a provisional space of discussion and experiment. This does not prevent other ways of thinking about values (such as in terms of principles or virtues) also operating as helpful stimuli to moral awareness and individual development.

Mill's own biography also provides an inspiring example of the development of individuality in response to the challenge of open feedback loops ('suffering') that stimulate new thinking. Given a high-pressure utilitarian education by his pushy father, Mill had a nervous breakdown as a young man, but this led him to reassess utilitarianism and question its narrower assumptions. He subsequently became more open to the Romantic movement with its challenge to narrow dependence on ideas of rationality, and also developed a close working relationship with his wife Harriet Taylor, who inspired him to offer one of the first critiques of the 'subjection of women'.

John Dewey (1859–1952) was a great pragmatic philosopher, psychologist, and educationalist whose vision of authentic human educational development was closely linked to his avoidance of dogma. He recognised the relationship between absolute beliefs and social group identity. He also recognised the importance of continuity, rather than erecting false absolute boundaries between facts and values, or between disciplines or areas of thought.[2] He saw provisionality as vital to democracy, and education as the means of developing it, so as to make society effective and overcome conflicts. The Middle Way for Dewey is thus often reflected in his vision for democracy, which goes far beyond the mechanics of electoral systems and is 'a form of moral and spiritual association'.[3]

Dewey's liberal recognition of the value of individual development is similar to Mill's, but he went much further in recognising the ways in which dogmatic positions could block that development. He also understood the dependency of those dogmatic positions on opposed social groups that form dualistic beliefs in counter-dependency to each other.

2 Dewey (1944) pp. 333–4.
3 Dewey (1993) p. 59.

> *The origin of these divisions we have found in the hard and fast walls which mark off social groups and classes within a group: like those between rich and poor, men and women, noble and baseborn, ruler and ruled. These barriers mean absence of fluent and free intercourse. This absence is equivalent to the setting-up of different types of life-experience, each with isolated subject-matter, aim, and standard of values. Each such social condition must be formulated in a dualistic philosophy, if philosophy is to be a sincere account of experience.*[4]

The development of individuality thus effectively requires an individual to find a Middle Way between their group of origin and the new challenging standards of other groups. Dewey's idealisation of democracy was to see it as a system in which this could occur. Like Popper, he made connections between the use of open feedback loops, effective scientific method, and the provisionality that is required to run society for the benefit of all its citizens. He thus developed a highly systemic form of liberalism, as well as living a long and admirable life that effectively integrated social, political, educational, and philosophical activity.

Jean-Paul Sartre (1905–80) was a French existentialist philosopher who focused on personal authenticity in terms of our acknowledgement of responsibility. It is he who makes clear the insight that we are responsible for our interpretations of whatever phenomena we encounter: not because of a metaphysical free will, but because we can experience options and thus provisionality.[5] A life of absolutisations, for Sartre, is one of 'bad faith', in which we deny the implications of our individual human awareness. For instance, when (following Kierkegaard) he discusses the 'anguish of Abraham', being apparently asked by God to sacrifice his son, he points out Abraham's responsibility for interpreting the voice he hears as God's and assuming that it is absolute and addressed to him.[6]

This calls out the extremely common appeals to tradition and authority that we find unjustifiably dominating religious traditions. The principle of interpretative responsibility, recognising that our readings are our own rather than to be attributed to the authority of God or the universe, is one that I have tried to follow in this book. If we ever need reminding how much the Middle Way is one based

---

4 Dewey (1944) pp. 333–4.
5 Sartre (1973).
6 Ibid. p. 31.

in our own judgements, whether we like it or not, I recommend turning to Sartre. He leaves us with the recognition that authentic integration requires an active engagement with zones of responsibility that will always be ambiguous.

None of these three figures was a meditator, but all made crucial contributions to our understanding of the Middle Way in ways that the Buddhist tradition does not. They all saw the value, in different ways, of avoiding absolutisations, not just in theory but in practice, in order to adopt a provisionality of individual judgement that is free of group pressure. They all saw the links between the integrity of the individual and the overcoming of conflicts in society. In different ways, they were both products of and shapers of liberal democracy, where it is believed that openness to alternative viewpoints can help shape society for the better.

The liberal Western society that their ideas helped to shape has gone further than any before it in its recognition of individuality and provisionality. However, its weaknesses centre around its relativism. Relativist thinking assumes that the contextual dependence of each individual's growth means that their development is only valuable in the terms of that individual, and thus that values cannot be justifiably compared or prioritised. Yet this involves a negative absolutisation: increasingly objective valuation and prioritisation are an unavoidable part of our embodied experience that is denied by relativism. Valuation also depends on the wider sense of meaning we feel as individuals, without which we may lack the confidence to judge reflectively.

The individual development process thus requires a continual balancing of provisionality of belief with both the sustenance of wider meaning and the even-handed avoidance of negative absolutisations along with positive ones. The mere denial of absolutes results either in the absolutisation of relative positions, or the defensive fundamentalist retrenchment of positive absolutes. It requires a carefully supported process of education to help each individual find a Middle Way approach, enabling development through each of the psychological stages charted by Robert Kegan (see chapter 4.e).

Dewey, at least, of these three thinkers, would recognise much of this need for a supported, meaningful, and even-handed path of development for the authentic and autonomous individual, rather than individuals being assumed to develop 'rationality' by themselves. However, his subtle arguments on the non-dualistic interpretation of liberal individuality are now largely ignored. Even though educational theory often tries to find an effective balance between structure and autonomy, much politically-driven educational policy today lurches instead between market-driven laissez-faire and ideological over-prescription. Without the basic sense of archetypal meaning that used to be provided by religion, individuals also often suffer crises of identity, with religion either absolutely prescribed by a repressive community or left as an apparently random individual choice. Without the critical thinking skills needed to discriminate between proliferating alternative beliefs, the modern products of a liberal society are also often left without the basic confidence they need to act sustainably in the world.

The liberal vision of developing individuality can thus greatly contribute to our understanding of the Middle Way in the modern context. However, that should not lead us to identify liberalism as a whole, let alone its manifestation in Western society, with the Middle Way. Instead, as with the Buddhist, Christian, or any other tradition, scrutiny is required to separate out those elements that help us to address conditions effectively from those that have given rise to new absolutisations. To do that effectively with modern liberal ideology would, of course, require another book in itself. In general, though, liberal thinking tends to emphasise provisionality and some aspects of integration, but to pursue scepticism and agnosticism only in unbalanced and selective ways, and to neglect the 'emotional' aspects of integration that cannot be so readily expressed in a shared framework of assumptions. Focusing on an individualistic ideal, it tends to neglect the complexity of the psychological conditions that actually shape individuals, particularly the conflicts within individuals that prevent them becoming 'rational'.

This neglect is not necessarily the fault of the three thinkers discussed above, or indeed of any other liberal thinkers, but rather the effect of the environment in which their ideas were interpreted. Just as Buddhist tradition can offer only a limited interpretation of the Middle Way as the most helpful insight of the Buddha, liberalism as it is lived out in the West can offer only a limited version of the Middle Way that may be developed from the insights of these three thinkers into the authentic development of the individual.

Conclusion

The final section has made clear that our understanding of the Middle Way may come from many different sources. It may not always be explicit nor always have that name, but nevertheless it is helpful to discuss it explicitly in order to understand its full implications. It is not a metaphysical truth, but it is a universal and synthetic practical theory. It is 'universal' in the sense that it springs from the structural needs of human beings (and possibly other organisms). We can thus confidently assume that it applies to all of them until we find reason to believe otherwise. It is 'synthetic' because that confidence increases from understanding its applicability in a very wide range of cases that we need to see in relation to each other.

The Middle Way is not merely a specialised term of Buddhist Studies, nor of any other pursuit. It is a practical theory, consisting in a set of provisional beliefs that are given their whole significance by being applied. That means that it has factual, moral, and technical implications, but that it is only understood by seeing those implications in relation to each other.

Those implications are huge. Factually, if we look beyond the limiting assumptions of any particular form of investigation we can see that the Middle Way has a significance that is not merely scientific, psychological, philosophical, ethical, religious, sociological, political, historical, or artistic, but all of these. Our accounts of each subject need to be much more synthetic. Morally, it provides us with a vision of the good that is not merely an idealisation, but rather an articulation of the edge of practicable challenge as we encounter it in experience. Technically, it can provide us with an indication of how to do each task better, from meditation to metalwork: absolutisations simply clog our blade.

However, the main focus of this book has been on the Buddha's account of the Middle Way, which is our first major source of understanding for it. I have argued that there is a substantial and feasible interpretation of the Pali Canon and Buddhist tradition that recognises the Middle Way rather than absolutised enlightenment as the Buddha's key insight and achievement. I have argued that all the major teachings of Buddhism – conditionality, the Four Noble Truths, the Eightfold Path, the Three Marks of Conditioned Existence, karma and rebirth, the significance of Awakening and of the Buddha, faith, and Going for Refuge – all need to be interpreted in terms of the Middle Way, *not* the Middle Way interpreted in terms of some prior, absolutised, interpretation of them. I have argued that absolutised enlightenment distorts our practical understanding of the Middle Way, so thus should not be an object of belief, although it can be an object of archetypal meaning and faith. All of this has been argued on practical, not historical grounds, with the use of texts from the Pali Canon to offer a helpful interpretation of the tradition rather than to offer proof in its terms.

I have also offered a positive analysis of the Middle Way into five sub-principles – scepticism, provisionality, incrementality, agnosticism, and integration – all of which overlap and are interdependent, but provide us with a straightforward way of testing new ideas in different contexts for their compatibility with the Middle Way. I have shown how these principles are rooted in the Buddha's life and metaphors as well as in a helpful interpretation of his teachings. The ways in which these principles can be found in a variety of other sources also supports the case that the Middle Way is not unique to Buddhism.

By comparison with my previous work, I have tried to engage positively and fully with the Buddhist tradition in this book. I thus hope that it will be useful for Buddhists and those interested in and studying Buddhism, who seek an interpretation that is above all practical and responsible, rather than enslaved to narrow traditional or scholarly assumptions. My aim is not to get Buddhists to give up Buddhism, but rather to interpret it in ways that are the most universal, whether at an individual or institutional level. If they do that they should find that many unnecessary conflicts both within Buddhism and with other religions or with scientific or other perspectives should fall away. The Middle Way, by focusing on the universal basis of our provisional beliefs in experience, is a tool of peace.

After reading this book, some people will probably consider me a Buddhist, others not. That does not matter. I seek only to remain inspired by the Buddhist tradition and to work with Buddhists as fruitfully as I can. I will personally call myself a Buddhist, though, only on those occasions when the basis of what people consider to be 'Buddhism' is clearly the Middle Way.

Bibliography

Bibliographical note:

Buddhist texts have been referenced using both the original texts and their translators, but are listed here only under their translators. In reproducing Pali and Sanskrit terms, diacritics have not been used, for three practical reasons: first, they create an unnecessary barrier for those unfamiliar with them; second, they can create problems in reproduction; and third, problems of ambiguity in transliteration, necessitating their use by scholars, are very unlikely in the context of this book.

Asch, Solomon (1956) *Studies of Independence and Conformity: 1. A Minority of One against a Unanimous Majority.* Psychological Monographs.
http://www.psycontent.com/content/h128830k244141t6
Ayer, A.J. (1946) *Language, Truth and Logic.* Penguin, London.
Batchelor, Stephen (2015) *After Buddhism.* Yale University Press, New Haven CT.
Beckwith, Christopher I. (2015) *Greek Buddha: Pyrrho's Encounter with Early Buddhism in Central Asia.* Princeton University Press, Princeton NJ.
https://doi.org/10.1515/9781400866328
Bett, Richard (2005) *Sextus Empiricus: Against the Logicians.* Cambridge University Press, Cambridge. https://doi.org/10.1017/CBO9780511815232
Bodhi, Bhikkhu (1994) 'Going for Refuge and Taking the Precepts'. *Access to Insight (BCBS Edition).*
https://www.accesstoinsight.org/lib/authors/bodhi/wheel282.html
Bodhi, Bhikkhu (1998) 'A Look at the Kalama Sutta'. *Access to Insight (BCBS Edition).*
http://www.accesstoinsight.org/lib/authors/bodhi/bps-essay_09.html
Bodhi, Bhikkhu (1999) 'The Noble Eightfold Path: The Way to End Suffering'. *Access to Insight (BCBS Edition).*
https://www.accesstoinsight.org/lib/authors/bodhi/waytoend.html
Bodhi, Bhikkhu (2000) *The Connected Discourses of the Buddha: A New Translation of the Samyutta Nikaya* (2 vols). Wisdom Publications, Boston.
Bruzina, D.A. (2002) 'Sextus Empiricus and the Skeptic's Beliefs'. Master's thesis, Virginia State University. https://pdfs.semanticscholar.org/30c7/cc4fd42b310f98e903d6f0bbf9a878cc5c8d.pdf
Burlingame, E.W., revised by Bhikkhu Khantipalo (2006) 'Buddhist Stories from the Dhammapada Commentary, Part 2'. *Access to Insight (BCBS Edition).*
http://www.accesstoinsight.org/lib/authors/burlingame/wheel324.html

Capra, Fritjof and Luisi, Pier Luigi (2014) *The Systems View of Life: A Unifying Vision*. Cambridge University Press, Cambridge. https://doi.org/10.1017/CBO9780511895555

Chabris, Christopher (2011) *The Invisible Gorilla: And Other Ways Our Intuition Deceives Us*. HarperCollins, London.

Conze, Edward (1951) *Buddhism: Its Essence and Development*. Bruno Cassirer, Oxford.

Curd, Patricia (2011) *A Presocratics Reader: Selected Fragments and Testimonia*. Hackett, Indianapolis IN.

Dewey, John (1944) *Democracy and Education*. Macmillan, New York.

Dewey, John, edited by Debra Morris and Ian Shapiro (1993) *The Political Writings*. Hackett, Indianapolis IN.

Drake, Stillman (1978) *Galileo at Work: His Scientific Biography*. Dover, Mineola NY.

Eddy, Mary Baker (1906) *Science and Health with Key to the Scriptures*. https://www.christianscience.com/the-christian-science-pastor/science-and-health

Ellis, Robert M. (2001) 'A Buddhist Theory of Moral Objectivity'. PhD thesis, Lancaster University, also published as *A Theory of Moral Objectivity* (2011) Lulu, Raleigh NC.

Ellis, Robert M. (2011a) *The Trouble with Buddhism: How the Buddhist Tradition Has Betrayed Its Own Insights*. Lulu, Raleigh NC.

Ellis, Robert M. (2011b) *Theme and Variations*. Lulu, Raleigh NC.

Ellis, Robert M. (2011c) 'The Master and His Emissary by Iain McGilchrist: Extended Review'. www.middlewaysociety.org/books/psychology-books/the-master-and-his-emissary-by-iain-mcgilchrist/

Ellis, Robert M. (2012) *Middle Way Philosophy 1: The Path of Objectivity*. Lulu, Raleigh NC.

Ellis, Robert M. (2013a) *Middle Way Philosophy 2: The Integration of Desire*. Lulu, Raleigh NC.

Ellis, Robert M. (2013b) *Middle Way Philosophy 3: The Integration of Meaning*. Lulu, Raleigh NC.

Ellis, Robert M. (2015a) *Middle Way Philosophy 4: The Integration of Belief*. Lulu, Raleigh NC.

Ellis, Robert M. (2015b) 'Cognitive Error as Absolutisation'. https://www.researchgate.net/publication/283460051_Cognitive_error_as_absolutisation

Ellis, Robert M. (2018) *The Christian Middle Way: The Case against Christian Belief but for Christian Faith*. Christian Alternative, New Alresford Hants.

Ellis, Robert M. (forthcoming) *The Jungian Middle Way: How Jung's Red Book Parallels the Buddha's Method for Human Integration*.

Festinger, Leon, Riecken, Henry, and Schachter, Stanley (1956) *When Prophecy Fails*. University of Minnesota Press, Minneapolis MN. https://doi.org/10.1037/10030-000

Flintoff, E. (1980) 'Pyrrho and India'. *Phronesis* 25(1): 88–108. www.jstor.org/stable/4182084, https://doi.org/10.1163/156852880X00052

Fox, Michael D., Snyder, Abraham Z., Vincent, Justin L., Corbetta, Maurizio, Van Essen, David C., and Raichle, Marcus E. (2005) 'The human brain is

intrinsically organized into dynamic, anticorrelated functional networks'. *Proceedings of the National Academy of Sciences USA* 102(27): 9673–8.
https://www.ncbi.nlm.nih.gov/pmc/articles/PMC1157105/

Fox, Kieran C.R., Nijeboera, Savannah, Dixon, Matthew L., Floman, James L., Ellamilla, Melissa, Rumaka, Samuel P., Sedlmeier, Peter, and Christoof, Kalina (2014) 'Is meditation associated with altered brain structure? A systematic review and meta-analysis of morphometric neuroimaging in meditation practitioners'. *Neuroscience & Biobehavioral Reviews* 43: 48–73.
https://www.sciencedirect.com/science/article/pii/S0149763414000724,
https://doi.org/10.1016/j.neubiorev.2014.03.016

Garfield, Jay L. (1995) *The Fundamental Wisdom of the Middle Way: Nagarjuna's Mulamadhyamakakarika*. Oxford University Press, New York.

Gokhale, Pradeep P. (1996) 'Essentialism, Eternalism and Buddhism' from Kalpakam Sankarnarayan et al. (eds.) *Buddhism in India and Abroad*. Somaiya Publications, Mumbai.

Govinda, Lama Anagarika (1966) *The Way of the White Clouds*. Rider, London.

Grossman, David (1995) *On Killing: The Psychological Cost of Learning to Kill in War and Society*. Back Bay Books, New York.

Gunaratna, Henepola (1995) 'The Jhanas in Theravada Buddhist Meditation'. *Access to Insight (BCBS Edition)*.
http://www.accesstoinsight.org/lib/authors/gunaratana/wheel351.html

Haase, Lori, May, April C., Falahpour, Maryam, Isakovic, Sara, Simmons, Alan N., Hickman, Steven D., Liu, Thomas T., and Paulus, Martin P. (2015) 'A Pilot Study Investigating Changes in Neural Processing after Mindfulness Training in Elite Athletes'. *Frontiers in Behavioral Neuroscience*.
https://www.frontiersin.org/articles/10.3389/fnbeh.2015.00229/full

Hadot, Pierre (1995) *Philosophy as a Way of Life*. Blackwell, Oxford.

Haidt, Jonathan (2012) *The Righteous Mind: Why Good People Are Divided by Politics and Religion*. Pantheon Books, New York.

Harris, Sam (2007) *Letter to a Christian Nation*. Bantam, London.

Hecker, Hellmuth (2009) *Similes of the Buddha: An Introduction*. Buddhist Publications Society, Kandy, Sri Lanka.

Heisenberg, Werner (1958) *Physics and Philosophy: The Revolution in Modern Science*. Harper, New York.

Horner, I.B. (1952) *The Book of the Discipline, Volume 5*. Pali Text Society, Oxford.

Hume, David (1978, 2nd edn.) *A Treatise of Human Nature*. Oxford University Press, Oxford.

Ireland, John D. (1990) *The Udana: Inspired Utterances of the Buddha*. Buddhist Publications Society, Kandy, Sri Lanka.

Janis, Irving L. (1982) *Groupthink: Psychological Studies of Policy Decisions and Fiascos*. Houghton Mifflin, Boston.

Jayawickrama, N.A. (1990) *The Story of Gotama Buddha (Jataka Nidana)*. Pali Text Society, Oxford.

Johnson, Mark (1987) *The Body in the Mind*. University of Chicago Press, Chicago.

Johnson, Mark (2007) *The Meaning of the Body: Aesthetics of Human Understanding*. University of Chicago Press, Chicago.
https://doi.org/10.7208/chicago/9780226026992.001.0001

Johnston, E.H. (1972) *The Buddhacarita or Acts of the Buddha*. Oriental Reprint, New Delhi.
Jones, Dhivan Thomas (2011) *This Being, That Becomes: The Buddha's Teaching on Conditionality*. Windhorse Publications, Cambridge.
Jung, Carl (1898) Zofingia Lectures, from *Collected Works Supplementary Volume A*. Routledge, London.
Jung, Carl, edited by Sonu Shamdasani (2009) *The Red Book: Liber Novus (Reader's Edition)*. Norton, New York.
Kabat-Zinn, Jon (2013, 2nd edn.) *Full Catastrophe Living: Using the Wisdom of Your Body and Mind to Face Stress, Pain, and Illness*. Bantam, New York.
Kahneman, Daniel (2011) *Thinking Fast and Slow*. Penguin, London.
Kegan, Robert (1982) *The Evolving Self: Problem and Process in Human Development*. Harvard University Press, Cambridge MA.
Kuhn, Thomas (1996, 3rd edn.) *The Structure of Scientific Revolutions*. University of Chicago Press, Chicago.
https://doi.org/10.7208/chicago/9780226026992.001.0001
Kuzminski, Adrian (2008) *Pyrrhonism: How the Ancient Greeks Reinvented Buddhism*. Lexington Books, Lanham MD.
Lakatos, Imre (1974) 'Falsification and the Methodology of Scientific Research Programmes' from I. Lakatos and A. Musgrave (eds.) *Criticism and the Growth of Knowledge*. Cambridge University Press, Cambridge.
Lakoff, George (1987) *Women, Fire and Dangerous Things: What Categories Reveal about the Mind*. University of Chicago Press, Chicago.
https://doi.org/10.7208/chicago/9780226026992.001.0001
Lakoff, George and Johnson, Mark (1980) *Metaphors We Live By*. University of Chicago Press, Chicago.
Lakoff, George and Johnson, Mark (1999) *Philosophy in the Flesh: The Embodied Mind and Its Challenge to Western Thought*. Basic Books, New York.
Langer, Ellen (1997) *The Power of Mindful Learning*. Da Capo Press, Boston.
Langer, Ellen (2010) *Counterclockwise: A Proven Way to Think Yourself Younger and Healthier*. Hodder, London.
Langer, Ellen J. (2014, 25th Anniversary edn.) *Mindfulness*. Da Capo Press, Boston.
Lerner, Melvin J. (1980) *The Belief in a Just World*. Plenum Press, New York.
https://doi.org/10.1007/978-1-4899-0448-5
Ling, Trevor (1973) *The Buddha*. Penguin, Harmondsworth Middlesex.
Macy, Joanna (1991) *Mutual Causality in Buddhism and General Systems Theory*. SUNY Press, Albany NY.
Marx, Karl, edited by David McLennan (1977) *Selected Writings*. Oxford University Press, Oxford.
Mates, Benson (1996) *The Skeptic Way: Sextus Empiricus's Outlines of Pyrrhonism*. Oxford University Press, Oxford.
Maturana, Humberto and Varela, Francisco (1992) *The Tree of Knowledge: The Biological Roots of Human Understanding*. Shambhala, Boston.
McGilchrist, Iain (2010) *The Master and His Emissary: The Divided Brain and the Shaping of the Modern Mind*. Yale University Press, New Haven CT.
Mill, John Stuart (1972 – originally 1859) 'On Liberty' from *Utilitarianism, On Liberty, and Considerations of Representative Government*. Dent, London.

Monier-Williams, Monier (2008) *A Sanskrit-English Dictionary*.
http://www.sanskrit-lexicon.uni-koeln.de/monier/
Morad, Natali (2017) 'How to Be an Adult: Kegan's Theory of Adult Development'. Medium online: https://medium.com/@NataliMorad/how-to-be-an-adult-kegans-theory-of-adult-development-d63f4311b553
Morrison, Robert (1997) 'Three Cheers for Tanha'. *Western Buddhist Review* 2. www.westernbuddhistreview.com/vol2/tanha.html
Murti, T.R.V. (1955) *The Central Philosophy of Buddhism: A Study of the Madhyamika System*. Unwin, London.
Ñanamoli, Bhikkhu (1962) *The Guide (Translation of the Nettippakarana)*. Pali Text Society, Oxford.
Ñanamoli, Bhikkhu (1991) *The Path of Purification (Visuddhimagga of Buddhaghosa)*. Buddhist Publication Society, Kandy Sri Lanka.
Ñanamoli, Bhikkhu and Bodhi, Bhikkhu (1995) *The Middle Length Discourses of the Buddha: A New Translation of the Majjhima Nikaya*. Wisdom Publications, Boston.
Ñanavira Thera (1987) *Clearing the Path*. Path Press, Colombo (also on nanavira.org).
Nussbaum, Martha (1994) *The Therapy of Desire: Theory and Practice in Hellenistic Ethics*. Princeton University Press, Princeton NJ.
Nyanaponika Thera (1962) *The Heart of Buddhist Meditation: A Handbook of Mental Training Based on the Buddhist Way of Mindfulness*. Rider, London.
Nyanaponika Thera and Bodhi, Bhikkhu (1999) *Numerical Discourses of the Buddha: An Anthology of Suttas from the Anguttara Nikaya*. Altamira Press, Walnut Creek CA.
Olendzki, Andrew (2013) 'Skinny Gotami & the Mustard Seed'. *Access to Insight (BCBS Edition)*.
http://www.accesstoinsight.org/noncanon/comy/thiga-10-01-ao0.html
Papadopoulos, Renos (2006) 'Jung's epistemology and methodology' from R. Papadopoulos (ed.) *Handbook of Jungian Psychology*. Routledge, London.
Payutto, P.A. (1994) *Buddhist Economics*. Buddhadhamma Foundation, Bangkok.
Perdue, Daniel E. (1992) *Debate in Tibetan Buddhism*. Snow Lion Publications, Ithaca, NY.
Pesala, Bhikkhu (2013) Quotation from translation of commentary on *Dighanakha Sutta (Majjhima Nikaya* 74) at
https://dhammawheel.com/viewtopic.php?t=16541
Popper, Karl (1959) *The Logic of Scientific Discovery*. Hutchinson, London.
Popper, Karl (1994) *Knowledge and the Mind-Body Problem*. Routledge, London.
Price, A.F. and Mou-Lam, Wong (1969) *The Diamond Sutra and the Sutra of Hui Neng*. Shambhala, Boston.
Pseudo-Dionysius, trans. John Parker (1924) *Mystic Theology*.
https://en.wikisource.org/wiki/Dionysius_the_Areopagite,_Works/Mystic_Theology, https://doi.org/10.1007/978-1-4899-0448-5
Ratnaguna (2010) *The Art of Reflection*. Windhorse Publications, Cambridge.
Ray, Reginald A. (1994) *Buddhist Saints in India: A Study in Buddhist Values and Orientations*. Oxford University Press, Oxford.
Reeve, C.D.C. (trans.) (1998) *Plato's Cratylus*. Hackett, Indianapolis IN.

Ross, Lee, Greene, David, and House, Pamela (1977) 'The False Consensus Effect: An Egocentric Bias in Social Perception and Attribution Processes'. *Journal of Experimental Social Psychology* 13(3): 279–301.
http://www.sciencedirect.com/science/article/pii/002210317790049X
Saddhatissa, H. (1985) *The Sutta Nipata*. Curzon Press, London.
Sangharakshita (1987, 6th edition) *A Survey of Buddhism: Its Doctrines and Methods through the Ages*. Tharpa Publications, London.
Sangharakshita (1989, 3rd edition) *The Ten Pillars of Buddhism*. Windhorse Publications, Glasgow.
Sangharakshita (1990a) *Vision and Transformation*. Windhorse Publications, Glasgow.
Sangharakshita (1990b) *A Guide to the Buddhist Path*. Windhorse Publications, Birmingham.
Sangharakshita (1990c) *New Currents in Western Buddhism*. Windhorse Publications, Glasgow.
Sangharakshita (1993) *Forty-three Years Ago: Reflections on My Bhikkhu Ordination*. Windhorse Publications, Glasgow.
Sartre, Jean-Paul, translated by Phillip Mairet (1973) *Existentialism and Humanism*. Methuen, London.
Sargeant, Winthrop (2009) *The Bhagavad Gita*. SUNY Press, Albany NY.
Shantideva, translated by K. Crosby and A. Skilton (1995) *The Bodhicaryavatara*. Oxford University Press, Oxford.
Stevenson, Ian (1974) *Twenty Cases Suggestive of Reincarnation*. University of Virginia Press.
Sunstein, Cass (2005) 'Moral Heuristics'. *Behavioural and Brain Sciences* 28(4): 531–42. http://www.ncbi.nlm.nih.gov/pubmed/16209802,
https://doi.org/10.1017/S0140525X05000099
Swearer, Donald K. (1995) *The Buddhist World of South East Asia*. SUNY Press, Albany.
Taleb, Nassim Nicholas (2012) *Antifragile: Things That Gain from Disorder*. Penguin, London.
Taylor, Donald and Doria, Janet (1981) 'Self-serving and Group-serving Bias in Attribution'. *The Journal of Social Psychology* 113(2): 201–11. http://www.tandfonline.com/doi/abs/10.1080/00224545.1981.9924371#.Uwn0cLnivIU
Thanissaro, Bhikkhu (1994) 'Sunita the Outcaste'. *Access to Insight (BCBS Edition)*.
http://www.accesstoinsight.org/tipitaka/kn/thag/thag.12.02.than.html
Thanissaro, Bhikkhu (1997a) 'Kucchivikara-vatthu: The Monk with Dysentery'. *Access to Insight (BCBS Edition)*.
http://www.accesstoinsight.org/tipitaka/vin/mv/mv.08.26.01-08.than.html
Thanissaro, Bhikkhu (1997b) 'Dhana Sutta: Treasure' (AN 7.6), *Access to Insight (BCBS Edition)*.
https://www.accesstoinsight.org/tipitaka/an/an07/an07.006.than.html
Thanissaro, Bhikkhu (2003) 'Avarana Sutta: Obstacles' (AN 5.51). *Access to Insight (BCBS Edition)*.
http://www.accesstoinsight.org/tipitaka/an/an05/an05.051.than.html

Thanissaro, Bhikkhu (2013) 'The Not-self Strategy'. https://www.accesstoinsight.org/lib/authors/thanissaro/notselfstrategy.pdf

Twenge, Jean M. (2017) *iGen: Why Today's Super-Connected Kids Are Growing Up Less Rebellious, More Tolerant, Less Happy – and Completely Unprepared for Adulthood – and What That Means for the Rest of Us*. Atria Books, New York.

Walshe, Maurice (1995) *The Long Discourses of the Buddha: A Translation of the Digha Nikaya*. Wisdom Publications, Boston.

Whitaker, Justin (2017) 'A Storm is Coming: Tibetan Buddhism in the West'. www.patheos.com/blogs/americanbuddhist/2017/11/a-storm-is-coming-tibetan-buddhism-in-the-west.html

Wijayaratna, Mohan, translated by Claude Grangier and Steven Collins (1990) *Buddhist Monastic Life According to the Texts of the Theravada Tradition*. Cambridge University Press, Cambridge.

Williams, Paul (1989) *Mahayana Buddhism: The Doctrinal Foundations*. Routledge, London.

Index

Note: sub-entries in this index are ordered by their initial appearance in the book

a priori beliefs, 153
abduction 82, 168, *see also* Five Precepts/sexual misconduct
Abraham (biblical) 278
absolute falsehood 66, *see also* absolutisation
absolutisation
   in Buddha's Three Considerations 16
   in going forth from palace 19–20
   in asceticism 28–9
   in relation to Middle Way 32–6, 100–1
   as Mara 39–40
   in interpretation of Awakening 41–7
   in Buddha's reluctance to teach 52–4
   in Buddha's First Address 57–60
   in the *Kalama Sutta* 67–70
   defusing 72
   in depression 74
   avoidance in discourses 77
   avoidance in Buddha's use of political values 80, 83–7
   avoidance in Buddha's approach to death 88–93
   in allegorical interpretation 99
   in wilful effort and slackness 106–7, 177–8
   in arrow analogy 109–13
   in response to pain 113–6
   in relation to discontinuity 118–20
   in dualistic dynamics 121
   as response to blindness 123–5
   as appropriation of the Middle Way 125–8
   in relation to integration 130–3
   in disabling doubt (*vicikiccha*) 139
   in selective scepticism 140, 156
   as ontological obsession 141–7
   wide range of 148–56
   clustering of 157–62
   in relation to psychological stage 165–8
   relaxation on Eightfold Path 170
   mindfulness as response 175
   as evil 180
   in ideas of truth 183
   in livelihood 186
   in interpreting right view 187
   of traditional forms 192
   in conditionality 198
   in interpreting Four Noble 'Truths' 200–1
   in interpreting impermanence 204
   in interpreting non-substantiality 205–6
   in relation to craving 209–11
   in interpreting karma and rebirth 212–17
   of the Buddha's authority 218–20
   in projection of archetypes 221–5, 252
   of 'Dharma' 226–8
   in relation to groups 228–30, 277
   in the monastic-lay division 231–3
   in interpreting the Three Refuges 239–41
   avoidance by Pyrrhonism 244
   found in Pyrrhonism 246
   in Christianity 247–50
   in scientific naturalism 255–7
   in categorisation 258
   avoided by embodied meaning 262–4
   in left hemisphere of brain 265–6
   in cognitive bias 269–71

292   *The Buddha's Middle Way*

in Langer's 'mindlessness' 272
avoidance in liberal thought 279–80
see also brain/feedback loops,
    dogma, metaphysics, ontology
absolutising: *see* absolutisation
absolutism, 13, 29, 127, 140, 160–1
abuse, sexual 234, *see also* Five
    Precepts/sexual misconduct
ad hoc reasoning: *see* fallacies
addiction 33, 60, 115, 176
adequacy 1, 35, 41, 53, 120, 183,
    186–7, 200–1, 218, 224, 255, 265,
    see also inadequacy
adiaphora 244, *see also* self
Adi-Buddha 223
adoxastous 245, *see also* no view
Aesop's Fables 98
ageing 14–15, 59, 202, 211
Aggañña Sutta 85
aggregates (*skandha*s) 59, 98, 144, 195,
    200, 203–5
agnosticism 40, 58, 66, 113, 196, 245,
    253, 257, 260, 274, 280, 282
    defined 36
    similarity to *parinibbana* 89
    in metaphor of blind people and
       elephant 121–5
    in metaphor of snake 125–7
    implication of *anatta* 205
    in Christian mysticism 249
    supported by embodied meaning
       264
Ajatasattu, King 78, 80, 82, 86, 136
aklineis 245, *see also* even-handedness
akradantous 245, *see also* agnosticism
Alara Kalama 23–5, 31, 36, 41, 52, 54
alienation 185–6, 209, *see also*
    repression
Allah 104, *see also* God
allegory 98–9
Amitabha 223
amygdala 39, 72, 106, 131, 175, *see
    also* brain
analogy: *see* metaphor
analysis 35, 52, 58–9, 83, 126, 141–2,
    153, 172, 178, 197, 216, 242, 282
    confusion with ontology 141
    role in over-specialisation 242
analytic philosophy 155

Ananda 80, 86, 88–92, 194, 208
anatta: *see* self, agnosticism
anepikrita (indeterminable) 244
Anguttara Nikaya 10, 14, 63, 66, 79, 86,
    105, 139, 173, 184, 203, 208, 210,
    237, 288
anicca: *see* impermanence
anima (archetype) 221
animus (archetype) 221
annihilationism: *see* nihilism
anterior cingulate cortex: *see* brain
appeal to authority: *see* fallacies,
    authority
appeal to moderation: *see* fallacies
appeal to tradition: *see* fallacies
appropriation **126**, 144, 206, 233, 236
arahants 79, 87, 217
archetypal imagery 234
archetype 26, 192, 206, 238, 240
    defined 191
    of Buddha 221–4
    of God and Christ 247–8
    in Jung 251–2
arhats: *see* arahants
Aristotelian scientific belief 256
Aristotle 243, 256
arrow (metaphor)
    poisoned arrow 64, **109–13**, 150
    second arrow 113–16
    Zeno's paradox of arrow and
       target 267
arts 263–4
Arya-Sangha 240
asavas: *see* taints
asceticism **27–30**, 32–3, 35–6, 42, 44,
    54, 131–2, 148, 157–8
Asch, Solomon 229, 284
Ashvaghosha 8, 10, 12, 15, 18, 37–9
Asian societies 219
association
    connections in brain 42, 95, 97, 99,
       132, 159, 192, 206, 209, 222
    social structure 234–5, 277
    see also brain/synaptic connections
astathmeta 244, *see also* impermanence
asymmetry
    of integration 55, 234, 240
    of integration in Buddha 133
    of power 185

ataraxia 244, *see also* integration
atheism 126, 161, 164
  appropriation of agnosticism 126
Athens 72
attribute substitution 145, 223, 269–70
authenticity 27, 276–80
authoritarianism 140, 234, *see also* totalitarianism
authority
  appeal to authority (fallacy) 2, 67, 156, 194, 224, 278
  historical authority of texts 4–5
  of Buddhist tradition 6, 9, 41, 68
  of teachers 26–7, 33
  Buddha and others' authority 52, 67–9
  Buddha's own authority 56–7, 68, **218–21**, 234
  Buddha's attitude to authority 65, 86–7
  as moral foundation in politics 84, 86–7
  of enlightenment 156
  in Asian societies 219
autonomy 27, 65–71, 92, 229, 259, 276–80
autopoiesis 258–9
avijja: *see* delusion
Awakening (enlightenment, nirvana, nibbana) 8, 20, 23–6, 31, 38,50, 56, 58, 60–2, 79, 85, 90, 98, 102, 105–6, 132, 148, 150, 163, 188, 207–8, 240–1, 244, 259
  absolutisation distinguished from meaning **41–9**, 218
  absolutised 54, 77, 125, 140, 156, 167, 171, 180, 187, 217, 219, 229, 282
  as goal of monasticism 78, 167, 232
  in relation to death 88
  discontinuity of absolutised enlightenment 120, 134
  archetypal meaning 124, 191, **221–4**
  unnecessary paradox about 146–7
  not basis of faith 236–8
awareness of alternatives 121, 246, 266, 272, *see also* provisionality
awe 24, 192, 222, 252
Ayer, A.J. 264, 284

Bahiya 116
baptism 132
basic-level categories 96
Batchelor, Stephen vi–viii, 2, 61–2, 78, 80, 88, 181, 284
Beckwith, Christopher I. 244–5, 284
becoming (*nidana*) 196–7, 216
belief in a just world 215
Benares 10, 56
bhavasava: *see* taints
bhava-tanha: *see* craving
bias (including cognitive bias)
  confirmation bias 104, 137, 161, 199, 206, 255, 269, 271
  information bias 111
  domain dependence 133
  attribute substitution 145, 223, 269–70
  in relation to absolutisation 153
  temporal biases 204: status quo bias 153; sunk costs fallacy 153, 269; neomania 153, 204
  group biases 229: false consensus, 229; group think 229; in-group bias 229; social proof 229
  actor-observer bias 269
  Kahneman and cognitive biases 269–71
  in relation to mindlessness 272–3
Big Bang Theory 112
Bimbisara, King 78, 86
birth
  human state 59, 202
  caste status 76–7
  discontinuity of conditions 119
  blindness from birth 122–3
  nidana 194, 196, 216
Birther (conspiracy theory about Obama) 162
blind people and the elephant 121–5, 242
blindness 123
Bodhi, Bhikkhu
  as translator 10, 14, 21, 23, 25, 27–8, 30–1, 37, 39, 44, 46, 47, 50, 53, 54, 56–9, 61–3, 66, 73, 79, 80, 85–6, 89, 99, 102, 104–5, 109–10, 113, 118, 125, 130–3, 136, 145, 148, 149, 150–1, 173–5, 182, 184–5,

187–8, 193, 195, 198, 200, 202–5, 208, 213–14, 284, 288
   on *Kalama Sutta* 68–9
   on Eightfold Path 171
   on meaning of 'refuge' 239
bodhi tree 39, 225
Bodhicaryavatara 142, 289
bodhisattva 146–7, 217, 241
bodhisattva's vow 241
body
   rejection in asceticism 27–30
   recognition in Middle Way 30, 37
   basis of awareness 40, 71
   basis of meaning 42, 95–6, 147, 267
   basis of shared meaning in metaphors 65, 99
   connection with right hemisphere 65, 265–7
   basis of confidence 67
   effects of depression on 73
   decay in old age 90–2
   tuned like lute string 106
   idealism about 115
   integration from mindfulness of 130–4
   Platonic rejection of 157–8
   relaxation of conflicts 170
   awareness in meditation 173–5, 179
   experience of self 206
   alienated craving to have 209, 211
   improbability of rebirth 215
   in group solidarity 229
   as system 258, 263
   see also mindfulness, body-scanning
body-scanning (meditation) 175
Brahma Sahampati 51, 53
Brahmajala Sutta 126
brahma-viharas (meditations) 182, 190
brahmin 22, 50, 74–7, 93, 118
Brahminical Middle Way 86
Brahminism 22, 75, 84
brain
   closed feedback loop **29**, 30, 75, 104, 106, 110, 114, 126, 145, 150, 178, 198, 200–1, 203, 210, 215–16, 247, 255–6, 259, 261, 268, 270
   limbic area (amygdala and striatum) 39, 72, 106, 131, 175, 210, 254

   synaptic connections 42, 45, 72, 96, 117, 173, 175, 188, 209, 214–5, 221, 260, 264
   prefrontal cortex (both hemispheres) 72
   brain lateralisation 97, **265–8**: left hemisphere (linguistic/goal area) 29, 97, 137, 182, 210, 265–8, 270–1, 273; right hemisphere 65, 97, 182, 188, 210, 265–8, 270, 273
   open feedback loop 104
   temporal lobe 124
   task positive network 173
   default mode network 174
   insula and anterior cingulate cortex 174, 210
brain lateralisation: *see* brain
breathingless meditation 28
brittleness: *see* fragility
Bruzina, D.A. 246, 284
Buddha, the (Siddhartha Gautama) *passim.*: refer to Contents (ix–x) for breakdown of topics in relation to Buddha
Buddhaghosa 23, 163, 196, 288
buddhas
   of past and future 9, 154
   enlightened beings in general 217
Buddhism
   partisan debates in 1, 144
   as source of Middle Way 2, 37, 109, 180
   recent reinterpretation of 2, 5, 198
   traditionally emphasised teachings 3, 44–8, 170–3, 176, 178, 180–4, 187–9, **193–241**, 259
   traditional accounts of Middle Way 3, 57, **135–69**
   conflicts with Middle Way 6–7, 44, 78, 115, 163–4
   traditional views of Buddha's life 14–16, 23–4, 41–2, 44–8, 88
   monk-lay division 22, 78, 163–4, 231–5
   Theravada v Mahayana divisions 50, 144
   traditional views of Buddha's status 54, 88, **218–25**
   interpretation of desire 60, **207–11**
   defences of absolutist view 68–9

use of allegory 98–9
emptiness and non-substantiality 115, 135, 140–3, 149, 158–60, 205–6, 227
misunderstanding of scepticism 135–6, 140
lack of interest in Middle Way 152
arguments for karma and rebirth 168, **212–17**
traditional practices 173–81, 190–2
use of term 'dharma' 226–8
faith and going for refuge 236–41
Buddhist metaphysics 155–6
Buddhist Studies, 4, 281
Buddhist tradition: *see* Buddhism
Burlingame, E.W. 83, 284

Cakkavatti-Sihanada Sutta 85
capitalism 16, 165, 185–6, 233
Capra, Fritjof 260–1, 285
care (political value) 83–4, 218
caste 74, 76, 85–6
categorisations 253, 258
Catholicism 126
causal theories 110–11, 153, 196, 212, 214, 258
cessation 25, 58–9, 61, 76, 120, 150–1, 196, 200–1, *see also* Four Tasks/Fourth Task, Awakening
Chabris, Christopher 176, 285
chanda: *see* desire
Chanda (name) 18
charitable interpretation 167, 243
China 233
Chinese 243, 264
Christ 218, 224, 247–9, *see also* Jesus
Christian Middle Way 5, 76, 247–50
Christian Science 115
Christianity 5, 119, 192, 223–4, 233, 236, **247–50**, 254
climate change 214
closed feedback loop: *see* brain
cognitive behavioural therapy 72, 271
cognitive biases: *see* bias
cognitive dissonance 104, 117
cognitive linguistics 262–4
cognitive models 97, 125, 160–1, 245, 262–3
come and see (*ehipassiko*) 118
comedy 74, 90

commitment 181, 184, 215, 217, 222, 235, **237–41**
communication 43, 66, 81–2, **183–4**, 263
Communist society 164
community (*sangha*)
  alternative spiritual group 17, 23
  political community 80–4
  Buddha's followers 90–1, 133, 231
  focus of moral stage 166–8
  group 229–31, 280
  Buddhist community 231–5
  Sangha Refuge 237–8, 240–1
  see also group
compassion 17–18, 24, 40, 54, 75, 172, 182, **190–1**, 222
complexity theory 199, 258
concentration, 51, 58, 170–2, **173–5**, 176–9, 198, 274
conditional language 273, *see also* provisionality
conditionality (*paticca samuppada*) 3, 47–8, 53, 97, 141–2, **193–9**, 206, 216, 258, 261, 263, 282, 287
conditioned arising: *see* conditionality
conditions, addressing 45, **47**, 85, 95, 115, 127
confidence 38, 48, 52, 54, 56, 67, 106, 127, 138, 176, 179, 189, 213–14, 224, **236–7**, 239, 248, 256, 279–81, *see also* embodied confidence
confirmation bias: *see* bias
conflict
  between Buddhism and Middle Way 6, 47, 57, 68, 215
  social conflict 12, 18, 48, 81–3, 171, 183, 186, 277, 279
  of values 13, 18, 33, 90–1, 181–2
  healed by integration 20, 30, 43, 63, 95, 107, 129, 133, 170
  psychological repression 27, 29, 39–40, 61, 114, 131–2, 139, 145–6, 221–2, 244, 274, 276, 280
  internal or external 36, 55, 58, 63, 180, 203, 232, 249
  between sources 68, 74, 122, 124, 209, 249, 282
  political conflict 78, 171
  between systems 259, 261
  from left hemisphere 268

conscience 238
consciousness 23, 143, 195–6, 205, 216, 230
conservatism 83, 85
contact (*nidana*) 195–7
container (schema) 96, 274
contingency 103–4
continuity of attention 176
conventionality 12–13, 33, 245–6
Conze, Edward 223, 285
cortisol 210, *see also* brain
cosmic law 35, 47–8, 59, 201–2, 213
cosmology 9, 45, 161, 261
counter-dependency 277
counter-group 230, *see also* group
craving (*tanha*) 39–40, 46, 59–61, 73, 88, 93, 130–2, 175–6, 179, 195–201, **207–11**, 216, *see also* desire
　craving for being (*bhava-tanha*) 59, 207, 210–11
　craving for non-being (*vibhava-tanha*) 59, 207, 210
　craving for sense-desires (*kama-tanha*) 59, 207, 210
creation (by God) 5, 112, 247
creativity 274
credibility 37, **68–9**, 86, 220, 234
crime 85
critical awareness 67, 69, 103, 126, 166
critical enquiry 231
crucifixion 247–8
cult 22, 117
Curd, Patricia 203, 285

damp piece of wood (metaphor) 130–2
death 125, 251
　in Buddha's four sights 14–16
　in *dukkha* and as *nidana* 59, 194, 196, 216
　of Buddha 63, 88–93, 154, 233
　in Kisagotami story 70
　whether enlightened survive 109, 112, 122, 148, 150
　discontinuity of conditions 119
　whether self survives 126, 169
　in relation to rebirth 212, 214–15
decision to teach, Buddha's 55

default mode network: *see* brain
deferred gratification 28, *see also* asceticism
delusion (*avijja*) 15–16, 27, 29, 41, 47, 51, 60, 67, 70, 88, 117, 123, 127, 141, 145, 176, 195–6, 207, **209–10**, 216, 219, 237, 271, *see also* absolutisation
democracy 218, 235, 241, **276–9**
denial (negative absolute) 58, 89–90, **137**, 150, 154, 162, 164, 205, 279
dependency 232–3, 277, *see also* counter-dependency
dependent origination: *see* conditionality
depression 73, 106
depth 128, 235, 241, 248, 252, 254
Descartes, René 136
desecration 87
desire 29–30, 34, 39–40, 46, 60, 65, 73, 105–7, 114, 129, 178, 188–9, 195, 197, 201, **207–11**, 223, 238–9, 256–7, 261, *see also* craving
chanda 207
determinism 149, 153, 161, 164, 185, 197, 206, 246
Devadatta 88, 133
devotional practice 190–2
Dewey, John 277–9, 285
dhamma: *see* dharma
dharma 17, 23, 25, 51–3, 62, 68–9, 91–2, 117–18, 122, 125, 151, 193, **226–8**, 236
dialectic 65, 126, 224, 247, 255
Diamond Sutra (*Vajracchedika*) 146, 238–9, 288
Digha Nikaya 9, 15, 17, 74, 80–1, 84–5, 89–93, 126, 136, 154, 175, 181, 194, 196, 290
Dighanakha Sutta 163, 288
direct knowledge 23, 25, 57–8, 148, 150, 208, *see also* insight
disabling doubt (*vicikiccha*) **139**, 221
discontinuity 78, **118–20**, 164, 187, 207, 231, 261, 267
　discontinuity of conditions 119
　practical discontinuity 119–20
　absolutising discontinuity 120
discourses (*suttas*) 63, 77–8, 231
discovery learning 65

ditthasava: see taints
divinity 251, *see also* God
dogma 3, 6, 16, 24, 212–13, 271, 277, *see also* absolutisation
domain dependence: *see* bias
Dona 93
dopamine 210, *see also* brain
Drake, Stillman 256, 285
dry piece of wood (metaphor) 130–2
dualism 36, 53, 83, **121**, 126–7, 151–2, 232–3, 243, 267, 273, 277–8, 280, *see also* absolutisation, metaphysics, fallacies
duality: *see* dualism
dukkha: *see* inadequacy

Earth Goddess 221
echo chamber (social media) 12
Eckhart, Meister 249
economy 11, 17, 87, 143, 164, 185–6
Eddy, Mary Baker 115, 285
edginess 224
education 70, 171, 174, 199, 230, 234, 257, 277, 279
eel wrigglers 136
ehipassiko: *see* come and see
Eightfold Path, 1, 3, 6, 58, 61, 86, 99, 129, 146, 148–9, 152, **170–2**, 173, 175, 177, 179–81, 183–5, 187, 189, 191–3, 200, 270, 282
  limbs of the path: *see* right effort, mindfulness, concentration, right action, right speech, right livelihood, right view, right aspiration
elephant 122–4, 142, 242, 271
Eliot, T.S. 132
embodied confidence 155, 236, 238, 248, *see also* confidence
embodied conditions 29, 40, 47, 86, 88, 108, 111, 114–15, 127, 135, 137–8, 142, 188, 199, 206, 236, 240, 252, 256, 270
embodied experience 35, 70, 92, 95–6, 100, 115, 117, 122, 137, 161, 170, 182, 207, 210–11, 240, 253, 264, 266–7, 279
embodied meaning 42, 95–6, 108, 117, 142, 154, 160, 239, 252, **262–4**, 266–7

empathy 182, 252, 265, *see also* compassion
emptiness: *see under* Buddhism
enlightenment: *see* Awakening
Epicureanism 245
epistemology 65, 67–8, 254, *see also* scepticism
epoché 244
equality 85, *see also* fairness
equanimity 23, 39, 40, 90, 129, 182, 190, 203, 222
equilibrium (schema) **100–1**, 108, 126
essentialism 77
eternalism (*sassatavada*) 135, 148–9, 156, **157–69**, 210, 232
eternality, 109–10, 112, 122, 148–51, 158–9, 211
ethics 1, 58, 64, 86, 157, 168, 179, **180–6**, 226, 233, 245, 260
  moral principle 1, 165, 181, 184
  moral objectivity 160
  moral awareness 168–9, 182, 277
  moral ideologies 168
  broader sense 180
  narrower sense 180
  see also Five Precepts, Ten Precepts, Eightfold Path, utilitarianism
eucharist 37
even-handedness 121, 149, 164, 167, 169, 201, 245
evil 90, 109, 154, 158, 163, 180, 213, *see also* Mara
evolution 104–5
existence 46, 59, 60, 126, **141–7**, 148–54, 157–60, 193, 200–2, 204, 206–7, 229, 238, 244, 247, 259, *see also* ontology, non-existence
existentialism 276, 278
experiential learning 70
expertise 86

fairness (political value) **83–5**, 218, 226, 258, *see also* equality
faith (*saddha*) 16, 68, 138–9, 198, 235, **236–8**, 241, 247–9, 278, 282, *see also* confidence
fallacies 153
  appeal to authority 2, 67, 156, 194, 224, 278
  appeal to tradition 41, 66, 194

ad hoc reasoning 44, 160, 187, 256
appeal to moderation 101
nirvana fallacy 201
false dichotomy: *see* dualism
see also bias
fallibility 20
false consensus: *see* bias/group biases
false dichotomy: *see* dualism
false speech: *see* Five Precepts
falsificationism 255
fast and slow thinking 269, *see also* bias/Kahneman
fear of wrongdoing (*ottappa*) 182, *see also* guilt
feedback loop: *see* brain
feeling
  as second arrow 113–14
  as object of mindfulness 175–7
  loving-kindness 183, 190
  as *nidana* 195–7, 216
  as aggregate (*skandha*) 204–5
Festinger, Leon 117, 285
festival 225
final goal: *see* goal
First Address (of Buddha) **56–62**, 170, 200, 202
First Noble Truth: *see* Four Tasks
First Sermon (of Buddha): *see* First Address
Five Aggregates: *see* aggregates
Five Precepts 164, 180–1, 183, *see also* ethics
  sexual misconduct 26, 85, 169, 181, 202
  killing 48, 78, 85, 99, **181–2**, 197, 214, 231, 258
  false speech 85, 135, 148, 173
  theft 85
Flintoff, E. 244, 285
forest 8, 18, **21–30**, 32–3, 35, 67, 69, 81, 95
Four Exertions 178, *see also* right effort, lute strings
Four Foundations of Mindfulness 175, *see also* mindulness
Four Noble Truths: *see* Four Tasks
Four Sights (of Buddha) **14–16**, 19
Four Tasks (Four Noble Truths) 3, 56, **58–62**, 69, 97, 116, **170–225**, 240, 282

First Task **58–9**, **200–6**, *see also* inadequacy
Second Task **59–60**, **207–17**, *see also* desire, absolutisation
Third Task **61**, **218–25**, *see also* Awakening
Fourth Task 61, 170–92, *see also* Eightfold Path, Middle Way
Fox, Michael D. et al. 174, 285
Fox, Kieran C.R. et al. 210, 286
fragility (of absolute beliefs) 118, 182, 206, 224, 233, 253
free will 149, 153, 160–1, 164, 185, 278
freedom (political value): *see* liberty
Freud, Sigmund 111
friendship 74, 78, 86, 93
frustration: *see* inadequacy
fundamentalism 112

Gaia 261
Galileo 256
Ganaka Moggalana 118
Garfield, Jay 159, 286
Gautama: *see* Buddha
generalisations 214
Genesis 5, *see also* creation
gestalt 182, 267
ghouls (metaphor for absolutisation) 227
globalisation 241
Gnosticism 253
goal
  limited in relativism 12
  final not reached in forest 24
  final self-undermining 25, 70
  absolutised 29, 114, 125, 137, 182, 210, 224, 265–6, 268, 273
  final as meaningful symbol 42
  social element 55
  embodied in schema 100–1, 108
  range of goals 105, 202
  in balanced effort 106
  implicitly assumed 138, **174–8**
  aspect of value 153
  nirvana as monastic 163, 171, 232
  integrating 237, 244, 274
  see also desire, craving, integration
God
  as absolutised source 11, 13, 219, 236, 247, 278

polarised assumptions 16–17
meaningful experience of 124, 127, 247–9
belief in 125–7, 158, 160, 206, 211
denial of 126–7, 164
archetype 191, 222–4, **247–52**
Gods 15, 182, 251
Going for Refuge 193, 236, **238–41**, 282
Going Forth 14, **16–20**, 21–2, 67, 85, 166
Gokhale, Pradeep 159, 286
government 78, 84–5, 87
Govinda, Lama Anagarika 216, 286
grace 26, 247
gradual training 117–18, 120, see also incrementality
grasping (*nidana*) 195–7, 216
group 11, 20, 22, 34, 43–4, 50, 52, 67, 75, 82, 107, 121, 127, 140, 161–2, 171, 186, 206, **229–31**, 259, 263, 268, 271, 277–9, see also bias/ group biases
groupthink: see bias/group biases
guilt 182–3, 202
Gunaratna, Henepola 174, 286
guru 26, 219, see also teacher

Haase, Lori et al. 176, 286
Hadot, Pierre 245, 286
Haidt, Jonathan 83–4, 218, 286
Harris, Sam 249, 286
hatred 27, 40, 46, 176, 178–80, 182, 195, 221–2, 252
Hecker, Hellmuth 99, 286
hedonism 12, 29, 148, 158, see also desire
Heidegger, Martin 243
Heisenberg, Werner 123, 286
Hellenistic philosophies 245, see also Epicureanism, Pyrrhonism, Stoicism
Heraclitus 203
hero (archetype) 15, 18–19, 221–2, 252
higher *jhana*s 23, 31
Hildegard of Bingen 249
hindrances 178, 209–10, see also craving, hatred, disabling doubt
Hinduism 22, 206, 226, 233, 243, see also Brahminism

hiri: see shame
history
non-historical approach to Buddha 4
avoiding appeals to 9
data, not facts 45
of Buddhism 50, 144, 219
origins of universe 112
historical determinism 164
of mysticism 249
of science 256
impact of brain on 265
homeostasis 259
Honeyball Sutta 145
Horner, I.B. 133, 286
Hume, David 136–7, 216, 286
humour: see comedy
hypnosis 216

idealisation 18, 224, 281, see also projection
idealism 115
ideology
ruling 11, 13
ascetic 28
political 80, 83, 87, 280
rivalry with neighbouring 136
monastic and lay 140, 164, 167
staged development of 166–7, 169
ignorance: see delusion
illness: see sickness
imagination 16, 21, 35, 65, 72, **96–8**, 172, 190, 252, 263, 269
imperfection 44, 64, 224, 247, 251
impermanence (*anicca*) 16, 71, 74, 90, 189, 201, **203–4**, 205
inadequacy (*dukkha*, 'suffering') 16, 50, **58–9**, 60–1, 66, 109, 115–16, 125, 150, 198, **200–3**, 204–5, 207, 215, 224, 239, 252, 277
incrementality **36**, 42, 53, 61, 68, 78, 86–7, 91, 107, 112, **117–20**, 121, 132, 140, 144, 146, 151, 160, 162, 164, 171, 195, 200, 205, 208, 211, 217–18, 232, 236, 245, 249, 251, 253, 257, 260, 264, 273, 276, 282, see also discontinuity
India 1, 8, 17–18, 21–2, 63, 99, 233, 244
individualism 230
individuality 146, 230–1, 277–80

individuation: *see* integration
inequality 11, 85, *see also* fairness
infinity 109–10, 112, 122, 148, 150
information bias: *see* bias
in-group bias: *see* bias/group biases
insight 4, 15, 41–2, 45, **46**, 50, 62–3, 69, 76, 94, 97, 112, 115, 124, 128, 156, 188, 191, 193, 197–8, 207, 222, 224–5, 237, 239, 251, 255, 265–6, 271, 276, 278, 280, 282
inspiration 4, 6, 37, 52, 63, 89, 167, **190–1**, 218, **222**, 240, 249, 251–2, 254
insula: *see* brain
integration
  defined **36, 129–34**
  Awakening as potential integration 43, 191, 222–4, 238, 247
  individual and social 50, 55, 146, 171, 180, 241
  incrementality of 55
  goal of teaching 63
  of meaning (imagination) 65, 263–4
  harmonisation 107
  delusion of totality 123
  basis of confidence 127, 138
  dependence on body 130–2, 263–4
  better model than Awakening 132–4, 156, 201
  asymmetrical 133–4, 240
  temporary and long-term forms 143, 179, 222
  interference from ontology 144
  Eightfold Path as method 170–2
  of belief 170–1, 190, 264
  in mindfulness and concentration 173, 175–7
  blocked by guilt 182
  supported by compassion 182
  in livelihood 185–6
  from open feedback loops 201–6
  of archetypes 221, 251–4
  supported by groups 230–1
  commitment to 240
  in Pyrrhonism 244–5
  in Christianity 249
  Jungian individuation 251–4
  needed in science 256–7
  in systems theory 260–1
  by right hemisphere over time 266–8
  better metaphor than container 274
  in learning 274, 276
  authenticity and autonomy 276–9
integrative practice 40, 44, 48, 72, 82, 105, 113, 118, 131, **170–92**, 200, 234–5
interdependence 61, 149, 180, 199, 210, 264, *see also* systems theory
intuition 123, 127, 253
invisible gorilla 176
Ireland, John D. 45, 116–17, 122, 196, 286
irony 93
Islam 33–4, 76, 243
Islamist terrorism 114
Israel 271
Izdubar (Jung's bull-god) 252

Jainism 226
Janis, Irving L. 229, 286
Japan 233
Jayawickrama, N.A. 38, 286
jealousy 60, 189
Jesus 26, 218, **247–9**, *see also* Christ
jhana: *see* meditation/*jhana* experience
Johnson, Mark 42, 95–6, 100, 161, 262, 286–7
Johnston, E.H. 8, 10, 15, 18, 37, 39, 287
Jones, Dhivan Thomas 196, 198, 287
Judaism 243
judgement 1, 27, 33, 49, 58, 89, 111, 121, 135, 146–7, 162, 165, 176, 201, 207, 219, 236, 243, 245, 266, 276
  Middle Way as principle of 3, **35–6**, 41, 162, 179, 220
  practical need for 13, 138, 152
  adequacy of 19, 258
  compared to achievement 24
  provisionality of 42
  incrementality of 53, 91, 247
  avoiding absolutised 59, 61, 153–4
  optimisation 64
  autonomy of 65–9, 92, 279
  confidence in 67, 236
  political 79–80, 82, 84, 218
  path of 100
  equilibrium in 101, 244

Index

not using Middle Way 101
discontinuity in 119–20
integrating 129, 261
fallibility 137
time-framed 138
better model than ontology 140–4, 193–4
moral 168, 180, 182–6
conditions affecting 195
in *nidanas* 197
flow of energy in 209
general effects of 212–15
group biases block 229
superiority of 234
effects of bias 269–70, 272
Jung, Carl 128, 191, 221–2, 244, 251–4, 287
Jungianism 254
justice: *see* fairness
justification 26, 68, 138, 151, 154, 166–7, 180, 182, **183**, 186, 213, 218, 232–3, 239, 256, 264, 273
justified true belief (definition of knowledge) 46

Kabat-Zinn, Jon 114, 287
Kabbalism 243
Kaccanagotta 151, 159, 188
Kahneman, Daniel 145, 223, 269, 270–1, 287
Kalama Sutta **65–9**, 79, 92, 231
Kalamas 65–9, 71, 79
kamasava: *see* taints
kama-tanha: *see* craving
Kant, Immanuel 253
karma (*kamma-vipaka*) 46–8, 60, 88–9, 97, 115, 120, 140, 149, 161, 168–9, 193, 197, 202, 211, **212–15**, 216, 282
kasina practices 174
Kassapa 149
Kegan, Robert 69, **165–8**, 230, 232, 260, 279, 287
Keynesian welfare economics 84
Khantipalo 83, 284
Kierkegaard, Søren 278
killing: *see* Five Precepts
Kisagotami 70–1
knowledge
definition **46**

three knowledges (of Buddha) 44–6
absolutised knowledge of Buddha 48, 51, 57, 62, 117, 120, 132, 148, 198, 226, 237
scepticism about 66–7, 194, 196
in representationalism 94
right view 187
delusion not lack of 210
in systems theory 258–60
container schema 274
see also direct knowledge
Kohlberg, Lawrence 168
Koliyans 83
Kosala 78
Kosalasamyutta 78, 86
Kuhn, Thomas 256, 287
Kutadanta Sutta 84
Kuzminski, Adrian 244, 287

laissez-faire 280
Lakatos, Imre 256, 287
Lakoff, George 42, 95, 100, 161, 262, 287
Langer, Ellen 176, 202–3, **272–5**, 287
language
of the Buddha 5, 64
embodied meaning of 42, **94–7**, 146–7, 252, **262–4**
adaptive use 77
practical judgements of definition 226, 228
conditional use of 273
lay practitioner 163
lay-people 78, 92–3, 165, 167, 185, 231–2
left hemisphere: *see* brain
Lerner, Melvin 215, 287
liberalism 83, 226, **276–80**
liberation 51, 85, 146, 161, 198, 208
liberty (political value) 61, 83, **85**, 138, 218, 244, 276
limbic system: *see* brain
lineage 66–7
linear causality 258
Ling, Trevor 22, 287
linguistics 262
literalism **94–5**, 97, 112, 118, 253
liturgy 225
living systems 258–9, 261
logic of four alternatives 150

logical positivism 264
love 248–9
loving-kindness (*metta*) 181–2, 190 *see also* compassion
loyalty, 66–8, 84, 86, 218–19, 234
Luisi, Pier Luigi 260–1, 285
lute strings (metaphor) 105–8, 173
lying: *see* Five Precepts/false speech

Macy, Joanna 199, 287
Madhyamaka 142, 144
Magadha 88
Magadhi (language) 64
maggavarana (conducive to path to nirvana) 163
Maha Kaccana 145
Mahaparinibbana Sutta 89–90
Mahasaccaka Sutta 44
Mahayana Buddhism 50, 140, 142, 144, 146, 148, 155, 221, 224, 233, 241
Majjhima Nikaya 21, 23, 25, 27–8, 30–1, 37, 44, 46, 53–4, 56–7, 85–6, 89, 102, 104, 109, 110, 118, 125, 130–1, 136, 145, 150, 174–5, 181–2, 184–5, 187, 213, 288
Mallas 93
Malunkyaputta 109–10, 112, 121–2, 136
Malunkyasutta 149
mandala 222, 224
Mara **38–40**, 90–1, 130–1, 221, 271
Marx, Karl 11, 160, 185, 287
Marxism 164, 233
Master and His Emissary, The **265–8**, 285, 287, *see also* McGilchrist
materialism 158, 211
Mates, Benson 244–5, 287
Maturana, Humberto 258–60, 287
McGilchrist, Iain 65, 97, 137, 182, **265–8**, 285, 287
meaning
　of Middle Way 2, 37, 224–5
　of religious sources 5, 17, 124, 127, 280
　of Buddha and his story 9, 20, 224
　new associations 21, 190–1, 206, 279
　of Awakening 25–6, 42–5, 218
　embodied 30, 42–3, **94–9**, 165, 191, 252–3, **262–4**, 266–7, 274
　integration of 36, 261
　of Buddha's teachings 49, 51–2, 125
　from metaphor 64–5, **96–9**
　cultural sources 82, 124
　representationalist view **94–5**, 112, 147, 153, 160, 264
　archetypal 128, 191, **221–2**, 251–3, 280, 282
　source of ontological obsession 142
　source of counter-dependent beliefs 161
　of words and sentences 162
　between desire and belief 189–90
　of rebirth 216–17
　of 'dharma' 226–8
　of faith 236
　of refuges 238–41
　in right hemisphere 266–7
medicine 110
meditation
　experience of Middle Way in 1, 72
　jhana experience 23–4, **30–4**, 36, 42–3, 67, 95, 117, 124, 143, 179, 191, 222, *see also* integration/temporary
　breathingless 28
　mindfulness practice 30, 114, **175–7**, 274
　Buddha's 38
　practice on path 58, 170, **173–9**, 180
　absolutisations as hindrances 109, 139
　withdrawal for 132, 231
　integrative effects 133
　on emptiness 142
　concentration **173–5**
　balanced effort **177–9**
　brahmaviharas 182, **190**
　in Buddhism 233–4
　misunderstanding of 274
meditative attainment: *see* meditation/*jhana* experience
metaphor
　Middle Way as 3, **100–1**
　in embodied meaning 42, 94–7, 160–1, 191, 253, 262–3, 267
　bounding beliefs 46
　Buddha's use of 64, **94–134**, 150, 214, 282

in right hemisphere 65, 97–8, 265, 267
allegorical reduction 98–9
specific metaphors: raft 102–5; lute strings 105–8; poisoned arrow 109–13; second arrow 113–16; ocean 117–20; blind people and elephant 121–5; snake 125–8; two mules 129–30; wet piece of wood 130–4; covering world with hide 142–3; thicket etc. for absolutisation 150; poison 186; sight 187; axle hole 202; boulder 214; rebirth 216; refuge 239–40; therapy 245; container 274
archetypes as metaphors 221
metaphysics 111, 140, **154–6**, 198, 253, *see also* absolutisation
metaphysical claims 35, 161
metaphysical beliefs 109, 121–2, 154–6, 158, 160–2, 167, 216, 244
metaphysical questions 109, 112, 136
metaphysical truths 204, 281
method, Buddha's Middle Way 3, 41, 52, 54, 63, 66, 68, 85, 126, 139, 142–5, 147, 188–9, 192–3, 224
proxy method 142
absolutised method 171, 234
scientific method 212, 234, 246, **255–7**, 267, 278
metonymy 111, 169
metta-bhavana (meditation) 182
Middle Way *passim.*
initial definition 3
priority in interpretation 3, 193
in relation to traditions 5–6
in relation to going forth 19–20
not specific achievement 24
Buddha's discovery of 31–7
five elements of **35–7, 102–34**
compatibility with Awakening 41–9
in decision to teach 52–5
in First Address 56–62
in Buddha's educative method 63–77
in Buddha's politics 78–87
in Buddha's approach to death 88–93

embodied meaning in 95
as a metaphor 100–1
misunderstanding of scepticism and 135–40
not ontological 141–8
avoids range of absolutes 148–56
not just eternalism and nihilism 157–62
even-handed 163–9
interdependence with Eightfold Path 170–2
in meditation 173–9
in ethics 180–6
in right view 187–9
in right aspiration 189–92
in interpreting conditionality 193–9
in interpreting *dukkha* 200–3
in interpreting impermanence 203–4
in interpreting *anatta* 204–6
in interpreting craving 207–11
in interpreting karma 212–15
in interpreting rebirth 215–17
in Buddha's authority 218–21
in Buddha as archetype 221–5
preferred to 'dharma' 226–8
in relation to groups 229–31
in Buddhist community 231–5
faith in 236–8
in interpreting refuges 238–41
in non-Buddhist sources 242–80 (refer to Contents for details)
Middle Way Philosophy 46, 152, 156, 160
Mill, John Stuart 276–7, 287
mindful walking 175
mindfulness 27, 30, 34, 58, 81, 114, 130, 149, 170, 172–4, **175–7**, 178–9, 202, 234, 272–5
mindfulness of breathing 175
mindlessness 272–3
ministry, Buddha's **50–93**, 98
minor ordination 232
miraculous events 248
mitigated scepticism 140
monarchy 219
monasticism 24, 82–3, 154, 163, 165, 167, 171, 185, 193, 219, 229, **231–5**
monastic community 82–3, 231

monastic 'debates' 233
monastic rules 154, 231, 233
Monier-Williams, Monier 226, 288
monks 10, 14, 23, 78, 81, 91, 93, 133, 167, 185, 232, 234, 272
Morad, Natalie 165, 288
morality: *see* ethics
Morrison, Robert (Sagaramati) 207, 209–10, 288
Muchalinda 221
mudra 225
murder: *see* Five Precepts/killing
Murti, T.R.V. 155, 288
Muslim Middle Way 76
mysticism 243, 247, 249

Nagarjuna 159, 160, 286
nagas (serpents) 128
name and form (*nidana*) 195–6, 216
Ñanamoli, Bhikkhu 21, 23, 25, 27–8, 30–1, 37, 44, 46, 53–4, 56–7, 85–6, 89, 102, 104, 109–10, 118, 125, 130–1, 136, 145, 150, 174–5, 182, 184–5, 187, 190, 196, 207, 213, 288
Ñanavira, Thera 197, 288
Nandabala 37
natural law: *see* cosmic law
naturalism 126, 161, 255–7
Nazism 5
negation 16–17, 142, *see also* denial
negative absolutes: see denial
negative atheism 126
Neo-Confucianism 243
neomania: *see* bias/temporal biases
network theory 258
neural connections: *see* brain/ synaptic connections
New Age Middle Way 76
New Atheists 249
Newton, Sir Isaac 1
nibbana: *see* Awakening
nidanas: *see* conditionality
Nietzsche, Friedrich 243, 253
nihilism (*ucchedavada*) 135, 148–9, 156, **157–69**, 210–11
nirvana: *see* Awakening
nirvana fallacy: *see* fallacies
Noble Eightfold Path: *see* Eightfold Path
no view 187

non-existence, 148, 151–3, 157, 164, 193, *see also* absolutisation, metaphysics
Norman, K.R. 4
novel distinctions 203, 272–3
Nussbaum, Martha 245, 288
Nyanaponika Thera 10, 14, 63, 66, 86, 105, 173, 176, 184, 203, 208, 288

Obama, Barack 162
obsession 60–1, 82, 106, 109, 111, 114, 127, 132, 140–2, 144, 147, 151, 177, 193, 204, *see also* craving
ocean (metaphor) 117–18
Olendzki, Andrew 70, 288
ontological obsession 141–47
ontology 141, *see also* metaphysics, absolutisation
opanayiko: *see* gradual training
open feedback loop: *see* brain
oral teachings 64
ordination 232, 234, 273
other-worldliness 83
ottappa: *see* fear of wrongdoing
over-specialisation 242

Padmasambhava, 224
pain, 29, 73, **113–15**, 175–6, 248
palace, 8, **10–13**, 14–15, 17–19, 25, 29–30, 32–3, 35–6, 44, 67, 85, 95, 118, 166, 230
Pali (language) 64, *see also* Pali Canon
Pali Canon 4, 8–11, 14–15, 23, 28, 31, 37–8, 42, 44, 50, 54, 61, 63, 70, 72, 77, 94, 97–100, 104, 125–6, 130, 134, 139, 144, 148–9, 151–2, 154, 175, 181, 184, 186, 196, 203–4, 213, 231, 239, 240, 282
Papadopoulos, Renos 254, 288
paradox 145–7
parinibbana 88–9, 115
Parmenides 203
Pasenadi, King 78–80, 86, 92
passions 93, *see also* craving
past lives 45, *see also* rebirth
path: *see* Middle Way
Path of Purification 196, 288
paticcasamuppada: *see* conditionality
patriarchy 219
Paul, St 119

Payutto, P.A. 207, 288
Perdue, Daniel E. 233, 288
Perfection of Wisdom (*prajna-paramita*) 146
Pesala, Bhikkhu 163, 288
philosophy (Western) 7, 26, 66, 153, 234, 243, 253–4, 262
    Marxism 11, 160, 164, 185, 233
    Socrates 72
    sceptical 135–40, 244–6
    ontology 141–7
    realism and idealism 151
    analytic 155
    Platonism 158, 171
    metaphysical beliefs in 160–1
    Parmenides 203
    Pyrrhonism 244–6
    of science 255–7
    logical positivism 264
    Zeno's paradoxes 267
    liberal 276–80
    existentialist 278–9
Piaget, Jean 168
Pilgrim's Progress, The 98
Plato 72, 203, 288
Platonism 158, 171, 253
pleasure 11, 17, 28–9, 30, 32, 36–7, 46, 57, 59–60, 79–80, 115, 131, 148–9, 157–8, 163, 175, 207, *see also* craving, hedonism
plurality 77
poisoned arrow (metaphor) 109–13
polarisation: *see* dualism
political correctness 122
politics 1, **78–87**, 241, 271, 276
Popper, Karl 255–6, 273, 278, 288
poverty 85
power
    absolutist ideology 13, 49, 140, 167, 219, 249
    group entrenchment 19–20, 76–7, 230
    flipping to opposite 29
    from limbic area 39
    in language 64
    concern of politics 78–9
    justification of political use 85
    monastic 140, 167, 231
    in unethical actions 181
    economic 186
    reciprocal 223
    challenged by meaning 264
practice, spiritual: *see* integrative practice
praise 203–4
Prajnaparamita 146
predestinarianism 160
prefrontal cortex: *see* brain
Price, A.F., and Mou-Lam, Wong 146, 239, 288
Prince Abhaya Sutta 183
probability 153
procrastination 38
projection 206, 221, 223, 237, 252, 254, 265, 271
proliferation 110, 145, *see also* brain/closed feedback loops
provisionality 42–4, 51, 119, 124–5, 129, 145, 151, 156, 158, 171, 199, 201, 216, 219, 226, 241, 267, 281–2
    definition **35**
    of four sights 19, 35
    mixed in with absolute 34
    versus 'knowledge' 46
    in generalisations 47–8
    other voices 53
    meditation supports 58
    intermediate positions 69
    relation to scepticism 103–4, 139–40
    open feedback loop 104
    adaptiveness 104–5
    adjustment 107, 113
    harmonisation 107
    overcoming discontinuity 118
    undermined by dualism 121
    of scientific method 126–7, 255–7
    applies before judgement 138
    compatible with basicness 155
    needed in stage transfers 167
    right view is provisional 187, 189–90
    supported by brahmaviharas 190–1
    in relation to conditionality 194–6, 199, 258–61
    applied to self 205
    applied to archetypes 206
    of 'karmic' claims 212
    of confidence in 'natural' events 214

positive effects 215
of belief in Middle Way 220
food for ghouls 227
group support for 230–1
partially lost in Asian Buddhism 233–4
supported by democracy 235, 277
undeveloped in Pyrrhonism 245–6
in crucifixion 248
imagination in 263–4, 266
in Langer's 'mindfulness' 272–3
supported by liberty 276–7
Pseudo-Dionysius 249, 288
psychological development 165, 230, 233
psychological stages 165, 279
psychology (Western) 153, 157, 257, 269, 271, 285, *see also* archetype, association, bias, brain, Haidt, Jung, Kegan, Langer, McGilchrist
Pudgalavadins 134
pumice 214
Pure Land Schools 223
purgative 208, 245
Pyrrho of Elis 244–5
Pyrrhonism 244–6

Rabbinic Judaism 243
raft (metaphor) 64, 94, 98–9, **102–5**, 106–8, 125
Rasiya 148
rationalisation 117, 211
rationality 252, 270, 277, 279
Ratnaguna 233, 288
Ray, Reginald 22, 288
reasoning 52, 66, 68, 133, 227, 265, 269–70
rebirth 28, 48, 97, 140, 161, 163, 193, 196, 202, 207, 233, 282
cessation of 43, 88–9
craving for being 210–11
karmic effects 212–15
supposed evidence for 216
desire to believe in 216
meaning 216–17
recollection of past lives 44
Red Book, Jung's 251–3, 287
Reeve, C.D.C. 203, 288

re-framing 129, 133, 144, 146, 151, 258, 268, 274, *see also* integration
refuge 91–2, 98, 115, 147, 154, 226, **237–41**
relativism **12–13**, 51, 160–1, 246, 279
relaxation 1, 21, 114, 170
religion 7, 9, 78, 180, 219, 226, 230, 247, 280
religious experience 33, 222, *see also* meditation/*jhana* experience
remorse 182
representation 38, 46, 52, 147, 177, 195, 263
representationalism: *see* meaning/representationalist view
repression 27, 40, 61, 132, 182, 249
reputation 34, 75, 86–7, 136
responsibility
experiential 33, 185, 278
social 82, 276
interpretative 116, 228, 246, 248, 254, 278
absolutised 149, 197, 206, 269
resurrection 248
revelation 54, 68–9, 139, 160, 236, 242, 247, 249
Rhinoceros Horn Sutta 231
right action **181–3**
right aspiration 170, 187, **189–92**
right concentration: *see* concentration
right effort 58, 170, 173, **177–9**
right hemisphere: *see* brain
right livelihood, 58, 170, 172, 180, **184–6**
right mindfulness: *see* mindfulness
right speech 58, 170, 180, **183–4**
right view 58, 170, **187–9**
role models 50–2
Romantic movement 277
rose-apple tree 29–32, 35, 42, 95, 166, 225
Ross, Lee et al. 229, 289
rote learning 272
rustic Pyrrhonism 246

Saccaka 85
sacrifices 19, 84
saddha: *see* faith
Saddhatissa, H. 187, 231, 289

saggavarana (conducive to better rebirths) 163
Sakyans 83
Samkhya 243
samma... (for each limb of Eightfold Path): *see* right...
sampajana (sustained awareness over time) **176–7**, 178, 266
Samyutta Nikaya 39, 47, 50, 57, 61–2, 73, 79–80, 86, 99, 113, 132–3, 148–9, 151, 163, 188, 193, 195–6, 198, 200, 202, 204–5, 213–14, 284
sanctity (political value) 84, **87**, 218–19
sangha: *see* community
Sangharakshita 45, 157–8, 167, 180–1, 188, 198, 221, 230, 232, 237–9, 289
Sanjaya Bellatthaputta 136
Sanskrit (language) 5, 64, 202, 284
Sargeant, Winthrop 202, 289
Sarnath 56, 229
Sartre, Jean-Paul 278–9, 289
Sarvastivadins 144
sassatavada: *see* eternalism
Satan 38
sati (breadth of awareness) 176–7
Satipatthana Sutta 175
scepticism 43, 58, 249, 253, 274, 280, 282
  in going forth 20
  element of Middle Way **35**
  in *Kalama Sutta* 66
  in raft metaphor 103
  misunderstanding in Buddhism 136, 139
  misunderstanding in philosophy 136–7, 139
  not denial 137, 205
  not impractical 138
  compatible with confidence 138–9
  not extreme 139–40
  selective use 155–6, 161
  based on embodiment 168
  about 'true' speech 183
  conditionality implies 195
  about generalisations 213–14
  Pyrrhonian 244–6
  in systems theory 260–1
  in embodied meaning 263–4
  challenge to left hemisphere 267

schemas **96**, 97, 100–1, 108, 117, 132, 160, 221, 262
  container 96, 274
  source-path-goal 100–1
  equilibrium 100–1
scholarship 4, 26, 76
science 1, 7, 34, 76, 112, 126–7, 158, 174, 180, 199, 212–14, 234, 241–2, 245–6, 253, **255–7**, 258, 260, 262, 264, 273, 278, 281–2
scientific method: *see* method
Scientific Middle Way 76
scientists 34, 45, 123, 158, 189, 211, 256–7
scripture 67, *see also* Pali Canon
second arrow (metaphor) 109, **113–16**
Second Noble Truth: *see* Four Tasks
Second Task: *see* Four Tasks
second-class Buddhists 232
selective scepticism 155–6, 161
self
  absolutised 27–9, 47, 144, 153
  expanded identification 43
  five aggregate analysis 59, 195
  after death 89, 126
  object v judgement 141
  fixed v 'no self' 148–50, 153–4, 193
  with other metaphysical views 157–9
  agnosticism 188, **204–6**
  'self' archetype 191, 206, 222, 249
self-indulgence 10, 12–13, 33, 148, 157
self-mortification 57, 148, 158
senses, the 122, 195–6, 216, 265
seven principles for preventing decline 81
sex 51, 78, 207, 231, *see also* Five Precepts/sexual misconduct
Sextus Empiricus 208, 244–5, 284, 287
sexual misconduct: *see* Five Precepts
Shadow (archetype) 221–2, 224
shame (*hiri*) 120, 182, *see also* guilt
Shantideva 143, 289
shramanas **15**, 17–18, 22, 28, 74–5, 77, 105, 122, 126, 132, 136, 230–1
shrines 81–2, 87
sickness 14–16, 59, 63, 114, 202
Siddhartha: *see* Buddha

Sikhism 226
simile: *see* metaphor
situationism 160
*skandha*s: *see* aggregates
skilful means 77, 140
snake (metaphor) 121, **125–8**
social media 12, 175
social order 11
social proof: *see* bias/group biases
socialism 83
socio-political integration: *see* integration/individual and social
Socrates 72, 76
Socratic questioning 65
solipsism 260
solitude 21, 55, 105, 231
Solomon, King 101
Sona 105
Sonadanda 74–7
Sonadanda Sutta 74–7
source-path-goal schema 100–1
Southeast Asia 223
speculation 111–12
speech precepts: *see* right speech
Spirit of the Depths (Jung) 252
spiritual community 80–1, *see also* community
spiritual practice: *see* integrative practice
Sri Lanka 197
status quo bias: *see* bias/temporal biases
Stevenson, Ian 216, 289
Stoicism 245
stream-entry 240
striatum: *see* brain/limbic area
striving 27, 37, 177
stupa 222
Subhadda 93
Subhuti (Buddha's disciple) 146, 239
substitution 170
    attribute substitution 145, 223, 269–70
    between positive and negative 164
subtractive (thinking) 255, 273
suffering: *see* inadequacy (in sense of *dukkha*), pain (in strict sense)
Sufism 243
Sunakkhata 88

sunk costs fallacy: *see* bias/temporal biases
Sunstein, Cass 224, 289
supernaturalism 161
supramundane Eightfold Path 171, 185, *see also* Eightfold Path
Sutta Nipata 38, 187, 231, 289
*sutta*s (discourses in general) 63–4, 70, 72
Swearer, Donald K. 223, 232, 289
symbolism (in general) 42, 95, 147, 191–2, 221–2, 262–4, *see also* meaning
sympathetic joy (*mudita*) 182, 190
synaptic connections: *see* brain
synthesis 76, 242, 271–2, 281
systems theory 199, **258–61**, 263, 266–7

taints (*asavas*) 44, 46, 48, 76, 120, 185, 198, 208
    bhavasava (taint of being) 46
    ditthisava (taint of views) 46
    kamasava (taint of craving) 46
Taleb, Nassim Nicholas 111, 289
tanha: *see* craving
task positive network: *see* brain
Taylor, Donald and Doria, Janet 229, 277, 289
teacher 22–3, 25, **26–7**, 41, 54, 56, 64–6, 68–9, 72, 92, 97, 185, 219, 220, 223, 233, *see also* authority
temporal biases: *see* bias
temporal lobe: *see* brain
Ten Precepts 181, 183, *see also* ethics
Thanissaro, Bhikkhu 84, 86, 139, 178, 206, 237, 289–90
theft: *see* Five Precepts
theism 160–1, 164; *see also* God
theory
    attachment to 34, 143
    applied 73
    ad hoc argument 160
    alternatives to 189
    modifying 255–7
    right hemisphere disrupts 267
    Middle Way theory 281
Theragatha 85–6
Theravada Buddhism 50, 118, 144, 163, 167, 169, 185, 197

Thinking Fast and Slow 271, 287
Third Noble Truth: *see* Four Tasks
Third Task: *see* Four Tasks
Thomism 126
Three Considerations (of Buddha) 14–16, 19
Three Jewels 226, 238–41
Three Knowledges 44–6
Three Marks (of conditioned existence) 149, 193, **200–6**, 244–5, 282
Three Times 154
Threefold Path 58, 170, *see also* Eightfold Path
Threefold Refuge 226, 238–41
Ti Ratana Vandana 118
time
    universality over 9, 46, 154, 242
    Buddha's teachings specific in 56
    needed to gain trust 79
    metaphors with space 100
    frames judgement 138
    absolutisations of 153
    provisional assumptions about 155
    awareness over 175–7
    right effort anticipates over 178
    occasion for speech 183–4
    temporal biases 204
    diachronic systems 258, 260
    hemispheric differences 266–8, 270
    fast and slow thinking 269
Tissa 73–4
top-down thinking 173, 273
totalitarianism 264
Trollope, Anthony 158
Twenge, Jean 175, 290
two mules (metaphor) 129–30
two truths 152

ucchedavada: *see* nihilism
Udaka Ramaputta 23–5, 31, 36, 41, 52, 54
Udana 116–17, 120, 122, 196, 286
uncertainty 35, 45, 60, 74, 89, 103, 110, 127, **135–40**, 156, 160, 181, 183, 220, 255, 264
universality 8–9, 15, 19, 24, 46, 52, 61, 65, 69, 76, 81, 94, 108, 121, 124, 164, 172, 192, 258

universe 35, 112, 123, 140, 148, 150–1, 157, 191, 193–4, 196, 199, 278
unsatisfactoriness: *see* inadequacy
Upaka 54–5, 62
upasaka 232
urbane Pyrrhonism 236
utilitarianism 77, 168, 276–7, *see also* ethics

Vacchagotta 150
Vajjian Confederacy 78, 80–2, 87
Vajrayana Buddhism 223, 233
Varela, Francisco 258–60, 287
Vedanta 243
Vedas 75
verificationism 255
vested interests 219–20
via negativa 249
vibhava-tanha: *see* craving
vicikiccha: *see* disabling doubt
violence 78, 83, 129, *see also* Five Precepts/killing
Vipassi (past Buddha) 9, 14–15, 17
volitional formations (*nidana*) 195–6, 205

Walshe, Maurice 9, 15, 17, 74, 80–1, 84–5, 89–93, 126, 136, 154, 175, 194, 290
Western teachers 198
Wheel of Samsara 195, 198, 216
Whitaker, Justin 234, 290
Wijayaratna, Mohan 231, 290
wilful effort 106, 132, 177, *see also* right effort
Williams, Paul 223, 290
wisdom 23–4, 40, 43, 51, 58, 76, 79, 82, 125, 128, 140, 151, 167, 170, 173, 178–80, **187–92**, 208, 219, 222, 249
Wittgenstein, Ludwig 136
worship 191, 223, 252
wrathful deities 224

Yogachara 144, 213

Zen Buddhism 176
Zeno's Paradoxes 267

www.ingramcontent.com/pod-product-compliance
Lightning Source LLC
Chambersburg PA
CBHW052053230426
43671CB00011B/1886